The Pope's MAESTRO

The Pope's MAESTRO

SIR GILBERT LEVINE

Foreword by John Tagliabue

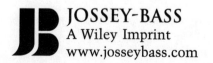

JOSSEY-BASS
A Wiley Imprint
www.josseybass.com

Published by Jossey-Bass
A Wiley Imprint
989 Market Street, San Francisco, CA 94103-1741—www.josseybass.com

Readers should be aware that Internet Web sites offered as citations and/or sources for further information may have changed or disappeared between the time this was written and when it is read.

Limit of Liability/Disclaimer of Warranty: While the publisher and author have used their best efforts in preparing this book, they make no representations or warranties with respect to the accuracy or completeness of the contents of this book and specifically disclaim any implied warranties of merchantability or fitness for a particular purpose. No warranty may be created or extended by sales representatives or written sales materials. The advice and strategies contained herein may not be suitable for your situation. You should consult with a professional where appropriate. Neither the publisher nor author shall be liable for any loss of profit or any other commercial damages, including but not limited to special, incidental, consequential, or other damages.

Jossey-Bass books and products are available through most bookstores. To contact Jossey-Bass directly call our Customer Care Department within the U.S. at 800-956-7739, outside the U.S. at 317-572-3986, or fax 317-572-4002.

Jossey-Bass also publishes its books in a variety of electronic formats. Some content that appears in print may not be available in electronic books.

Library of Congress Cataloging-in-Publication Data

Levine, Gilbert,
   The Pope's maestro / Gilbert Levine. – 1st ed.
      p. cm.
   ISBN 978-0-470-49065-5 (hardback); 9780470608333 (ebk); 9780470608340 (ebk); 9780470608357 (ebk)
   1. Levine, Gilbert, 1948-   2. Conductors (Music)–United States–Biography.   3. John Paul II, Pope, 1920–2005–Friends and associates.   4. Catholic Church–Relations–Judaism.
5. Judaism–Relations–Catholic Church.   I. Title.
   ML422.L667A3 2010
   784.2092–dc22
   [B]

                                                                                    2010027000

Printed in the United States of America
FIRST EDITION

HB Printing   10 9 8 7 6 5 4 3 2 1

CONTENTS

In Memory of

*His Holiness Pope John Paul II, for his trust and
faith in me and in the power of my art*

and

*Margit Raab Kalina, survivor of Tarnow Ghetto, Kraków-Płaszów,
Auschwitz-Birkenau, and Bergen-Belsen, for inspiring me
always with her quiet voice that said, "We live."*

FOREWORD

It is hard for me to think of religion without music: great Jewish liturgical song, Gregorian chant, the choral works of Orthodox Christians. It is equally difficult for me to think of music without religion: Bach's B Minor Mass, Mozart's Great Mass in C Minor, Mahler's Eighth Symphony. It is against the backdrop of this symbiosis that I like to view the relationship of my friend Sir Gilbert Levine with Pope John Paul II.

I first met Gilbert in December 1987, the beginning of a long and enriching friendship, I hope, for both of us, when he had just begun a tour as music director and conductor of the Kraków Philharmonic, in then-Communist Poland. He was the first Western conductor to have become the principal conductor of an Eastern European orchestra, and I traveled to Kraków to interview him for the *New York Times*.

Already then I felt a religious dimension to his music. Yes, he conducted his Dvořák and his Mahler with wonderful élan. But Gilbert's grandparents had been immigrants from Poland, and Kraków's fringes housed the Auschwitz-Birkenau concentration camp, where millions of Jews were killed, and of which Gilbert's mother-in-law was a survivor. In the spring of 1988, in commemoration of the end of World War II, he conducted Brahm's Requiem—"German art, with texts from the Old and New Testaments, and music speaking directly to the soul," he told me.

But Kraków had also been the archdiocese of Karol Wojtyla before he became Pope John Paul II. And it was through Wojtyla's successor, Franciszek Cardinal Macharski, that Gilbert came to the Pope's attention. The Cardinal sent a *Newsweek* article about Gilbert to the Pope, and in February 1988 Gilbert was summoned to the Vatican. He later recalled John Paul greeting him, with a twinkle in his eye, by saying, "How are you treating my orchestra?" But then quickly adding, "How are they treating you?"

Later that same year he was invited to bring the Kraków Philharmonic Choir to Rome to celebrate the tenth anniversary of John Paul's Pontificate. On that visit Gilbert brought his mother-in-law. Few popes could credibly have claimed Jewish friends, though many medieval popes boasted Jewish doctors. But John Paul, who had grown up alongside Jews in Wadowice, Poland, before World War II, remained close to some survivors of the Holocaust.

I like to think that the Italian word *maestro* means not only orchestra conductor but, originally, teacher, for each of these men, over time, became a teacher to the other. I saw, over the years, how the Pope opened avenues to Gilbert that would have been otherwise closed; Gilbert, for his part, brought the Pope more deeply into the world of music than he would have otherwise gone.

Perhaps the most moving interaction of the two that I was privileged to observe came in April 1994, when John Paul, who repeatedly sought to heal the strife between Christians and Jews, officially commemorated the Shoah, for the first time, with a concert held on the day Jews have set aside for the memory of the millions of European Jews killed by the Nazis. It was also the first time that Rome's Chief Rabbi—Elio Toaff at the time—was officially received in the Vatican as the honored public guest of any pope.

Emphasizing the equal dignity of their faiths, the two men sat on identical gilt and brocaded thrones, I recall, next to the President of Italy, in the immense audience hall next to St. Peter's. With Gilbert conducting London's Royal Philharmonic Orchestra, the American cellist Lynn Harrell performed Max Bruch's Kol Nidre, a composition by the German Protestant composer that evokes the prayer chanted at the start of the Jewish Day of Atonement, Yom Kippur. We all noticed that John Paul was most visibly moved as the actor Richard Dreyfuss recited the Kaddish, the Jewish prayer for the dead, to Leonard Bernstein's music. Many of us wept.

I like to think that both men, Gilbert and the Pope, never really wandered far from their roots, regardless of the heights they reached in later life. Gilbert, who had studied at Juilliard, Princeton, and Yale and had later worked with Nadia Boulanger in Paris and Sir Georg Solti in London, never really shed his blunt and exuberant Brooklyn manner. John Paul, despite his climb through the Church hierarchy to the summit of the papacy, never lost touch with the village of Wadowice. Yet together they worked a kind of magic.

To honor Gilbert's work, the Pope made him a Knight-Commander of the Pontifical Equestrian Order of St. Gregory the Great. My wife, Paula, and I attended the ceremony in Paris, where the sword of a papal knight was presented to now Sir Gilbert by His Eminence Jean-Marie Cardinal Lustiger, a close friend of both Gilbert and John Paul, and a Jew, whose father had survived the war but whose mother, turned in by a French neighbor, had been murdered at the very concentration camp Gilbert's mother-in-law survived.

After the Holocaust concert, I recall talking to Jack Eisner, a survivor of the 1943 Warsaw Ghetto Uprising. Jack, who died in 2003 and whose friendship I shared with Gilbert, said he told the Pope earlier that day that he was the sole survivor in his family, though his Grandma Masha had twenty grandchildren and his Grandma Hannah, eleven. He told John Paul that as a boy growing up in prewar Poland, he was afraid to cross the sidewalk next to a Catholic Church. "Now, some fifty years later," Jack told the Pope, "the unthinkable is happening."

Indeed, I've been convinced since that day that the friendship of these two men, Gilbert Levine and John Paul II—the Jewish conductor from New York and the Polish pope—somehow made the unthinkable possible.

John Tagliabue
June 2010
Paris

Stanislaus Cardinalis Dziwisz
Archiepiscopus Metropolita Cracoviensis

Krakow, November 10, 2009

Maestro Gilbert Levine had the extraordinary privilege of conducting concerts for His Holiness Pope John Paul II for 17 years. I was proud to collaborate closely with him as he created such events as the Papal Concert to Commemorate the *Shoah* and the Papal Concert of Reconciliation which helped immeasurably to bring the Pope's message of Peace and understanding to Christians and Jews, Muslims and peoples of all faiths throughout the world.

Sir Gilbert's inspiring book about his journey to Krakow, the Vatican and beyond will enrich everyone who reads this unique and ennobling story.

Stanisław Card. Dziwisz
Archbishop of Krakow

Yis—ga-dal v'yis-ka-dash shmay ra-bo, b'olmo dee'vro chir'usay—
May the great Name of God be exalted and sanctified,
throughout the world.

Alone, bareheaded, standing in front of one of the two velvet-
covered chairs set out before Pope John Paul II's tomb in the crypt of
St. Peter's, I recited the Kaddish, the ancient Aramaic Jewish prayer
for the dead. A few paces behind me stood the Prefect of the Pontifical
Household, who had, to my astonishment, arranged for me to be
brought here alone, after the basilica had been closed to the public for
the night, so that I could pay my respects to His Holiness in private.
On this late afternoon of December 7, 2006, I had come back to the
Vatican for the first time in many months. I had neither seen nor
spoken to anyone in the Apostolic Palace since the Papal funeral in
April 2005.

*Oseh sholom bimromov, hu ya'aseh sholom olaynu, v'al kol yisroel;
vimru Omein*—May there be abundant peace from Heaven, and life
upon us and upon all Israel; and we say, Amen.

After I had finished saying Kaddish, I prayed on silently for as
long as I thought I could. I stepped back from the tomb, and motioned
that I was ready to leave, feeling that the Prefect and the two guards
from St. Peter's who had accompanied us might be anxious to get on
with their duties. The Prefect stepped forward, put his arm gently on
my shoulder, and whispered that I could take as long as I wished.

I sat down heavily in the red velvet chair, letting images of His
Holiness over the seventeen years that I had known him pass gently

through my mind. There were so many memories. So much music I had made for him. So many moving moments created together. From among these many visions three came to my mind most vividly.

First I saw the young and vigorous Pope John Paul II, striding onstage, beaming as he put his arm around me at my first Papal Concert in 1988. I thought of the lyrically lovely "Ave Maria" of Brahms and the unadorned yet beautiful Mass in D of Dvořák, which I had just conducted and which His Holiness had seemed to appreciate so deeply. "Thank you for going to Kraków, and thank you for bringing Kraków to me," I heard his still-clear voice whisper in my ear at concert's end.

Next came the painful, sad memories of the music we had made for the Papal Concert to Commemorate the Shoah in 1994. I heard the mournful tones of Bruch's "Kol Nidre," and the universality of the Adagio from Beethoven's Ninth. Bernstein's "Chichester Psalms" and "Kaddish" had moved Pope John Paul deeply, almost to tears, as he sought to reach out to comfort the survivors of the Holocaust. "These victims: Fathers, mothers, children, brothers, friends. In our memory, they are all present, they are with you, they are with us," he had told us all, as the six-candle Holocaust menorah burned brightly in the Vatican's great auditorium, the Aula Paulo VI.

Finally, still lost in painful thought, I felt the presence of the bent, frail, and gnarled, yet still strong-of-spirit Pontiff listening with rapt attention to our music at the audacious Papal Concert of Reconciliation in January 2004. In my mind's eye, I saw him once again, sitting on his wheeled throne, watching intently, as I led the musical journey of Mahler's "Resurrection" Symphony in its ascendant quest towards our reunion with God. "Yes! We must find within us the courage for peace. We must implore from on High the gift of peace," he had said then, his lungs gasping for air, his voice halting, but his words potent nonetheless.

We had done such marvelous work together. Although I could not presume to think so, many who knew us and our work together considered us friends. A special kind of friendship. One whose musical witness had been viewed throughout the world. A friendship that transformed my art and my faith in inestimable ways. Our time together was over now. There would be no more encores, no more collaborations in service to his powerful goals of peace and reconciliation through music.

In the deep silence of the crypt, inside a hushed Saint Peter's Basilica, I felt crushed. I missed him terribly. His warmth. His humanness. And his profound concern for the spirit of the world. I walked forward and laid my hand gently on his tomb, as though my hand were the fringes of my tallis, my ritual prayer shawl, as if I were touching the passing Torah as it is carried reverently through the synagogue on Shabbat. I finished the ritual by touching my hand to my lips, my eyes tightly closed, holding back my tears.

I backed away, turned, and walked slowly out of St. Peter's, with the Prefect and the basilica's protectors following silently close behind.

It was not until later, after I had bid the Prefect good-bye at the entrance to the Apostolic Palace, and had walked out past the Swiss Guards into the pink and orange sunset spreading out over the Bernini columns in Saint Peter's Square, that it dawned on me.

I had prayed to my Polish Pope in the spoken language of his Savior Jesus, the Jew, in the great church built on the model of the Second Temple in Jerusalem. It is a prayer as old as my faith—and his. A prayer intoned in celebration as often as it is in mourning. A prayer Jesus would have recited every day of his life. I knew in my heart that Pope John Paul II had heard my prayer and had understood it also, every ancient word. And with that thought, the smallest smile crept back onto my face, as I remembered all we had accomplished, working together, in music and in spirit, over the seventeen most privileged years of my life.

The Pope's
MAESTRO

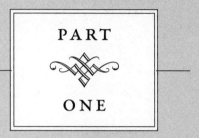

PART

ONE

Ave Maria

If all roads lead to Rome, in this story my road began in Kraków, the place that eventually led me to Pope John Paul II.

In 1987, I was in the middle of a series of guest conducting engagements in San Francisco, Philadelphia, and Hamburg, among other cities. For one of these musical weeks, I was scheduled to go and conduct in Kraków. I had heard the Kraków Philharmonic in Symphony Hall in Boston on their 1986 American tour. And my grandparents on my father's side had come to America from Poland. Generations of Levines had lived their lives in Warsaw. I thought it might be interesting, both musically and from a family heritage point of view, so I went.

But I went with great trepidation. My wife, Vera, was born and raised in Bratislava, in what was then the Czechoslovak Socialist Republic. The city she grew up in lay just sixty kilometers from Vienna, one of the great musical capitals of the world, but it was surrounded by a barbed-wire fence and an expanse of no-man's-land, which placed it a million miles away, well behind the Iron Curtain. Vera knew the hardships of the socialist East Bloc all too well. She knew what I could expect on my short weeklong sojourn in Communist Poland.

I also knew a bit about it. In 1986, I had spent a week conducting the famed Dresden Staatskapelle. At that time, living and performing in the Saxon capital, now located very deep in East Germany, one of the Soviet system's worst police-state outposts, I had loved the music-making. Who would not? The Staatskapelle is one of the marvels of the musical world, with a unique tradition dating back to its founding in 1548 and a renowned way of making music. They were an ensemble that had survived the Thirty Years' War and both World Wars, and now they would outlive, they were sure, the Communist commissars. Their music would conquer all.

But my week in Dresden had tested me greatly. The Staatskapelle might have been able to steel itself institutionally, but I was alone against the Socialist system. The walls, and everything else, seemed to have ears. I was followed and harassed by the dreaded Stasi, the East German secret police, even though I was supposedly an honored guest of the German Democratic Republic. I was glad to leave with my body intact, but thankfully, my soul was artistically refreshed.

So I felt a tug in two directions when I went to Kraków. I was anxious about the Communist government and what came with it but at the same time curious and full of anticipation, both as an artist and from the point of view of my family's heritage.

My first journey to Kraków took place in February 1987, but even my stay in Socialist Dresden did not prepare me for my initial impressions in the Polish city. It was incredibly gray. A pall of industrial pollution pervaded everything, blowing in from the east, from belching furnaces of the "workers' paradise" town of Nova Huta, and from the west, from the heavy industries in Katowice. The buses had no antipollution devices and spewed a heavy foulness that trailed along after them for fifty yards or more. They seemed to be running on belching smoke. The nights were even worse than the days. Everyone, it seemed, used soft coal, or peat, for heating, which added soot to the day's accumulation of factory-generated filth. It was no wonder that everyone seemed to have a chronic upper respiratory infection.

Then there was the secret police, a central part of the totalitarian Communist system. Their aim was total control of everyone's life, even the lives of visitors from the West. The secret police kept a close eye on the local population, and a special eye on artistic guests like me. For them, control was everything. When I arrived at the Warsaw airport, I was transferred to an airport hotel. I knew I wasn't supposed to be staying overnight, so I thought that was a bit odd. I was, in fact, per my itinerary, meant to have transferred to another flight on to Kraków. But all of a sudden, without a word of explanation, I was driven to downtown Warsaw and put alone on the next train to Kraków. I didn't speak a word of Polish, and in those days, few Poles would have wanted to be seen talking with a stranger so obviously from the West. In any case, I was not given a choice in any of this. I was an honored musical visitor to the People's Republic of Poland, but if this is what it meant to be their honored guest, I wondered if everyone would have been treated in such an arbitrary manner. The secret police and the Communist authorities made me know they were in charge right from the start.

Luckily, the train was a nonstop, Warsaw-to-Kraków express. I just sat in my seat and stared out at the Polish countryside, at the sleepy towns, the fallow farmland, and the small stands of trees. The surprising mix of old and new. On a stretch of country road, trucks jostled with heavily laden horse-drawn carts driven by men in pointed triangular hats. Old farmhouses and smaller villages passed by in a blur.

I arrived in Kraków, and through the mists I began to see a city like no other. Even through the polluted haze this place was a marvel. Left intact by the Nazis when they occupied it, Kraków was a city of beautiful architecture: baroque palazzi, moats, and barbicans, and real Renaissance graffiti—beautiful geometric designs painted permanently on the walls of some of the city's oldest edifices. Many of the buildings were crumbling from the chemicals that were eating them away, but they were resplendent with historical detail, nonetheless. It seemed far removed, at least on the outside, from the influences of the twentieth century. At night, when I walked around the city's main square, the Rynek Glowny, everything was very dark and mysterious, and extraordinarily atmospheric. The radiating cobblestoned streets of the city center were dimly lit, seemingly by gaslight. (They were in fact lit by electric lights, but with wattage so low, it felt like a time before the modern age.)

I had never been in a city with so many churches. I had the immediate sense that even in Communist Poland, the Church had unmistakable power. The activity of people hurrying to these churches on the Sunday after I arrived made it very clear to me that 1987 Poland was as much a Catholic country as it was a Communist country, and maybe much more so.

In that first week, I began looking for my Jewish roots, for something to tell me that my people had once been there. My mother-in-law, Margit Raab Kalina, had had her entire family annihilated in the Holocaust. Her brother and many aunts, uncles, and cousins had been murdered at Auschwitz-Birkenau, which is about a forty-five-minute drive from Kraków. I had made a promise to her that if I went to Kraków, which she had not visited since she had passed through its railway station on the way from one horrendous concentration camp to another, that I would go to Birkenau to say a prayer for all her murdered family. I would also try to look for the remnants of the culture that she and her family had represented in prewar Central Europe. She wasn't from Poland; she was from the neighboring region of Moravia in the Czech lands, but the culture was very similar. And her grandparents did indeed come from Rzeszow and Przemyśl in the heart of the province of Galicia, in Poland, of which Kraków is the ancient capital.

One morning I went for a walk from my cell-like room in the Soviet-era Krakovia Hotel to find Kazimierz, the Jewish section of Kraków that had been the home of the Jews for eight hundred years prior to 1939. I went walking, and the first thing I noticed were the synagogues, which are as plentiful in Kazimierz as churches are in the rest of Kraków. Within the space of ten square blocks, there were six or seven Jewish houses of worship. But now, after the Shoah, most no longer resonated with the sound of prayer. One was a museum, open even on the Jewish High Holy Days. Another was used by the city as a book repository. Only one, the exquisite Renaissance jewel called the Remuh, was still functioning as a synagogue, but only barely. I went there for Shabbat services and found a tiny group, made up exclusively of older people, trying to put together a minyan of ten men so that they could conduct their Sabbath service. There was no rabbi, no cantor. At that time, my family and I attended a Conservative synagogue on Long Island where there were four separate services on the

High Holidays, one bigger than the next. At the Rosh Hashanah and Yom Kippur services, the main sanctuary held fifteen hundred people. The overflow crowded into the downstairs ballroom, the synagogue's library, and vast tents set up on the Temple's grounds. I was used to vibrant Jewish life. All I found here in Kraków was the Remuh, a beautiful remnant of a near-extinct Jewish heritage.

When I walked through the Jewish Quarter, I saw mezuzahs on the doorframes, not removed but painted over with coat after coat of paint, so you couldn't see that iconic symbol that marks the doorpost of every Jewish home, but you could still see the outline of the small box where the tiny prayer scroll had once been stored.

Unlike the rest of the city, in Kazimierz there was a tremendous silence. People lived there, but ghosts inhabited it, too. And neither stirred. In Kazimierz, I also felt the powerful silence of voices that had been stilled. As I walked back to my hotel, I felt a terrible chill, a painful empty cold, devoid of all human warmth.

The next afternoon, I took a taxi to Auschwitz to honor my mother-in-law's request. I was immediately taken by my Polish taxi driver to Auschwitz 1, which is now a museum. It is the place where everyone goes to see the exhibits: grotesque heaps of eyeglasses that were ripped off noses, of hair that was shorn off heads, of suitcases piled one on top of another with the addresses in Czechoslovakia and Hungary and Romania and France and Belgium still visible. That was terrible.

The numbers in each pile were almost unimaginable.

But my mother-in-law hadn't spent any time in Auschwitz 1. For it was the site of a more antiquated form of barbarism. Hundreds of thousands were martyred there. One by one by one. It is the site of the infamous "Block of Tears," an execution ground where Poles and many others met their tragic deaths. The highly mechanized, twentieth-century innovation in lethal cruelty was to be found at Auschwitz 2. When the Nazis decided they wanted to murder thousands upon thousands of human beings a day, they invented a new and more efficient system, the killing factory at Auschwitz 2, called Birkenau.

So I asked my driver to take me there. He said, "You don't need to go. There is nothing left to see."

And I said, "Yes. I really do. Please just leave me at the entrance. I will come and find you later."

He took me grudgingly to Birkenau. I got out of his taxi, and went through the infamous brick gates through which the railroad tracks once ran: one-way tracks for all those people, for my mother-in-law and many of her relatives. Gates that led to a hell on earth. And millions never made the return journey.

It was a cold, snowy, smoggy, unpleasant day, and I was glad it was so. If it had been a day of sunshine in June, I'm not sure the contrast would have been understandable in God's creation. I walked a very long way along the railroad tracks to get to the first area that I remembered Margit speaking about. The place where she was taken off the train and where the "selection" was done. Some people went to the left, almost everyone to the right. On both sides of the tracks, I could see wooden barracks, some of which the poor Polish people who lived in the villages around the camp had begun to disassemble, because they needed the wood for fuel in the bitterly cold winters after the war. There were still some, though, that were completely intact. I peered inside. They were not barracks; they were more like chicken coops, with floor-to-ceiling stacked shelves and only ten or twelve inches between them, where lice-ridden sacks had been placed for people to sleep on, piled one on top of another. To call them places of human habitation is a gross exaggeration. Humans lived there, so they were indeed a habitation, but they were hardly fit for even a despised animal.

I imagined my mother-in-law there, and I imagined her surviving for months on end. People died every minute of every day, even those who were "selected for life." There were no sanitary facilities, just holes in the ground. People were so close together that if someone had a cold, everyone in the barracks would have a cold, or worse, the next day. If someone had dysentery, everyone had dysentery; if someone had typhus, everyone had typhus. A confoundingly enormous number of people died of disease, so that the Nazis didn't then have to doom them to "special treatment." They only had to burn their corpses. Every day was execution day, whether one was sent directly to the gas chambers or not.

I walked farther down the tracks and saw in the distance, hidden by some trees, the crematoria. Margit had told me that she had participated in dynamiting the crematoria, forced to by the Nazis in an attempt to destroy the evidence and cover up their horrendous deeds when they abandoned the camp. I couldn't see the ovens as they had been, only the remnants of the death buildings and the red brick chimneys of the furnaces, lying akimbo on the ground, as if they had been dynamited only yesterday. As if the earth would not accept this awful detritus from the foulest human mind and hand.

My mother-in-law, Margit, had always talked about the horrible stench, the stink of the burning flesh that permeated the camp and got into every fiber of what was left of her clothes. It was clear that the odor of death could be smelled and felt for many, many miles around. The wind would have born its terrible message of death in all directions, depending on which way it was blowing. Everyone nearby would have known, though it may have been just too terrifying for them to give that smell a name.

While I was near the crematoria, I bent down and picked up some earth; it was very light, like ash mixed with dirt. Forty years later, there were, incredibly, still pieces of human bone in the loam. I realized in horror that I was walking on graves. Perhaps the graves of Margit's brother, or one of her dozens of cousins and aunts and uncles. Or someone's wife, husband, or most terrifying of all, someone's little child. It was a shattering, smothering dirt that I felt I would never be able to wash away.

I went to Birkenau many times after that, but this was a sobering first day. In February in Kraków, the days are very short, and by four o'clock it was getting dark. I returned to the waiting shabby old Polski Fiat taxi, glad to get out of the bone-chilling cold. I went back to my hotel and felt emptied of all human warmth. God, I wondered, why had I ever come to this place?

But the next day, Monday, I remembered what had drawn me to Kraków in the first place, and what had made me feel I needed to be there: the music-making. Aside from my mother-in-law and my heritage, I was drawn back to Central Europe for an artistic experiment. As in Dresden, when I was returning to the roots of the Weber and the Beethoven I conducted there, here in Kraków, in Galicia, I was going back to the Austro-Hungarian roots of Mahler and Mozart. With the Kraków orchestra we performed the Mozart D-Minor Piano Concerto, one of the greatest piano concertos by one of the greatest musical geniuses who ever lived, and the Mahler Fourth Symphony, which, strangely, in the last movement sets words describing a child's idyllic vision of heaven. I was so in need of that after what I had seen at Birkenau.

I also felt something very special when I walked through the door of the Philharmonic Hall to work with that orchestra. These musicians, who on the outside were victims of the Communist system, of its pollution and grayness—inside these walls, these orchestral players seemed free. When they walked through the door, they were artists first and political pawns second. They entered sometimes a little bit hunched, but when they came onto their stage, they walked with pride as the dedicated musicians they were. They were inheritors of the great Central European orchestral tradition that Kraków represented. And I was there to partake of it all with them.

Kraków, which was the seat of Polish kings during the "Golden Age" of the fifteenth and sixteenth centuries and beyond, had a rich musical heritage in Chopin and Szymanowski, but it was also, from about 1800 to 1917, the capital of Galicia province, a part of the Austro-Hungarian Empire, the very heartland that bred Haydn, Mozart, Beethoven, Schubert, Dvořák, Brahms, Bruckner, and Mahler. Cracovians spoke German, along with their native Polish, during the whole of the nineteenth century and, it is said, relatively happily so. If the music of these legendary composers is alive in Prague, their works live on vibrantly in Kraków also. The culture is more similar to Vienna than one could imagine. In 1987, Cracovian ladies could sometimes still be seen promenading on Sundays arm in arm up and down on the embankments of the Wisla River under Wawel Castle, as I had seen them do in Stadtpark or Prater in the Vienna of those days.

When I stood on the podium and made music with these Kraków musicians, we needed no interpreter, even though my Polish at the time was nonexistent. My German and my English served us well enough, but it was music, the universal language, that made us understand one another instantly. It is one of the true miracles of my art which never ceases to amaze me.

We started our rehearsals with Mahler's ethereal Fourth Symphony. From the opening gentle sleigh bells, played by musicians for whom *sanie*, as they are called in Poland—sleds drawn by horses with bells around their necks—were still a part of their country's winter landscape, to the glissandi-slides in the violins, which were played so naturally you would never have thought they were a rarely called-for effect, I was hearing a Mahlerian tone-palette as the composer himself might have imagined it. The clarinet sound was different from any clarinet sound I knew, except perhaps in Prague. The sound of the strings was almost edge-less, something akin to what I had encountered in Dresden. It had a glow about it, like the glow you would see in the hearth, in the ash-gray coals that remain after a long quieted fire. These sound embers were very soft and warm, not hot, about to burst into flame. The whole orchestra made a burnished sound, like brushed and polished brass.

This Kraków orchestra was about bringing alive the folk tunes and nature sounds in Mahler, sounds that were very much in the composer's ear, hailing as he did from Margit's Moravia, just south and east of Kraków. These musicians recognized those Mahler folk tunes intuitively, as part of their inchoate musical vocabulary. They didn't play as virtuosically as American orchestras, but they played in a special way nonetheless. One that was their own.

I knew that part of the intensity of my Mahler Fourth that first week, part of the spark of making music in Kraków with that Polish orchestra, came from my visit to Birkenau. Part of the reason I could lose myself in the incredible dreamlike quality of the heavenly aspects of Mahler's fairy tale was that I needed to leave that cruelest of imaginable worlds for the creative one that came out of the same roots, the same imagination, that same soil and culture. I needed to conduct that magical work of Mahler's that week. It became my salvation, the musical and artistic release for all that I had seen. It was my way of coping, of righting myself after confronting the hell of Birkenau.

This was the gift that this Mahler performance gave to me. Whether the members of the orchestra could sense this, I don't know. But I do know that only the Mahler Fourth could have healed the hole in my heart and soul. It became my saving grace.

For the first time as a conductor, I experienced a personal unity, in an ethnic and religious sense, with the salvation that was represented by my musical and artistic sensibility, in a way I could not have imagined before. Music had never served quite that purpose for me. It was truly cathartic. It was like connecting with the best in life after having seen the worst. From the hell of Birkenau to the heaven of Mahler Four.

The orchestra played the Mozart concerto with a quiet elegance, sitting back and letting the music develop by itself without forcing it. There is much talk these days about original performance practice in eighteenth-century music. Here in Kraków, in 1987, I heard a seamless stylistic line, handed down from generation to generation, which might have been in the spirit of the Austro-Hungarian Empire that Mozart himself would have recognized as his own.

Then we performed the Ives Third Symphony, a very American but also a very spiritual work, and very accessible for Ives, who is one of our most iconoclastic composers. Other orchestras had performed Ives in Poland, and there was, strangely, a vogue for his work. His Third ends with church bells that are supposed to be superimposed on the ending of the work. We had the idea to record the bells from one of Kraków's many spires, and to play them back in the Philharmonic Hall at the work's conclusion. But which bells? There were so many churches. We recorded the sounds of this church and that, and finally found one that really worked. The connection between Ives and these Kraków players was much more than just their church bells, however. They seemed to connect spiritually with Ives, as if the New England Congregationalist organist and these Kraków Catholics felt the same underlying touch of the hand, of a being higher than themselves. They seemed quietly moved by the religious calm that pervades the symphony's last movement, entitled "Communion," with its sonorous, bell-pealed close.

Much to my surprise, at the end of the concert, Krzysztof Penderecki, a renowned composer as well as the dominant figure in the Polish official musical establishment of that time, jumped up and started applauding enthusiastically. He even led the wonderful European honor of rhythmic applause. His approbation was clear.

Afterwards, at a postconcert reception, Penderecki approached me and said, out of the blue, "Gilbert, this concert went very well, don't you think? How would you like to be Music Director of the Kraków Philharmonic? I believe the time is right."

The time is right?! This was 1987. The tanks had just been removed from in front of the U.S. Embassy after the lifting of martial law. It was not a place for a permanent position for anyone from the West, and certainly not for an American. But Penderecki seemed serious enough, and he kept repeating his idea over and over. I smiled back at him. But I couldn't imagine this would ever come to be. I tried my best to put it out of my mind.

When I left Kraków the next day, Krzysztof Penderecki and his wife, Elzbieta, followed me right out to the plane. I had first met Penderecki when I studied for my master's degree at Yale, and encountered him again later in 1984, when he and I shared conducting duties for a subscription series with the Minnesota Orchestra. In each of the four concerts, he conducted his own violin concerto on the first half of the program, and I conducted Shostakovich's searing Fifth Symphony on the second. At one performance, Penderecki and his wife sat in the audience for the second half, evidently sizing up this young American for a possible future in Poland. I was completely oblivious to this possibility when he invited me to his home city to be a guest conductor. It probably didn't hurt that the review in Minneapolis was titled "Levine Soars in Twin Cities Debut." The reviewer went on: "The Shostakovitch symphony received a performance as vibrant and vivid as any in my listening experience."

That February morning of my departure from Kraków, Penderecki kept saying over and over, "I mean it, Gilbert. Please think about this position with our orchestra. You could get so much done here." I supposed he had not thought at all of the incredible difficulties involved. How could he? What I was about to embark upon had never been done before.

The Kraków Philharmonic is considered one of the three most important ensembles in Poland, along with the Warsaw Philharmonic and the Orchestra of Polish Radio in Katowice. The Kraków Philharmonic was now looking for a Music Director, which would be a normal process for most orchestras involving the best candidates from around the world. But Kraków just happened to lie behind the Iron Curtain. In Poland, since 1948, the Communist artistic hierarchy had always sought a talented Pole for such a position, someone who had seniority and had waited patiently for this plum assignment. Past Music Directors of the orchestra had included Stanislaw Skrowaczewski and Sir Andrzej Panufnik, Polish conductors who had both later made distinguished careers in the West. But the reverse, a Western conductor, let alone an American going to the East to hold this position in Kraków, had never, ever happened before.

Apparently, however, my guest stint in Kraków had been part of the Philharmonic's Music Director search without my having known anything about it. A search that was intended to be way out of the ordinary. (And who would have believed them if they had said it was ordinary? Surely, not I.)

The background to this turn of events, however, was part of a far grander political design. Mikhail Gorbachev, then General Secretary of the Soviet Communist Party, had begun reaching out to the West, a gesture called *glasnost*, to find links that would be nonthreatening to communism but that would open it up to some degree. I hadn't thought about it when I went to Poland, but Penderecki most certainly had. He had close ties to both the Polish government and the Soviets. He always seemed to know everything about everything. That's what had impelled him, and his fellow members of Poland's musical ruling elite, to think that there was a possibility of having a Westerner as Music Director. The offer was as startling to me as it was to the members of the Kraków Philharmonic themselves. Neither they nor I thought this was remotely a possibility until Penderecki popped the question.

I flew from Kraków to Berlin via Warsaw. On the plane from Warsaw to Berlin, I sat by chance next to an official from the American Embassy in the Polish capital. I took the opportunity to tell him about this strange offer, just out of curiosity to see how he might react. He looked at me as if it were the craziest thing he had ever heard. It was inexplicable. Living in Warsaw as a member of the American diplomatic delegation, he could not imagine how such a thing was possible from the point of view of the Polish Communist hierarchy. "You know," he said, "they just removed the tank from in front of our embassy. Protecting the Americans, they had said. Martial law was just lifted in '86. It is the coldest of cold in the Cold War. Yes, there is glasnost, and Gorbachev seems like he wants to make things better, but this is nuts, an American Music Director sitting, unprotected, in Kraków?

"You know," he went on, "you'd be on your own. You would not be official. There would be nothing we could do to protect you on a daily basis. You'd be a sitting duck for their security people. And the Kraków secret police are worse than the guys in Warsaw. You know, there has not been so much as a multiple-entry visa for an American in Poland. Ever! And now you'd be a Polish state official. Do you really want to do that?

"You want to be a guinea pig?"

I was stunned, but after what I had been through, not so very shocked.

I think he thought he had talked me out of even considering this offer. He kept a bemused smile on his face the whole rest of the flight. And he probably reported it back to our embassy as a lunacy that would soon die its natural death.

After my week's guest engagement, I went as usual to Berlin to debrief my agent, the famous Dr. Witiko Adler, the manager of some of the greatest conductors in the world. The shock of arriving in West Berlin had never been greater. I was going from Communist Kraków to this vaguely decadent, glitzy, but artistically very advanced enclave of the West in the middle of East Germany.

First of all, I took a shower. The grime and soot had to come off and with it, the eerie loam of Auschwitz. How odd it was, taking that shower in Berlin, of all places. The sole synagogue functioning in Berlin at that time was in the Fasanenstrasse, around the corner from the Hotel Kempinski, where I was staying. Historically, the whole thing was slightly creepy. I had flown from Kraków, which the Nazis had occupied, to Berlin, which had been the very epicenter of their regime.

I went downstairs and had dinner with Dr. Adler and his wife, Jutta, in my hotel. I said that I had the strangest story to tell them. I told them about my week's conducting in Kraków and that it had been musically very rewarding. I reminded him that for this Kraków engagement I had been paid only in Polish zlotys, which were worthless in the West. His commission was in the form of a hand-carved wooden statue I had bought for him in the Sukkienice Market in Kraków's central square. Then I dropped the bombshell.

"Penderecki has offered me the Music Directorship of the Kraków Philharmonic. I have no idea how serious the offer is or whether it is really all that interesting. But what do you think?"

Both their jaws dropped. They didn't speak for at least a minute. But then a look came over Dr. Adler's face, as though a light had just gone on in his head.

The import of this invitation was more apparent to them, of course, than it was to me. They had more of an inkling of the East-West aspect of this, because living in West Berlin, they knew in a more tangible way about the musical interchange between East Germany and West Germany and between the East and the West generally than almost any other Western agent might have. So they weren't going to dismiss this idea out of hand. They were the ones, in fact, who had arranged for me to conduct the vaunted Dresden Staatskapelle deep inside Communist East Germany the season before.

Finally, Dr. Adler said, "I've never heard of such a thing. But you know, Gilbert, maybe this is not so crazy after all. Maybe this could be possible. You say you enjoyed the music-making, yes? It's a good orchestra. They tour all over. They record even, no? And maybe, just maybe, the time is right. Of course," Adler said, "you will have to get some real money!"

But money was not my primary concern. I had had a terrible time politically. I had no idea that I could even survive another week in that society, let alone live there.

"I just don't know. I have to think this through very carefully, and I have to talk this over with my family as well."

I went back home to New York and raised it first, of course, with my wife, Vera. She shuddered at the thought because she had escaped communism. She left Bratislava for Israel in 1965, a year and a half before the Six-Day War. Her family had fled because communism was choking them. They had desperately needed to get out. Now I was proposing to go back in.

I started telling her about what my week was like. And as I rattled on to her about the musical experience, she saw the glow in my face. She knew on some level then that if all of the hurdles could be worked out, that I was going to do this. She saw it in my eyes. The music-making had clearly been very special.

I knew, however, that there was something else I had to do before I could engage in even one more conversation with the Poles, with my agent, or with anybody else. I had to pay a visit to my mother-in-law, Margit. I had to share with her what I had experienced at Birkenau. I feared it would be a very difficult conversation.

Margit and I settled into the overstuffed chairs in the living room of her Upper West Side Manhattan apartment. She and her husband, Laci, had made many moves in their difficult lives, to be sure, but New York was where they had retired so that they could be near Vera, Vera's brother Yuri, and their grandkids.

"Margit," I said, "I know less now than I did before about what it would mean for you to have lived in Birkenau. It is inconceivable to me that you survived even one day in that hellish place, let alone eighteen months. I don't understand how you did it!"

She didn't need my description of what I had seen because for her it was still alive, in her mind's eye, every day of her life since the day she left on the Death March from Birkenau to Bergen-Belsen. But she let me talk, because it was important for me to tell her.

After I had told her what I had seen at Birkenau, I went on to the strange tale of my new opportunity.

"Margit, I have something I need to tell you. You're not going to believe it. I've been offered the job of Music Director of the Kraków

Philharmonic. Musically, I have to say, I had a wonderful time, but even more than in East Germany my encounter with communism was very rough. And my time at Birkenau was just terrible. I'm glad I went, for your sake, but it was awful nonetheless. Am I crazy even to think about this? I won't go if you say so. I would never desecrate the memory of your family, if that's what you think this will do."

Margit had lived under communism for many years, from 1948, three years after her liberation from the concentration camp at Bergen-Belsen, until 1965, when the Kalina family had left Czechoslovakia for a new life in Israel. She looked at me at first as though I was indeed talking crazy, as she would say. Then she thought for a good long while, all the time looking at my face. Finally, she began:

"Musically, I cannot judge. You say it's good, it must be good, or you would not even be considering it. As for communism, you know, I had very close friends in Bratislava, but the system is terrible. I would never, ever go back.

"But let me tell you something; if you go, you would really be doing a good deed. You would be showing everyone, all over the world, that yes, millions of us were killed, but the Nazis did not kill the Jewish people. Even though they murdered my whole family, they didn't kill Jewish culture. You know, we were in Poland for so many centuries. My family and millions of Jews. Not all those years were bad. We really did great things there. Yes, Hitler tried to kill every last remnant of our culture, to destroy our past so we would not have a present. But he didn't succeed. Go back. Show them all that they failed. By taking such a prominent position in Kraków, where the General Government, Hitler's terrible government for Poland, was headquartered, and which they left standing as an architectural monument, you would be showing the world that that maniac and his murdering regime didn't succeed. That we still live."

I was stunned. I couldn't say a word. Her witness was just so powerful.

I left her feeling that what Vera had said was true; that if everything could be worked out, I was going to go. That I had the right to go. Maybe a duty to go. What a statement my Margit had made!

There remained one more stone to touch. One more person I had to consult. And that was Elie Wiesel, the Nobel Peace Laureate and the world's most recognizable Holocaust survivor.

Even after I had talked to my mother-in-law, I still felt I had to talk to Elie before I could go forward, before things got too serious. I had met Wiesel during the early 1980s, flying back and forth on the shuttle between Boston and New York. When Vera and I lived in Back Bay and I was frequently on my way south, he was living in New York and teaching at Boston University. Elie and I used to sit in the front of the plane with our feet up talking about Beethoven at thirty-five thousand feet. Elie has a deep appreciation for classical music. I always loved our talks. So on this matter I called Elie and said that I really needed to speak to him about something very important.

I went to visit him in his East Side apartment, which looked at that time like nothing so much as an ancient rabbinical study, piled high with books from floor to ceiling, well-worn volumes falling off the shelves and all over the place. Elie invited me into his study, and I described to him what had been proposed, this musical invitation to Kraków.

"I don't know," he said quietly and with sadness in his eyes. "I really don't know that I can advise you what to do. What does your mother-in-law think?"

"Margit? She thinks that I should go. She thinks it would be an important demonstration of the vibrancy of Jewish life. That we still live! That they did not kill the Jewish people, even though they murdered so many millions of us."

"You know, Gilbert, I believe that no survivor's opinion is more important than any other's. All survivors," he said in his light Yiddish and slightly French-inflected accent, "each one of us, has the same right to the memory of the Shoah. If your mother-in-law says that you should go, then you should go. Who am I to say anything else?"

It wasn't the answer I had hoped for. I had wanted him to say that he too thought it was a positive idea. But he had shared a profound and generous truth, nonetheless. And I was grateful to have received his wisdom, if not his blessing. His *heckscher*, as we say in Yiddish, would have to wait for another day, or so I hoped.

After that, the business negotiations began, if you can call them that given the very small amount of hard currency the Poles were able to offer. At root, mine was a business contract: I was being offered the post of Music Director for a set number of concerts a year, for so many dollars. I was going to make a tenth of what I would have received someplace else as Music Director, plus, it is true, quite a lot of Polish zlotys. But you couldn't take the zlotys out of the country or convert them into foreign currency. Having this much Polish currency did mean, however, that I could live very well in Kraków. I could eat in whatever restaurants I liked, though there were very few open at the time. I could buy what was available, although what was truly worthwhile was only to be bought for dollars at the Pewex shops, set up by the Polish government just for that purpose. But in dollars I would be very poor.

There were also political and diplomatic aspects that had to be discussed as well. Artistic freedom, for example. One didn't have to be an expert, or read Solomon Volkov's *Testimony*, the posthumously published biography of Shostakovich, to have heard the tales about the horrendous interference of Communist apparatchiks in the functioning of East Bloc musical institutions. It would be no different for me: I was to be the American head of an East Bloc orchestra. I had exalted notions about artistic freedom and the ability to choose my programs and artists. The Polish answer was always, "Of course, of course, of course. You can have everything. What stories have you read? We are artistically very free. You will see." I was naive enough to believe it was true. Until I lived there, in their culture, it was impossible to know what it would really be like.

The fact of the matter was that the political wheels ground very slowly. Penderecki and the Kraków musical establishment over which he had tight control had decided on the night of my concert in Kraków that they wanted me. The Polish state musical authorities in Warsaw, too, had decided this was going to work out one way or another. But this was a decision that had to be made at the highest level of the Polish government. The philosophical impetus—glasnost—may have come from Moscow, but it had to involve all of the various practical mechanisms that go into decision-making in an authoritarian regime. It took months for the decision to go ahead to be made in Warsaw. I think that, as in every society, the security authorities were the most suspicious. They must have been asking, "Who is this guy? What do you know about him? Is he a CIA plant?"

It took George H.W. Bush to solve the problem. That official from the U.S. Embassy whom I had met on the plane from Warsaw to Berlin went back to John Davis, the Chargé d'Affaires in the American Embassy, and told him of the proposal for me to go to the Kraków Philharmonic as their Music Director. At about that time, George H.W. Bush, who was Vice President in 1987, was running for President, and that meant a trip to Poland to shore up the Polish vote back home. In late August, before the Vice President left on his Eastern European trip, I received a call from Washington.

"White House Signal," a voice intoned. "Mr. Gilbert Levine?"

"Yes?"

"Please hold for the Office of the Vice President."

"Mr. Levine, this is Donald Gregg, National Security Advisor to the Vice President. I understand that you have been offered a position with the orchestra in Kraków. What's the holdup?"

"I don't know," I said hesitantly. I'd never received a call from the White House before. "We've pretty much solved the issues, as far as I'm concerned. It's a wonderful opportunity if things could be worked out, but if politically it isn't the right thing to do just now, then I don't want to go."

"No, no. We think it would be great. We'll see what we can do."

Perhaps it was he who saw my appointment as the 1987 equivalent of the 1970s ping-pong diplomacy, which paved the way for Richard Nixon's visit to China. I doubted that Mr. Bush himself would be all that concerned. But in any case, I was pretty convinced that would be the last I would hear about this from Donald Gregg.

When a high-ranking American politician goes to Warsaw, it is for state business, where the real business of any high-level Polish trip takes place. There is usually, however, a weekend visit to Kraków, for a kind of cultural tourism; there might be a lunch with the Mayor, a visit to Wavel Castle, where the treasures of royal Poland are viewed, and a tour around the magnificent old town square. I am surmising that in Vice President Bush's case, as at all official meetings, there were "talking points"—things that the Vice President of the United States could say to the Mayor of Kraków over their official lunch. My Music Directorship was probably about Point Number 5.

I imagine it going something like this:

Vice President Bush: "I understand that a gifted young American conductor, Mr. Gilbert Levine, is under consideration to become Music Director of your Philharmonic Orchestra. Wouldn't that be a wonderful signal in fostering better Polish-American relations?" Or something like that. The Kraków Mayor's side of that talk I can't even conjure up, given the political climate in Communist Poland at the time.

Whatever actually occurred, shortly after the wheels were up on Air Force Two as it left Poland, I got a call at my West Side Manhattan apartment. On a crackly line, a highly accented Polish voice said, "Mr. Levine, you must please come to Cologne to finalize negotiations for Kraków post. Right away. Next week is fine? Yes?"

After nine months of halting political stalemates, the process had been reenergized. Donald Gregg and his boss, the Vice President, had had a real impact, stiffening the resolve of the Polish Communist regime to go forward bravely with this unprecedented cultural opening.

I flew to Cologne and spent a day and a half with my agent, Witiko Adler, Krzysztof Penderecki, and a Communist functionary from PAGART, the Polish Artists Agency, talking about my contract. In the dining room of the five-star Hotel Excelsior, the hotel where the Pendereckis were staying, the agreement was worked out for the grand sum, I remember, of $18,000 a year, plus all the zlotys I could possibly spend, plus tickets back and forth on Pan Am, which would be helping, in this way, to sponsor my Kraków post. And so it was that in December 1987, my appointment as Music Director and Principal Conductor of the Kraków Philharmonic would begin, ten months after I had left, thinking I would probably not see Poland again for a very, very long time.

Once my appointment was announced to the press, there was an amazing outpouring of interest. *Newsweek*, the *New York Times*, National Public Radio, and ABC News, among many others, called for interviews. I hadn't really thought about the public aspect of it; my concerns had been more private: my mother-in-law's reaction, my Polish-Jewish roots, and of course, the music-making. But I couldn't have imagined it would be such a news story.

The media interest led me to believe that there could indeed be larger issues at work than I had thought. I was going to Kraków as the first American head of an artistic institution in the East Bloc in this period of glasnost. So I began to think of myself and my Music Directorship in somewhat more historic terms. It was more than a little daunting. This added political dimension made me nervous and very uneasy.

It went beyond the surveillance of the Polish secret police, or SB, as they were known. I now knew I would have to face them head on, something I dreaded just from the week I had already spent in Kraków. My uneasiness was even more acute than the reality of Auschwitz-Birkenau, which I would have to confront in its constant proximity, reminding me every day of the worst tragedy in the history of my people. It even went beyond the challenge of building a relationship with my new orchestra. I would have had to do that if the Kraków Philharmonic had somehow been transplanted to

Chicago. That's what musicians and their conductors do. They find a way to be together that makes them larger than the sum of their parts.

No, what was truly beginning to seem overwhelming was my being an American in Poland, a member of the society of the West in the Communist East, of living behind the Iron Curtain as a vulnerable pioneer. I found the idea of being a political guinea pig distasteful. The secret police would be looking at me up and down and sideways: to intimidate me, to keep me in line. That was one thing. But to think that my activities would have larger international implications was something I had not fully considered. The intense press interest made me understand that I would never be able to do my work in Poland without the eyes of the world following my every move.

The realization of my larger role in turn led me to think about the fact that there was now a Polish Pope and that Kraków was his hometown. But, I thought, what could the relationship possibly be? I was Jewish, from New York, Pope John Paul II was the leader of more than a billion Catholics worldwide. Why would he conceivably care about me? It had been just about the farthest thing from my mind. Still, now I began to wonder. Could there somehow be such an implausible connection? Could the world be so strange?

After all, I knew so very little about the Church before I went to Poland in 1987. My only vague recollection about popes up until then was that when they were elected at the Vatican, the smoke rose white out of the chimney of the Sistine Chapel, and that their coronations were most impressive. Up until that time, I'd never even met a Catholic priest in my life. It was a very, very long way from there to any conceivable encounters with a pope.

Before my first trip in my new position, Vera and I sat down for a serious talk about our family, and how this would affect us and our son. Vera had a job at a bank in New York. My new Polish position would involve a serious financial sacrifice as it was. We could not also give up her income. And, Vera told me, "In any case, I don't think it would be good for David. He's only three years old, and there would be no American kids his age. I think it's better if we come back and forth to visit you, as often as we can afford."

I finally arrived in Kraków at the end of November 1987, and promptly began rehearsing for my opening concert as Music Director of the orchestra. I wanted to begin my Music Directorship with a truly great work: Mahler's Third Symphony fit the bill to a tee. It is a strong and optimistic statement of Mahler's love for all creation. Musically, though, that was a huge mountain to climb, because it is one of the most gargantuan of all symphonies. At eighty minutes of uninterrupted virtuosic musical challenge, it requires an enormous orchestra of one hundred–plus musicians, a women's chorus, a children's chorus, and a mezzo-soprano soloist. The Kraków Philharmonic had never done this work before, so it was a way for us to come together musically by learning something new. Once we had climbed this artistic mountain, we could feel that much stronger about our musical future together.

If this sounds like the beginning of a marriage, in a way it was. Orchestras and conductors have to learn to respect and admire each other to make good music together. Different conductors may work better or worse with different orchestras. And not all Music Director–orchestra relationships are meant to be. But in this case, the Mahler Third on our first program and the subsequent program of Brahms' Violin Concerto and Dvořák Symphony No. Eight, which we performed the next week, made for an auspicious beginning. In one realm at least, the musical one, which I knew the best, we would be OK. My art would be there for me to rely on as I faced the other challenges of my new Polish post. I hadn't been in Kraków more than five days when something happened that was, to say the least, totally new for me. It was the Wednesday of the week of rehearsals leading to our Friday and Saturday subscription series concerts. Completely unexpectedly, I received word via the U.S. Consulate that I had been called in to meet with His Eminence Franciszek Cardinal Macharski, Archbishop of Kraków.

I walked across the ring road in front of the Philharmonic Hall, across the Planty, the park which surrounds the old city, and proceeded down the street to the Curia Metropolitana, the offices of Kraków's Archbishop.

After I entered the courtyard of the Curia, I turned right and went along a sheltered walkway then up two flights of stone steps covered by straw matting. All around was quiet, so all I could hear was the crunch, crunch, crunch of my shoes, disturbing my own discombobulated thoughts. This would be my first-ever conversation with a Catholic priest. What would this meeting be like? Try as I might, I couldn't stop my feet from making that awful noise. As I got to the top of the stairs, I noticed oil paintings of the Cardinal's predecessors as Archbishop of Kraków. One of the last I saw was the most recent portrait, that of Cardinal Karol Wojtyla, now His Holiness Pope John Paul II.

I knocked on the heavy wooden door, and an older man who was not a priest answered. He led me into an antechamber where I took off my coat. Then we walked together into the Cardinal's waiting room, which was filled with people who had come to make a call on the Archbishop that day. Occasionally, His Eminence would come out and look around to find his next petitioner. When it was my turn, the Cardinal ushered me into his inner office, a room right out of *Anna Karenina*, filled with samovars and paintings and Persian rugs. Very elegant in an understated way. His Eminence was tall and gaunt and very patrician-looking. He fit right in with the rows of paintings I had seen outside his door. He said to me in a very courtly English, "Welcome to Kraków. How are you, Maestro? Please do sit down."

Cardinal Macharski and I began a meandering conversation about Kraków, and how much he admired the Kraków Philharmonic. He asked how I, an American, liked his medieval city, coming, as he knew I did, from the bustling metropolis of New York. He said, as if reading my mind, that if our interview, as he called it, had taken place before 1939, it would have been with the Chief Rabbi. I said I thought Kraków was a beautiful city, which I did, that the Kraków Philharmonic was a wonderful orchestra, which I also believed, but that there were some aspects of life that took some getting used to. Poland, I said, as His Eminence well knew, was not the United States. I looked out of the Cardinal's window in the direction of the offices of the Communist Mayor of the city, which were just down the street. Without saying another word, we both knew what I meant. One didn't talk openly about these things, but they were very much in the air.

After twenty minutes or so of this back-and-forth, the Cardinal said, "Well, Maestro, good of you to come. You must tell all that you have told me to the Holy Father."

I looked at him like I hadn't heard him correctly. It took me a minute to even realize who it was His Eminence had meant by "the Holy Father." I only thought that if the occasion arose, it would indeed be wonderful to have the opportunity to meet the Pope.

I left the Curia and went straight back to my hotel. I went on with the rest of the week and the weeks that followed, not really thinking about what had been said in the Cardinal's private office that day. I had much too much else on my plate to be thinking about what I was sure was an offhand comment.

I was preoccupied, as I had been from the beginning, with the oppressive nature of the surveillance that went on. I wasn't completely taken aback by it. I had lived through the week with the Dresden Staatskapelle and the East German Stasi, and then a period during the Prague Spring Festival with their Czech "colleagues," and my week in Kraków the February before. But there was an aspect to the intensity of the attentions of the Polish SB that I found newly oppressive.

One condition of my contract was that I be able to come and go as I needed, something no one else in my orchestra could hope to be able to do. Getting a visa out of Poland in 1987 was a rare gift that went only to the most reliable of artists, who could be counted on to come back to communism even after they had tasted the fruits that the West had to offer. So my multiple-entry visa, which allowed me to come and go as I pleased, a first in all of Polish-American relations to that point, was an object of some serious curiosity, and no little envy among my Kraków musical colleagues.

Yet one of the really big fights that first week was not about my visa but about where I would live. The orchestra, and I was sure the

SB, wanted me to live in the apartment that was reserved for the Music Director. It was, by local standards, a nice small apartment in a relatively new if drab apartment block. As far as space was concerned, there was nothing wrong with it. And it was located relatively near the center of the city, something very difficult for most members of the Philharmonic to find.

But this apartment didn't have a phone, and in those years in Poland there was no prospect of ever getting a phone. The wait could last years! And the building didn't have a guard downstairs, who although undoubtedly would have reported on my movements to the authorities, would have at least been a witness should anything untoward have occurred. If I took this apartment, I would be totally cut off from the outside world. This was a frightening prospect, given that I was subjected to constant secret police surveillance. There was no way I would stay there. God only knows what might have happened to me, and no one would have ever been the wiser.

So I turned down the apartment and, after much contentious back-and-forth with the authorities, moved into the Holiday Inn, which was then the best hotel in Kraków, although it was a fifteen-minute drive outside of town. It had desk clerks downstairs and telephones that worked. I thought I would be much safer in the Holiday Inn than I would have been in the apartment, but nothing was ever that simple.

The secret police decided they would make my decision about where to live seem as oppressive and as foolish as possible. The hotel put me on the fifth floor, which was where every delegation from the West seemed to stay. I assumed that was because that floor was the most electronically advanced, in terms of secret police surveillance. After my move, administrators in the Philharmonic would comment on something that they could only know if they had been privy to my private phone calls made from the hotel. I surmised that members of the security apparatus must have told very select members of the Philharmonic hierarchy some of the things I said on the phone. I was safer than I would have been in the Music Director's apartment, but I still had no semblance of privacy. But then, I don't think anyone did in Communist Poland.

One nice thing about the Holiday Inn were the regular visitors from Project Hope, a Christian organization that brought in doctors and nurses who wanted to volunteer at the Kraków Children's Hospital. They would come in for a week of intensive work, ministering to Polish kids, performing lifesaving operations, even open-heart surgery—all for free. Project Hope eventually rebuilt the entire Kraków Children's Hospital, and the Kraków Philharmonic and I gave a concert in honor of its dedication. I enjoyed the good old American camaraderie I had with those Project Hope medical folks. It gave me a little less sense of isolation to share a dinner or two with them in the dining room of our common home away from home.

Life in the hotel was never easy. One day I left the hotel and got down to my orchestra-provided taxi before I realized it was raining. I decided to get an umbrella, and ran back up to my room. In the time it had taken for me to get downstairs and back upstairs, something weird had happened. I tried my key in the door, and it wouldn't work, although it was the same key I had used a few minutes before. I went down to the front desk and asked what was going on. The Polish lady behind the desk looked at me with great concern. She made the sign of the cross and said, "If I were you, I wouldn't go back up there. If you can't get in, it means you are not meant to get in. If I were you, Sir, I would just get back in your car and be on your way."

When I got back from my rehearsals that afternoon, I found that things had been moved. A suitcase that had been on one bed was now on the other bed. Other things had been moved around ever so slightly but enough for me to know. I am not an expert on espionage, but I know that if people don't want you to know they've been in your room, you won't know it. These people knew what they were doing, which was scaring the heck out of me, showing me that no place was safe. I imagine they wanted me to conclude that I might as well move into the apartment, or just leave Poland altogether. It ran through my mind that even though the authorities in Warsaw wanted me there, the Kraków SB apparently did not.

I picked up the phone and called the American Consul General, Michael Hornblow. I said, "I'm not staying here anymore. It's not healthy."

He said, "What do you mean?"

"You know what I mean. Things have gotten out of hand. I am really at my wit's end." I was speaking very ostentatiously because I knew, and he knew, that whoever had switched my suitcases was also listening in on our conversation.

Hornblow waited a second and then said, "OK, Gilbert, come to us. Please come stay in our home."

Moving into the Consul General's residence was not what anyone had in mind, especially not Michael and Caroline Hornblow. Yet, with my wife and son, who had long been scheduled to come to Kraków for a visit, I spent some peaceful days in the Consul General's lovely Christmas-decorated house. It was completely surveilled by the men in trench coats ever present on the outside, and probably by microphones planted on the inside, but at least I had peace of mind that this experiment in international living was not to be undone in one week by the thuggish tactics of the Kraków secret police.

The provocations didn't end there. Once, when Vera and David were safely back home in New York, I went out to the movies. At the end of the show, a very pretty, ostentatiously dressed girl approached me afterwards to say, "Oh, are you American? Can I show you around the city?" She was lovely but obviously a plant. It was pretty heavy-handed. They wanted to see if they could get me in a compromising position, and take a few pictures for their files.

For somebody with no training or preparation, not even a one-day State Department course a foreign correspondent might get, it was scary. And I was the Music Director of the Kraków Philharmonic, not a guest conductor. I wasn't leaving after a single week. I was committed to the orchestra, responsible for their musical and, to some extent, financial future through the tours and recordings, and all the things a Music Director does. I couldn't just leave. My contract was for three-

and-a-half years. So, as far as I was concerned, I wasn't going anywhere.

In the end, the music-making made everything worthwhile. I had heard the Kraków Philharmonic in Boston on one of their U.S. tours. They toured regularly to America and to Western Europe, and had won a Grand Prix du Disque. I was an admirer of their artistry and their tradition.

Now I was proudly conducting them as their Chief.

We found a common ground, especially in Beethoven and Brahms. I came from a strong European tradition. My mentors had been Sir Georg Solti and Klaus Tennstedt. Solti was a Hungarian and a galvanic Wagner and Beethoven interpreter. Tennstedt, an East German refugee enormously successful in those years in the West, was one of the greatest Brahms and Mahler conductors of the second half of the twentieth century. I could learn from the Kraków orchestra's tradition and also bring them something of my own musical perspective. Every time the secret police tried to knock me out of kilter, the orchestra brought me back, reminding me of just why I had come to Poland.

At the time, I was leading rehearsals with the orchestra in English or German. There were then two concertmasters in the Kraków Philharmonic, an English-speaker named Mieczyslaw Szlezer, who had studied at Indiana University and whose English was very good, and the other an older gentleman who spoke German. So when the orchestra was being led by the concertmaster who spoke German, I spoke German (a language in which I felt completely comfortable). He would translate what I said into Polish. I didn't speak any Polish, so I didn't know what was being said. When Mr. Szlezer was the concertmaster, I spoke to him in English and he translated into Polish.

Sometimes I said something about the music in fairly elaborate terms, but when he translated it, it came out as just one sentence. And sometimes, after that one sentence, they would look at me very oddly. I wasn't always 100 percent sure that Szlezer was translating exactly what I had said, nor saying it with quite the degree of politeness which I always tried to use in relation to my orchestra. I had enough to do to understand the orchestra on a musical level. Our different spoken languages just added to the complexity of it all.

I did have a rather interesting relationship with Mr. Szlezer, who was always looking for American magazines—*Newsweek* or *Time*—or whatever other Western publications I had brought with me into the country, which were not then available to the general Polish population. Szlezer would sit with me and practice his excellent English. I enjoyed it as well. Having a conversational partner in my native language was something I truly looked forward to.

My concertmaster's religious background, however, was always a bit of a puzzle. His family name sounded Jewish, but I was never sure. At one point my curiosity overcame me:

"Szlezer—isn't that a Jewish name?" I asked.

He answered, "Yes, Maestro. I am of Jewish heritage."

"Was your mother Jewish?" I inquired. By Jewish law, if his mother was Jewish, then so was he.

"Yes, yes she is."

"And your Father?"

"Yes, he is also."

"So," I said, "you are Jewish then."

"No, Maestro; as I said, I am of Jewish heritage."

I pressed him no further, and returned to other things.

After what the Nazis (and the Russians) had done to Poland during the war (both of Mr. Szlezer's parents were Holocaust survivors), and with some in the most extreme elements of Polish society still harboring strong anti-Semitic sentiments, I could well understand why he might be uncomfortable with his religious identity. But our conversation still made me very sad.

Then, early in the winter of 1988, after reading an article about Polish politics in *Newsweek*, I asked Mr. Szlezer what he thought the future might bring to his country. "You know, Maestro, I truly believe my grandchildren will live under communism. I see no end to this system. It is our Polish fate. There is nothing to be done." His dark vision for what lay in store for his country made me even sadder still.

The other person whom I met, who befriended me without linguistic bridge, was a man named Czeslaw Pilawski. Czeslaw was a violinist and the Personnel Manager of the Kraków orchestra. Then in his mid-fifties, he was old enough to have seen the war firsthand. On our Sundays off, he would pick me up at my hotel and drive me into the Polish countryside to proudly show me his homeland. He didn't speak English, and I didn't then speak Polish, but somehow we made ourselves understood. On other occasions, he even invited me to share a meal in his home. That openheartedness, and his ever-present smile, were as precious as they were rare.

I went back to Birkenau again and again. I had made a commitment to my mother-in-law to do so and to never forget. I also sought out the Kraków Jewish community for the first time. I went into Kazimierz and found the Jewish community center, a kind of disheveled suite of rooms on the second floor of a nondescript apartment building. I met the Jakubowiczs, a quintessential Polish-Jewish family who had come to Kraków after the war and established themselves as a kind of nucleus of the two hundred Jews who were left out of the eighty thousand who had lived there before 1939. Czeslaw and his brother Tadeusz were fascinated by me, an American Jew. They were less nervous about me than were other people, most of whom were scared of having anything to do with me. Associations like that could be trouble; conversations could be misinterpreted or reported to the SB, so it was not at all easy to get close to Poles, even those in my orchestra, during that period. And outside the job, I wasn't finding many other opportunities for Polish friendship.

But the Jewish community was more welcoming, not because they were any less afraid but because they needed the outreach to a larger Jewish world. I was from New York, one of the world's biggest Jewish communities. We talked about what Jewish life was like in New York. And we talked about their lives in Kraków. Small in numbers and resources, their lives were just so different. They asked me a lot of questions: Can you help us with reconstruction? Can you help bring us a Rabbi for the High Holy Days?

They invited me to go to the Remuh Synagogue to pray with them, to partake of their Jewish lives. I wasn't especially close with these people; we didn't have a lot in common. In New York, one doesn't get close to someone just because they are Jewish. But in Kraków, I was a Jew alone, and these people were, effectively, my only kin. I wanted to do what I could to help them, but I didn't really know what that would be. Still, they were a link to my mother-in-law, to the survivors who had stayed in Poland. There was a connection that gave me a sense of Jewish history in that place that was not just in dead buildings and painted-over mezuzahs. I would try to do what I could.

I went home for my winter break, feeling wonderful about the music-making and beginning to digest the many different things that had happened. There was nothing so sweet as getting on a Pan Am plane, settling back in my seat, and realizing that for all intents and purposes, I was free again. What a relief.

My stopovers in Frankfurt on my flights home became an oasis. There people were free to say what they wanted. In Frankfurt, I felt normal. I was finally on my way to the West. West to New York, my family, my friends, and the bright lights of my hometown.

CHAPTER

FOUR

W hen I returned to Kraków after my winter break, I was
greeted by the artistic administrator of the orchestra, Pan
Jacek Berwald, at the door of Philharmonic Hall with a
strange question:

"Pan Direktor, why do you want to meet our Holy Father?"

I didn't know how to respond. I just stared at him, my face
scrunched in puzzlement.

I had not discussed my meeting with Cardinal Macharski
with anyone in Poland besides the American Consul General. I certainly knew nothing of any actual meeting with the Pope. So the
question simply seemed rather odd. Also, the way it was put was,
well, off-putting. The "you" and the "our" of it. "Why do you want to
meet our Holy Father?" I was a Jew, not a Catholic, and an American,
not a Pole. So, for Pan Berwald, at least, I was decidedly not one of
them.

"I have no idea what you are talking about, Pan Berwald," I said,
and climbed the broad cold stone steps then walked down the hall to
my third-floor office.

There in the middle of my otherwise empty desk was an elegant,
oversized envelope, obviously no longer sealed. I smiled. This was
Communist Poland. I was not the first to read this letter. Just how
many readers had there been?

I picked up the envelope and turned it over to see whom it
was from. The beautiful calligraphy read *Curia Metropolitana*

Krakowska—Office of the Archbishop. I took the rich-textured note card out of its envelope and began to read:

> Dear Pan Direktor Levine,
>
> His Eminence Cardinal Macharski has just returned from the Vatican where he had occasion to speak with the Holy Father about you. His Eminence believes you may now be received by His Holiness. When you are in Rome in February, please kindly telephone to:
>
> Father Konrad Hejmo—Responsible Party for Polish Pilgrims [followed a seven-digit number] or
>
> Monsignor Stanislaw Dziwisz—telephone number 6982.
>
> Yours in Christ,
> Fr. Bronislaw Fidelus

Questions immediately began to spin in my mind. Was I going to Rome in February? In any case, to do so I would need a specific travel permit. My contract stipulated that I needed the Kraków Philharmonic's permission to enter and exit, per my special-status Polish visa. Would I get the management's OK? What would I tell the Polish authorities about why I was going to Rome? The note from Father Fidelus left that matter vague.

As it turned out, there was indeed some official resistance to my making this trip. Relations between the Vatican, even with a Polish Pope at its head, and the Communist government of the Pope's home country, were not yet even on an official basis. I had to go to police headquarters to have my visa reviewed before permission would be granted. The authorities asked me questions about the nature of my Vatican trip, questions which I could not really answer. I consulted the American consulate, as this was a bilateral visa matter, but they could be of no help. I was in the hands of the security apparatus. They would have to decide whether I could go to Rome or not. They were evidently not going to make this easy.

In the end, I was summoned to the police once again and received my exit and, most important, reentry visas. Though I had a never-before-granted multiple entry visa, I had to report all my comings and goings to the authorities. The orchestra General Director gave his official permission as well. So early one Tuesday in February, I boarded a flight for Rome.

Flights from Kraków to Rome flew twice a week. During those years, they mainly served as a means of transit for priests and nuns from Kraków back and forth to the Vatican. Very few tourist or business links existed between Italy and Poland. My flight was no exception. I was one of the few nonecclesiastical passengers on the plane. I felt oddly secure.

I had made the reservation for my hotel room in the Eternal City via the concierge at my hotel in Kraków, so I knew I would be sure to have a place to stay. By so doing, however, I had also naively given my Roman whereabouts directly to the Polish secret police, although I'm sure they would have had the information from their many informants in any case. The SB were still intensively tracking my every move, and their contacts in Rome were ever present as well.

On arrival at the Hotel Napoleon, near Roma Termini, I dutifully called the first name on my short list of Polish priests. Father Hejmo's number was not only listed first but had seven digits. He was clearly the more important of the two, or so I thought. It was Tuesday afternoon at about 5 P.M. His telephone rang and rang, but for whatever reason he never picked up.

I was impatient. I was in Rome for a short time, and there was this other name on my list, so after two or three further attempts to reach Father Hejmo, I decided to give the other one a try. I dialed the four digits and eventually a female voice answered "*Vaticano?*"— something like, "Offices of Vatican City?" Wow, I thought, it was the Vatican switchboard. For this I had to come all the way to Rome?!

Plunging on, I said, in Italian, "May I speak with Monsignor Dziwisz, please?" only I am sure I mangled the name. It is pronounced *Gee-vish*, which is not exactly how it looks on the page. The good sister on the other end of the line was surprised. Her tone changed instantly. I had clearly unintentionally overstepped.

"Please may I ask, who gave you this name?" she asked with polite sternness.

"His Eminence Cardinal Macharski," I answered, now newly timid.

"*Vediamo*—we'll see—kindly hold the line."

Then there was silence.

After some moments, a sonorous baritone voice intoned.

"Pronto?" Nothing more.

I started a rambling explanation in Italian about how I had gotten the number, still not knowing with whom I was now speaking. Monsignor Dziwisz stopped me short after a sentence or two and said, continuing on in Italian, the lingua franca of the Vatican:

"Maestro, I was expecting your call. Cardinal Macharski has told me about you. Please come to the Portone di Bronzo tomorrow at 5 P.M."

"Where is that?" I asked.

Monsignor Dziwisz laughed a warm and hearty laugh. "Just ask anyone. I know you'll find your way," he said, and put down his receiver.

Instead of being put off or embarrassed at how little I knew of the Vatican, I was now more and more curious. Who was Monsignor Dziwisz? He had seemed quite friendly on the phone. I was anxious to meet him and, most of all, to see where all this would lead.

The next morning, I dutifully asked the hotel concierge where I might find the Portone di Bronzo. "Oh," the desk clerk replied, "that's the main entrance to the Apostolic Palace, the residence of the Pope. When you reach Saint Peter's Square, follow the Bernini Columns to the right in the direction of the Basilica until you reach a large staircase that leads to the Bronze Door. There, where you can go no further, ask the Swiss Guard. You can't miss it."

I might as well have asked, "Where's the East Gate of the White House? You know, just outside that large mansion in the middle of Pennsylvania Avenue!" I had been a bit of a fool. And not just about the location of the Pope's Palace in Rome.

Monsignor Stanislaw Dziwisz, it turned out, was the longtime Private Secretary of His Holiness Pope John Paul II. John Paul had brought him specially from Kraków when he was elected Pope. Esteemed for his keen intelligence and his impeccable good judgment, Dziwisz was now one of the most influential figures in the Vatican. However, he was rarely seen in public, except as a discreet presence behind the Pope at important functions. But his effectiveness on behalf of John Paul was immense, because he was so completely trusted by the Pope to do and say only that which His Holiness might wish. In sum, Monsignor Dziwisz lived his life completely in service to Pope John Paul. Father Fidelus' note had not begun to prepare me for such a potent Vatican encounter.

Well in advance of the appointed hour, I approached the Portone di Bronzo, the immense and famous Bronze Door at the entrance to the Apostolic Palace. Two Swiss Guards stood at right angles to each other at the top of the stairs, on either side of these giant portals. One faced me down as I walked up the steps, the other thrust out his halberd (a Renaissance lance with a half-moon scimitar-shaped blade at the end) just in case I didn't get his fellow guard's cautionary message. When I reached the top step, the guard facing me asked whom I had come to see. When I said Monsignor Dziwisz's name, I was shown into a small office off to the right. Two men in civilian clothes sat behind what looked like a post-office window. The walls of the room were festooned with calendars and the neatly hung black capes of the color-fully clad Swiss Guards who were on duty just outside. The clerk behind the open window telephoned someone "upstairs" to verify my appointment. Then he stamped my blue Apostolic Palace pass and sent me on my way.

An officer of the Swiss Guards seated at a desk just inside the Bronze Door had seen me go into the office, had witnessed my being given the blue-colored pass, and still asked to examine it before letting me go any further into the Palace. He directed me towards three long flights of wide stone stairs that led to a landing, where another Swiss Guard, just inside the opening to a vast inner courtyard, checked my paper pass once again.

One guard led to another and to another through a seemingly endless series of checkpoints. Up the stairs, across a courtyard, up a small elevator I went until finally I found myself on the Seconda Loggia, the Papal Palace's second level.

When I exited the elevator, I thought I was finally alone. I walked out into a magnificent hallway, my eyes drawn upwards to ceilings some forty feet high, painted resplendently in high Renaissance style. Staring up, I began to walk from the elevator vestibule out into the hallway itself when, abruptly, another Swiss guardsman appeared out of nowhere to my right. He gestured once again for my pass. He examined it and pointed to my left, towards the end of the glorious glass-sided hallway.

There I was stopped by a massive shuttered wooden door. I looked back for the Swiss Guard. He had disappeared. I stood there a minute, as if waiting for the door to magically open by itself. Finally, I knocked. After some time, a beefy man in formal morning clothes opened the door from the inside. I entered the Papal Palace proper.

The man who let me in was one of the Pope's Sediari, those that carry the chair; it is a name that means what it says. Until the reign of Pope Paul VI in the 1960s, no pope's feet could touch the ground at public ceremonies, so he was carried in a chaise, a grand throne transported by the forebears of these same Sediari who greeted me now.

The first room I entered beyond the wooden door was the Sala Clementina, the grandest reception room I had ever seen. It is immense, with gleaming parquet floors and very high painted ceilings with the Seal of Pope Clement in the very center. It was a room so resonant that I immediately heard beautiful Renaissance polyphony that seemed to have been trapped for hundreds of years in its exquisite walls. It was a *trompe d'oreille*—a trick of my musician's ear. The room, of course, was absolutely silent.

Through a door on the other side of the Sala Clementina, I could see a desk and another of the Sediari seated behind it. I was asked to approach. The desk was elegant but simple, with a lamp and a phone, and a very thin ledger placed in the middle. The Sediaro greeted me with a smile.

These were the first people I had met in more than half an hour who seemed to acknowledge that I was indeed welcome, expected, not alien to these august surroundings. They greeted me instead of looking me up and down. The Sediaro behind the desk disappeared with my blue permission slip into a corridor through yet another door. I was then guided by another of the Sediari into a proper waiting room, also exquisitely decorated and majestically high-ceilinged. It had antique chairs set far apart, with a table on which one could leave a briefcase or a coat on the near wall. The entire north side was lined with curtained windows, which looked out onto the Pope's private gardens at the back of the Vatican itself.

I spent a few moments staring out the windows, imagining the Pope taking in this remarkable view. A tap on my shoulder brought me back into the real world. I was led by the first of the Sediari down a corridor that led from this grand ceremonial space to the working part of the Palace, a place of day-to-day papal tasks. Coming from the magnificently proportioned Sala Clementina, I found this all much more to human scale.

Just down this corridor I was met by yet another man, this one dressed in a formal black business suit. He smiled cordially, and showed me into a small room, perhaps twelve feet square, with very high painted ceilings showing the seal of Pope John XXIII. There was a small, slightly worn Persian carpet in the center of the floor. The odd proportions, small room, very high ceilings, made this room feel like an elegant cell. My latest guardian-companion smiled again, and left me there.

I was finally alone. At last, I could catch my breath.

I looked around to make sure I didn't miss any details; I knew I would not likely see this room again. In the middle of this cell was a small rectangular desk, Baroque period–appropriate, but nondescript, with two chairs on either side. An ornate Baroque clock sat on an equally ornate gold-cornered marble table, to my left. Besides the clock, the table was laden with gifts. I imagined they were gifts, perhaps brought by other visitors who had hoped to give them personally to the Pope. A hand-painted folk art portrait of Pope John Paul, dressed in red cassock and standing in front of a simple wooden church in his native Poland, hung on the wall above the table. It seemed out of place in this room, but then this Pope did come from simple stock.

On the right side of the room was a very small two-tiered credenza with two telephones perched side by side. One was black with buttons for multiple lines, the other red, with one line only. Next to the telephones was a single pen and a sheaf of elegantly embossed note papers, and a very thick, red clothbound book with the gold Papal Seal on the cover.

(I would later learn that this was the Annuario Pontificio, the yearly directory that is laid out to reveal the structure of the Roman Curia, the Vatican's governing body, and which contains every published relevant telephone number in the worldwide Roman Catholic Church.)

The room was still. Although I knew that Rome with all its traffic and cacophony was only a stone's throw away, here, in this room, behind the ten-foot thick walls of the Vatican, it was remarkably quiet. In that stillness, the Baroque clock's ticking became unbearable, like the buzzing of a mosquito on a still summer's night. I could hardly wait any longer, but it was only 4:55, still five minutes before my appointed hour.

Right then, I realized just how nervous I was. Even though it was February, I was sweating. I don't know if it was all the probing check points, the long silent wait, or the centuries of my people not belonging here, but it suddenly dawned on me just where I was. And I wasn't very comfortable at all.

Finally, at the very stroke of five, in the corner of the room opposite my chair, a door I hadn't noticed before opened. And through that door walked a smallish, middle-aged priest in a simple, long, well-worn black cassock, that swished as he walked the very few paces to his side of the desk.

I rose and offered him my hand. He held it firmly, looking straight into my eyes. For the next half hour those eyes would never leave me. It was as if he wanted to remember everything about me and what I said, so that he could relate what he had come to know of me to person or persons unseen.

Monsignor Dziwisz looked much younger than his forty-nine years. Dressed in a long Roman cassock with buttons down the front, he was all polite business. He did not introduce himself. I guessed that in these hallowed halls he didn't need to. He called me Maestro. We spoke Italian. And that was good, because my Polish in those first months of my tenure in Kraków was nonexistent.

Monsignor Dziwisz's manner was keenly intelligent, straightforward, and sincere. He immediately won my trust. He asked me a series of questions, very similar to those that Cardinal Macharski had asked. How did I feel in Kraków? What did I think of his city? How did I find the orchestra? They were all very general, but there was no reference at all to my religion. With that last exception, it was almost as if Monsignor Dziwisz and Cardinal Macharski had been working from the same script.

The Pope's private secretary too seemed to be looking for something that would give him the answers he was looking for, although to what precise end it was not yet apparent. He just kept staring at me across the narrow table, his brow slightly furrowed as he silently probed my every word.

Finally, without further preamble or connecting phrase, he asked:

"And what would you say to the Holy Father?"

It was the first time in thirty minutes that the Pope had even been mentioned. Ah, I thought, the point of all these interviews was now clear.

I told Monsignor Dziwisz that "I would tell the Pope how much I have taken to Kraków. Particularly to its people and to its cultural life. That I love its ancient architecture, and the feeling it gives me of living in its history. I would tell the Pope of the kindnesses that the ordinary Polish citizens of his city have shown me. Of the understanding I had come to have for their daily struggle in the face of the clear hardships that his people have endured."

I felt like an honorary Cracovian. I genuinely thought that that is what I might say, if given the chance. Monisgnor Dziwisz stopped me mid-sentence.

"Fine, Maestro, please come right here at 12:00 noon tomorrow. Is your wife with you? Please invite her to join you as well."

And with that, he stood up and walked me out through the narrow corridor, just as far as the desk of the Sediari. He offered me his hand and bid me good-bye.

"Maestro, *a domani*—until tomorrow." And he was gone.

I walked out as I had entered. Out the wooden door, under the high ceilings, no longer noticing a thing. Down the elevator, across the courtyard, past all the Swiss Guards, and finally, out the Portone di Bronzo into Saint Peter's Square. I was deep in thought. The crisp February Roman air hit my face and woke me from my daydream.

Tomorrow was going to be a very interesting day. Now I only had to wait nineteen more hours to find out just what might be in store.

Immediately, though, I phoned Vera, in New York. "You won't believe it, but I just met with the Pope's private secretary. He says I will be meeting with His Holiness tomorrow. It would be so important if you could come. Can you get here? And David should come too. If you can get on a flight, it would be so important if we can meet him together."

"I will try," she said. I could hear the shock in her voice. "I'm sure I can get some flight or other that will get me there in the morning. That should leave enough time for me to come to the hotel and dress."

I hung up the phone feeling much more comfortable, knowing that Vera and my boy would be with me on this important day. We would meet the Pope together.

In the meantime, I needed some very important information. I had no idea what to expect. But I knew exactly whom to ask. That evening I had dinner with Consul General Michael Hornblow and his wife Caroline at Grappolo d'Oro, one of their favorite trattorias near the Piazza della Cancelleria. The Hornblows had "coincidentally" decided to come down from Kraków to spend this particular week on a Roman holiday. They just happened to have informed me where they were staying and happened to be free to meet me this particular evening for a meal. In retrospect, it was quite a convenient coincidence.

That evening, I regaled Michael and Caroline with my visit to the Papal Palace. Up until his move to Poland, Michael had been the Deputy Chief of Mission at the U.S. Embassy to the Holy See, with an office not far away on the Aventine Hill, so he knew all there was to know about Papal audiences. Visiting Americans, from Senators, Congressmen, and Cabinet members to high-class and not so high-class businesspeople, would all come to him seeking a meeting with the Pope. It was part of his job to give them the lay of the land. A lucky few would be accommodated. The vast majority would not have any chance of getting in to see the Pope. He tried to be as diplomatic as he could with everyone.

After listening intently to my morning's tale, Michael laid it out as best he could. He was even more soft-spoken than usual. We were surrounded by fellow diners just inches away.

"Well, it's Wednesday evening, so you won't be in the front row at the Wednesday Morning Audience," he said ironically. "Prima Fila, it is called. It is where I would have bet you would be, getting a picture taken with the Pope as he walks down the row nearest to his throne. He shakes hands and stops just long enough for the treasured photograph for the grandkids. It's not exactly private. It all happens in front of the thousands that come every week just to be in the Pope's presence.

"No, by the sound of things, I think you'll have a Baccia a Mano. You and Vera will be positioned somewhere in one of the reception rooms of the Apostolic Palace. As the Pope walks by, you will be quickly introduced, and three or four pictures will be taken during the twenty to thirty seconds of your interaction. Don't prepare anything. No speeches. There won't be time for anything more than formalities. Still, it's a step up from the Prima Fila, and the backdrop for your photo will be the Palace itself. You should feel quite pleased.

"For completeness only," he went on, "there is also the Rolls-Royce of Papal audiences. It is called a Tête-à-Tête. It takes place in the Pope's Private Library, but that is reserved for visiting Cardinals and Bishops on their *ad limina* visit, once every five years, and for heads of state, the leaders of world religions, and others of very high rank. For those audiences, there is usually a priest secretary and, if needed, a translator present. In my experience, one is almost never truly alone with His Holiness. In any case, the list of such audiences is published the next day in *L'Osservatore Romano*, the Vatican newspaper. It goes into the official record for anyone around the world to see. It's a kind of public private audience, if you know what I mean. But again, I add this just so you know the full range of the Pope's audiences. In my years of working at our Holy See Embassy, I have never heard of anyone like yourself being accorded a Tête-a-Tête. Please don't take offense, but that's how it is. The Pope's time is very precious.

"Gilbert, you should be truly honored that he will greet you at all. It will be a memory for a lifetime. And again, don't prepare any speeches. There won't be any time."

Michael Hornblow had tried to be kind, and encouraging. At least now I had a very good idea what we might expect. Duly briefed, I walked back to the hotel to wait out the night.

CHAPTER

FIVE

The next morning, bright and early, the telephone rang. Luckily, it wasn't Vera saying there had been a travel delay. It was a producer from ABC News.

"Well, Maestro, what's going on? Are you seeing the Pope?"

I had forgotten all about this TV crew. They had begun filming a story on my appointment to Kraków back in December. The producer had gotten wind of my trip to Rome, and had asked whether they could tag along just in case.

"Yes, I'm sorry. I've been told to be at the Apostolic Palace at 12:00 noon. I have no idea what's going to happen, but somehow I'm going to be meeting the Pope."

"Fine," she said. "We know what to do. We'll see you in there."

At least one of us knew what to do. ABC had probably done this many times. For me, it would be the first and last such visit; of that I was sure.

Vera and David arrived on time at Fiumicino at 8:00 A.M. and came directly to the Hotel Napoleon, arriving about 9:30. She had slept very little (although David had dozed off as soon as the plane took off), but it didn't matter. She was very excited about just the possibility of meeting the Pope. Sleep could come later.

We dressed in the fanciest clothes we owned, and just after 11:15 A.M. hailed a plain tiny Fiat taxi to take us across the city to Saint Peter's Square. Getting anywhere in Rome on time is iffy. The combination of a Papal audience and the snarl of cars from Castel

Sant'Angelo all the way up the Via della Conciliazione to the Vatican was maddening.

When we finally arrived, I was in quite a state. My three-year-old son was with us when we arrived at the Vatican. We had not been able to find a sitter through the hotel on such short notice, and we had no idea what we would do, but a walk through the elegant audience halls of the Apostolic Palace with a toddler didn't seem to fit the occasion.

Just as we were approaching the Portone di Bronzo, I caught sight of a kindly-looking, white-bibbed, middle-aged nun, her head fully draped in black as I had seen on the streets of Kraków. She was sitting just outside the entrance to the Palace, in full view of the Swiss Guards. I looked at Vera, and she looked back at me, and out came these unthinkable words in my best Italian:

"Sister, I am Maestro Gilbert Levine from the Pope's home city of Kraków. My wife and I are on our way to meet His Holiness. This is our son David. Would you possibly be so kind as to look after him while we are with the Pope? I'm sure we won't be long."

We would normally never have thought to do such a thing, but here, in the Vatican and after my time in Catholic Poland, we somehow had faith that this was exactly right.

The good sister answered, "Of course, it would be an honor. Leave him here with me. I will keep him safe until you return."

It may seem very strange, and we both shudder at the thought to this very day, but neither my wife nor I gave it a second thought. David would be just fine. And in the end he was. He and the sister were smiling and playing happily when we came back out of the Palace. She was the first nun I had ever met face-to-face in my life. I don't know her name, and we never saw her again after that day.

After leaving David, we walked the short distance to the Bronze Door. As we proceeded into the Palace, all the same precautions and the Swiss Guards were in place. Up the stone stairs, through the magnificent hallway, and through the great wooden doors. Finally, we approached the Sediari desk just inside the Sala Clementina, and our progress came to a halt.

This time, we waited in the large sitting room with the windows looking out on the gardens, where the corridor to Monsignor Dziwisz's tiny office went off to the right. Now I noticed something I had not had time to see the day before. Back behind a wall was a small elevator. As we waited, a priest emerged from the elevator carrying a well-worn light-brown leather briefcase. He did not quite fit in with these elegant surroundings. He was dressed in Roman collar but wore a faded parka which was unzipped to reveal a gray sweater, instead of a cassock. Something else caught my eye. The good father wore gray leather shoes, the color of the year in Communist couture. So I knew this priest was most likely from Poland. And he was coming up the back elevator without any fanfare to meet with his Polish confreres, or perhaps with the Pope himself. I felt proud that I knew that. Proud that he and I shared at least some things in common from our shared Polish heritage.

The priest in gray shoes stepped off the elevator and walked purposefully across the parquet floor and down the corridor towards the office of Monisgnor Dziwisz. In an instant he was gone.

At last another priest, in conventional Roman dress, appeared to act as our guide. We were ushered through the next doorway into yet another room. We waited there. And walked to the next room. Walk and wait. Walk and wait. We were in a sort of queue whose end we couldn't see. The Pope could appear at any time, if Michael Hornblow was right.

We were moving from room to room along the outer perimeter of the Palace. Each room was approximately the same, with windows looking out and a throne on the inner wall. Before each throne was a microphone set at an angle. Behind each throne was a door. It appeared to us that the Pope might enter any of these rooms through the door from behind the throne. We would be introduced, pictures would be taken, and he would be gone.

We moved along until we came to the corner of the Palace. There we found a sitting room with chairs and a couch. At the moment it was occupied by a group of African red-capped Bishops, gathered in a tight circle conferring among themselves. They held what were clearly beautifully wrapped gifts. For the Pope, no doubt. We had none. I began to feel unprepared and very nervous.

The African bishops did not throw us even a sideways glance. After a few moments, they went on into the next room, and we were asked to sit where they had sat. Some minutes later they came back out to where we were, excitedly speaking amongst themselves. Their gifts were no longer in their hands. We moved on to the next room, around the bend of the Palace and into a small antechamber; it did not feel like the Pope would enter here. It had no regal dimension. It felt like a holding room. There was an upholstered bench on the wall and two more priests. One, in a plain black cassock, spoke in perfect American English with my wife, while another, in a black cassock with a red sash and red buttons down the front, greeted us with official decorum. He smiled, but seemed stiff and on guard. He held a red leather-bound folder in his hands.

I was still of a mind that the Pope would be walking by, in whatever room it might be. I had no reason to think otherwise. The red-buttoned priest then asked me to come and look out the window. I went over, and he showed me a different view of the Papal gardens than I had seen the day before. He pointed into the distance to the east and said, "That's where His Holiness' helicopter lands."

With that, he swung around and opened a door by the window, and with no further preamble, he nudged me into the next room of our seemingly endless sequence of chambers.

While the small antechamber had been dark, with only one somewhat narrow window lighting its red-lined walls, this room was bright and large. Its floors were of shiny white and green marble. Along its walls were bookcases lined with white leather-bound books. The room's many large windows were covered in sheer fabric that made it feel airy. The priest in red introduced me to a figure in white who stood up from behind a desk. And then the priest was gone.

His Holiness Pope John Paul II rose to greet me. He looked so much younger than his sixty-seven years. He was thin and balding, with a wisp of whitish hair just peeking out from under the white zucchetto that covered his head. It looked like the yarmulke that we wear in synagogue on Yom Kippur, except for the point of thread that sticks straight up from the center. His white cassock had a sash trimmed in gold, which ended with his own Papal seal. The large cross around his neck was fastened by a gold chain.

He was human sized, I was surprised to see, and much smaller than I had expected, although I'm not sure why. I looked around to see who else was there with us in the room. Where was the photographer? Where was my wife? Neither was to be seen. We were alone.

The Pope invited me to sit down next to him in a chair at one end of his desk and said, "Maestro, I know your story. We must talk."

I hadn't been prepared for this at all. For a brief moment I thought of getting up and excusing myself, saying something like, "You must have mistaken me for someone else. Really, I should be going." He knew my story? How much of it? Had Cardinal Macharski sent the Pope the *Newsweek* interview concerning my appointment to Kraków that had appeared in its International edition back in December? The next few moments would tell.

I was feeling very anxious at being alone in the presence of the Pope. The Pope must have sensed this, because he reached across the corner of the desk and put his hand on mine to soothe my nerves and quiet my fear. He kept his hand right there for the entire time we talked.

His Holiness' hand was a bit rougher than I might have imagined it to be. It had done real work in a quarry during the war, I had read. That too made him seem more real. More fully human. Not like any of the pictures I had seen of him on TV but a direct, compassionate man, trying to put his guest at ease.

He began by asking the same questions that Cardinal Macharski and Monsignor Dziwisz had already asked. It was as if he had dictated the questions and wanted to vet my answers before posing them himself.

His first words were in English. I answered him in German, thinking that would be easier for him. That was foolish. He continued in English, because in his politeness he knew that English was truly easier for me. His inquiry, in whatever language, was much more immediately personal than the priests before him. Much more direct and from the heart than the others'.

"How is my orchestra treating you?" he asked, with a warm smile of understanding. "You know, Maestro, they are not much fun for conductors."

His orchestra. How extraordinary. And he knew their professional reputation. That he shared it brought us closer. We were immediately two citizens of the same city. He made me feel as if I were in his city now, which was also my city and thus ours. In fact, within minutes we were talking about Kraków as if we were sitting in his old office at the Curia Metropolitana, down the street from my Philharmonic Hall.

The Pope told me he had often gone to concerts there. That he loved the music of the great masters. He asked me how I really felt in his city. The heartfelt, solicitous sincerity he showed made me less afraid. And he seemed pleased when I told him that I had opened my heart to his Polish people.

Now that he had established our kindred love for his hometown, he moved on to the next topic on his agenda. And there did indeed appear to be an agenda. He guided the conversation. He had some things he seemed to need to know.

He asked about my mother-in-law. About her family and what had happened to them in the war. He asked me how I felt as a Jew, being her son-in-law, in Poland. He told me he had lost many close Jewish friends in the Holocaust, how he had grown up with them in his hometown of Wadowice, and how their memory was with him still.

I told him that I knew that Jews had been welcomed in Poland for centuries, and that although terrible things had been done to my people over those many years, there had been many good things as well. I told him what my mother-in-law had said when she urged me to take up the position in Kraków. That I had to go, to show that we still lived.

The Pope listened with great attention. He was, it seemed to me, deeply moved. He sat leaning towards me, with his hand on mine, and looked me closely in the eyes. He, like Monisgnor Dziwisz, didn't want to miss anything I said, nor how I said it. His look was penetrating, forceful, yet it eased my nerves still more. In this short time, he had made me feel a shared humanness of spirit that I had never felt before. He had touched a stillness in me that I had only ever felt through music.

Whether it was that lessening of tension or something else that transformed me, I will never know. But as I began to think of Kraków and of Margit, and of my terrible day at Birkenau, I said something which came from the depths of my soul. Something I had not rehearsed nor could have imagined I would ever have the chutzpah to have said to anyone, let alone the Pope.

As if it were another person, I heard myself say:

"I believe, Your Holiness, that it is you who can achieve the coming together of our two peoples after so many centuries of misunderstanding and of hate. I believe you were sent by God to do just that."

The minute I said it, I knew I had crossed a bright red line. I had been lulled into crossing it by his empathy and his support. I wished I could take it back. His unlined face showed pain. He grew visibly uneasy.

Time went by. Perhaps a minute or more. I thought he might say something. I would have welcomed it, whatever he would have said. But he was silent, looking down, no longer at me. He seemed deep in thought.

I was growing more and more mortified. Every second was excruciating. I couldn't take it back, and it would all be over in an instant. About that, at least, I was right.

Suddenly, doors opened on two sides of the Papal Library. Vera walked in with the red-buttoned priest. A slew of photographers and the crew from ABC News came in from the opposite side of the room as well. The Pope stood and guided me, his arm on my shoulder, to the middle of the room. His touch was strong, muscular, athletic even, directing me where he wanted me to go.

Pope John Paul stood between my wife and myself. He greeted her cordially, welcoming her to the Vatican. He asked her where she was from. When she said that she was from Bratislava, he immediately started to speak to her in her native Slovak. He used simple phrases, but it made her smile. We all smiled. But the Pope kept looking down. He was being Papal, thoroughly gracious, but he still seemed lost in thought.

Another priest came in bearing an ornate silver presentation plate on which were placed two white boxes, one square and the other slightly smaller, with rounded corners. When the Pope reached for the boxes, the priest showed concern. His Holiness had begun to give me the rounded-corner box, and Vera the other, square one. But that was backwards. The priest knew I should get the square one, which held a Papal Medal, and Vera should get the rounded one, which contained pearl devotional beads. His Holiness realized his mistake and crossed his arms awkwardly, looking down as if in disbelief. This was a ceremonial part of his life that he had presided over countless times before. Something must have been preoccupying him.

And I was sure I knew what it was. He was still dismayed by the boldness of my comments. The temerity! Telling the "Vicar of Christ on Earth" what his destiny should be. No, more than that: what he was preordained by God to do during his Pontificate. If the Pope was thinking what I was thinking he was thinking, I was in big trouble.

As quickly as they had come in, the photographers and video crews were gone. In an instant, Vera and I were alone with the Pope once again. His Holiness walked towards a door on the opposite side of the room. Just as he was about to exit, he hesitated, and he looked back towards me.

The Pope smiled warmly, looking me straight in the eyes once again, and said, "Maestro, I will see you at your concert." And then he was gone.

I was dumbfounded. "What concert?" I tried to say to the closing door.

Vera and I walked the whole way out the many rooms of the Palace at the double-quick in silence. I couldn't say a word. Not yet.

Room by room faded behind us until we reached the desk of the Sediari. There, just before we were about to leave the Palace proper, we were met by Monsignor Dziwisz. The door through which the Pope had exited the Library led to the corridor down which Monisgnor Dziwisz's office is located. It was all one big loop. Monsignor Dziwisz had cut us off at the crossing point.

"How was it?" he asked in Italian.

"*Incredibile*," I answered, also in Italian.

He took good note of the word. "*Incredibile*," he repeated. "*Incredibile.*"

It was as if he wanted to remember it exactly.

Then Father Dziwisz said, "Maestro, the Holy Father wishes me to tell you that he thinks you have a great soul."

My jaw dropped again, and I stared into his eyes. I was beyond tears.

Then, as if an afterthought, he turned to me again and said, "And Maestro, he meant what he said about your concert!"

"What concert?" I asked, this time out loud. But all I saw was the back of Monsignor Dziwisz's cassock as he made his way down the corridor. As he reached the bend, beyond which I could have no longer made him out, he simply raised his hand as if to say, *Arrivederci*—until we meet again. And with that, he too was gone.

Vera and I walked out the rest of the way, back downstairs, in silence. My wife looked at me quizzically the whole time. She wanted to know just what had happened in there. But I could not speak. It would take a while to recover. Anyway, I had no idea what to say to her just then. "Great soul!" I thought. What had just happened hadn't even begun to sink in.

We walked out the Bronze Door, kissed our son, and thanked the kindly nun profusely. We continued out under the Bernini Columns and passed into Saint Peter's Square before I said, "You won't believe this. Let's sit down and have a coffee. I want to try to tell you what just happened."

We found a café on the Borgo Pio near the Porta Sant'Anna. I started to recount my story as best I could, but I was at a loss for words. Instead of a photo and good-bye, something truly *incredibile* had begun that day. Something that would affect both our lives immensely.

That much I knew. I just had no idea *what* exactly, or just how it would all turn out.

For now, it was a dream. A dream which grew out of the most improbable soil of Birkenau, and of the Philharmonic Hall in Kraków, and which now had the promise of a next step. And that step would be musical. That itself was too good to be true. What came after this, what that concert would be, I couldn't wait to find out.

The next morning we picked up a copy of the official Vatican newspaper. There it was, staring back at us in black and white, the official list of His Holiness' Private Audiences from the day before:

**L'Osservatore Romano—Friday, February 12, 1988—
Nostre Informazioni**

The Holy Father received in Audience yesterday morning:
Gabriel Zubeir Wako, Archbishop of Khartoum, President of
the Bishops Conference of the Sudan; along with Joseph
Abangite Gasi, Bishop of Tomura-Yambio (Sudan) Paolino
Lukudu Archbishop of Juba (Sudan) of Sudan, and Paride
Taban, a Bishop of Bururi (Burundi) In Ad limina
Apostolorum;

as well as Henryk Muszynski, Bishop of Wloclawek.

The Holy Father also received in Audience this morning
Maestro Gilbert Levine, Conductor of the Kraków
Philharmonic with his wife.

The musician who met the Pope in February 1988 had considerable experience as a conductor but nothing that could have prepared him for his first Papal event.

After the Pope's parting remark, "See you at your concert," I didn't hear anything from the Vatican for months. I was perfectly willing to believe that the experience I had had in that astonishing private audience with His Holiness was complete unto itself. I had encountered the man whom I saw as the greatest spiritual leader of our time; we had exchanged meaningful words; I had received his blessing; and then I had been sent on my way. And if it had been left at that, it would have been enough.

But in August 1988, I was invited to Castel Gandolfo (a small hilltop town twenty-three kilometers south of Rome, where the popes spend the summer months) to meet with Monsignor Dziwisz. He wished to extend the Pope's invitation for me to conduct the concert to commemorate the tenth anniversary of His Holiness' Pontificate in the Vatican that coming December. Monsignor Dziwisz said, "Maestro, you are our artist." What an incredible phrase, I thought, and one that didn't sink in at first but that would come to have great resonance in the months and years ahead.

This was my second meeting with Monsignor Dziwisz, the first since I had met him prior to my audience with the Pope. Castel Gandolfo is very different from the Vatican and not just because of the soothing, cooling wind that blows there or because of its beautiful setting, high above a lake, with lovely gardens where the Pope loved to take his summer walks.

When I arrived, I was welcomed as an expected visitor. It was an entirely different atmosphere from the Apostolic Palace. Castel Gandolfo is very well guarded, to be sure, but it has the feeling of an Italian palazzo, grand yet intimate at the same time. That is something one could assuredly not say about the Vatican.

At Castel Gandolfo, once you are past the Swiss Guards at the entrance, there is a huge white awning that protects the entire interior courtyard from the blazing Italian summer sun. It billows like a sail in the gentle breeze. It puts a visitor immediately at ease.

When I met Monsignor Dziwisz in a small sitting room on the second floor, I was there to discuss the business at hand. It was very different from "How are you feeling in Kraków?" In fact, I was being introduced for the very first time to the workings of the Appartamento of the Pope, the Vatican term used to describe His Holiness' innermost circle of advisors and trusted confidants, of whom Monsignor Dziwisz was the closest of all. This was the man who, as the Pope's Private Secretary, assisted the Pope in overseeing the entire range of affairs as leader of the largest Christian church in the world.

The upcoming concert was an important occasion. The Pope clearly had decided from all he had heard in Kraków and from our first meeting that I was the person to conduct on this occasion. This was not only a wonderful surprise but also something of a shock. The tenth anniversary concert would be *the* concert for the year at the Vatican. High Vatican officials, leaders in all walks of life, and political dignitaries, including the President of Italy, would also attend, and it would be broadcast throughout the world. I both cherished and was humbled by this degree of Papal trust.

Before a standard concert, there is a little bit of back-and-forth about the program. I would have a conversation with the artistic administrator of an orchestra. I would then submit three programs, and they would come back and say which one works for their upcoming season. It's fairly straightforward. But the conversation I had with Monsignor Dziwisz was only the beginning of a two-month process about what should be on this Papal program and, even more delicately, which orchestra and chorus should participate. I was being led into a world in which every decision has all kinds of unseen ramifications.

My guide in all this was Monsignor Dziwisz. The requirements of a Papal Concert are very strict, from the length to the selection of the works. The works to be performed had to be appropriate for a concert before this Pope, John Paul II. However, Monsignor Dziwisz was not literally organizing, nor was the Vatican paying for the concert. That was the honor of the RAI, the Italian television network, which was offering this concert to His Holiness in honor of his tenth anniversary. Monsignor Dziwisz told me at the end of our meeting at Castel Gandolfo that I would be receiving a call at my hotel from Dr. Biagio Agnes, the Director General of the RAI, who would take over the preparations for the concert on the RAI's behalf.

In fact, the RAI was astonished to hear that the Pope had selected the conductor for this annual concert, which was the network's pride and joy. The RAI had always held this concert out as a plum for a major conductorial figure, a Zubin Mehta or a Carlo Maria Giulini, who would have loved to conduct the RAI's very best orchestra on this august Vatican occasion. The Pope's selection of me, the Music Director of his hometown Kraków Philharmonic, was unprecedented.

Because I would be leading it, all the musical elements of this event were now in discussion, including which orchestra would have the great honor. Naturally, I wanted the Kraków Philharmonic to participate. I knew they would have done anything to perform for their Polish Pope. And I, their Music Director, couldn't imagine not bringing them with me in December. But as I soon learned, Papal Concerts can become huge political footballs. They are the ne plus ultra of musical prestige in Rome. The RAI, the broadcasters, and sponsors would not hear of bringing in the Polish orchestra for the concert. A fight ensued: the Kraków orchestra versus the orchestra of the RAI Roma.

Unexpectedly, I received an invitation to conduct the RAI Roma Orchestra in September. I came down from Kraków to lead them in the Tchaikovsky Fifth Symphony and the Penderecki Viola Concerto.

The RAI saw this September event as paving the way for our working together in December, and this preliminary concert allowed me to develop a relationship with the orchestra, which otherwise I would have been conducting for the very first time before the Pope.

Eventually, a compromise was worked out. The chorus from the Kraków Philharmonic would be invited for the Papal Concert to be accompanied by the orchestra from the RAI. There was a balance. For the Church, the choice of chorus is certainly at least as important as the choice of orchestra. Everybody got to save face. Judicious wisdom, that was always the way with Pope John Paul.

Then, after much back-and-forth with the RAI, the program for the "Concert to Celebrate the Tenth Anniversary of His Holiness Pontificate" was set. We would perform the enchanting Brahms Ave Maria, a rare work based on a Catholic text by the great Protestant composer from Hamburg. Then the Penderecki Stabat Mater, perhaps the greatest portion of his greatest work, the Passion according to Saint Luke. And the concert would conclude with the Dvořák Mass in D, a composition of deep devotion written for a small chapel in his native Bohemia, which he later expanded for full orchestra to be performed in the huge Crystal Palace Exhibition Hall in London, an auditorium not unlike the Sala Nervi, in which we would perform it for the Pope.

The setting would be grander than anything I had ever experienced, the occasion historic by its very nature. But most of all, it was the musical program that would make it so extraordinary.

John Paul was a Marian Pope, which I learned meant that he held Mary as a very special figure in his religious devotion. Thus, it was important to have the Ave Maria and the Stabat Mater, both Marian prayers, on the program. And the Mass was the most natural piece for us to perform as the main work on the Papal Concert.

Up until that time I had been a symphony conductor from New York, for whom all music was art music—beautiful and worthy of the investment of all my musical powers. But this performance for the Pope would be made up entirely of Christian liturgical music. It was held at the Vatican, with all the Church listening and watching my every gesture. It would challenge the very basis of my cultural understanding.

How, I wondered, would I invest these works with the proper devotion, the proper reverence? How would I return the extraordinary trust of the Pope in selecting me for this honor?

If you have studied Mozart or Beethoven or Haydn, then you know the great works: the Mozart C Minor Mass, the Haydn Nelson Mass, and the monumental Beethoven Missa Solemnis. These are compositions which reach the highest level of artistic achievement. But they are more than that. They were, I now know, for their creators expressions of a most profound Catholic faith.

In 1988, I was only just beginning to understand what they meant. Up until that time I had never set foot in a Catholic church other than to visit the great cathedrals, Notre Dame de Paris, the Duomo in Siena, Wawel Cathedral in Kraków, or so many others around the world, just to admire their beauty. Indeed, for many of my colleagues, myself included, conducting a Mass in concert, however beautiful, was just another musical assignment. That would not be nearly enough for this occasion. I knew that right away. I was being called upon to conduct the Ave Maria of Brahms, the Stabat Mater of Penderecki, and the Mass in D of Dvořák under sacred circumstances. The Pope had set me quite a test.

When December finally came, I left a German tour of the Kraków Philharmonic Orchestra after our last concert in Munich. I felt bad that I was not bringing my orchestra with me to Rome. But if they were angry or resentful, they did not show it in the Beethoven or the Tchaikovsky we performed on that tour. Our concerts were filled with wonderful music-making. I was sad to leave them behind as I boarded my flight south to begin my rehearsals for this most important Vatican concert.

The RAI Roma Orchestra had been performing these annual Papal Concerts for a number of years and was, by now, accustomed to them. For the Kraków Philharmonic Choir, on the other hand, this would be a huge occasion. It was the first time they would perform for their Polish Pope in the Vatican. They were simply in awe. I think they would have had a hard time opening their mouths to sing, if not professionally required to do so.

It is safe to say that this was by far the most important concert I had conducted in my life. It was the first time I had conducted an entire concert for international television. And though I had performed many works by these composers over the course of my career, I had never conducted any of these particular works before. But this alone is not so unusual for experienced conductors. We are always called upon to broaden our repertoire, to expand our artistic horizons. No, it was the sheer magnitude of this Papal occasion that made it so different.

When we were finally all assembled in the Vatican, the Kraków choir and the orchestra from Rome, and four excellent international soloists, the rehearsals went as in a dream. No language barrier, no political differences could prevent the unity we all felt in preparing for this great musical occasion. We would all be ready to make music for the Pope.

I anticipated that I would somehow be meeting His Holiness at the concert. My mother-in-law had joined me in Rome, together with my wife and my son, David. Vera and Margit were now getting ready to attend the concert that evening. At the intermission of our dress rehearsal, though, a priest from the Pontifical Household came to my dressing room. The priest said that the Holy Father wished to see me that very morning, together with my wife and my mother-in-law. I asked, only partly in jest, if he saw the way I looked. By the time the rehearsal was over, I told him, I would have sweated through every garment I had on. Conducting requires more vigorous physical exertion than many people think. My question, of course, was rhetorical. Even I knew that one doesn't go to an audience with the Pope looking like that.

I immediately called our hotel and told Vera and Margit about the unexpected honor of our audience with the Pope. They needed to come along to the Vatican right away, and I asked Vera to please bring me a fresh shirt and a suit, so that I could get out of my sweaty rehearsal clothes.

At the end of the rehearsal, Margit, Vera, and I were led by that same priest from the Sala Nervi to the Apostolic Palace through the back way for the first time. We went behind St. Peter's Basilica, directly to the courtyard of the Apostolic Palace, and up, past the Swiss Guards and the Sediari, into the same private library as before. I couldn't imagine what this last-minute request to see the Pope on the day of the concert might mean. All three of us were filled with great curiosity and nervous anticipation.

When we were shown into the Pope's private library, His Holiness was already there. Instead of sitting at his desk as before, the Pope was standing in the middle of the room. There was a wonderful sense of inclusion in his welcome. He greeted me with a huge grin, as if this were a great day for us—for me and for him. He cordially welcomed my wife and then my mother-in-law. As soon as he and Margit came together, it was clear, there were at least two purposes to our meeting that morning. One was to see his conductor on the day of the concert; the other was to meet and spend a bit of time with my mother-in-law, about whose suffering during the Holocaust he already knew.

His Holiness approached her gently, and asked her very quietly, in English, where exactly she was from. She answered him in Polish, which I did not understand. She would later recount the conversation to us word for word.

"I am from Moravian Ostrava," Margit said, diffidently, almost inaudibly. She seemed so very nervous.

The Pope looked intently and calmly into her eyes, and said in his native language, "Oh, from Silesia, like myself, but from the Czech side."

With these words, he acknowledged that they hailed from the same tiny part of the world. Their stories began to entwine.

His Holiness put his arm on her shoulder and looked deeply into her eyes. Margit had not known what this Papal meeting was to be about. I am not sure she was at all comfortable. She had always told us that she waited for someone, anyone, to tell the world to stop its madness, all the time she had been at Auschwitz. But no one ever did. Now, this Polish Pope had invited her son-in-law to conduct a concert in the Vatican. That in itself was surely a great thing. But what did this have to do with her?

"Why does he want to see me?" she had asked as we hurried on our way to the audience.

The answer came in the profound empathy the Successor to Saint Peter was showing towards her now.

It was very clear from the moment he addressed her that the Pope wished to be in deep communion with her. He wanted somehow to reach out to her, to touch her soul. I didn't understand everything they were saying. They spoke very softly. But I could see from both their faces that the brief conversation was extremely serious and meaningful for both of them, meant for their ears alone. The atmosphere in that Papal Library was now very intimate, filled with deep meaning. They gestured and spoke to each other in a language, beyond words, that only those who have seen the greatest unimaginable evil could possibly understand. The rest of us in that room could only look on in humbled awe. Vera stood off to the side of her mother. She had tears in her eyes. She could tell how emotional her mother had become.

Suddenly, the mood in the Papal Library changed. Leaving my mother-in-law's side, Pope John Paul came over to me and put his arm around me conspiratorially.

"Have you had enough rehearsal time?" the Pope asked.

"Why, Your Holiness?" I replied.

"It's a very important concert, you know. I hear the Pope is coming this evening." The Pope smiled broadly as he told his joke, and it made me laugh out loud.

It was so wonderful because up until that moment I had indeed been extremely nervous. Especially watching him with Margit. Even before that, though, I had been tied up in knots. I am not normally very nervous before concerts, but this was something so very different. Worldwide television. A new orchestra, new repertoire, and yes, a momentous event being celebrated in the Pope's honor in the Vatican that very night. Somehow, whether it was because he had been an actor himself in his earlier life, or just out of extraordinary human empathy, His Holiness knew just how I felt, knew exactly what to say to calm me down so that I could do my best for him, for myself, and for the world that would be watching. He clearly appreciated my laughter and returned it with a warm smile of his own that lit up his whole face.

Now that the audience was over, the warmth of the Pope's visage told me that he was feeling that he had accomplished the two things he had wished to do that afternoon. The three of us left the Apostolic Palace walking in silence. Margit, the Pope's Silesian sister-in-spirit, looked somewhat bewildered by what had just occurred but with a sense of a coming peace that she had not known in the decades since the war. The Pope had indeed begun the healing of her soul.

I returned to our hotel with renewed confidence in the performance, and I set about the remainder of my concert-day routine: lunch, nap, and score study.

After our dress rehearsal, after my Papal audience, I was certain I could pass on to my orchestra and chorus a part of the humanity and warmth that the Pope had shown to me that morning. We would make wonderful music together. Everything was going to be just fine. I couldn't wait for this special concert to begin.

The event was to start at six o'clock. As I entered the Paul VI hall and made my way to the podium, I heard only a smattering of applause. That evening, people were there to enjoy the music surely, but even more, they wished to be in the presence of their beloved Pope. They felt honored to be there with him to celebrate this tenth anniversary of his Pontificate.

When His Holiness arrived, I realized I had never before seen him up close in a public forum. The hall was electric. The applause began to swell from the very back of the hall, when people in the last rows saw him walk in from the foyer at the rear of the Sala Nervi, almost a hundred yards away. People rushed to the edges of the aisle. It was like a rock star making an entrance. Normal people, middle-aged or otherwise, acted as if an incredible, perhaps once-in-a-lifetime event was at hand. And for many, it would be just that. For many people, but for Catholics especially, just being in the presence of their Holy Father is an unheard-of privilege. If they could touch him, be touched by him, they believed, their lives would be changed.

The Pontiff began to shake hands with as many as he could, walking vigorously, as he was still able to in 1988. For the full ten minutes it took him to walk down the aisle, the applause didn't stop. The orchestra, the chorus, the soloists, and I were all standing there, watching with smiles on our faces; many of us joined in the applause ourselves in a show of respect and affection for the singular personage for whom that audience had gathered that night.

It was awe-inspiring to give a concert under those circumstances, knowing I was adding to the aura of an evening already made historic by the presence of the Roman Pontiff. What he meant to these people was very powerful. It inspired me, and it must have had the same effect on everyone on the stage. I could especially see the effect Pope John Paul had in the faces of his Polish chorus. They were straining to get a glimpse of him, and they were glowing just to be in his presence. This was their countryman, and he had reached a height no Pole, no king, no general, no great artist had ever reached before. After ten years of his Pontificate, they could still not get over their national pride that one of theirs had reached the pinnacle of their Holy Church.

The Pope sat down and we started our music-making. It was like we were in a zone, reaching heights far beyond where we had gone in our rehearsals. The Kraków chorus performed the Penderecki choral work—crisply, accurately, and confidently with all its atonally challenging elements. The rarely performed Brahms Ave Maria had a lilt, a sweetness, an unaffected aspect that fairly floated on the Roman air. And the Dvořák was delivered as the reverential country devotion that it was, yet all dressed up and made grand as the composer had finally wished. The Czech master would have been so proud that his exquisite Mass in D was being performed at a command performance for the Pope in Rome and for viewers and listeners around the world.

As each work ended, I turned to bow, and His Holiness looked back at me. The Pope caught my eye as if to say, "Well done, and thank you. Now, Maestro, let's go on to the next." By the end, after the Dvořák had finished its pianissimo *dona nobis pacem*, there was utter silence in the Aula. As well there should have been. It was as if the whole audience, all seventy-five hundred of them, wished to preserve the sacred atmosphere of the evening before disturbing it with their applause. Finally, the ovation began, led from the outset by the man sitting on the Great Throne in the middle of the hall.

A microphone was brought to His Holiness, and he began to speak simply and directly in his beautifully intoned Italian. He noted with what efficacy our music had entered into the heart and soul of all who had listened that evening. Music, he said, is truly a language of God. Then he thanked all of us for celebrating this wonderful anniversary with him, and wished those lucky enough to be there and everyone watching around the world, *Buon Natale a Tutti!*—a very Merry Christmas to All!

There was great anticipation that the Pope might be coming up on the stage. As the audience continued to clap, he got up from his chair, and with both hands clasped in front of him in a sign of approbation, he began to walk towards the podium. As he approached the bottom of the stairs, I descended from the podium to meet him. He held my hands in his and repeated over and over, "Wonderful, wonderful." Simple words, but under the circumstances, he could have been the *New York Times*: there was only one critic in that house whose review would have mattered, and the Roman Pontiff seemed pleased.

The Pope walked with me up the stairs and onto the stage, put his arm around me for all to see, and then whispered in my ear, "Thank you so much for going to Kraków. And thank you for bringing Kraków to me."

It was clear from that expression of Papal gratitude that this concert was important to him because of the presence of the American conductor who had gone to Poland, to his beloved hometown, and because of the Polish chorus that had come to the Vatican, to make music for him on this special day. He shook the hands of the front desk players of the RAI Orchestra. Each one was proud, joyful, and seemingly speechless in his presence.

Just before I walked him downstage, the Pope stopped, whispering again in my ear. "Where is your mother-in-law?" he asked, gesturing faintly with his finger towards the large audience in front of him.

"Holiness, I'm afraid I don't know," I answered.

The Pontiff seemed genuinely disappointed that she was somewhere lost in that crowd, and unable to be located at precisely that moment. I think the Pope had actually wanted her to come on stage, or perhaps he wanted to greet her in the hall. He seemed to have been so touched by his meeting with her that morning that he wanted to greet her once again. In the end, he just looked at me with a smile of deep satisfaction, knowing that just by asking after her, he had clearly expressed his deeply caring interest.

The Pope walked out of the hall, shaking hands again as he went. The chorus of hurrahs only ended when he got into his car and drove off. I walked back to my dressing room to change and greet my family and friends who had come from America and from Europe to share this day with me. Among the first to reach my room were Vera and Margit. (Our son had stayed in the hotel with a babysitter to watch Daddy on the television.) When I told Margit that the Pope had asked after her, she looked at me in complete disbelief—which, of course, was totally appropriate. Until that day, she could not have imagined ever meeting a Pope. And now, twice in one day, His Holiness had reached out to her, cared for her, wanting so much to make right things that had once, many years ago, gone so terribly, awfully wrong.

Also coming to my dressing room that evening were two most unexpected guests, who had dined with the Pope that day: the great Saint Louis Cardinal ballplayer Stan Musial and his close friend, the wildly popular American author James Michener. Stan the Man offered his congratulations, and the most valuable player's trophy he had at hand—an autographed ball signed "To my biggest fan, Maestro Gilbert Levine."

Michener, for his part, held forth in the middle of the Persian rug in the center of the room, describing vividly just how important this evening had been. He would later include his account of the concert in his memoir, *Pilgrimage*, which chronicled a trip that had begun the week before in Poland and was ending that night in the Vatican at the concert for Pope John Paul.

Everyone had left, and our postconcert dinner was a pleasant memory; I had had the experience of a lifetime. I was sure that my almost unbelievable association with Pope John Paul was now over. There was nothing more fantastic any artist could wish for: a Papal command performance broadcast throughout the world.

What had begun at the audience in February 1988, had completed its circle. I had had the unique experience of conducting for the Pope. I had had the joy of bringing His Holiness and my mother-in-law together in a way that was meaningful for her and, now clearly, for Pope John Paul.

I had brought the Philharmonic chorus from Kraków to the Vatican to perform for their Polish Pope. I felt a tremendous sense of completeness and satisfaction at all that had taken place. Little did I know that this was just the beginning. And if you had told me then, on that special night, I would not have believed you.

I would be going back to Kraków now to an uncertain future. The all-powerful Penderecki would surely be jealous that it was I who had conducted for his Polish Pope on this momentous occasion. I was willing to encounter those difficulties, and any others that presented themselves, because of the incredible gratification this Papal Concert for Pope John Paul's tenth anniversary had given me, and the peace it had begun to afford my family.

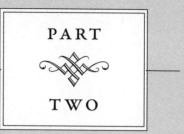

Kaddish

CHAPTER

SEVEN

I n the spring of 1989, I was sent by Cardinal Macharski of Kraków to meet his fellow Prince of the Church, His Eminence Jean-Marie Cardinal Lustiger.

The small street where the Archbishop of Paris lives is like many other streets in the 7th arrondissement on the Left Bank. Elegant, without being showy, La Rue Barbet-de-Jouy is lined with fancy residences turned into official buildings, embassies, an elite private school, and at the end, a few tasteful shops filling the various needs of its upper middle class inhabitants.

At the far end of this one-way street is a typical Parisian bar, complete with *habitués du quartier*. A foreigner sticks out like a sore thumb to even the casual Parisian observer worth his savoir faire.

I sat at the bar, looking like a very odd duck indeed, what with my upscale briefcase, made of the very finest Florentine leather, and my out-of-place proletarian Polish *czapka*, a woolen cap out of *The Grapes of Wrath*, made for me by the last remaining private shop owner allowed to operate in all of socialist Kraków.

I nursed my café crème endlessly, and mused about the man I had come to Paris to meet, the famous man who lived down the street at No. 32. The Jewish Cardinal of Paris. Yes, a Jewish Cardinal! And the more I thought about it, the more fascinating that oxymoronic concept became. I couldn't quite get my mind around it.

This is what I knew: Jean-Marie Lustiger had been born Aaron Lustiger, of Polish-Jewish immigrant parents in 1926. His family came from Benzin, a town in Galicia not too far from Kraków. When the Nazis invaded Paris in 1940, his parents had sent him and his sister to the French countryside, where they had been blended into good Catholic families for safekeeping. The whole experience cannot have been easy.

While his children were in the countryside, Aaron's father had stayed in Paris, hiding in one garret or another, passing for Aryan on false documents when he could, dodging the Gestapo, always on the run. His story was atypical—he survived in Nazi-occupied France.

Aaron's mother had not been nearly so fortunate. She was rounded up, like so many, many others, and sent to the infamous deportation center at Drancy, and from there straight to annihilation at Auschwitz-Birkenau.

Of the rest of the Cardinal's unique story, I knew only the barest facts. He came back to Paris after the war, having had a profound, life-changing, and mystical religious experience, one so powerful that it led to his conversion to Catholicism and eventually to his ordination as a priest in 1954. He had changed his name from the prototypically Jewish Aaron to the equally typical Catholic Jean-Marie.

He was, as I came to know, an academic at heart, and so it was that he became the Catholic chaplain of the Sorbonne, where he would have remained, contentedly, one suspects, for the rest of his priestly life, but for the intervention of one man, a character who functioned as what the ancient Greeks called a deus ex machina, a larger-than-life figure who changes everything in an instant. That figure was Pope John Paul II.

Only a year after his own election Pope John Paul had plucked Father Jean-Marie Lustiger from obscurity and had elevated him to great prominence in an unbelievably short time. He was ordained Bishop of Orleans in 1979, elevated to the coveted seat of Archbishop of Paris in 1981, and created Cardinal, a Catholic title meaning a close advisor to the Pope, in 1983. Twenty-five years of obscure academic contemplation had ended in four years of rocket-like advancement. And that's about all I knew.

Except, that is, for two seemingly contradictory facts. One was that he still considered himself a Jew; as he said, just like Jesus and his disciples. And two, that he had worked long and hard to help resolve the controversy of the Carmelite nuns, who had established themselves at Auschwitz to pray for the souls of all who had been murdered there, Catholic, Protestant, and Jew alike. That was an activity that, understandably, was not welcomed by Jews the world over. His Eminence worked with His Holiness and with prominent Catholic and Jewish leaders over several years to help resolve the resulting controversy.

I was in Paris for a quite practical reason, to make final arrangements with the Cardinal and his staff for a grand concert of the Kraków Philharmonic in, of all places, the legendary Cathedral of Notre Dame de Paris. Concerts in that awesome place are rare, more like events than ordinary concerts. And this one would have the added significance of being the first occasion for the Catholic and Jewish communities of France to get together since their falling out over the Carmelite nuns at Auschwitz. The concert would also be dedicated to the free spirit of Poland, which was now experiencing a rebirth of Solidarity, their national movement of freedom. What a musical meeting this promised to be!

I had arrived at the bar around the corner from the Cardinal's residence much too early, in great anticipation, and the wait for my 4 P.M. rendezvous seemed endless. I filled the time with my fantasy of what was to come.

In my imagination, this was to be an even more imposing meeting than almost any I had experienced thus far, except perhaps for those with His Holiness. In my mind's eye, this would be a regal meeting with a princely head of the Church, the successor to Cardinal Richelieu. True, it was to take place in the Cardinal's private residence and not in the Offices of the Archdiocese or at Notre Dame, but still, I imagined a palace the size of Fontainebleau, right in the middle of Paris. A residence as grand as the Élysée Palace, where the President of the French Republic resided, something akin to the Apostolic Palace, where I had met the Pope. Something grand like that, at least! I could hardly wait.

Finally, the time arrived. I pulled myself up, straightened my tie and cap, and walked out of the café and across the street along the even-numbered side of the Berbet-de-Jouy looking for No. 32. The few corner storefronts right across from the café soon gave way to a seemingly unending high wall. Anyone who has walked the streets of Paris will recognize the mystery of a wall right in the middle of the city. And this high wall that hid everything from view only fed my overripe majestic fantasies as I looked impatiently for an opening, to glimpse the private world beyond. I'm convinced the wall was meant to do just that: impose privacy and, yes, mystery, in the midst of urban nosiness. My curiosity was piqued. What lay behind this impertinent wall?

At last I came to No. 32. No fancy gate, no bronze door, no Swiss Guards, just a number on the wall, "No. 32," in simple black numerals on a white square; and next to the number, a button below a small, quite ordinary-looking intercom.

I rang. Once, twice, not even waiting for an answer.

Finally a disembodied female voice said, *Oui ... ?*, stretched out forever as only a Parisian can manage with this one-syllable word.

"It's ... it's ... Gilbert Levine for the Cardinal," I responded. "I, I uh, have an appointment," I added unnecessarily. Of course I had an appointment; who else would ring this bell?

The reply came like a tape recorder, the same monosyllabic *"Oui!"* *Oui!* And nothing more. But this time, a bit shorter, as if with a soupçon of recognition that I might actually not be an intruder. I wondered, was my name on the list of those expected?

A buzzer sounded, and the door opened, letting me enter. I walked through it, leaving the noise of the street behind, and entered the quiet world behind the wall.

I came in under a covered walkway that led into a compound much like what one would find anywhere in France. On the right was a small porter's lodge, and there the owner of the disembodied voice presented herself. She was the spitting image of the woman tending the bar I had just left on the corner of the street, the same petite, attractive French feminine form, and the same instantaneous, automatic ability to size one up. To my surprise, though, she was not a nun, or at least she wore no habit. I had somehow, in my fantasy at least, expected a white-hatted nun.

She invited me into the anteroom of the porter's lodge to wait briefly as she used the phone, making sure that it was all right to send me on to the next station of my visit. No Sediari, just a French porter, doing her job.

Getting the proper reply to her call, she nudged me out into an open-air cobblestone courtyard, which was large enough to lend a sense of proportion to the whole complex of buildings which lay before me.

On the far side of the courtyard was a large, handsome house, imposingly titled the Hotel de Rambuteau, three stories tall, but not nearly as grand as the residence of the Pope or the President of the Republic. It had beautiful large windows, high up on the second floor, making the facade both open and somehow remote at the same time. To the right of this large house was another building much more functional looking, and to the left, a practical single-story structure that looked something like a community center.

The man who lived here worked here as well. He was important; his house said that. But work was also done here. And I was in the right place, too, to do the work I had come to do.

Without any ceremony, I was escorted across the courtyard and shown into a downstairs side entrance on the far left of the main building. Past this entryway I entered a small room; there was only a simple chest-high table, placed hard against the window facing back out into the courtyard, and several unused chairs, which lined the drab walls. A single bright light hung from the center of the ceiling, illuminating a map that was laid out on the table with paperweights on the top two corners.

Hunched over this map was a middle-aged gentleman in civilian, that is, nonpriestly clothes, a Monsieur François Girard, who introduced himself as the Chief Administrator of Notre Dame Cathedral. Monsieur Girard greeted me politely and without any ceremony.

He proceeded to draw my attention to a plan of the interior of the Cathedral. He pointed out where the orchestra would be placed, the chorus, the soloists, and, oh yes, incidentally, the conductor. He asked me at every turn whether what he had marked made sense.

"*Pardonez-moi*, Maestro, but I am not a musician, you know. And we have so few concerts in Notre Dame; it is hard to remember how we might have set it up the last time. But it's important to get it right, *n'est-ce pas?*"

I saw without seeing. I hardly heard what he said. For just looking at the plan of the Cathedral brought me into a dream of what it would be like to make music in that astonishing spiritual space. I was lost in this reverie, which must have lasted for some time, when I was brought back to reality by the sound of someone walking into the room. He was a priest, dressed in simplest black with Roman collar. A small cross hung from his neck, much smaller and more discreet than I had come to expect from my experiences in Poland or in Rome.

The priest, perhaps sixty-five, had a pear-shaped face with five o'clock shadow, a receding hairline, and thin black nondescript glasses. He spoke English with a heavy but intelligible accent and seemed quite amiable and down-to-earth. He apparently had a special affection for Monsieur Girard, whom he seemed to know quite well. He shook hands with him and with me, and asked in a slightly gravelly voice whether everything was clear for the concert. Just that: "Clear?"

Monsieur Girard and I both said yes. The priest and I exchanged a few nonspecific pleasantries, about the fine weather in Paris and about my trip from Poland. Then, without further ado, the priest turned and left, departing through the back door as quietly and as unobtrusively as he had arrived.

I thought nothing much of it. He apparently was just one of the many assistants to the Archbishop. This interruption over, I turned my attention back to Monsieur Girard and the business at hand. But no sooner had the priest left, then Monsieur Girard rolled up his plan of Notre Dame, saying, "I believe we have covered it all. I will look forward to seeing you and your orchestra in September. If you have any questions, please don't hesitate to let me know."

He gave me his card and started on his way.

"Wait, Monsieur," I said. "*S'il vous plait.* I can't go yet; I am here to meet Cardinal Lustiger. The Archbishop of Paris. I can't possibly go until I have met him. That's why I have come. I mean ..."

Monsieur Girard turned back and looked at me with a bemused expression, then left the room by way of the door leading back out to the courtyard, his map rolled up and tucked neatly under his arm. He looked like nothing so much as a man on his way home after a long day's work.

I remained in the room a few moments longer, collecting myself. I was disconsolate at having come so far for such an important meeting, only to be left alone, and in the Cardinal's basement at that. Finally, pulling myself together, I exited out into the courtyard and headed in the direction of the door in the wall that led out to the street.

I only got about halfway across the courtyard before something stopped me. For as my eyes adjusted to the bright light of the Parisian midsummer afternoon, I caught sight out of the corner of my eye of a figure standing on the high outer staircase, leading to the formal entrance to the three-story main house. He was right next to the windows which had seemed so imposing when I had first entered the compound.

Although not very tall, the figure seemed somehow regal in bearing. He was elevated by the staircase, to be sure, but there was something else, something intangible, which gave him a kind of distinctive stature. I looked up at his face and saw an impish grin grow as he said in his thickly accented English:

"So you do not believe you have met the Archbishop of Paris; perhaps you have been in Kraków a bit too long, Maestro."

There he was, to my utter embarrassment: the same simple priest I had met only minutes before, now standing at the top of the staircase, beckoning me to come into his—the Cardinal's—home.

As I walked up the steps to greet him, he stretched out his arms and grasped my hands, locking me in a warm smile. It seemed as though he would tolerate this need to show off his station in life, but only this once, and only as a demonstration for his Polish country cousin. Although I was a Jewish conductor from New York, at this moment I was more a representative of the Church in Kraków. But at the same time, I was a Jew of Polish origin being greeted by his Parisian cousin, a cousin who had emigrated before him. But then, of course, in reality, he was the Cardinal of Paris.

His Eminence showed me in through the formal vestibule, past the beautiful, gold-framed artwork and gilded walls, turning right into a formal sitting room. Two large chairs sat solemnly before a picture window letting in the light of a large walled-in garden that seemed in need of a gardener's care. Perhaps Monsigneur Lustiger liked it that way.

"Please, won't you sit down," the Cardinal said. "Now Maestro, do you see? I am indeed the Archbishop of Paris." The warmth of his tired smile was as genuine as the depth of his concern that I not go away disappointed.

"You will see, the French church is not like Poland," His Eminence said. "We are much less formal here. But I do have this room for my important guests. I hope you will feel welcome."

For what seemed like an eternity, I studied his face. I couldn't help it. I wanted to see if I would recognize Aaron in the face of Jean-Marie. All I saw for the moment was deep intelligence and empathy. And a bit of impatience to move our talk along.

I hesitated, not really knowing what to say. "Your Eminence, I apologize for persisting, but I have a message for you from Cardinal Macharski. I was only afraid I would not have the chance to—"

He stopped me short. "I know. Cardinal Macharski wrote to me. He is very fond of you, you know, and the Holy Father, too. And I hope so much that your concert will help to bind the wounds caused by the problems of the Carmelites at Auschwitz."

With the word *Auschwitz*, he fell silent. His face fell imperceptibly. His eyes glistened. I knew the look. I had seen it in my wife's mother's eyes and in my wife's also. I let the silence lie.

Finally, I said, "You know, Eminence, my mother-in-law survived Birkenau. But her family was completely decimated. I—"

He clasped my hands to stop me from going any further with my family's tragic tale. He said nothing, saying everything.

At last, he asked, "How is it with you in Kraków? How do you feel there? Life in Poland now is very hard. Have you been to Auschwitz? You know, I have never been. I must go, I know it. But for now, I feel, I cannot."

"I tell you what is strange, Eminence," I said. "It is the Church that has made me feel welcome. The Church and my music. Otherwise, I don't know how I would do it. I have been to Birkenau, even in the spring, and it is so cold. Thank God I have His Holiness to support me."

What a strange thing to say, and in the first ten minutes of meeting this man, this Aaron, this Jean-Marie. But I believe he understood exactly what I meant.

He rose, and I rose with him.

"Let me know how I may be of assistance with your concert. It is important to me. I will attend with great anticipation," His Eminence said. "And Maestro, please send my regards back to Cardinal Macharski when you return to Kraków, and to His Holiness, of course, when next you see him."

And with a gentle sweep of his arm around my shoulder, he walked me to the door, following me with his kindly eyes all the way out into the Rue Barbet-de-Jouy. I seemed to feel his gaze long after I had left the quartier, and Paris, and all the way back to Kraków.

CHAPTER

EIGHT

On the third of September I found myself back in Paris, this time standing in the near-empty Notre Dame Cathedral waiting for the Kraków Philharmonic Orchestra and Chorus to arrive. At seven in the evening, this great spiritual space was empty. It gave off a strange and eerie feeling. I had been in Notre Dame many times before, joining the hundreds, if not thousands of tourists who mixed with the religious faithful in a strange mélange of the sacred and the mundane.

Just inside the massive processional doors, round white votive candles are for sale, to be lit in prayer at one of the many shrines to the myriad saints whose spirits inhabit the Cathedral. Votive candles are a ubiquitous and essential element in the Catholic world, from the smallest church to the greatest cathedrals. All these man-made structures are made lighter by these small, frail tapers. They gain their strength in the thousands of tiny flames, lit one by one, adding their warmth one to another, contributing their prayer-inspired illumination to many cold stone walls.

Mothers light a candle when someone in the family is sick or deeply troubled; a wife lights one for a wayward husband; a family lights one on the birth of new child. For me, as a Jew, they are like the small pieces of paper stuffed into the crevices of the Wailing Wall, the Western Wall of the ancient Second Temple in Jerusalem. Pieces of paper laden with prayers are stuffed into the cracks of the only solid connection we Jews have to a place we know God once dwelled. To think that the Ark of the Covenant was once not a hundred feet away in the Holy of Holies within the Temple of Solomon! Just so, for Catholics, votive candles bear their message of light to the spirit of God which inhabits the living places of their faith.

Standing in the apse of the Cathedral, surrounded by light, both from the candles and from the softly filtered sun, I remembered a strange experience I myself had had with a votive candle in a cathedral a continent away, in what seemed now like another life.

Two years before, when I was thinking about whether to accept the position as Music Director in Kraków, I knew a woman named Carmen Perez, an employee of the artists' agency in New York that represented me in the United States. As a devout Catholic woman, Carmen seemed to me at the time such an anomaly—a profoundly spiritual person in a business known for its sometimes raw-boned politics.

When she heard that I had been offered the position in Kraków, Carmen began fervently urging me to take it. I asked her again and again what made her so sure this was the right thing to do. She couldn't give me any specific answer, but somehow she said she just knew.

In October 1987, when I returned to New York from the final negotiations with the Polish Communist officials in Cologne, when I knew that I would indeed be going to Kraków, Carmen asked me to do her a great favor.

"Please don't think I'm crazy, but promise me you'll do what I ask. Go to St. Patrick's Cathedral in New York, go inside, and find the statue of St. Jude. When you do, would you please light a votive candle in the Saint's honor?"

"Are you nuts?" I said. "Carmen, you know I am Jewish. This is the strangest thing anyone has ever asked me to do. Do you even know why you want me to do this?"

"Please just do it. I feel something very, very important is happening. I feel it has something to do with me also. With all of us. You know, I was taught by the nuns to trust my faith. I know this is important. The Pope is from Kraków. You will think I'm crazy, but you two will find each other. And something wonderful will happen, something you can't even now imagine. Please, do this for me! Will you?"

She had never spoken to me in this way before. Her boss at the artists' agency was Jewish. Maybe that had motivated her in some way. But I don't think so. I believe she simply had some inner vision for what my going to Kraków might mean. It was her vision, but one I felt strangely compelled to follow.

With as odd a feeling as I have ever had in my life, I entered St. Patrick's to perform an act of Catholic devotion, a mitzvah as we Jews say. But a mitzvah for whom? For Carmen, for me, or for all of us, as she had so directly said?

I snuck into the Cathedral and walked around the outside of the pews, looking at each statue until I found the one of St. Jude. I bought a votive candle, putting my money in a metal box provided, and said the only prayer I knew, which is the Jewish prayer for the lighting of candles that we say on the Sabbath and on holidays. I lit the candle and placed it into the votive rack before the statue. Then, looking over my shoulder both ways, I walked very quickly out the door and onto Fifth Avenue. I was hoping to seamlessly blend into the crowd before anyone saw me. If someone had asked me to recount the strange ritual I had just performed, I would have been hard put to find the words. Luckily, I made a clean getaway.

I walked north a couple of blocks to the St. Regis Hotel, went to a lobby telephone, and called Carmen. She was overwhelmed. I'm not sure she thought I would actually follow through, but she was so moved that her tearful reaction almost made the whole strange trial worthwhile. I was still shaken by what I had done. But in a way, I also knew it was right.

I somehow knew that my upcoming Kraków journey would entail many such strange border crossings of faith. In fact, some essence of that experience has stayed with me every day since then, in ways that not even Carmen could have imagined. Yet I have never again been tempted to perform a Catholic devotion. My Jewish soul endured, was even deepened by that one oddly uplifting day in St. Patrick's

Cathedral in New York. And for that, I will always be grateful to Carmen Perez for sharing her Catholic faith with me.

As my thoughts came back to Notre Dame, the silence of the church began to give way in my mind to the music that would fill that silence in less than an hour's time, when we began our rehearsal. The devotional peace of these ancient stone walls would be replaced by the prayerful sounds of Schubert's setting of the Ninety-second Psalm: a setting in the original Hebrew by that most Catholic of Viennese composers for his friend Solomon Sulzer, the most famous Austrian Cantor of his day. These walls, which had heard all manner of music, from the chant of the Middle Ages and the polyphony of the Renaissance to the voluptuous Romanticism of Fauré, and which had even endured the shrill cries of the French Revolution, had never, ever heard anything like this small, unassuming a capella choral work. For there had never, ever been a work sung in Hebrew, the language of the Torah, in the more than 750-year history of this, one of the most famous landmarks of Christian France.

When I had discussed putting this work on the program, Cardinal Lustiger had said yes immediately.

The baritone for our Schubert performance in Notre Dame was, incredibly, also a Cantor. An Israeli, resident in London, Raffi Frieder had never set foot in any Catholic Church, I think, until that very night.

All in all, I became so lost in the wonders of this privileged experience about to come that I almost did not feel Monsieur Girard's nudge on my shoulder.

"You know, it's almost eight and there is no sign of your orchestra," he said indignantly, in perfect English, honed from working for IBM in France for almost thirty years before he was lured to run Notre Dame for his friend the Archbishop.

For Monsieur Girard, this concert was a pain in the neck. It meant longer hours and more and more details to take care of. But he knew that Cardinal Lustiger personally wanted it to happen and that he would attend it. So there was nothing to be done but to get on with it. Which was exactly the problem. How would we get on with it? My orchestra and choir had not arrived!

The rehearsal, the one rehearsal that we would be allowed, could only take place after the Cathedral had been closed to the public for the day at 7 P.M. Then, with a bit of time to tidy up and arrange the chairs around the altar, we could begin at 8 and be gone by 11, when Monsieur Girard would be safe at home, snuggled in his bed, having left the closing of the church to an assistant.

So here it was, almost 8:00, and there was no sign of the Polish musicians. I could almost hear him muttering under his breath.

"I told the Cardinal this would be trouble, just trouble. Leave the concerts to the concert halls, that's what I say. But no, he wouldn't listen. If it must be then, it must be. But, you'll see, this will be nothing but trouble!"

It looked as if Monsieur Girard was about to lose his Gallic temper.

Meanwhile, Cantor Frieder was pacing up and down the aisles of the Cathedral, talking to his agent, who had accompanied him, and anyone else who would listen, nervously wondering what he had gotten himself into. "First a church, then a Polish choir, and now, nobody here?! This is what you book me for in Paris?!"

I must say the delay surprised even me. The orchestra was coming that day from La Chaise-Dieu, a medieval festival town in the very center of France. It wasn't exactly the *banlieue*, but the distance was easily covered in a day, even with Polish buses on French roads. I was positive they would show their faces very soon, so I assured Monsieur Girard all would be well. Hope was speaking louder than faith.

At 8:30 Monsieur Girard, Pere Guiard (the Chief Priest of Notre Dame), and I retired to the vestry behind the altar to discuss what to do next. We couldn't for the life of us puzzle out why there had been no communication, not a single heads-up, about what might have gone wrong. This was, after all, the orchestra from the Pope's home city, coming to play a special concert in one of the truly great cathedrals of the world. What could be keeping them?

At 9:00 P.M. the phone rang in the vestry. As far as I know, this was the only phone in the Cathedral proper. And it was, coincidentally, in the room in which we had all just happened to have gathered.

It was Pan Janusz Pietkiewicz, the Polish agent for our tour. He asked to speak with me. He was calling from the Paris hotel where the orchestra was just checking in, he said.

"Pan Direktor, there has been an accident with one of the buses, the one with the orchestra's principal players and its management. It went off the road into a ditch somewhere near Lyon. No one was hurt, mind you. But there needs to be a bit of sorting out before we can head out again for Notre Dame. Oh, and by the way, just how late will the Cathedral remain open for a rehearsal?"

I repeated the question to Monsieur Girard and Pere Guiard. Monsieur Girard fairly grabbed the phone from my hand.

"The Cathedral will stay open all night, if need be. We will stay here until every note has been rehearsed. Do you hear me?" he fairly screamed into the telephone. This was definitely more IBM than INRI. He pressed the phone back into my hands.

Neither he nor I believed the story about the bus accident. I suspected that Pietkiewicz, who had close ties to the Communist regime and to Penderecki himself, was trying to see whether he could somehow sabotage our performance in Notre Dame Cathedral, which was to be dedicated to the enduring spirit of Poland, and to the Solidarity movement that was now getting closer to achieving its ultimate victory back home.

"We'll see what we can do," Pietkiewicz purred into the receiver. "We'll be there as soon as we can."

It was two more hours before the orchestra and chorus arrived from a hotel that was at most a half hour away from the Ile de la Cité. The buses parked on the far side of the Cathedral, away from the Seine, and loaded in the largest instruments, the double basses and timpani. I expected heavy going to get my musicians to rehearse at that ungodly hour. But no, the entire orchestra, the chorus, even the Polish soloists and Cantor Frieder, all stayed and rehearsed every note, just as Monsieur Girard had said they would. Our last note did not sound until after 1 A.M., and smiles of satisfaction spread over the faces of all concerned for having beaten the mischief makers at their own game.

These Polish players seemed to say, "Here, in this house of God, a Polish orchestra and choir, from the Pope's home city. Here you would have us play politics?!! Now you see what we are made of and what we will do to honor our collective spirit."

I'm sure the musicians had never been more bone-tired than that night, and yet never more proud of themselves for what they had accomplished. The concert would be a piece of cake after a night like this.

Two days later—or a day and a half if you consider that we had ended the rehearsal so long after midnight—the concert finally began. The Cathedral was packed with five thousand people, of whom half at least must have been expatriate Poles, there to show their solidarity with their touring orchestra and their struggling, politically awakening nation.

There was a political-religious atmosphere in the Cathedral that night whose force could be felt all the way back in Kraków and Warsaw, as well as in Rome. It was electric. The Agnus Dei, a hymn to the tragedy of the Polish people after the declaration of Martial Law in 1981, roused the audience's patriotic passion. If these thousands of Poles had their way, the regime of General Jaruzelski would be in the River Wisla, thrown from the parapet of Wawel Castle, Kraków's ancient seat of Polish kings. I have never felt anything like it. It was as if eight years of suppression and forty years of Communism came to an end, if only spiritually, that very night in Paris. Chopin himself would have been very proud.

The Schubert Psalm was another matter entirely, intended to soothe the waters ruffled by the Carmelite nuns of the convent at Auschwitz. Major figures in the French Jewish community were present, including Theo Klein, a stalwart fighter for interfaith understanding and an old friend of Cardinal Lustiger. They sat together, for this evening, again, as one.

This first-ever performance in Hebrew in Notre Dame brought the Jewish-born Cardinal Lustiger to tears. I cannot imagine what thoughts must have been going through his mind. Of his mother, and her martyrdom, and of his own roots, which I know he felt so deeply.

"How good it is to give thanks unto the Lord"—that is the beginning of the psalm's text. And to hear those words sung in Notre Dame by the voice of a cantor sent tingles down my spine as I conducted my Polish choir in that ancient Hebrew scripture.

Afterwards, following this draining, emotional evening, the Cardinal came to me and just held my hand. For a long time he could say nothing. Then, just "Thank you." He hugged me so hard I was immobile in his embrace.

Then, when he moved on to greet Cantor Frieder, he saw that he was not wearing a yarmulke. "What's the matter? Do you need me to lend you one?" His Eminence joked, pointing to his orange Cardinal's skullcap. "I have many of these; they're all the same color, but I would be glad to share."

Cantor Frieder, a bit lacking in humor, said nothing. He is orthodox, *frum* as we say, and he had intentionally not worn his *kippah* out of religious conviction, not out of sartorial forgetfulness. For him, just the act of singing in a church was enough unorthodoxy for one evening. He moved off to consult his agent, in some sense I think not understanding his extraordinary role in this historic evening.

I was the last one out of the Cathedral. The square in front of Notre Dame was still bustling with people going from Left Bank to Right and back, or sitting in the cafés on the Left Bank at the Place Saint Michel across the Seine. The Polish mass that had packed the Cathedral had blended back into the Parisian tapestry, and I was off to Chez Bébert to find a fragrant couscous and a welcome bottle of good French wine.

CHAPTER

NINE

After the concert in Notre Dame, I flew back to New York for a week at home before returning to Kraków to begin our season. I felt great about the ultimate triumph of the Paris event but still uneasy about the drama surrounding it. It would be good, I thought, to have a few days to think things through.

Weighing on my mind, besides the Kraków Philharmonic events of the previous week, were widespread news reports about East Germans rampaging in front of the Czechoslovak and Hungarian embassies in East Berlin, desperately seeking political asylum. Although the great crumbling of the Soviet Empire that would transform the map of Europe had only just begun, powerful change was definitely in the air. It was as exciting as it was unsettling. And I would be watching all of it unfold from my unique perch behind the Iron Curtain, which was just beginning to come apart at the seams.

On the Sunday of my week off, I visited my in-laws, Margit and Laci, in their West Side apartment, as Vera, David, and I did almost every week. As we feasted on her old-world Czech cuisine, I told Margit about all the nefarious goings-on in France—about buses going off the road on their way to Paris, the chorus and orchestra's curious late-night arrival for our one and only rehearsal in the great cathedral, and about the ominous edginess we had all felt leading up to the event. I also told her about the audience's palpable patriotic fervor, how the atmosphere in Notre Dame seemed almost like a

Solidarity rally. Most of all, I told her about the way our music had seemed to soar in that great sacred space.

Margit listened quietly, at first saying nothing, her lips pursed together in her characteristic pensive expression. But then, over the best homemade tortes in all New York, she opened up full blast, in her equally familiar no-nonsense way:

"Gil, I have been following closely what is going on in Poland. I read all the news, and I have to tell you, I have seen this all before. In 1956, in the revolution in Hungary; in 1968, with the Prague Spring in Czechoslovakia. The Soviets brutally crushed them both, killing thousands in cold blood. And just like they did then, they'll send the tanks into Poland now. So, I'm sorry to say it, but I just don't think things will be safe there for you now. Anyway, Vera and David should not go with you anymore to Kraków. It is too dangerous. You don't know this. For you it's all about music. But I do know. I lived in a Communist country for seventeen years. Yes, maybe the times were different, but I know them. Especially now, when they are under such pressure, these Communists, they will be very, very dangerous. Now you will see; you will become a threat to them. Everything American they will hate, those old comrades and, what we used to call in Czechoslovakia, their collaborators. They will want to shut down everything and everybody that comes from the West, if they still can. They will do anything to keep themselves in control. They may have wanted you there when they were secure in their power, but now you are expendable. Believe me."

"Margit," I said, "don't get so upset. I can take care of myself."

"No, Gil. Against them you cannot," she went on. "Believe me, they will do things to you. And I don't mean they would just say bad words. I mean terrible, terrible things could happen. A rock could come falling down from a building. A big one. Right on your head. Who's to say where it came from? A truck will come right at you at night and crush your car. You drive through the night to Warsaw on small roads, right? Via Kielce and Radom you told me, no? So, small roads. Very dark. No one will ever know what happened. Or even right in Kraków someone will beat you up in an alley. Who can say who it is?! I'm telling you, this is no joke anymore. You have to be very, very careful. Things are not in order there. In any case, I won't have your wife, my daughter, and my precious grandson put in danger. I won't! I have seen enough tragedy in my life. If you want to go back, you go back. I can't stop you. But Vera and David are not going with you if I have anything to do with it. I'm sorry Gil, but that's how it is."

Margit was as upset as I have ever seen her. Now Vera was also getting visibly upset. And this tirade was making me think things through all over again.

I knew so much less about the Communist system than Margit did. But from what I did know, what she said had the ring of truth. The suppression of the Czech and Hungarian revolts under the boot of Soviet troops had indeed been brutal. The Hungarian revolt had been too long ago, but I remembered the events of the Prague Spring of 1968 ever so vividly. I had been in Paris when it all unfolded. Elation. Freedom. Followed by crushing defeat for the forces of liberty. The television pictures of Soviet tanks rumbling into Wenceslas Square in the center of Prague scared the heck out of me, even six hundred miles away. Margit's premonitions of disaster seemed all too plausible from where I now sat.

What she had said about getting beaten up also rang a bell. I remembered what Michael Hornblow, the American Consul General, had once told me. In 1986, at a particularly tense time in Polish-American relations, Michael had been waylaid in one of the tiny streets that lead from the Rynek, the central square in Kraków, to the American Consulate on the Ulica Stolarska. He had been pummeled pretty badly by men he called "hooligans," but who, he was pretty sure, were plainclothes agents of the Polish secret police. I had not experienced anything so physically damaging, but I knew I could have been in real danger. If the U.S. Consul General could get beaten up, then so could I.

I also remembered with tremendous unease something strange that had happened towards the end of the previous 1988–89 season.

I had arrived late at night in Warsaw after one of my concerts in Kraków, and had been shown to a room at the Hotel Victoria that, quite oddly, did not have a functioning lock. I went back to the reception clerk, who told me that it was the only room available. It was very late. I had no place else to go, so I decided to stay. No sooner had I turned out my lights than I heard a key in the unlocked lock. Whoever it was just put the key in and out, in and out, without pushing the door open, or even actually turning the key. I lay there in my bed, scared out of my mind. But I knew it would be useless to call the hotel clerk. In those days, no one entered a Polish hotel without being closely observed. Hotel staff would have had to be complicit in whatever was going on. Nothing happened that night, thank God. But I had been totally petrified, which was perhaps the goal of the entire exercise.

There were many more public things as well. I remembered one evening late in that same spring of 1989 when, as I entered the Philharmonic Hall for a concert, I was met by teary-eyed members of the Kraków orchestra. "What's happened?" I asked, expecting perhaps to hear that someone, one of our colleagues, or some beloved public figure, had passed away.

"No, Pan Direktor," they said. "It's not that at all. There was tear gas fired at a demonstration across the tram tracks in the Planty Park. The police and some of their thugs broke up the rally, shoving people to the ground. Everyone that we know of escaped unharmed. But it was no joke. Perhaps we should delay the concert for a half an hour while our eyes and noses clear up. The audience will be slow in getting here this evening, in any case. Things are still a little chaotic outside." It turned out that I had missed the tear gas because I had walked up the street from the opposite direction, and entered the Philharmonic Hall through the side stage door.

Although I had not experienced the kinds of horrors Margit had when she had lived in the Communist Bloc, I had seen enough to know that her fears were not unfounded.

I began to think that the "mishaps" leading up to the concert in Notre Dame, and the incidents from my recent past in Poland, may well have been a wakeup call that maybe I should heed. If the still predominant Communists, fully aware of the threat to their absolute rule posed by the Solidarity labor movement led by Lech Walesa, could try to hijack something so innocent as a concert in Notre Dame Cathedral, what else might they try to do? How might they seek their revenge on me? On my musicians? Margit's tough talk again gave me pause.

Still, I loved Kraków and my wonderful orchestra. I didn't know if there was more trouble to come, but I just knew I had to go back. I told myself that maybe I had seen the worst. Even now, I can't say why I was so resolute. Any sane person would probably have left. The money, after all, was terrible. I lived life on permanent public view scrutinized by the secret police in every way one could imagine. And now I would be alone. Vera and David would not return to Poland for many months, just as Margit had wished. I would have to face whatever came next without them. Still, I know that had I not gone back, I would have missed so very much: my new city, my brave orchestra, and an incredible front-row seat to history. The fall of Communism was happening before my eyes. And it all started right there in Poland.

The lure for my return was musical as well. Before Margit's jeremiad, I had been eagerly looking forward to the 1989–90 season of the Kraków Philharmonic. We had great events and great repertoire scheduled. We were to open the season with a major concert performing Mahler's powerful Fifth Symphony in commemoration of the fiftieth anniversary of the beginning of World War II. Shortly after that, we would be embarking on our first-ever tour to South Korea, then a return tour to the United Kingdom, and visits from wonderful guest artists from the West, like Emanuel Ax, who would be performing with the Kraków Philharmonic for the very first time.

I was looking forward also to one of my busiest guest-conducting seasons. I was scheduled to lead orchestras in Spain, Germany, the United States, and Italy. I would also be making my first visit to Israel to conduct the Israel Chamber Orchestra at the invitation of my friend and colleague, the violinist and conductor Shlomo Mintz. I was excited just thinking about my calendar. I couldn't wait to begin all this fine music-making.

Our season began with a linguistic surprise. When I had arrived in Kraków in August for the preparatory rehearsals for our upcoming year, my musicians were amazed. Over the course of that summer, I discovered that my musician's ear had finally put all the Polish I had been hearing into coherent form, in much the same way that a child who has been listening carefully to his parents suddenly comes out with his first words.

When I raised my baton and greeted my orchestra that Monday morning in the late summer of 1989, it was with a hearty *"Dzien dobry panstwo,"* and not my usual "Good morning, ladies and gentlemen" or *"Guten morgen, meine Damen und Herren."* The entire Kraków Philharmonic sat openmouthed with astonishment. This they did not expect. "Wow, the Chief speaks Polish!" was written all over their faces. Now we could communicate in a common tongue, musician to musician, without the need for any translation. Of course, they corrected me when I made many obvious grammatical errors in their impossibly difficult language, but the whole atmosphere in the Philharmonic suddenly changed, and for my part, only for the better.

As I look back on this, I imagine that it was not only the orchestra that would have been surprised by my sudden linguistic ability. The secret police, who had counted on my having only very limited contact with most of my musicians, let alone the broader citizenry of Kraków, must have been more than a little taken aback. I don't want to say that I had suddenly become fluent. Far from it. But I could make myself understood with almost everyone I now met. And just as it made my association with my colleagues much easier, it must have made the job of those watching me that much more complicated. They would have many more contacts to monitor, more paperwork to file, and many more conversations they would now have to transcribe.

My new abilities in Polish also meant that I became more fully aware of the profound transformation that was taking place in my adopted country. I could understand the talk on and off stage about how the incredibly fast political changes were affecting my musicians' daily lives. I could also, with some difficulty, understand the larger political picture from the Polish perspective. I would not be getting my current events secondhand, only from old editions of *Newsweek* or the *Herald Tribune* passed along by members of the U.S. diplomatic community or the odd American tourist who made his way to Kraków in those years. I could basically understand the Polish press myself. Now I could know what my musicians knew, what Poles knew, or at least what their government wanted them to know. I became so much more in tune with the people of Kraków and their courageous struggle for a new way of life.

The Kraków of August 1989 was indeed a place of great foment, one of the epicenters of the headlong charge toward freedom in the entire Eastern Bloc that had begun in Poland just two months before. The parliamentary election of June 4, 1989, had brought a landslide victory for Solidarity. The writing was on the wall. Lech Walesa and his comrades had won 99 percent of all the seats in the Senate and the mandated limit of one-third of the seats in the National Assembly. General Wojciech Jaruzelski, whose name was the only one the Communist Party allowed on the ballot for the presidency, had won by just one vote in the parliamentary vote that brought him to power. With this election, the Communist Party's fifty-year monopoly on political power had begun to crumble, a full five months before the fall of the Berlin Wall.

It was amazing to behold. Just one year after my concertmaster, Mieczyslaw Szelzer, had told me, "My grandchildren will certainly live under communism," the whole totalitarian system was coming apart at the seams.

Now all the avenues of power, including those relating to the control of the cultural life of the country, were suddenly up for grabs. For me, the concert at Notre Dame had been the opening salvo in a quiet struggle over who would control the Philharmonic: the old guard Communists or the emerging voice of Solidarity itself; the secret police, who had surely engineered the buses going off the road, or Polish people themselves, represented by the huge crowd of patriotic, solidarity-loving Poles who had crowded into Notre Dame that great and fateful night.

The subtle battle raged for months to come, and in ways that were entirely unconventional. In early October, the Kraków orchestra was booked on a tour to South Korea. Not an uncommon occurrence for Western orchestras, but a first for any ensemble from the entire Eastern Bloc. There were as yet no diplomatic relations between the Republic of Korea and the People's Republic of Poland. We would be playing our music as ping-pong diplomacy against the background of a larger East-West struggle. In the newly emerging environment of artistic freedom and Solidarity bravado, no one had cleared our trip with the Polish Communist musical authorities still in control in Warsaw. We just made our plans to go, and off we went. The authorities retaliated by holding up our plane from Kraków to Amsterdam (supposedly because of "air-traffic control" difficulties) for more than two hours, long enough, they must have thought, to prevent us from arriving on time for our connecting flight to Seoul.

But it didn't work. KLM wasn't about to forgo the fares of one hundred paying passengers. The blue-and-white jumbo 747 waited patiently at Schiphol Airport in Amsterdam until our Polish orchestra finally arrived and all the musicians and their instruments had made the connecting flight. The shenanigans didn't end there: slipped in among the orchestra's entourage were agents of Polish security, as they were politely known. They would keep tabs on these seemingly free Polish artists as they encountered the Wild West (East) in Seoul.

Now we knew that the political games which had begun in Notre Dame were going to be played out in earnest. No rocks from buildings, but strong-arm tactics, intimidation, and obstruction nonetheless.

Despite the Polish authorities' undermining efforts, the world was watching and supporting the movement toward freedom in Poland and throughout the East. We felt the cheers of encouragement from all over Western Europe and, of course, from the United States.

On November 15, 1989, before he had even been elected President of Poland, Lech Walesa was honored by being asked to give a very rare address to a joint meeting of the U.S. Congress, and I was asked to play a small role in that momentous event. In a show of support from three of the most powerful leaders in the House of Representatives, Speaker Tom Foley and Chairmen Dan Rostenkowski and John Dingell, I was invited to sit near Walesa at the special dinner in the Capitol rotunda on the evening of his congressional speech. I was introduced to this courageous Polish patriot as an important American cultural ambassador to his home country. The irony of my meeting with Walesa that evening in Washington was powerful. This was the same Lech Walesa whom I had encountered sixteen months before, sitting alone in the far corner of the dining room of the Holiday Inn in Kraków. Walesa was there on his way to join Elie Wiesel and four other Nobel Laureates on their visit to Auschwitz. At that time, in January 1988, Walesa was officially so shunned in the Communist People's Republic of Poland that he could only be referred to in whispered tones, as "the Mustache." And now he was the honored guest of the leadership of the United States Congress on behalf of an admiring nation.

That January 1990 I made my first trip to Israel, joined by Vera and David, who true to Margit's word, had not visited Poland all that fall. There was something extraordinary about being in Israel, a country from which my ancient ancestors had been dispersed almost two thousand years before. I saw the whole array of world Jewry, from deeply religious Haredim in their silk caftans and fur-trimmed hats, a costume modeled on that worn by the Polish nobility in the fifteenth century, to secular Jews dressed as anyone else did in the Western world of 1990, going about their daily lives, much as my family and I did back in New York.

In Israel, Jewish life in all its manifestations was as vibrant as it was nearly dead and almost forgotten back in Kraków. After post-Holocaust Poland, I felt in Israel like I was home.

The Israel Chamber Orchestra was made up largely of immigrants, many of them Russians like their conductor Shlomo Mintz. To them, Israel was an oasis away from the same brand of communism I had encountered when I first went to Kraków. In Israel, their promised land, they breathed the air of political and artistic freedom, precious hard-won rarities that were finally beginning to show themselves again in Poland.

During my time in Israel, I gave many interviews. People there were curious about how a Jew could live in Poland, a country they associated with terrible anti-Semitism. I told them that I had not found that to be true, at least not in my case. I told them frankly that things were extremely challenging for me and for my orchestra, but whatever was going on with me in Poland, whatever difficulties I was facing, they were not because I was Jewish. Professional jealousy perhaps. Political chicanery and worse, absolutely. But not anti-Semitism directed towards me, at least not that I could discern. I told the Israelis this, but I'm not sure how much they believed me. I also told the Israeli journalists that I wanted to help my Polish musicians in any way I could; that things were tough indeed for Polish artists. With so many Soviet immigrants flooding into Israel during this period, the newly arrived Russian-Israeli musicians could have certainly grasped the dire straits of their Polish colleagues with no trouble at all.

On my return to Kraków a few weeks later, the political turmoil that had started in the fall was continuing at full boil. No bricks were being thrown at me from rooftops, but life was getting tough for many ordinary Poles, and not least because the economy was only going from bad to worse. They were achieving their freedom, but it would come at a price. Things that were difficult to find in stores under communism were now being hoarded. Salami became a rare delicacy. Shoes were too expensive. Trying lives were being tried still more. The lives of my musicians were not getting any easier as Poland's politics became increasingly unclear. The end of Communist tyranny was in sight. Change was bracingly in the air. But it would not come all at once.

The makeup of the Polish government kept changing, with more and more control coming into the hands of Solidarity and their allies. Still, the Interior Ministry, the home of the nefarious internal security services, remained firmly in the hands of the old guard. General Czesław Kiszczak, a hardliner from the most virulent, irredentist wing of the Polish Communist Party, was still in charge of overseeing the population's daily lives. People lived in fear that he and his cohorts would open their secret police files at any moment. Important figures from all segments of Polish society—cultural, political, and academic—would come up to me and say, "Don't believe what you might hear about me in the next few days or weeks. I was by no means the only one who was informing to the police. So and so was much worse. You will see." And then they would mention the name of someone we both knew whom they were offering up as an example of true evil. They cast themselves as the lesser transgressors, whom I should, of course, continue to trust. But for me trust was a rare commodity in those days.

Under Kiszczak's ongoing oversight, the problem of surveillance intensified in the so-called post-Communist period of the late winter of 1990. I found it strange that although a new Solidarity government had taken over six months before, the secret police could still be up to their old tricks. All my phones were still bugged. Snippets of my private conversations in my office, my backstage greenroom, on stage at the Philharmonic, and even in the car that was used to shuttle me around Kraków were fed back to me verbatim, just so I would know that I was never truly alone.

This made sense in a way. Warsaw may have changed its political colors, but the people around me, or should I say, surrounding me, were all the same. Robert Wydra, who in his guise as vice-mayor for culture in the Communist-run Kraków municipal administration, was still the manager of the orchestra. When I would try to talk with him about artistic affairs, he would tell me, "This is beyond my competence. I only know about organization." He had not changed his political stripes, just the address of his office. The orchestra members themselves could hardly believe that their world had truly changed with Pan Direktor Wydra still in his office on the orchestra's top floor.

And I still had my orchestra-provided driver taking me to work and back every day. He supposedly spoke no English but had an uncanny ability to understand my native language when it was spoken privately in the backseat of his cab with whatever guest happened to be in Kraków visiting me or the Philharmonic. I could see in his rear-view mirror his uncontrollable reaction to provocative things said in his cab, in ways that let on that his understanding of spoken English must have been pretty good indeed. In all, in the winter of 1990, I was still as closely surveilled as I had ever been.

When, therefore, in late February of that year, Burt Quint of CBS News contacted me about participating in a story he was developing about continued secret police activity in post-Communist Poland, I was at once all too eager and more than a bit hesitant to tell Burt my story on air. As we went back and forth about the project, he assured me that although I would be the only American interviewed, a number of Poles at the highest levels of the Solidarity government were also going to give him interviews. Burt Quint knew Poland as well as any foreigner could; he had covered the country for CBS for many years. He was also someone who had reported from the Vatican for a long period during the Pontificate of John Paul. In the end, I had to trust his judgment.

The interview was finally taped on March 2 and 3, 1990. We thought we were being very careful. At my insistence we conducted our on-camera talk, not in my office at the Philharmonic or in my hotel room, but on a bench in the Planty Park opposite the Jagiellonian University. Although long-range microphones were in existence and could never be discounted, no one but myself, Burt, his Polish camera-man, a sound man, and a driver was present for our taping.

On returning to the Forum Hotel, my home away from home, with Burt and crew, I went to the reception desk on the right-hand wall about halfway through the glassed-in lobby. The desk clerks there worked twelve-hour shifts, and by now I knew most of the young men and women who were lucky enough to get a job in what was then the best hotel in Kraków. I knew what to expect from these folks, or I thought I did. But the clerk on duty that particular day was new to me. He was a tall, dark-haired young fellow in glasses. He seemed at the same time stiffer and more obsequious than most of the others. Over the course of my time in Poland, I had developed a second sense about who could be trusted and whom it was best to avoid, if one could. Anyone who lived in a Communist country cultivated such mild and sensible paranoia as part of his daily survival kit. In any case, my visceral reaction to this particular clerk was very negative. As I approached the desk and asked for my key (I was always given Room 502), the clerk bent down and took the key from the row before him. As he handed it to me, he flashed a forced grin and asked, "Sir, may I ask you, for what network did you give your television interview?"

"What interview?" I retorted, in a bit of a shock. "That's none of your business."

Looking steadily at me, he said, unabashed, "It is most definitely our business. So I repeat, sir, for what television station did you give your interview just now? We need to know this."

I looked at him for a long time, trying to see any shame on his face for having revealed himself to me as someone who was working for people other than the management of the hotel. I said nothing and went up to my room, feeling newly nervous about what Burt and I had just done for CBS.

When I came down a few minutes later to join the crew for lunch in the Forum's dining room, I was the first to arrive, followed shortly by the Polish cameraman. I began to relate to him what had just happened with the reception clerk. I thought, this being the "new Poland," that he would be sympathetic. Instead, he said something that shocks me to this day.

"Maestro, you know, you shouldn't judge us Poles too harshly. Informing was just a part of our lives. Really. We had to do it. Everybody told about foreigners, and even about our fellow Poles to the proper authorities. It was just something we had to do. I personally think that only those who committed terrible crimes, you know, murderers and such people, only they should be punished, or even publicly named."

This would have been a disappointment coming from any Pole, but from someone who had worked for CBS News in Warsaw for many years, it was deeply disturbing. Was he saying that in all those years he had been telling the secret police about Burt's interviews, about his stories, as they were being developed? No wonder people were paranoid about any contact with the foreign press, when its

Polish "colleagues" were the ones they could not trust. In the end, I
think Burt must have known all this and done his journalistic best in
spite of the risks. He was truly one of the great unsung heroes of
Western journalism behind the Iron Curtain.

I doubt if the reception clerk, or anyone else in Poland, actually
saw the interview when it aired on CBS on March 10, 1990. If they
had, they would have seen the power of a free press to tell a story that
no one else wanted to touch. In the end, they would also have seen
that I was the only one brave—or foolish—enough to be interviewed
on air for the story. Every Pole, even members of the Solidarity leadership, who had been asked by Burt to do an aired interview for this
story had politely declined. Perhaps Burt's cameraman had inadver-
tently told me why.

Within a month after my CBS interview, Comrade General
Kiszczak was finally gone from the Interior Ministry, and Poland was
beginning to be truly free. But it would take years for the fear to
subside. The secret police files Kiszczak and his cohorts left behind
would haunt Poland and many of its most prominent citizens for years
thereafter. Memories of who did and who did not collaborate with the
Communist regime would dominate the national debate and pit colleague against colleague.

It is easy to look back and say that Margit Kalina had been paranoid, alarmist, or worse. Poland was a difficult place to live and work
for me in 1989–90. I was living in a fishbowl. But no harm came to
me, and relatively few Poles were actually killed in their courageous
march towards freedom. But it could easily have been so different. In
December 1989, my friend, the longtime *New York Times* foreign correspondent John Tagliabue, then resident in Warsaw, was sent by his
paper to cover the anti-Communist protests in the Romanian town of
Timisoara. Timisoara is an old Austro-Hungarian city close to the
Hungarian border. It has a philharmonic orchestra with a rich past.
Béla Bartók appeared with the orchestra as a piano soloist, and the
great Austrian maestro Bruno Walter was its principal conductor early
in his career. By a small twist of fate, I might conceivably have ended
up there instead of Kraków.

The Communist regime of Romania made very different choices in defending itself against the rising tide of freedom from those made by their Polish counterparts. They fired live ammunition directly into crowds of protesters in Timisoara, killing many Romanians and grievously wounding my friend John, who just wouldn't let that historic story go unreported. John came within an inch of losing his life, having to be medevacked out of Romania to Germany, where he lay between life and death for many months. Yes, things were different in Poland, thank God. There I had protectors, and the regime was not so crazy or brutal as to lethally attack its own. But Margit was not all wrong; she was off by just a few hundred kilometers, and in a country lacking the moral and spiritual guidance of Pope John Paul.

And so, in Kraków, I felt throughout this period that I had a number of guardian angels who kept those proverbial bricks from falling on my head.

The American diplomats who had seen me through my earliest days in Poland had also been an enormous help during these many trying months. I made sure to call them when I entered Poland, on landing in Warsaw or in Kraków, just to let them know I was in-country and still safe. They in turn showed tremendous public pride in what I was accomplishing for Polish-American relations. They would host me and my Polish counterparts at the consulate and at the embassy. They even put out a compendium of all my successes with the Kraków Philharmonic, both in Poland and abroad—reviews, testimonials, a list of recordings and tours—to counter any attempts by remnants of the old regime to undermine my ongoing relationship with the Philharmonic.

But most of all, throughout all the trying events of the fall of communism in Poland, Pope John Paul and Monsignor Dziwisz followed the events of my life in Kraków with keen and solicitous interest. Monsignor Dziwisz would even comment on reviews of my Philharmonic performances that he had read in the Kraków newspapers, which were forwarded constantly via priestly channels to the Apostolic Palace. If a particular tour of ours went especially well, he would even send me a congratulatory note. I knew I was being watched from Washington and from Rome, and that kind of "surveillance" was most welcome indeed.

As the spring of 1990 burst forth, Poland was finally seeing real and credible change. By May, Solidarity was in full control. They had won the local elections, which the Poles themselves believed were free and fair. And it was during this time that I attended the first-ever solidarity meeting of the Kraków Philharmonic itself.

Members of the orchestra, the choir, and I gathered quietly in the Zlata Sala, the Golden Hall, our rehearsal room on the second floor of the Philharmonic Hall. We observed a moment of silence for all those in the Philharmonic as a whole who had suffered at the hands of Communist tyranny over the past forty years. I felt privileged to be trusted enough that I could be part of that moment of solemn remembrance. Though I could easily have left Poland during this difficult time—and indeed had many lucrative opportunities to do so—I did not.

There were undoubtedly elements among the Communist dead-enders who would have been only too happy to see me go. But that meeting of solidarity in the Philharmonic Hall, and the great spiritual presence from Rome that I felt constantly with me, strongly encouraged me to stay on in Kraków. I enjoyed the music-making, and these powerful positive forces were keeping me on track. If the Polish people could so courageously find their way out of communism to freedom, if the Polish Pope could honor me in the profound ways he had, then maybe I could repay them, these fierce Polish spirits, with my own steadfastness.

CHAPTER

TEN

Ever since Ibrahim ibn Jakub (a Jewish traveler, merchant, and diplomat from Tortosa in Spain) visited Kraków in 965, Jews have been a part of Kraków's rich history. It is almost impossible to believe in light of the Shoah, but Poland was such a haven for the Jewish refugees from Western European persecution during the Middle Ages and early Renaissance that many in the Jewish world at that time even called it Paradisus Iudaeorum, the Jewish Paradise.

Starting in the fourteenth century and continuing until the Holocaust, Kazimierz, an ancient city district bordered by the slow, meandering Wisla River, was the center of Jewish life in Kraków. Many synagogues were built there over many centuries. A Jewish market filled the quarter's central square. There were ritual bathhouses, called *mikvahs*, and so many yeshivas (Jewish schools) that Kraków became one of the greatest centers of Talmudic study in all of Central Europe. Kazimierz was a testament to a seemingly invincible, vibrant Jewish life, in Kraków and in Poland.

It is a twenty-minute walk from the Philharmonic Hall, past Wawel Castle, across a grand nineteenth-century boulevard called Dietla into Kazimierz, but it might as well be a world away. I walked there many times during the period of my music directorship in Kraków. I often found myself in the Renaissance-period Remuh, as it was still the only synagogue still functioning in the city.

But there was another synagogue, not far from the Remuh, but not actually still a part of Kazimierz. It was called the Postepowa or

Templ Synagogue, and it was located on the Ulica Miadowa. It had been built in the middle of the nineteenth century, at the time of a flowering of assimilated Jewry, that is, Polish-speaking Jews who didn't speak Yiddish or knew it only as a second language. The nineteenth-century Jews of the Templ viewed themselves as Poles who were Jewish. They considered themselves Polish patriots, just as much as their Catholic brothers and sisters. They were, they believed, a firm part of Polish society, unlike their coreligionists at the Remuh, who lived largely separated lives.

Walking through the Rynek Glowny, the central square of old Kraków, a member of the Templ would not have thought there was a difference between himself and his Polish Catholic counterpart. A shopkeeper was a shopkeeper. A professor at Kraków's great Jagiellonian University was a professor. A Jewish musician thought himself the same as his Catholic colleague, a dedicated artist who served a great Polish musical institution. Until Friday night, that is, when the Jews of the Templ celebrated the Sabbath together in the Ulica Miadowa. Then they joined their fellow Reform congregants on their day of rest and prayer. Until the Nazis came. The Nazis made no distinction between a Reform Jew and his brother who worshiped at the Remuh. All were condemned, no matter how observant they were.

The Templ was a place where I would have felt at home and my family would have felt at home. But it was now completely empty. The Reform Jewish community, as all the Jews of Poland, had either been killed during the Holocaust or had fled in the political purges of 1968, during which thousands of the survivors of the Holocaust were forcibly exiled from their native land. The Holocaust and the great exile left the Templ cold and desolate when I found it that first time.

I had wandered by it many times, but one day in 1990 my curiosity became too great. I peered in through one of its filthy stained-glass windows; I could see very little of the interior and decided to knock on the door. I knocked and knocked again. No answer. I was about to go on my way when a small man in dusty overalls came and unlocked the door. He was the beadle, hired by the community that now worshiped solely in the Remuh to take care of this place. It is an exaggeration to say "take care." Mostly, he was there just to keep the doors locked and the leaves swept off the Postepowa's back steps and, I suppose, to keep intruders like myself safely on the outside. But the beadle heard my insistent knocks, looked out through the window beside the door, and decided to let me in.

What I found inside amazed me. The Templ Synagogue is a jewel. It was dusty, dirty, and cold, to be sure, but a hidden jewel nonetheless. Its ceilings are high, with wooden columns topped with flourishes, all in gold. The ceiling too was layered in gold, with gilt-edged chandeliers hanging down almost to my head. These lights would have illuminated the large congregational space, both the downstairs, reserved for men, and the upstairs gallery, where the women sat. In a word, it was grand; if, that is, you could see through the years of neglect.

Behind the *aron-ha-kodesh*, the Ark where the Torah scrolls would once have been kept, I found prayer books piled high in uneven stacks, a disgrace that testified as much to the haste with which the congregation must have fled as to the desultory care the beadle had been providing. The Postepowa was also uncommonly cold, even for that blustery March day. There was either no working furnace or, more likely, there was no coal purchased in those desperate economic times just after the fall of Communism, to stoke the furnace fires.

The walls and everything inside this sanctuary were chilled, and I shivered all the time I was there. I walked outside just to warm up. As I did, I looked up to the steeple at the front of the Templ. There was no Star of David perched atop its spire. The Nazis, who had used the Templ as a stable during the war, had pulled it down, depriving this ghost ship of even the smallest outward marking of its original sacred purpose.

I got it into my head that I was going to warm those walls. I was going to bring life to this place. And being a musician, the gift of life I knew best was music. I decided I would conduct a concert with my Polish orchestra in this place and let its walls resound once more with our living, breathing art.

In order for a concert to take place, however, a certain amount of refurbishing—I wouldn't dare call it renovation—had to take place. Just enough to make it hospitable, perhaps to the point where one could see what needed to be done to return the Templ to its former glory.

But all this would not be easy. First I had to get the permission of the Gemeinde, the Jewish Community Council in Kraków. That meant the Jakubowicz family. They were the arbiters of all that concerned the official Jewish life of Kraków. I approached Czeslaw, the elder of the two Jakubowicz brothers, with my idea of a concert in the Postepowa. His reaction was astonishment, and not a little bit of skepticism. Czeslaw could not remember in the entire history of Kraków's Jewish community a similar concert in a synagogue, especially one involving a symphony orchestra. Not before the war, and certainly not after. This would be a first, Czeslaw exclaimed.

"Concerts in churches—they happen every week here in Kraków. But in a synagogue? Never. Who will come? We are only two hundred here in the Jewish community, and among the very orthodox, they might not approve, so not even all of those will probably attend. And Poles, do you think they will come? You are from New York; you don't know Kraków very well yet. You'll be conducting for yourself. And, do you really think the Philharmonic itself will consent? Most of those musicians have never been inside a synagogue. What will they think? What a strange idea? And anyway, who will pay for this? The Templ is, as you have seen, in a terrible state. It is cold, and unheated. It's filthy inside. No one uses it. But, if you wish, please, by all means. Try your best. I will be there. More than that, I cannot promise."

With that tremendous encouragement (I was happy just to have his permission!) I went looking for assistance elsewhere. And it came from an unexpected source. The United Jewish Appeal was planning one of their frequent missions to Poland. They visit places of former European Jewish culture before going on to Israel. The UJA's goal was to give two hundred young Jews a sense of their heritage. They would be in Kraków in October and generously agreed to support this "Concert of Remembrance and Reconciliation" in the Postepowa

Synagogue with their presence and, importantly, with their subvention. Funds did come from them, and from the Ronald S. Lauder Foundation, so that we could at least wipe away the soot from the windows and the grime from the floor and buy enough coal to begin to heat the furnace. Polish Guraly, the devoutly Catholic mountain people of the nearby Tatras were famous for their skill in constructing and repairing the steep-pitched roofs so common in southern Poland. These simple but open-hearted people donated their special expertise to repairing the roof of the synagogue so that it would not leak during our performance.

Ronald Lauder and I had had a previous encounter in another synagogue, three thousand miles away in Crown Heights, Brooklyn. We had both had the honor of meeting the great Lubavitcher Rebbe Rav Menachem Schneerson earlier that year, at Simchat Torah, the Rejoicing of the Torah, a celebration marking the conclusion of the annual cycle of Torah readings, and the beginning of reading the holy book anew. We had been introduced by a Chasidic Rabbi, Chaskel Besser, who was then working for the Lauder Foundation, concentrating on its work in Poland. The Simchat Torah service at 770 Eastern Parkway, the Lubavitch world headquarters, was a noisy, song-filled affair, with thousands of the Rebbe's followers singing and chanting, as the Rebbe himself clapped loudly in strict rhythm and sang along with them in his gravelly baritone voice.

At the end of the service, the Rebbe greeted a line of well-wishers, including Ronald Lauder, Rabbi Besser, and myself. When Rabbi Besser introduced me to the Rebbe, who had been married in Warsaw and fled Europe before the Holocaust, he told him I was the permanent conductor of the Kraków Philharmonic.

The Rebbe replied, "A Yid in Polin! A Yid in Polin! A Yid in Polin!"—A Jew in Poland!, which he kept repeating over and over.

With each repetition he expressed more and more disbelief, and he then gave me a dollar and a bottle of vodka, a huge honor befitting the fact that he had given me his *heckscher* or blessing.

Then the Rebbe added, "You should find Jews in Poland to share this vodka with you. That will be your mitzvah," your good deed.

Right afterward, in June, at the end of the 1989–90 season, I gathered as many Jews as I could in my suite at my hotel in Kraków, and we drank the Rebbe's blessed vodka, according to his command. And now, Ronald Lauder was helping me to share the blessing of the Rebbe even further, by supporting the cleaning of the Templ Synagogue in preparation for this special concert.

These practical matters attended to, I approached the Kraków Philharmonic and said, "I would like to do a concert in the Templ Synagogue. We've done concerts in churches, gone from church to church making our music in spiritual spaces all around the city. Now I'd like to bring a concert to a Jewish house of worship, the Postepowa on the Ulica Miadowa." The director's face was blank. I'm not sure how many of our orchestra he thought had even been to Kazimierz, let alone seen this particular synagogue. So it would be the first time for nearly everyone in the orchestra to perform in a synagogue.

In the end, he asked the orchestra, and they said yes, as I knew they would. We had Notre Dame behind us, and by now, in 1990, our mutual respect as musicians was great; my being Jewish seemed to play little if any role in our artistic relationship. It didn't hurt that by now, a full year and a half after beginning my work in Kraków, I spoke conversational Polish. The Templ Synagogue concert would be just another date on our busy calendar, or so they thought.

Then, I went back to Czeslaw Jakubowicz with the news that my discussions with the Philharmonic, the UJA, and the Lauder Foundation had been successful. Jakubowicz now brought the idea of the concert to the Gemeinde and received their official approval. Now the question arose, besides the two hundred Jews from the UJA and the few Jewish souls left in Kraków, who would attend this event? If you're going to do a concert in this city, it's largely going to be the Catholics who come, and first among them their Archbishop and my old acquaintance Franciszek Cardinal Macharski.

However, when I went to see Cardinal Macharski, he didn't seem to embrace the idea, for reasons I don't really understand to this day. I had had wonderful conversations with him that indicated his understanding of the Jewish heritage of his city. He was a committed member of the Catholic-Jewish dialogue both in Poland and world-wide. But this concert didn't spark his interest, and he would not be attending. I was crestfallen. I couldn't imagine this historic concert going forward without a high-level presence on the part of the Church. I decided to consult a close friend about the best way to solve that problem.

Monsignor Dziwisz seemed to know why I had come to see him in Rome. Sitting with him in his small office in the Apostolic Palace at the Vatican, I was about two minutes into my exposition about the upcoming concert in the Templ Synagogue, and the "problem," when he stopped me short and went out through a door to his right. Minutes went by, five minutes, ten minutes—I am really not sure, although the Baroque clock to my left ticked and ticked and ticked incessantly—until I couldn't think of anything but the time passing and just what had made Monsignor Dziwisz leave so hurriedly, without saying a word.

He came back as suddenly as he had left and said, "Come with me." I followed him through a corridor in the Apostolic Palace across a narrow foyer and into a very small elevator. We traveled down to an inner courtyard of the Palace where a car was waiting for us. The driver took Monsignor Dziwisz and myself through covered tunnels past traffic lights, some manned by Swiss Guards, passageways I had never known existed inside the Vatican. We went out past the back of St. Peter's Basilica, past the Vatican gas station, and out a gate to the opening of the Paul VI Hall, the Sala Nervi, which I knew very well from my concert there in 1988.

Monsignor Dziwisz and I exited the car. I followed him only as far as the foyer when he commanded me to wait for him right where I stood. He proceeded immediately to the far end of the foyer of the

Aula and vanished. The large space was now totally empty. To my right was a staircase. A few moments passed.

Finally, I noticed a figure descending the staircase at a hurried pace. It was my old friend Cardinal Lustiger. He looked at me. I looked at him. He couldn't have been more bewildered. I had no idea why I had been brought at this particular time to this particular place. From the look on his face it was clear that I was the last person His Eminence could have imagined seeing at just that moment there in the Vatican.

"Maestro, what are you doing here?" he said. "Excuse me, but I have no time to see you; I am in the middle of the Bishops Synod. In fact, I am one of the Chairmen of the Synod. And just now, the Holy Father has called me urgently to meet with him."

Sure enough, just as he said that, both of us caught sight of Pope John Paul walking purposefully across the vast foyer in our direction, with Monsignor Dziwisz just behind him. His Holiness gestured with two fingers of one hand for some people across the foyer to come and meet him in the middle, where he had stopped. Cardinal Lustiger knew exactly whom he was pointing to, namely, Cardinal Lustiger. I, however, had no idea to whom that other Papal command was being directed. I looked around to see whether he was perhaps looking for someone else, someone I hadn't seen, perhaps standing just behind me. Finally, Monsignor Dziwisz pointed to me directly: "Maestro, you as well." Cardinal Lustiger and I walked to the middle of the foyer, which had instantly become a restricted Papal space.

I couldn't have stuck out more. There were no civilians here, only Bishops and Archbishops and Cardinals in their various robes circulating around us. His Holiness was dressed in simple white, the holiest of holy garbs. My blue blazer and gray slacks might have been an elegant outfit on normal occasions, but I certainly stood out in the midst of this huge sea of high-level ecclesiastical personages.

The Pope immediately started speaking to me in Polish, with Cardinal Lustiger standing on his other side. "I understand you are planning a concert in Kraków. It's going to be in Kazimierz, yes? Maestro, tell me about it, please."

"Yes, Your Holiness, it will be called a 'Concert of Remembrance and Reconciliation.' It will be held in the Postepowa Synagogue. Not exactly in Kazimierz, but just outside."

"I know this place," the Pope said. "I remember that synagogue; is it open? I knew the people of that synagogue. They were professors at the Jagiellonian University, doctors and lawyers."

"Yes," I said, "that is the place. It will be opened now. We are doing a small amount of refurbishment to make it fit."

Then His Holiness asked, "What would be on the program?"

"The Eroica Symphony of Beethoven, the Dvořák Cello Concerto," I said, "and we'll begin with Kol Nidre and all three national anthems: Polish, American, and Israeli as well. The program will accentuate the common European heritage of all who might attend. We expect that there would be members of the Kraków Jewish community there." I paused, then continued, "And many Catholics as well, of course, and there will be a delegation of Jews flying in specially from America."

Then I told the Pope that I had talked to Cardinal Macharski about it and that it did not appear that His Eminence would be able to come, but I hoped very much that someone from the Church might be in attendance. The Pope stopped me in midsentence and began to translate what had been said between us in Polish to Cardinal Lustiger, in French.

All this time, Cardinal Lustiger had a growing look of astonishment on his face. He had been standing there, listening to a conversation in Polish, a language he did not understand. His family came from Poland, it is true, but they had been Yiddish-speaking, so the Pope's language with his Maestro was strange to him indeed.

By contrast, my French is certainly good enough to understand what was now being said between these two titans of the Church. The Pope said, "There is going to be this wonderful event in Kraków. It is going to be the first time there will be a concert in a synagogue, and there will be members of the Catholic community there and members of the Jewish community also, and I wish you to go to represent the hierarchy in Cardinal Macharski's stead."

Cardinal Lustiger could not possibly have looked more surprised. He looked stupefied. He and the Pope went back and forth, talking about the date and other arrangements. Finally, the Pope said to me, "You'll keep Cardinal Lustiger apprised. This is a wonderful idea. Please let me know how it goes." And then he was gone. He walked out past both of us, with Monsignor Dziwisz trailing him, into a waiting car.

All during our conversation, members of the Catholic hierarchy, who had seen the Pope leave the Synod, began to leave for their lunch break. They had been walking out through the foyer of the Aula but not very close to His Holiness, Cardinal Lustiger, and myself. They had all kept their distance, watching the end of this conversation, some of them with slight smiles on their faces, bemused, as if they could not imagine what they were seeing. This unknown layperson, gesticulating madly in the face of the Holy Father. The Pope gesturing just as animatedly right back. They were just as surprised by all of this as Cardinal Lustiger had been.

After the Pope left, Cardinal Lustiger and I exited the Aula and went out into the Roman sunshine, making our way to Saint Peter's Square. We walked side by side in silence for the longest time.

Finally, he turned to me and said, "Are you a Galicianer?"

I couldn't believe my ears. This was the Cardinal-Archbishop of Paris asking me about a nomenclature—Litvak versus Galicianer, people of Lithuanian-Jewish descent versus South Polish–Austro-Hungarian Jews—words I had not heard since the Bronx, when my grandmother regularly made such distinctions among her friends. The Litvaks had the supposedly intellectual, cooler heads, while the Galicianers were the more earthy, warmhearted, and wily southerners, who somehow had the gift to do things that other people couldn't imagine. And now the Cardinal-Archbishop of Paris was asking me whether I was a Galicianer.

"No, Eminence," I said, "in fact my family comes from Warsaw, and I guess that would make us Litvaks. But in any case, what do you mean?"

"Do you have any idea what took place in there? Did you know what was going to happen?" Cardinal Lustiger gently demanded.

"No, Eminence. I did not."

"Well," he answered, "I have never seen anything like that in my life. I had no idea you had become so close to the Holy Father. And it just seemed so odd that His Holiness was conversing with you, and then translating for my benefit. Please forgive me, but I am just so amazed by all of it. Your concert in Kraków clearly has gained the Holy Father's blessing. For that, you should be very proud."

Galicianers or no, Cardinal Lustiger and I parted ways a few paces farther on. As he left me, he turned and gave me a warm smile as if to say, "Don't worry, Maestro, we are still good friends"; and then His Eminence walked on through the Bernini Columns, towards the Via della Conciliazione, still shaking his head.

In the week of the concert in the Postepowa Synagogue, the
Kraków Philharmonic and I went to the Templ to begin our
rehearsals. The Kraków musicians had been in and out of churches
their entire lives, playing in the city's great Catholic spaces, Saints Peter
and Paul, the Basilica of Saint Mary, and so many others. But before
that first rehearsal, they stood outside the synagogue not knowing
quite what they would find inside. This was 1990, long after the Shoah.
These musicians, most of them, had never set foot inside a synagogue,
as far as I could tell. Czeslaw Pilawski, the orchestra personnel manager
and by now my friend, gathered them together on the street, and
calmed their nerves.

When they finally went in and saw the beautiful interior of the
Templ, they soon relaxed and began to play as if they immediately
felt at ease making music in that sacred place. Our Beethoven, our
Dvořák, felt as at home in the Postepowa Synagogue as they had in
any of the churches in which we had made music so often. The Kraków
Philharmonic went to work to make our Templ performance the very
best it could be.

The night of the concert turned out to be a night of surprises.
The first was that the synagogue and the entire area around it were
cordoned off and guarded by large military vehicles. It's true that
important diplomatic personages were attending: Israel's Ambassador
to Poland, Mordechai Palzur, signaling a newly warming bilateral
relationship; Thomas W. Simons, the United States Ambassador to

Poland; and Jan Majewski, the Polish Deputy Foreign Minister. But I am not sure that the security protocols required this kind of cordon sanitaire around the concert. To this day I don't know what kind of security threat was perceived, but it gave the event an otherworldly look.

The entire exterior of the synagogue was floodlit, and there were backlit armored personnel carriers and soldiers, not in riot gear but in combat gear with semiautomatic weapons at the ready, guarding every entrance to the sanctuary and all the streets immediately surrounding it. Certainly, I felt much more nervous on this occasion than I had felt that morning at the dress rehearsal. It was as if something very strange and very dangerous was taking place on the Ulica Miadowa that night.

Our concert program began with the playing of the three national anthems, those of Poland, the United States, and Israel. Everyone stood for all three. The playing of the first two was stirringly patriotic. Pride could be felt throughout the hall. The reaction to Hatikvah was heartrending. Here in this congregation-less Polish synagogue, desecrated in the Shoah, the song of a resurrected Israel rang out mournfully, strong and deep. I did all I could to keep from tearing up right there on the podium.

The symphonic music-making that evening was natural and unconstrained. Bruch's Kol Nidre and the Dvořák Cello Concerto, both with the wonderful young cellist Matt Haimovitz as soloist, and the Eroica Symphony of Beethoven were perfect for this concert. They were, after all, Central European music being performed in a nineteenth-century Central European Reform synagogue and thus were all of a piece with the culture of those who had once worshiped there: committed Poles of Jewish faith. This was their music, every bit as much as it was the Central European music of the Polish Catholic community. Our music was at home in this place.

One part of the evening's program was a rededication of the synagogue. It wasn't for us to sanctify it as a place of worship, but it needed to be rededicated as a place of Jewish memory nonetheless. The Nazis, who used this synagogue as a stable for their horses, had pushed aside the pews and the bimah, where the rabbi reads the Torah. How ironic it was, I thought, that the machine of Nazism that had murdered and destroyed Jews and Jewish property in Poland had chosen to leave Kazimierz intact as a kind of memorial, a ghostly museum to nine hundred years of Jewish culture in Kraków.

As I had previously noticed, the Nazis had ripped down the Star of David from the synagogue's steeple. The United Jewish Appeal had a gold Star of David specially created for the Postepowa and had it brought to Kraków to be reinstalled by Rabbi Ronald Sobel of Temple Emanuel in New York during the concert. At intermission the audience gathered outside in the dark night and listened silently as the Rabbi said the prayers of reinstallation. The floodlights that had so startled me as I arrived, illuminating the armored personnel carriers as they ringed the synagogue, now served as the stark lighting for this ceremony. Having a military presence there lent our ceremony a very odd aspect as prayers were recited for the reconsecration of the star on this Jewish house of worship.

After we all reentered the sanctuary, Czeslaw Jakubowicz, wearing a brown Polish *czapka* instead of a yarmulke, rose and spoke to the audience. As he looked around at the huge crowd that filled the Postepowa to the bursting point, he gave me a look as if to say, I guess you pulled it off. His talk was simple and direct, welcoming one and all to this synagogue, a vital part of his fragile domain.

Then Father Fidelus, Cardinal Macharski's secretary, read a letter from the Archbishop, which expressed His Eminence's regret at not attending our concert. It was a letter which quoted extensively from words of Pope John Paul, honoring the spirit of reconciliation between Jews and Catholics, the very goal we had striven mightily for on that night.

Finally, unexpectedly, a member of the audience rose and asked permission to speak. It was Father Stanislaw Musial, a deputy editor of the *Catholic Weekly*, where the Pope himself had maintained very strong ties. Dressed in simple Jesuit garb, Father Musial was not a high official of the Church but a quiet man of powerful intellect, well known in Kraków circles, Catholic and Jewish alike. His request came out of the blue, but I had come to know Father Musial well during my time in Kraków. He had become a friend. I was only too happy for him to say his peace. And peace is indeed what he intoned.

"Forty-five years ago a tragedy occurred on Polish soil like the world had never seen. Our Jewish brothers and sisters, who had lived among us for hundreds of years, were torn from us before our eyes. The Lord knows what dangers we Poles faced if we lifted a hand to help. But some of us did. They are Christian heroes, what are called in Israel the 'Righteous Among the Nations.' Many sadly did not. They feared for their lives and the lives of their families in our Polish homeland, which was under terrible siege. For the heroes, they sought no reward. They received none on this earth. Their reward is in God. For the others, who could have done much more—in this I include myself and my family—we ask your forgiveness, although we know you do not ask it of us.

"If I may, I will finish with this very short prayer. It is one that is said by Christians and by Jews alike:

"May the Lord Bless you and keep you. May he cause his countenance to shine upon you. And may he give you Peace. Shalom. Amen."

Then there was silence. Tears ran down many faces. Those of Jews and Catholics alike. It was a powerful statement, and one which clearly came from the heart. Father Musial had expressed our atonement or, as I have always believed it, our "at-one-ment" with the spirit of the physically absent Pope John Paul. However, the heart and soul of His Holiness was clearly present with all of us in the Templ Synagogue that night.

The performance of the Eroica Symphony, which we played after those deeply felt words of Father Musial, was one of the most powerfully motivated I've ever done. The Marcia Funebre, or Funeral March, the symphony's heroic slow movement, seemed to memorialize all the victims of World War II, and the millions who lost their lives on Polish soil. The finale, with its stirring and uplifting close, expressed our musical wish for a new beginning in the tortured relations between our two faith communities.

Some weeks later, I went to Rome and saw Monsignor Dziwisz. He had a smile on his face and said, "It was really wonderful, wasn't it?" And I didn't even have to ask what he was referring to. I also didn't need to know what had happened to Cardinal Lustiger. For me, understanding the relationship between Kraków's *Tygodnik Powszechny* (*Catholic Weekly*) and the Pope, and knowing of the warm friendship between its deputy editor and His Holiness, I was sure that although the Pope had not penned the words of Father Musial, he had most certainly inspired them. The fruit of that most special meeting that I had had in the Vatican with Cardinal Lustiger and the Pontiff was revealed in those extraordinary words, which had given such meaning to our concert in the Templ Synagogue.

CHAPTER

THIRTEEN

If you had asked me in 1987, before I embarked on my journey into Poland, whether a concert in a synagogue would have been a great event in my tenure as Music Director in Kraków, I would have told you that was extremely unlikely. Prior to going to Kraków, I had never conducted a concert in *any* house of worship, synagogue or church. That was not where music was made. Not by me, at least, up until that time.

The weeks and months before and after the synagogue event were busy ones in my ongoing professional life, both with the Kraków Philharmonic and as guest conductor with other orchestras in the United States and Europe. A special musical treat that spring had been my concerts in Stockholm and the United States with Esa-Pekka Salonen's New Stockholm Chamber Orchestra. I had had the privilege that June of leading them in their North American debut at Lincoln Center as part of the First New York Festival of the Arts. The program was Stravinsky, Bartók, and a deeply affecting performance of Britten's "Les Illuminations" with the distinguished Metropolitan opera star, Elisabeth Soderstrom.

And by October 1990, the Kraków Philharmonic and I had performed a great many subscription concerts in our Philharmonic Hall consisting of orchestral repertoire that spanned the entire range of Western classical music: from the eighteenth century to the twentieth, from Mozart to Messiaen, and everything in between. Great soloist friends of mine, with whom I had made music in the West, visited to share their wonderful music-making with us, and showed Poland their great generosity in the bargain.

Garrick Ohlsson, an early winner of Poland's prestigious Chopin Piano Competition, came to Kraków and performed and recorded Shostakovich, bringing his eighteen-foot Bösendorfer Imperial grand piano with him from Vienna. In a remarkable collegial gesture, Garrick not only recorded the Shostakovich Concerto for Piano and Trumpet, with the amazing London Symphony principal Maurice Murphy as his partner, but took his place in the orchestra itself performing the piano part in the Soviet-era Russian composer's First Symphony as well. Garrick even arranged for that luxury boat of a piano to be left behind on our stage to be used by other visiting artists for a year, as a gift to the Kraków Philharmonic.

The inimitable Emanuel Ax came back to his native Poland (he was born in Lodz) to share his elegant, powerful interpretation of the Brahms Second Piano Concerto with us, for a small fraction of his Western fee. Manny's courtly disposition and perfect Polish brought a sunny warmth to the cold Kraków climes and to his fellow Polish musicians as well. For me, he brought the gift of American camaraderie, at least for one wonderful week.

Shlomo Mintz, the talented Israeli violinist, joined us for our concert in the Warsaw Autumn Festival. He played a wonderful performance of the Prokofiev Concerto No. Two, and actually donated his entire fee to our orchestra.

Yo-Yo Ma also came to Kraków to share his immense talent. His experience was, by contrast, not so very pleasant. Yo-Yo gave a solo recital in our hall. I was so pleased that he had made time in his extremely busy schedule, and I had expected the Polish musical establishment to have rolled out the red carpet for our distinguished international guest. His concert was sold out, and Yo-Yo played wonderfully, as always. Afterwards, I went backstage to say hi. Yo-Yo and I had known each other since the early days, when we were both just starting out on our musical careers. I wanted to welcome my now very famous friend to Kraków and to see whether there was anything I could do to help him in my new "home" city. He said yes, he needed a room for the night, and an early morning car to get to Warsaw to catch a flight.

Curiously, these had not yet been arranged.

No problem, I said, there was undoubtedly room at the Forum Hotel, which by now was my place in Kraków. A voice over our shoulders broke into our conversation. "No, Mr. Ma will be going to Warsaw this evening. We'll take care of him," said the representative from Pagart, the Polish Communist government artists' agency. I said, "OK, I understand," and bid Yo-Yo good-bye. I told him I would probably see him at the airport the next day, as I was flying out of Warsaw myself.

When I did reach the Warsaw airport, at about 9 A.M., and had checked in for my flight, whom did I see crumpled up on a bench in the departure lounge? Yo-Yo. He looked exactly the way one looks after a night of no sleep. "What's up? What happened to you?" I asked. "They dropped me here at the airport early this morning. We drove very late. Everything seemed to get mixed up," Yo-Yo replied. "They said something about there being no good hotels." I apologized profusely, although it had been no fault of mine. But I don't think Yo-Yo came back to Poland until the Communists were mercifully out of power.

That same year, the Kraków Philharmonic Orchestra and I had also toured together to Germany, the United Kingdom, and the Far East. We had even made that harried first-ever visit by any ensemble from the People's Republic of Poland to the Republic of Korea, including a broadcast concert for KBS (Korean Broadcasting Service) from their home studios and a concert in Seoul's Catholic Cathedral. The secret police had failed to stop our groundbreaking musical diplomacy. The Polish Pope's presence was never far away from his hometown orchestra, even halfway around the world.

Tours, with concerts day after day in city after city, are great ways for orchestras and their conductors to form strong musical and personal bonds. Even performances of the same repertoire, played night after night, as happens on tours, can change with each new city.

Acoustics change from hall to hall, of course, but more, everyone learns and grows with each assay of a challenging score. Details are highlighted that then reveal a larger structural arc, which lets the story of a musical work shine through. From these repeated performances comes an organic unity between the conductor and his or her musicians, a more complete trust that makes the musical experience come alive, freshly minted every day, for performer and listener alike.

We had also performed numerous broadcast concerts for both radio and television, playing all manner of repertoire, and in the process spreading our collaborative music-making far and wide. One of the most memorable such television appearances happened when CBS "Sunday Morning" decided to send their culture correspondent, Eugenia Zuckerman, to report on me and my work with the Kraków Philharmonic. For their "Time in Poland" profile, as they called it, I suggested to Genie, whom I had known in musical circles in New York, that she bring her flute and take the occasion of her television story to join us in making some music. We quickly settled on "Halil" of Leonard Bernstein, a work which eulogizes a member of the Israel Philharmonic who fell in the 1973 Yom Kippur War. The piece had never before been performed in Poland. It made a remarkable statement about the musical and spiritual connection I had formed with my Kraków players, and their understanding of the world from my perspective as well as theirs. In short, we had done everything one could wish for in a high-level professional musical relationship.

But even as satisfying as all these wonderful professional concerts had been, still there is something very special that stands out about that night in the Templ Synagogue. Our Eroica, which we had performed many times before, was more powerful, our Dvořák, more heartfelt. We were made larger than our musical selves because our music-making was used in the service of a higher purpose. We were finding that ineffable intersection between music and spirit that is at the heart of a truly transcendent artistic experience. And we, those of us who made the music and those who witnessed it, had as our guide an unseen but ever so strongly felt presence: the Polish Pope in Rome.

The meaning of the relationship of Pope John Paul to "his artist," as His Holiness and Monsignor Dziwisz were fond of calling me, was becoming ever more clear. And for the first time, after that Templ concert, I began to think that maybe all this was truly fated, *beshaert*, as my grandmother would have said in Yiddish. That I had come to Kraków and met the Pope to fulfill some larger purpose.

I had endured long absences from my family, lived in a country haunted by the ghosts of the Shoah, and felt the repression of the Communist secret police for a reason. A reason beyond the artistic fulfillment I now felt in the music-making with my new orchestra. And that reason, that higher purpose, was somehow shared by His Holiness. To bring peace through music to all for whom this noble vision would resonate. To accomplish the very thing that I had so boldly told the Pontiff at my first audience:

"I believe, Your Holiness, that it is you who can achieve the coming together of our two peoples after so many centuries of misunderstanding and of hate. I believe you were sent by God to do just that."

After the concert in the Templ Synagogue a light went on in my head. Maybe I too had a role to play in this. Maybe I could help in bringing about this long overdue reconciliation between my people and his.

My path had indeed, improbably, led from Kraków to Rome and the Pope, and back to Kraków again. And then I had found this deserted synagogue. Everything that had happened up until then was part of my search for something higher, and deeper, than even the pure, profound love of music could have revealed. In fact, I had found a meaning in music which I had known was there since my childhood. Not a meaning that came from hours and hours of practice drilling my fingers, my ears, and my hands, but rather one that comes from the power of music to express the content of the human soul. Music, I now knew, could heal, foster remembrance, and ultimately bring reconciliation, all through its wordless power to reach the soul directly. I had learned this through my work in Kraków, and my coming to know Pope John Paul.

The special nature of our synagogue concert, and the questions that would not go away afterwards, also had a great deal to do with my mother-in-law. I heard Margit's plaintive words on my departure for Kraków: "Do not forget us. Do not forget the six million: my mother, murdered by the Gestapo, my father, killed on his way to work by the Luftwaffe strafing the town we fled to ahead of the Nazis, my brother Poldi, the smarter of the two of us, who would surely have gone on to do great things, murdered on arrival at Birkenau because there was no more room in the barracks. Birkenau, where I myself would cling to life for eighteen more torturous months. For each of these in my family," she had said to me, "there are uncountable families, each with a similar story. Do not forget any of them, or their relatives, their friends, their entire communities, all murdered on the false altar of man's inhumanity to man." After the Templ concert, her image stayed with me, haunted me.

And when I came back to New York, there she was, sitting directly across the table at our Passover Seder. Without saying any words, she spoke powerfully to me, lighting a fire of imagination and audacity.

I have to say that no two Holocaust survivors are alike. Each has suffered his or her distinct torment. All, individually, must have the freedom to express themselves in relation to their world in their own way. In this, I remembered Elie Wiesel's wise counsel: "Each of us has the same right to our unique memory of the Shoah." This showed itself once again in the tortured life of my father-in-law, Laci. He could take no interest in any of this. He had survived in Bratislava, much as Anne Frank had, hidden in an attic with strangers, opposite Gestapo headquarters. For Laci, there could be no pope who could have any understanding whatsoever of what he and his family had gone through in the war. He wanted nothing to do with Catholics, or even with very many Jews, for that matter. He even mocked Margit for her foolish interest in the promises of hope coming from the Pope, or his son-in-law's journey back to a Central European world he was only too happy to have left behind. He thought my going to Kraków was folly, pure and simple. His soul was closed to outside light.

But my mother-in-law's faith in the fact that there was something special in Kraków was abiding. My soul-opening experience in Kraków, the Pope's deepening interest in me, and my growing belief in the spiritual power of music were about to come together.

Some time after the concert in the Templ, in the winter of 1991, I had an idea that crystallized all these elements. I knew there had been concerts to commemorate the Shoah all over the world. Maybe, I thought, my growing relationship with the Pope could allow me to organize such a concert in Rome that His Holiness himself might attend. This would be unprecedented. And how wonderful that would be! I had organized the concert in the synagogue in Kraków, so it seemed at least plausible that I could do something similar in Rome.

As close as I had become to the Pope, it seemed far-fetched that I could be the source of an idea for such a concert. There were so many reasons why it would not work. The Vatican bureaucracy would stop it. The Jewish community would object. Still, His Holiness had been very supportive and directly involved in the birth of the concert in the synagogue. His encouragement had seen me through many difficulties along the way to that success. But that was in Kraków. This new idea for a Shoah Concert in Rome seemed a step too far.

I asked my mother-in-law what she thought. "This would be wonderful," Margit said, "if, that is, you could actually do it."

I spoke to several other friends who had lived through the Shoah. They were disbelieving but said, like Margit, that if it happened, it would be incredible. They simply did not think that this pope, any pope, would actually show such sympathy and understanding about the Jews' most profound pain. And no matter what, I did not want to offend anyone, least of all the survivors of the Shoah, for whom this concert would be intended.

Thus encouraged, I decided to test my idea on my priestly friend in Paris, His Eminence Cardinal Lustiger. Since I first met him in the spring of 1989, our relationship had only grown closer. We had achieved the concert in Notre Dame together, which was, he told me, a great event for him and for his Cathedral. Our chance meeting with His Holiness in Rome had not diminished our friendship at all, as his look back at me had promised. In fact, it had even made us closer. And in the intervening year and a half, whenever I went to Paris, he would invite me to lunch or dinner, alone in his private dining room on the lower floor of his elegant home. Over shared stories of Poland and Rome accompanied by glasses from the rare vintages in his cellar, we had become closer still. We were two people from a uniquely shared background, both of us having been brought up as Jews and both having a close relationship with the Church (his, infinitely closer than mine).

I went to Paris to tell His Eminence about the Shoah concert idea that had been rattling around in my head for some time. Meeting upstairs this time in his light-filled drawing room, I began to unfold the idea as best I could. He listened carefully and was kind enough and solicitous enough to say that he thought it interesting. He said that he would be going to Castel Gandolfo that summer and would be meeting the Pope. He would certainly raise the idea with His Holiness, he said.

Perhaps Cardinal Lustiger knew already that he would not do so. In any case, when I asked him about it in September 1991, after he had visited His Holiness at Castel Gandolfo, His Eminence said, "Oh, Maestro, I did not have a chance. I am so sorry. It just didn't come up." He had his reasons, I was sure. And these reasons became clear years later, when he told me that he had thought I was "crazy" to have proposed such a thing to him at all. That, in his view, the idea was simply impossible to realize in the then prevailing, often hostile atmosphere between Catholics and Jews. He told me that he had simply not wished to tell me this at the time, for fear of offending a good friend.

In any event, I was now on my own. I suppose I could have dropped the whole idea. Cardinal Lustiger knew vastly more than I did about the Vatican and what was and was not possible in the sphere of Catholic-Jewish relations. But the idea would not leave my imagination. I had come to believe it was indeed *beshaert*—fated. Or perhaps I was simply too foolish to know when to quit.

I could imagine at least two very bad outcomes. I would organize the concert, and in the end the Pope would not attend. This would be perceived as a major snub to Jews and would set back Catholic-Jewish relations even further than where they already stood. Or His Holiness would think me as crazy as did Cardinal Lustiger and want nothing more to do with me. That crossed my mind as well.

But then everything about my relationship with Pope John Paul was beyond improbable. If it had ended the day of our first audience, it would have been enough. If I had conducted the concert for his tenth anniversary, well, what a grand opportunity! That too would have been more than I could ever had expected in two lifetimes. If he had helped me bring alive the "Concert of Remembrance and Reconciliation" in the synagogue in Kraków, he would have added immeasurably to my life. So, I thought, what did I have to lose? Shoah concert or no, I might never see or speak with His Holiness again. Those thoughts went through my mind every day.

In the end, I decided to go to Rome and see where this bold idea would lead. I had to take the risk. It was an opportunity I simply had to explore.

Once again, I made an appointment to go to the Vatican to meet with Monsignor Dziwisz. I walked into his now-familiar small office in the Apostolic Palace and said, "I have an idea. I would like to organize, here in Rome, a concert to commemorate the Shoah [I was very careful to use the Hebrew word], and I would like very much for His Holiness to attend."

Monsignor Dziwisz looked at me for some time, staring right into my eyes. He sat there, carefully considering what I had just said. The silence grew longer and longer. Finally, he said, "Excuse me, Maestro. I will return in a moment."

The moment stretched to five minutes. Then more. I grew nervous, then apprehensive. Finally, Monsignor Dziwisz returned and sat down with a smile on his face:

"We think it is a wonderful idea. Maestro, *Va avanti*—Please go ahead."

His Holiness' study is very close to where Monsignor Dziwisz and I were meeting. I was now sure that the good Monsignor had taken my idea right to the Pope. That he had felt that the Pontiff had to hear it immediately. What was incredible was the rapidity with which my idea had clearly found root in the Pope's imagination.

His Holiness' reaction had been instantaneously positive; I was as elated as I was amazed by this rapid assent. There was no equivocation. There was no "Yes, well, interesting. Let us think about it." The Pope had said yes to the Shoah concert immediately, and now we were on our way.

But now what was I to do? A synagogue concert in Kraków is one thing. A major event in Rome is absolutely another. I had no experience whatsoever in organizing a major international concert such as this.

I began to think about the details: the venue, the orchestra, the repertoire, who should be invited. A month later, I went back to Monsignor Dziwisz and said I'd been thinking about this, but there were many, many unanswered questions about which I needed his advice.

Instead, when I sat down with Monsignor Dziwisz in his office, it was his agenda we would be following. It seems there had been further discussion between himself and His Holiness. Now the questions would come from him to me.

"Where in Rome do you think to have this concert to commemorate the Shoah?" Monsignor asked.

"It should be in a place with a very special meaning. I had thought about the Ardeatine Caves, the place outside Rome where Italian Jews were held before they were deported to Auschwitz."

"Isn't that a bit too cold up there?" Monsignor Dziwisz replied. "It is not really suitable, is it?"

"Yes, yes, of course. Then what about the Auditorio della Conciliazione? Isn't that concert hall the property of the Holy See? Wouldn't that be appropriate?" I next proposed.

"Yes, you are right. But it is too small, Maestro," he said. "Don't you think it would be too small?"

The concert hall on the Conciliazione seemed large enough to me, but by now I was beginning to think Monsignor Dziwisz and, most importantly, the Pope, had some very particular place in mind.

"Monsignor, might I ask, do you perhaps have an idea?"

"Yes," Dziwisz answered, smiling. "Maestro, we do. And you have already conducted there. Don't you like our Auditorio Paulo VI? Wouldn't that be a grand place to have this very special concert?"

Suddenly, everything was clear. His Holiness wished to make this a Papal Concert. It would become a Vatican event. And by according it his Papal presence, it would immediately be imbued with worldwide significance, beyond anything I could ever have imagined or dreamt to achieve on my own.

"Yes, Monsignor, of course," I answered, deeply moved and a little stunned. "That would be extraordinary. I didn't dare suggest it."

Dziwisz's smile broadened. I beamed back. The "Papal Concert to Commemorate the Shoah" had just been conceived.

The implications were enormous. The Pope wished this to be an event to which the Vatican, and he as the Roman Pontiff, would be inviting Jews, especially Holocaust survivors, from around the world to come together with him and the Catholic Church in commemoration of the greatest tragedy in the history of the Jewish people. It was breathtaking, audacious, and only he, the Pope, could have imagined it was possible. I was in awe of his courage.

Monsignor Dziwisz had one more important question. And with this his face became very serious. "If we do this, Maestro, if we have this 'Concert to Commemorate the Shoah' here in the Vatican, will the survivors come? If we hold out our hands in welcome, will the Jews come to join us?" Dziwisz said, extending his hand outward towards me. "Will our hand be met by their hands coming back to meet ours? His Holiness wishes to know. Please understand, Maestro, we will do this in any case—the Holy Father believes it is very important—but you are our artist. I ask you please to go and find out the answer to this question."

I wanted to burst out and say, "Me, Monsignor, you're asking me? How can I know? I am just an artist!" But of course I said nothing of the kind. Rather, I answered, "Yes, Monsignor, of course, I will find out all that I can. And I will let you know as soon as I have some answers." And with that, the incredible meeting was over.

But my challenges had only just begun. How would I, a conductor, not a rabbi, not the head of any Jewish organization, not the spokesperson for the survivors of the Shoah, if there was any such person—how would I be able to answer the Pope's momentous question? But before I could find out about my Jewish brothers and sisters, there was the matter of just what to do next to set this concert in motion at the Vatican.

I returned to Monsignor Dziwisz on my next trip to Rome. I didn't yet know the answer to the Pope's query about whether Holocaust survivors would attend a concert to commemorate the Shoah. That would take many months to find out. What I did need to know was whom I should speak with at the Holy See to properly proceed with our plan. The Vatican is a complex institution, with an intricate bureaucracy. I needed an address, an office, that could move things along.

Monsignor Dziwisz gave me the name of a Monsignor Pier Francesco Fumagalli, the Secretary of the Pontifical Commission for the Relations with the Jews. Monsignor Dziwisz wrote down his name and number on a simple but elegant piece of Vatican notepaper and asked that I keep him informed of my progress.

The next afternoon at 5:00 I walked a short distance from Saint Peter's Square down the Conciliazione to the Via del Erba, there to find the office of the Pontifical Council for the Promotion of Christian Unity, under which the Commission for the Relations with the Jews is organized. I knocked, and was shown by a well-dressed attendant into a small conference room on the third floor. The room was fitted with four chairs placed around a Persian carpet. There was a telephone, with a glossy, paper-bound Vatican directory next to it, sitting on a small stand on the sidewall. The drapes were drawn across a wall of windows, keeping out the late afternoon Roman sun, so that the light was diffused, softening the sharp angles in this small, square, austere-feeling room. I was lulled into a sense of quiet calm, patiently awaiting what might come next.

Finally, Monsignor Fumagalli came in through a door on my left. He was thin, small of stature, and earnest-looking. He looked at me, and immediately put his hands together in front of him as if in prayer. Then, touching his right fingertips to the tips of his fingers on his left hand, he said, in Italian:

"Maestro, the Vatican is like this, like a pyramid. You, Maestro, you come from here. From the top. So, tell me, what is it that I can do for you?"

For a moment, I thought I should begin to tell Monsignor Fumagalli all about my conversations with Monsignor Dziwisz about our Shoah concert plan, which had just been born. About the Pope's intense interest. But some instinct made me stop. Something about this did not seem right. No, as solicitous as Monsignor Fumagalli was being, something told me that this wouldn't be the right way to make our dream come true. So, using words the provenance of which I still do not understand to this day, I declared, "Monsignore, please kindly convey to His Eminence that I wish to speak with him."

The Vatican is exquisitely hierarchical. Monsignor Dziwisz had arranged for me to speak with Monsignor Fumagalli. That was appropriate, without a doubt. But here I was jumping over four layers of rank, asking to see the President of the Pontifical Council, His Eminence Edward Idris Cardinal Cassidy. Chutzpah does not even begin to cover my temerity.

I waited, looking at Monsignor Fumagalli, who kept looking back at me. Finally, he replied, "*Vediamo*—We'll see. Maestro, you will please wait here." Then he left by the same door he had entered, looking more than a little dismayed by what had just occurred. I thought, what a mistake. I was sure I had just doomed our concert. Monsignor Dziwisz would hear of this foolishness, immediately, no doubt, and feel he could trust me no more. And that would be it. What had possessed me to do this?

I waited, something one gets used to in the Vatican. Five minutes. Perhaps more. I even looked for something to read to ease my anxiety, to take my mind off my obvious affront. There was nothing but the phonebook. I was getting more and more nervous. I agonized again and again over my audacity, every second that I was left alone. Indeed. What had possessed me to do this?!

Finally, His Eminence Cardinal Cassidy entered the room and sat down in the chair opposite my own. Cardinal Cassidy is an Australian, who was then in his late sixties. He had come to the Council for Christian Unity from a career in the Vatican Secretariat of State, which is the very nerve center of the Holy See's governing bureaucracy. He was then elevated by Pope John Paul to the rank of Cardinal and given the prominent position he now occupied as President of the Vatican office charged with fostering better relations with all the other Christian Churches and with the Jews. He was one of the Pope's senior advisors, one of the twenty heads of the Vatican's main offices, called Decasteries. He was as experienced in Vatican protocol as I most decidedly was not.

His Eminence came right to the point. "Maestro, good afternoon. What may I do for you? To what do we owe this visit?" The Cardinal had a most serious, if not annoyed, look on his face.

"Please, let me introduce myself," I said. "I am the Music Director of the Kraków Philharmonic, and I—" His Eminence stopped me short.

"I know, Maestro, I was at your concert in December 1988. The one to celebrate His Holiness' tenth anniversary. In fact, may I say, I enjoyed it very much. I am a concertgoer, you see. A regular subscriber at the concerts of the Santa Cecilia Orchestra right down here on the Conciliazione. I must say, I especially appreciated the Dvořák Mass you conducted. A really lovely work. But, please, what can I do for you?" he said, in his strongly Australian-accented English.

"I have had conversations with Monsignor Dziwisz. I have shared with him and he has shared with His Holiness my idea for a concert to commemorate the Shoah, to be held here in Rome. I am so pleased to tell Your Eminence that the Pope has expressed his strong support. In fact, His Holiness wishes this concert to take place here in the Vatican."

His Eminence looked puzzled.

The Vatican's relations with the Jews came under Cardinal Cassidy's jurisdiction. He had to deal with every Jewish organization, every Jewish personality in the world who wanted to get the ear of the Vatican. And now a layperson, a Jewish conductor, was coming to him with a message from the Appartamento, from the Pope's inner circle, suggesting a Shoah memorial concert? He kept gently rubbing his forehead.

The more I spoke of the concert, the more uncomfortable His Eminence seemed to become. And he had his reasons.

In late 1991, when this meeting occurred, relations between Catholics and Jews were strained. And Cardinal Cassidy was on the front lines. The controversy concerning the Carmelite nuns praying for the posthumous conversion of Jewish victims at Auschwitz had finally been resolved but only after direct Papal intervention. It had left deep wounds, as yet unhealed.

Also, there were in that year, 1991, no formal relations between Israel and the Holy See. Years of drawn-out disputes of various kinds had kept the two states apart. Full diplomatic relations would be finalized only in December 1993. This lack of formal recognition was an enduring cause of angst in the Jewish community worldwide.

And most of all, the long-delayed development of the Vatican's "We Remember" document about the Church's history in the Holocaust, so exquisitely and delicately difficult to realize, was just beginning to be drafted by Cardinal Cassidy and his Jewish brethren in dialogue. It would be seven long years in its birthing process.

Everything in the relations between these two faiths, so closely linked through the Torah—the Old Testament—seemed tortuously problematic to resolve.

Still, His Eminence remained gracious. He asked many absolutely appropriate, respectful questions. When might this take place? Where did one think to hold the concert? What music did I think to include on the program? Which orchestra might be invited to perform? Who did I imagine might attend? I had few answers, but I gladly shared what I knew. After ten minutes of, at this point, a mostly one-sided conversation, His Eminence rose and gave me his card. He asked that we keep in touch. And we bid each other good-bye or, more appropriately, *arrivederci*, until we might see each other again. The Cardinal's face still registered serious concern as he courteously saw me to the outer door of his offices.

I called Monsignor Dziwisz that night at 9:00. It was long past Vatican business hours, but he had asked me to report back, without fail, after I had seen Monsignor Fumagalli. So I did. Monsignor Dziwisz picked up the phone quickly, and asked:

"So, Maestro, how did it go today?"

"Actually, Monsignor, I had quite an interesting first conversation with His Eminence Cardinal Cassidy, and he—" I began, intending to go on in a bit more detail.

Monsignor Dziwisz laughed and stopped me short: "*Bravo*, Maestro, *bravo*. *A presto*—See you very soon. *Buona notte*."

Whew! Somehow my speaking with Cardinal Cassidy had been the right thing after all. At least Monsignor Dziwisz thought so. I had passed the test without even knowing there had been one. Now I could finally relax, if only for a moment.

I walked out of the Hotel Sant'Anna, left into the Borgo Pio, and on over to Saint Peter's Square for a late night stroll to collect my thoughts. The Vatican fountains were gurgling. The obelisk in the center of the Square stood silent and stolid as always. And the windows of the Pope's rooms, high above to the right on the facade of the Apostolic Palace, still glowed intensely against the dark Roman sky. I didn't know what would happen next. But I had lived through today, and that was good for a start.

The next morning, I reported back to Cardinal Lustiger in Paris by telephone. "His Holiness liked the idea immediately," I fairly yelled in German, now our preferred language with each other. "Eminence, the Pope wants to go ahead. He's even asked that it be brought into the Vatican, as a Papal event. It is unbelievable."

There was a momentary silence on the line. I waited nervously for His Eminence's reply. Finally, Cardinal Lustiger said, "Maestro, that is literally unbelievable. I congratulate you. Really? So fast! When are you next in Paris? We must speak about this further. You must tell me how this came about. So fast, so fast ..." His Eminence's voice trailed off. And then, "*Also, gute Nacht*, Maestro. *Bis bald*—Until we meet again." And he too rang off.

Alas, my schedule would not bring me to Paris for many months, but Cardinal Lustiger and I would have a totally unexpected chance to speak about this and many, many other things when we met in the Hyatt Hotel in Denver in August 1993.

CHAPTER

SIXTEEN

World Youth Day was created by Pope John Paul II in 1984 as a way to energize and inspire young Catholics from all over the world. It still takes place every other year in a city specially designated by the Pope. These great mass youth jamborees have occurred in places as far-flung as Paris, Manila, Rome, Buenos Aires, and Czestochowa, in John Paul's beloved Poland. They all follow a highly scripted plan: a gathering of Catholic youth from across the chosen country and around the world on a Thursday and Friday. Then a Papal Vigil Service takes place on Saturday night, where young Catholics bear witness to their faith. To be followed by a Papal Mass on Sunday that can attract upwards of two million Church faithful, adults and youth alike.

Concerts had never been part of World Youth Days, much less one conducted by a Jewish conductor. But in 1993, at World Youth Day VI in Denver, that's where I found myself, conducting the music for the Vigil Service for the Pope and representatives of the entire Church: Cardinals and Bishops, representatives of the Roman Curia and five hundred thousand enthusiastic young Catholics from around the world accompanied by their bishops, parish priests, and locally resident nuns.

It all began in 1992, after beginning the long preparations for the Papal Concert to Commemorate the Shoah. In one of my meetings with Monsignor Dziwisz, I mentioned to him that I had noticed the announcement that His Holiness would be going to Denver in

August 1993 for World Youth Day. As we discussed this, I said that I would be pleased to lend an artistic hand, if the Pope so wished. I was so full of gratitude for all the warmth and respect that the Pope had shown me and His Holiness' willingness to hear and take seriously my creative ideas that I was ready to do anything I could to help.

The ever thoughtful Monsignor Dziwisz thanked me for the offer and said, "We don't normally have classical music at these events. Not of the kind that you, Maestro, would usually be involved with. But there will, as always, be a Vigil Service on the Saturday night of World Youth Day. There is always music of some kind at the Vigil. Maestro, perhaps you could be of assistance with that. It could be very beautiful, no? I would suggest that you speak with Archbishop Keeler in Baltimore. He is now the President of the United States Bishops Conference. Please tell him I sent you. He is one of those charged with organizing this World Youth Day for us. Archbishop Keeler is a very good man. He will know whether what I have suggested would fit in with their plans."

When I was next back in the States, I went down to Baltimore to meet Archbishop William Keeler at his stately mansion on North Charles Street, just behind Latrobe's grand Basilica, America's first Cathedral. The Archbishop's house is set right in the middle of the city, open to the street. Its windows let in bright light, but its thick walls protect it against the noise of the bustling city thoroughfare on which it sits. Portraits of Archbishop Keeler's predecessors line the mansion's walls. I was shown in by His Excellency's household helper, who led me into one of the gracious sitting rooms off to the left of the entrance foyer.

Archbishop Keeler came down the steps from the second floor, having just finished celebrating Mass in the Basilica. He began our conversation cordially, but cautiously as well. If I had to guess, I think His Excellency found it curious that this American conductor was coming from Poland to talk to him about a conversation he had had with Monsignor Stanislaw Dziwisz, the Private Secretary to Pope John Paul II. By now, after my first Papal Concert of 1988 had been on PBS television a number of times, he may possibly have known something about me and my nascent relationship with Pope John Paul. If he did, he didn't let on.

Archbishop Keeler knew Monsignor Dziwisz simply as the priest-secretary who "takes such good care of the Holy Father," as His Excellency once told me. I don't think he, or many others in the Church hierarchy in America, knew what an important role Monsignor Dziwisz played in the Vatican of John Paul. That knowledge would come for Archbishop Keeler, as for so many, somewhat later.

His Excellency and I began to talk about what might conceivably be possible in the way of serious music for the Vigil Service. I asked questions about what was expected, about the purpose this music would serve. This was a service in every sense of the word, and the music needed to fit with its sacred purpose. Through our conversation, Archbishop Keeler began to imagine that classical music could help them reach the Catholic youth of America and the world. His Excellency became a strong supporter of my participation in World Youth Day at Denver. What remained was exactly how I could best be of service.

In the end, as with so much in the Church, many hands would be involved in the decision-making surrounding the realization of this idea. The Secretary of the Bishops Conference, Monsignor Dennis Schnurr (now Archbishop of Cincinnati); Archbishop of Denver, James Stafford (now a Cardinal of the Roman Curia); and Monsignor (now Archbishop of Spoleto) Renato Boccardo of the Pontifical Council for the Laity all were intensely involved in seeing that every *i* was dotted and every *t* crossed in the preparation for this Papal visit, including the music for the Vigil. For this immense occasion, it was now clear, I would not be the maestro but simply a humble part of the Papal panoply. These priests would be the masters of this ceremony, but I knew the Pope would nonetheless wish me to give World Youth Day my creative all.

The decision about the orchestra would be the first example of this evolving mixture of Church and art. At first, I thought that the Colorado Symphony, which I had conducted a number of times on their normal subscription series, would be the natural ensemble for this event in their home city. But no, I was soon told in typical elliptical Church fashion: one wished to have a youth orchestra, befitting the essential nature and purpose of World Youth Day. Fair enough. And lo and behold, there was a national youth orchestra that met every summer in Breckenridge, Colorado, high in the Rockies above Denver. The National Repertory Orchestra, I soon found out, was wonderful. A perfect fit for this occasion. The Church's choice was right.

Then came the musical questions, and there were many. What repertoire would we perform? What soloists might we engage?

The event would include Catholic prayers, a whole liturgy, to be decided on by those same Vatican and American churchmen. So there was no chance for important music-making. Or was there? I was so pleased to find John Kuzma, a wonderful Colorado orchestrator, who could turn even the simplest hymn into a rich orchestral tapestry. When he came on board, he even transformed a prayer set to the stirring melody of the "Ode to Joy" into a replica of the actual Finale of the Beethoven Ninth Symphony, from which that tune originally came. It made the members of the youth orchestra so pleased to be able to test their musical skills, while also fulfilling the requirements of the occasion.

Then I had an even bolder idea. There have to be interludes, I thought. His Holiness is going to be praying, so we have to find music to support those moments of prayerful devotion. This is World Youth Day, yes, but we are in America. American musical culture is broad and deep. The Pope and all those Catholic kids have to hear our very best composers. What if I were to find some Copland or Bernstein that fit just these important points in the Vigil? I asked myself.

When I proposed these two wonderful composers, Monsignor Boccardo, the most vocal of my liturgical advisors, said, "Well, I suppose we can think about this if you, Maestro, think they are appropriate. But remember, the music must always serve the spiritual moment. It is not there for art's sake alone." So I searched the rich range of Bernstein and Copland compositions to find the perfect musical matches for the Vigil Service.

I fought for and finally won approval to use excerpts from one of Bernstein's most interesting works, his Mass. One portion, the Sanctus, sets a text which comes directly from the Hebrew prayer Kadosh. They are identical except for the language, Latin for the Sanctus and Hebrew for the Kadosh. Even in this World Youth Day Vigil Service, then, I was able to honor the Pope's belief in the unified wellspring of the Jewish and Christian faiths. And through it all, I would succeed in making the music as artistically meaningful as I could.

After months of planning, I came to Denver in mid-August 1993. For some reason, I was put up in the same hotel as all the Bishops from the United States and throughout the world. It was a very strange feeling. World Youth Day had taken over the entire hotel. Other Catholic lay leaders may have been staying there, but they and I got lost in the sea of red and orange hats of the Bishops, Archbishops, and Cardinals filling the elevators, corridors, dining rooms, and lounges of this immense business hotel in downtown Denver. Even the ballrooms, which normally host corporate meetings (when they are not being used for weddings and Bar Mitzvahs), were taken over as vestries for the Bishops to change into their priestly garb before being loaded onto buses for the half-hour trip out to Cherry Creek State Park, or the other venues throughout the city where their youthful delegations were housed.

One of these delegations, from France, was accompanied by their spiritual leader, my old friend Jean-Marie Cardinal Lustiger. When we first eyed each other across the hotel lobby, we did a mock double take. We had communicated beforehand, so our meeting was no surprise, and not anything like the intense impromptu colloquy we had had with His Holiness in the Sala Nervi at the Vatican in October 1990.

Cardinal Lustiger told me of the strenuous schedule his young French charges were keeping him to. But staying at the same hotel made it convenient for the two of us to get together in the Archbishop's rare but treasured downtime. We took to spending at least part of our afternoons over those days taking long walks together in downtown

Denver. Beyond affording me the opportunity to tell him all about the plans for the upcoming Papal Concert to Commemorate the Shoah, it also gave him the chance to share with me something more about his complex past. We had a bit of time, there in the relaxed atmosphere of World Youth Day, away from the rigors and formality of the Archdiocese of Paris or Vatican City. And His Eminence seemed in a mood to share.

One day, while circling around one of Denver's inner-city parks, he started to tell me the story of the beginnings of his conversion to Christianity, that moment when he knew he was no longer destined to remain in the Jewish tradition.

"You know, Gilbert," he said in his heavily French-accented German, calling me by my given name for the very first time, "I was born into a very typical immigrant Jewish family. Probably like yours, I would suppose. My family was not very religious, but proud of their faith nonetheless. One day during my twelfth year, my father came home from work with a rabbi by his side. A chassidic, orthodox man, dressed in traditional long black kaftan, wearing a black silk yarmulke on his head. He had a worn brown satchel under his arm, filled with books, all in Hebrew, which he laid down, one after another on our foyer table.

"My father introduced this rabbi to me, and told me he was there, in our home, to begin preparations for my Bar Mitzvah, to take place, he reminded me, shortly after my thirteenth birthday. The rabbi would teach me the Hebrew language and some general Bible study. Most important, he would prepare me for the chanted recitation of my Haftorah, the reading from the Book of Prophets in the Sabbath service of our synagogue, an occasion which would mark my passage into Jewish manhood. You know this well, Gilbert. You were Bar Mitzvah, no?"

"Of course, Your Eminence," I replied. "All my Jewish friends were Bar Mitzvah. And for me, especially, it was a very important day. That was the day I truly began to find my Jewish identity."

"Well, so you understand my story," the Cardinal went on. "That is just how my father thought. He told me this matter-of-factly, as if there was no question about it. I would be starting my Bar Mitzvah preparations with this rabbi that very day."

"Then the rabbi began to speak. His French was heavily accented by the Yiddish of his Polish birthplace, something like my father's, but much stronger. He and my father spoke in fact in Yiddish, which I understood a bit. Like you, Gilbert, no?"

"Yes," I said, "like in our house. My parents didn't have Yiddish accents, but they were raised bilingually, Yiddish and English. And they used Yiddish when they didn't want us children to know what they were saying to each other."

"So you see, you understand the situation," the Cardinal said with an empathic smile, but all the while trying to read my face to see whether I was truly sympathetic to his tale. He went on with his story. "The rabbi said he was looking forward very much to teaching me. My father had told him what a smart boy I was. As the rabbi said, 'the best student in your class, no? Your father is so proud of you, Aaron. There is so much to learn, and so little time. We must begin right away.'

"My father, standing next to him, nodded his assent. They had it all worked out between them," the Cardinal went on. "Now, at that time, this was in Paris in early 1939, my family associated mainly with Jews, so many of my childhood friends were Jewish. I had heard from them about their Bar Mitzvah preparations. Some were going to Hebrew school, Yeshiva, and some, like me, were to be tutored at home. So I knew very well what this was about. I had even expected that something like this was sure to happen to me in the very near future. I have to say, it was not a complete surprise.

"But suddenly a feeling came over me. A very strong feeling that I could not suppress. I knew in that instant that I could not go through with this. I looked at the rabbi, at all that he represented in his strict Jewish faith, and I just knew I did not belong."

As he relayed this experience, Jean-Marie Cardinal Lustiger looked stricken, as if he were reliving the moment and all its sadness— what it felt like for Aaron Lustiger to deny his faith. Feeling the family trauma, all over again.

"So I told my father to send him away," His Eminence continued. "Right then. Immediately. I did not want to take even one lesson. This was not for me. I was sure. My father and I fought bitterly right there in our flat. He was shocked, but I was adamant. My mind was made up. My father was crushed. Finally, he had to give in, at least then. With deepest apologies, my father told the rabbi his services would not be needed that day. The rabbi too was shocked. He couldn't believe his eyes and ears. This had never happened to him in all his years. He left our home in disgust.

"I actually think my father thought this all would pass, that I would soon come to my senses, and realize the consequences of my stubbornness. In his mind, it was unthinkable that I should not be Bar Mitzvah. That I should not take my place with the generations of Lustigers who had been Bar Mitzvah when the family had lived in Poland, and before that, no doubt, for thousands of years going back to the time of the beginning of the Diaspora. But in my mind, it was just as unthinkable that I should. I had no commitment to Judaism. I didn't then know why. The call to Christ had not yet come to me. But I knew that, in any case, this would not be my way."

Jean-Marie Cardinal Lustiger was one of great men of French letters. He was even a member of the Académie Française, the most elite of French intellectual institutions. But I had no idea he knew our Jewish history so well. His intellectual interests were indeed most catholic.

"I loved my father very much," the Cardinal went on. "He was all I would have left after my mother was rounded up and sent to the transit camp at Drancy, and then to Auschwitz, to be murdered by the Nazis."

I thought I could see His Eminence's eyes tear up. The loss of his mother, now more than forty years before, still clearly hurt him deeply.

"But then and there," he went on, "I knew I was no longer really a Jew in my father's understanding of our people. The war, and with it the terrible separation from my family, would intervene. And at the end of that, much to my father's total shock, I would become a

Christian and a priest, in heart and in soul. My sister even became a nun. His loss, as he saw it, was complete.

"My dear Gilbert, I know this will be hard for you to understand. So many Jews think I have deserted the faith. But I have come to believe that I was, and am, a Jew in the same sense as the original Apostles of Jesus were Jews. A Jew who has found his savior in Jesus Christ. Maybe it was Kristallnacht, maybe the war that was already in the air, but whatever it was, that day in our home in Paris, that was a path I simply could not go down. It broke my father's heart. My God, that was difficult. But I could see no other way. I have never told anyone outside my family this story. But you, Gilbert, who have become so close to the Church, and whom I feel so close to, you, I felt I had to tell. My conversion is real, it is powerful, and it started, I think, very young, at twelve years old, at that turning point in the life of every young Jewish man. I had to take another path. And I have never been sorry about it. In fact, it has made me so deeply satisfied. Except for the pain I caused my father. For that, I am still so sorry every day."

When he finished, he looked at me to see how his narrative had affected me. He needn't have worried. I felt incredibly close to him. He had shared this story which came so much from his heart. I looked at him, and then gave the Cardinal a hug. It felt strange at first, but His Eminence needed comfort. It was the least I could do for this man who had just bared his soul to me.

After that, we kept walking around and around the same small park. We didn't speak again for a very long time. For that day, there was nothing more to say. We walked back to the hotel and went our separate ways.

I had never doubted his conversion. After all, I knew him only as a priest. But it was a very important story for me to hear. It helped me understand him so much better. Somehow, internal to that Jewish boy, Aaron Lustiger, had been a turmoil that would lead him away from Judaism. And towards his Christian faith. No one had converted him. He had found his way himself. And when he heard the calling, it was with no thought in mind other than to serve his Savior. He had

had no thought that he would ever rise in the hierarchy of the Church when he was ordained a priest after the war. He had simply wanted to dedicate his life to Christ.

As he told me on another of those walks, it was beyond his wildest imagination that he would be plucked from obscurity by Pope John Paul. That he would go from serving as the University Chaplain of the Sorbonne, to being ordained Bishop of Orleans, and then being created Cardinal-Archbishop of Paris, all in the space of six short years. I always had the impression that he had accepted these responsibilities because His Holiness had wished him to. But he had not sought a life in the hierarchy of the Church. It had come to him, and he served as best as he was able.

Our relationship began to round itself out with these exchanges. I was on one side of the divide, firmly in the Jewish tradition. His Eminence had made a different choice. We could grow closer nonetheless.

On the night before the Saturday Vigil, the National Repertory Orchestra, the chorus, and our soloists, who now included the Christian music legend Michael W. Smith and Metropolitan Opera star Harolyn Blackwell, came to do our dress rehearsal in the immense arid park that had been transformed into an outdoor cathedral for this historic purpose. The decision of the Church and the city fathers of Denver was a practical one. Cherry Creek was the only park in or near Denver that could accommodate five hundred thousand to a million people. But it was in the middle of the prairie, completely open to the elements.

When we got to the park on the Friday night before the Vigil, there were very big, obviously heavy television lights hung on stanchions very high above our specially built performance stage out in the middle of an open field. Sure enough, just in time for our one and only rehearsal at the site, the wind came up suddenly and ferociously. It howled at forty, fifty miles an hour to the point where the lights were swaying ten feet from side to side, high above the orchestra, the chorus, our soloists, and the whole crew. After a few minutes of rehearsal in these very dangerous conditions, the Fire Marshal came up to me and said, "Forget it. We gotta stop. One of these things is gonna come down on all you folks. People will get hurt. So that's it. Everybody out."

I didn't have time to say, "But this is our only rehearsal all together." And if I had, it wouldn't have mattered. As soon as the Fire Marshal gave the word, everybody started to scatter, and in five minutes torrents of rain started coming down, collecting in growing streams that coursed through the park. We were lucky to get our instruments packed up and safely stowed away before the deluge hit.

By early next morning, hundreds of thousands of people started trooping into Cherry Creek State Park, in preparation for the Pope's arrival. We had had our one chance for a rehearsal, and it had been washed out. Only providence and our wits would keep us making music together for this event, which would be broadcast for all to see, literally around the world.

The day of the Vigil came and not only were the Swiss Guards omnipresent but so was the Secret Service. Once heads of state like the Pope come onto U.S. territory, they are protected not only by their own security detail but by the United States Secret Service as well. I have never seen such elaborate security. Folks with earpieces were seemingly everywhere.

Three immense podiums had been set up for the Papal Vigil; the one in the center was for the Pope. It was where all the evening's ceremonies would take place. The podium to His Holiness' right was for all the assembled Church hierarchy, hundreds of Bishops, Archbishops, and Cardinals who had come to Denver to be with the Holy Father and his youthful flock. The platform to the Pope's left was ours: the orchestra, the choir, the soloists, and myself.

The soloists and I were given a dressing-room trailer behind the podium area. It would also serve as a quiet place where we could sit during the two hours between the time we were required by security to be on site and the actual beginning of the Vigil Service.

My family was with me. Vera had her hands full with our two boys, David, eight, who was very nervous for his dad, and Gabriel, nineteen months old and blissfully oblivious to all the ruckus going on around him.

When it was finally time for me to mount the podium to begin the musical program of the Vigil, I grabbed my scores, straightened my bow tie, and walked out the door of my trailer. I got as far as the back of the staging area, just behind the three giant podiums, when I was stopped quite forcefully by a man with a gun in his side holster. This stern-faced gentleman of the U.S. Secret Service said, "Stop right there. Where do you think you are going?" Dressed in white, and clearly on my way to join my orchestra, I replied, "Right over there. I am Gilbert Levine. I am conducting the music for the Pope's service this evening." "Not on your life, you're not," said the agent. "Where's your identification badge? You're not going anywhere without it."

I was caught in limbo between my trailer, where I had left my badge, and the podium, where my orchestra was waiting for me. Suddenly, out of the corner of my eye, I spotted Monsignor Dennis Schnurr, the Secretary of the U.S. Conference of Bishops, who was trying to sort out some last-minute details with one of the youth groups that was to greet the Pope on His Holiness' arrival that evening.

Monsignor Schnurr came over, smiled just a bit at my predicament, and assured the Secret Service agent that I was legit. The agent then said, "I'm sorry, Father, this man can't go anywhere near the Pope. Not without his badge. He has to go back to his trailer to get it. I'll watch him from here as he does."

I walked quickly back to my trailer. There was no time to lose. No sooner had I entered and found my badge than I noticed something really crucial, which I had left sitting in front of my mirror on the far side of the trailer. It was my baton. In my haste, I had left that behind along with my ID. Whether it was providence or just luck, if I had not been stopped by that beefy U.S. guard, I would have been conducting for the Pope and all the world using a pencil instead of a baton. It wouldn't have been the first time. But elegant and Pontifical it would surely not have been.

CHAPTER

SEVENTEEN

hen it finally came down to it, conducting the Vigil turned out to be great fun. There were five hundred thousand kids, with their Holy Father beaming from ear to ear from the joy of being in their midst. I'd never seen His Holiness as alive and connected as he was with those young people. Kids were coming up to him, participating with the Pope in one aspect of the Vigil or another, and being blessed by His Holiness throughout the ceremony. He interacted with all of them as if they were his own children, which in a way they were. Hearing half a million kids chanting, "John Paul Two, we love you!" was beyond stirring. Hearing the Pope chant back, "John Paul Two, he loves you!" was heartwarming for everyone, clearly for the Pope as well. His Holiness seemed to have lost years, becoming younger at heart in communion with his youthful flock. In truth, in the summer of 1993, he was still a youthful-looking, vigorous man of seventy-four years, very much an athlete in both body and spirit.

It was a tremendous thrill to be there and also very nerve-racking, because it was all so scripted. Every piece of music had to go off in the time allowed, in the order prescribed. By the time I had finished consulting with the Church liturgists both from the Vatican and from the U.S. Bishops Conference, there was a playbook of thirty-eight numbers I was supposed to follow exactly, with no deviations.

The Bernstein and Copland pieces, which had been subjects of endless discussion with the liturgists, fit in perfectly with the spirit of the Vigil Service. Other than the Sanctus, the other section of Bernstein's Mass that we chose was the Prayer for the Congregation. I know of no more beautiful, spiritually whole setting of a chorale than this simple, short prayer. The great master Bach, in the Chorales from his St. John and St. Matthew Passions himself provides the only antecedent, incredible company for the Jewish boy from Lawrence, Mass-achusetts.

Bernstein, who had died three years before, in 1990, was my idol. He was also the reason I had become a conductor. His televised Young People's Concerts were mesmerizing for my young musician's imagination. Before him, no American could really aspire to be a full-fledged maestro.

When I was twelve, my mother became alarmed that I might be taking my music a bit too seriously. For many years, since I was five, she had watched as my fascination with everything musical grew and grew. She couldn't pull me away from the piano. I would bang away at chords that had a beauty only I could seem to hear. Then came the clarinet, and finally the bassoon. I was getting very committed indeed. But my poor mother knew nothing of the musician's life. She could only guess that it was very hard and not quite appropriate for her boy. She needed advice about what to do with this crazy child of hers who would not stop practicing the piano or going on and on about being a conductor like Leonard Bernstein.

Without my knowledge, she wrote a letter to Maestro Bernstein asking what she should do with her son, the obsessed young musician. Some weeks later, she received a handwritten reply from Helen Coates, Bernstein's longtime private secretary. It said:

"Maestro Bernstein suggests that you find someone of impeccable musical credentials to hear your son play. Ask that person to give you a completely open and honest answer about your son's talent. He thinks that is the best way to find out whether your son has the talent necessary to succeed in this extraordinary profession."

My mother had heard me talking about a bassoon teacher named Stephen Maxym, the principal bassoonist in the Metropolitan Opera Orchestra. All the young bassoonists I had met had been telling me how extraordinary Maxym was, as a teacher and as an artist. They said, however, that he almost never took students as young and inexperienced as I was. He auditions so many, they told me, and takes almost nobody outside his Juilliard and Manhattan School of Music college-level classes. Right away, to my mother, that meant that he must be someone of impeccable credentials. So she called Mr. Maxym out of the blue and asked that he audition her son, and that he report back to her (and not to me!) his honest thoughts about my talent and prospects for a life in music.

I excitedly trundled off from Cedarhurst on the South Shore of Long Island, where my family now lived, into Penn Station in New York City, to change trains for Manhasset on the North Shore of Long Island, where Mr. Maxym lived. That was a journey of two and a half hours each way, what with all the waiting time between trains.

I played my heart out for this middle-aged, slightly paunchy man with a round, kindly face, thinking I was merely taking a one-off lesson, not knowing that my mother had set this up as the audition that would, in her mind, determine my future. At the end, Mr. Maxym thanked me for coming and playing for him, and bid me a polite good-bye. He smiled me to the door, but otherwise revealed nothing of his honest answer to the burning question in Sara Levine's anxious mind.

I walked home from Cedarhurst Station, my bassoon weighing heavily at my side, exhausted from my day on the rails. I was disgruntled at the lack of feedback. I thought, in all likelihood, that my lesson had not gone very well. When I arrived at our home at 37 Adele Road, my mother stood beaming in our kitchen doorway at the side of the house.

"Now I can tell you," she said. "I wrote to Leonard Bernstein, and he advised me to find someone to assess your talent, and so I set up this lesson with Stephen Maxym. Please don't be mad at me. Not now. It went really well. The moment you left his house, he called, sounding very excited. He told me, 'Your son is a great talent, Mrs. Levine. If you agree, I would really love to teach him. If he works very hard, and practices like mad, trust me, he has an extraordinary future ahead of him as a really wonderful professional artist.'"

I couldn't believe my ears. The first part made me mad, of course. Why hadn't she told me about this in the first place? But then I was so pleased. Pleased that Maxym had liked my playing and that my mother might now stop worrying, the way every Jewish mother does, about how her son was going to make a decent living in a world as foreign to her as that of classical music.

So I can really say that Bernstein and Maxym together saved my life. They made it possible for me to continue my studies, to go on breathing music like everyone else breathes air. I went on to study privately with Mr. Maxym for seven more wonderful years. What a gift. Because of that history, and so much more, it was absolutely right to put Leonard Bernstein's music in this Papal Service. It was the least I could do. And in the end, of course, his wonderful Mass fit this Vigil, oh so well.

The Copland we performed was "Fanfare for the Common Man." The Church liturgists had objected to the piece on the basis of the title. "Maestro," they said, "His Holiness is not a common man." "No, of course, it is not meant to refer to His Holiness," I told them. "Copland means all men are of one common spirit, rich or poor, and of whatever creed. I believe the Pope would share that view from the bottom of his heart." That argument won the day, and Copland's noble "Common Man" stirred all assembled, as it always does.

After the Copland came a ceremony in which a single candle in each section of that massive crowd was lit, and its flame passed from youth to youth, from priest to nun, one penitent person at a time. Pretty soon, the entire enormous field was one sea of soft illumination, lighting up the dark Colorado sky. The park had come alive with dancing, shimmering light. It took my breath away as I gazed out over its immensity.

About two-thirds of the way through the service, during one of the Pope's extended homilies, Monsignor Dziwisz, who was standing at the back of the Papal podium, looked past the Swiss Guard and the Secret Service who were between him and me, and gestured for me to come over. I couldn't imagine what he wanted. I was on the podium. There were five hundred thousand people there; although they weren't looking at me at that moment, because they were looking at the Pope, I was on display nonetheless. Finally convinced that his gesture was meant for me, I went over towards Monsignor Dziwisz, approaching the barricade set up by the Secret Service.

Monsignor Dziwisz said, conspiratorially, "Reverse Numbers 38 and 37."

I said, "But we have it all settled. How will I tell the musicians?"

"Maestro, kindly please do this," Dziwisz said, decisively.

I thought, *It is his show, so I will do as he wishes.* If I didn't obviously scratch my head on my way back to my podium, I certainly felt like I should.

Number 38 was a rousing rendition of the then famous tune "We Are the World," meant to accompany the sight of the Pope's helicopter as it rose above the park and took the Papal party back to Denver. Number 37 was a more ceremonious piece, a decorous work more fitting to be performed in the Pope's presence at the end to the evening. I thought it was strange to have the helicopter music first, but OK. I somehow got word to the orchestra, and we made the switch.

We got to No. 38, and I started conducting. The piece involved big gestures and a lot of energy, all meant to keep the orchestra and the choirs together. I was, as always, very intent. About a half-minute into this piece, I noticed that the double basses were not looking at me; they were looking past me and had stopped playing. I looked over and gave them a gesture that says, "What are you doing? Stay with me here." Then the cellos, just in front of the basses, followed suit about ten bars later. One by one, they too stopped playing. Then the violas, then the violins. Pretty soon, the concertmistress was looking to where the other members of the orchestra and the chorus were looking. Fewer and fewer musicians and members of the chorus were following me at all. When the concertmistress turned her head and looked right past me, I finally turned around. There, about four feet behind me, was the Pope.

His Holiness was arrayed in a beautiful red cape, and he had an impish grin on his face. I looked at him, and he looked back at me. I couldn't have been more shocked. The Pope came over and put his arm around me saying:

"Maestro, I am sorry. Did I disturb you? Can't you go on? The music is so beautiful!"

What I really wanted to do was give the Pope my baton. The Supreme Pontiff of the Universal Church had stolen the orchestra's entire attention. The Pope had played his joke. And it was all set up by his collaborator, Monsignor Dziwisz. My shock lasted for exactly two seconds, after which I couldn't get a huge smile off my face. We were both standing there in front of all those kids enjoying the moment, and each other.

The Pope then turned to the orchestra and told them how much he appreciated their music-making that evening. How much it meant to him that they had joined him on this very special occasion. He turned back to me and gestured with his arm, as if to say, "Now you can continue. Really, do go ahead."

Later, looking at the video, I saw that during the time when I had been oblivious to the Pope's sneaking up behind me, His Holiness had actually been imitating my energetic conducting style, with that mischievous smile spread all across his face. The Pope had enjoyed himself immensely.

And he had again taught all of us such an important lesson about friendship. His Holiness did all this in front of a half million Catholic kids and on television for hundreds of millions watching throughout the world. He did it in front of all the priests who had accompanied all their young parishioners from all those countries to Denver, to learn what it meant to be a person of tolerant, loving faith. He had done this in front of the Bishops, Archbishops, and Cardinals, whose job it is to lead by example in their home dioceses. The Pope was showing them that they too needed to reach out to members of other faith communities in their home cities, as he had reached out to me.

And he had done it in front of all the members of the Roman Curia who had accompanied him on this pilgrimage. He knew, and I knew, that he and I would be climbing an even bigger, more difficult mountain together, which would eventually require the Curia's understanding and full support. The Papal Concert to Commemorate the Shoah would soon be a reality. His affection for his Maestro was now known throughout the Church and throughout the world. The reason for my conducting at the Catholic Church's World Youth Day in Denver was now clear. The holder of the keys of Saint Peter had yet again shown himself to be a remarkable teacher.

Cardinal Lustiger told me afterwards that his mouth had been open the whole time. That he had, again, never seen anything like this in his life. For his part, Monsignor Dziwisz had a wholly satisfied look on his face, as if to say, "His Holiness wished this; I planned it out so carefully; didn't it work wonderfully?"

The Pope, Monsignor Dziwisz, and the Papal entourage walked away, back to the center podium to finish the Papal Vigil Service, and the orchestra, the chorus, and I went on with No. 37 in our approved Church liturgist's playbook. Then, in just a few moments, he was gone. Up in the helicopter, into his Papal Plane, flying back to the Vatican. His Holiness landed safely on Italian soil the next day. Me? I didn't come down from the clouds for days.

CHAPTER

EIGHTEEN

B
ut come down I did, and faster than I would have ever believed possible. The Papal Concert to Commemorate the Shoah, which had been embraced so quickly by the Pope, would be the hardest creative challenge I ever undertook. It became my full-time preoccupation from the moment I left the podium in Denver in August 1993.

Already the previous year, I had encountered obstacles to this seemingly purely virtuous initiative. The Vatican had chosen a winter 1993 date for the concert and then made a singular, initial private inquiry to Rav Elio Toaff, the Chief Rabbi of Rome. The Rabbi, who was a true friend of the Pope, was the spiritual leader of the Jewish community of Rome, which had been in continuous existence since well before the fall of the Roman Empire. The Rome Synagogue's liturgical rite is thought to be the closest form of Jewish observance to that which the apostles of Jesus himself would have known. The Great Synagogue, a nineteenth-century edifice, stands not more than a mile from the Vatican. In 1986, Rav Toaff had officially invited Pope John Paul II to make the historic first visit of any pope to any synagogue in the world. As it has been said, it took two thousand years for any Roman pontiff to make this journey of less than a mile across the Tiber. Now, eight years later, the Papal Concert to Commemorate the Shoah would be the Pope's return invitation to this great Rabbi to join him in the sacred sphere of the Vatican.

During the planning stages of the Shoah concert, I had made it a point to pay my great respects to Rav Toaff. I wanted him to come to know the person who had initiated this unprecedented Vatican event. The Chief Rabbi had to believe that the concert we were planning would be deeply respectful of the victims of the Holocaust, Italians and non-Italians alike. And he had to know that it was greatly hoped by all concerned that he would play a historic role as the Jewish personage who would represent our people alongside His Holiness before the world on this occasion.

When I entered his office, up the stairs, just behind the sanctuary of his synagogue, Rav Toaff greeted me with warmth, kindness, and just a hint of suspicion. He was then a man in his late seventies, with a scholarly mien, and a goateed, wizened face that had seen more than its share of the terrible tragedy that humankind is capable of inflicting on itself. He addressed me in Italian, asking simply, "How is it, Maestro, that you come to know the Pope? Our community is a bit anxious about this proposed Papal Concert to Commemorate the Shoah. Please do tell me about it, so I can, I hope, allay their fears."

"You know, Rabbi," I said, "the story of my knowing the Pope is a strange one. I am not surprised that you have questions. In a way, so do I. But I think the best way for me to tell you is to say I think it was somehow fated. I went to Kraków in 1987 to conduct the Philharmonic Orchestra there. I had never met a Catholic priest in my life before that time. And the next thing I know, I am sitting in the Pope's private library in the Vatican, talking about music, about Kraków, and about the Jewish people."

Rav Toaff leaned back in his chair. He looked at me for a very long time. His face softened just a bit, but the pain never left his eyes. They had seen too much of the pain of the world for that, I supposed.

"Yes, Poland ... Kraków ... Now I understand. Someone told me you conducted the concert in honor of the Pope's tenth anniversary. They said that they saw it on television.But your story, this I am hearing for the first time. So you have actually met the Pope several times? And this concert for the Shoah, I have been told it was your idea?"

"Yes," I answered. "The Pope has treated me with great respect, and has helped me so much with my work in Kraków. He even assisted with a concert I conducted in the beautiful Templ Synagogue in Kraków. And it was after that that I had this idea of performing a Shoah concert here in Rome. One to which we could invite the Pope. But it was the Pope who changed that. It was he who decided to make it a Papal event in the Vatican. I hope very much you will be able to come and that you will bring your congregation with you. Without you, the concert would not have the right meaning. As I have been told by the Vatican, without your presence we cannot go forward."

"Maestro, I will communicate with the Vatican," Rav Toaff said finally. "When the time is appropriate, they will have my answer. But now at least I understand much better what this is about. Thank you most kindly for coming to see me. Maestro, *buona giornata*."

Rav Toaff seemed to me to be a very cautious man but also a man capable of great things. His historic invitation to Pope John Paul to visit his synagogue was proof enough of that. But he was wise as well. He would need to have his community with him when he crossed the river to visit the Holy See.

This great Rabbi surprised everyone but His Holiness, therefore, when he demurred, saying he would not be able to attend the concert scheduled for January 27, 1993. He would unfortunately not be able to accept this most gracious Papal invitation, he said, because the concert had been scheduled for Saturday evening at 6:30. Even though, in January, this would be a full hour after sundown, the official conclusion of the Shabbat observance so important to the Roman Jewish community's Orthodox congregation, Rav Toaff noted that this would be too late. Although the Rabbi could imagine that a special motorcade might well be provided to him and his closest aides so that they could easily be in their places at the appointed hour, this would not be true for his congregants who lived scattered throughout all of Rome. Many of them, he asserted, would undoubtedly be stuck in the thick of Roman traffic, unable to reach the concert on time. In addition, tightened security had become an unfortunate part of the routine surrounding Papal events since the assassination attempt on John Paul in 1981. With this, there might well be a large crowd of very disappointed Jews with, God forbid, Holocaust survivors among them, left waiting outside the Vatican gates while the Holy See's commemoration of one of the greatest tragedies in human history took place inside without them.

There were those in the Vatican who saw Rav Toaff's negative reply as an opportunity to allow the project to fade away. One Vatican official said to me, "Oh, Maestro, we are so sorry that your Rabbi has decided not to come. But it was a wonderful idea, wasn't it?" But the Pope did not agree. He knew that what the Rabbi had said was true. He also had much too much respect for Rav Toaff not to be sensitive to whatever other issues might be behind this decision. In the end, His Holiness wished Rav Toaff to come, with all his congregants, in wholehearted support of the goal of reconciliation that this Vatican concert promised. The Pope would wait patiently for the Rabbi to be able to say yes.

As testament to his belief in a positive outcome, the Pope asked me immediately to find another date that would be completely free of any foreseeable complications. One which would prove to one and all that Rav Toaff was sincerely interested in grasping the hand that the Pope had offered him. The Rabbi just needed a bit of time to make sure that he was not alone.

Once again, John Paul's wisdom and his powerful understanding of the human heart proved true. I put forward a new date, April 7, 1994, a Thursday, and not coincidentally the exact date of the international Jewish commemoration of Yom Ha-Shoah—Holocaust Memorial Day. No sooner had the "official" Papal invitation gone out than Rav Toaff replied right away in the affirmative. He would come, and he would bring his congregation with him to this historic Papal Concert. Whatever persuading the great Rav Toaff needed to do inside his own community was well rewarded. His wisdom would be heeded in the end.

So now the concert date was set. The Pope and the Chief Rabbi would attend, and the Vatican could go forward with all that was needed to make this the grand occasion that every Papal event so naturally becomes.

The only thing left was, well, everything else!

Would any survivors from outside of Rome be willing to come to the Vatican on that April day? Would the major Jewish organizations worldwide give the event their blessing and would their leaders, like Rav Toaff, also grace this historic Pontifical act with their presence? In other words, would there be a positive answer among Jews worldwide to the Pope's earnest, heartfelt question: "If I do this, will there be a Jewish hand to meet ours when it is outstretched?"

Beyond all this, as an artist, I was by now just six short months before the Papal Concert to Commemorate the Shoah, going to be standing completely alone on the platform, conducting in the air in front of the thousands who would crowd the Sala Nervi and the millions more who would be watching on television around the world. I had no orchestra, no choir, no soloists. I had an empty slate that needed to be filled with musicians of the highest caliber for what would surely be the most historic day of my artistic life. My plate suddenly became very full, and the responsibility placed on my shoulders by the Pope began to register its awesome weight.

The world Jewish community's response was tepid at best. Relations between it and the Vatican in those years before formal diplomatic recognition between Israel and the Holy See were often rocky. And the Shoah was the most sensitive subject of all. Added to this was the little matter that none of these Jewish community heavyweights had any idea who I was. Who was this conductor who was now approaching them with this fantastical tale about a Papal Concert to Commemorate the Shoah? They were Rav Toaff times 50. *Skeptical* is much too mild a word for their reaction.

Up until that time, few in the Jewish community had heard my name. Mine was a professional reputation, not a religious one. Perhaps some of these heads of major organizations had seen the *New York Times* or *Newsweek* articles or the network television reports about my appointment to Kraków. There had been many of those, and not in the cultural pages alone. Perhaps they had seen the broadcasts of my first Papal Concert in honor of Pope John Paul's tenth anniversary, which had aired repeatedly in the years since the concert was first shown in 1988. Still, even if they had known who I was, a symphony conductor with a Kraków connection to the Pope, these heads of the most powerful Jewish organizations in the world had their own entrée to the Vatican. They all knew Cardinal Cassidy. They all had been working in the vineyards of relations between the Vatican and the Jews for years. It didn't compute that I would be bringing them word of such an audacious step forward in the carefully scripted high-level Vatican-Jewish dialogue, to which only they were supposed to be privy.

So the reaction of virtually all of the heads of the major Jewish organizations—the World Jewish Congress, the American Jewish Congress, the Anti-Defamation League of B'nai B'rith, and on and on— was uniformly negative. Even Miles Lerman, the head of the United States Holocaust Memorial Council, whom I had met in Poland and who I thought would be intensely interested in this endeavor—even he said, "No, Gilbert, I know you are only trying to help, but the time is not right." Miles even wrote a letter to Cardinal Cassidy to that effect, suggesting that this event be put off to some indeterminate date when the atmosphere between the Vatican and world Jewry had improved. In any case, if and when it took place, Miles thought that it should be in Washington at the Holocaust Museum, with him, of course, as the host. Cardinal Cassidy showed me this letter, gently trying to persuade me that this concert, however well-meaning, would not likely be met with a positive reception in the worldwide Jewish community.

I told the good Cardinal, with whom I was by now on fairly close terms, that it was not up to me. I was at the Vatican's disposal. As far as I knew, His Holiness continued to be strongly supportive, and I was communicating every response to Monsignor Dziwisz, who was of course only guided by the Pope's wish, whatever that might be. His Eminence seemed unconvinced.

It is my understanding, confirmed later in a conversation by Cardinal Cassidy himself, that he had approached His Holiness directly with his concerns and that the Pope remained undeterred. The

Pontiff knew in his heart that what he was doing was the right thing, and that in the end our Shoah concert would surely be a great success.

It was incredible to me that the Pope believed so strongly in my idea. He had made the event so much larger by making it his own, by supporting it so stalwartly inside and outside the Vatican. Now I knew why Denver had been so important. Through his most public show of support for me, whom he and Monsignor Dziwisz called "Our Artist," he was showing the entire hierarchy of the Church his faith in me and the mission he had sent me on. It was all part of his plan. The Pope and his Maestro could show the world by their example just how powerful human understanding could be, how it could tear down the walls of hatred and suspicion, no matter how ancient and how thick those walls might seem to be.

I too continued then my search for Jewish support. It seemed a thankless task. In the end, after all my entreaties, I found not a single official organization of Holocaust survivors that would participate in what seemed to me to be an incredible Papal gesture offered solely in their honor. None.

Sometimes, though, it only takes one man.

In Kraków, some years before, I had met a one-person dynamo, a Polish Jew then living in New York named Jack Eisner. Jack had survived the Warsaw Ghetto uprising and numerous stations in the Nazi system of murder and terror, finally being freed from the Flossenbürg concentration camp in Bavaria, in 1945. On hearing the tale of this Papal Concert, Eisner offered instantly to lead the effort of gathering survivors from around the world, one by one, if need be, to join his march to the Vatican, to add their vital witness to this groundbreaking event.

Along with Jack, only one important Jewish organization heeded my call. The American Jewish Committee, encouraged by its interreligious affairs expert Rabbi James Rudin, grasped the enormity of this historic project right away. Rabbi Rudin worked tirelessly with Cardinal Cassidy on aspects of the event that only men of the cloth could possibly accomplish. The Rabbi brought the Cardinal some peace of mind by carrying the AJC's full official blessing along with him. In the end, Rabbi Rudin was rewarded with a place of honor, sitting in the middle of the hall, not very far from the Pope. After the AJC showed its support, so did the International Jewish Committee on Interreligious Consultation, the IJCIC. They were the official liaison between the Vatican and the Jewish world. With this important body's assent, the Shoah concert could finally receive Cardinal Cassidy's official approval.

So now, safe in the knowledge that there would be survivors present and that the Pope's outstretched hand would indeed be met with a Jewish hand coming back, I set out to gather a circle of important artists for whom this event would have very special meaning.

My first thought for *the* appropriate orchestra was the Czech Philharmonic. Artistically, they are one of the world's top ensembles. For that reason alone it would have been a pleasure to make music with them. More specifically, they and their wartime Chief Conductor, the internationally renowned maestro Raphael Kubelik, had endured the Nazi occupation of Prague, all the while protecting their Jewish colleagues for as long as they possibly could. They had come out of the war with their honor intact. Maestro Kubelik had in fact been quite heroic. He had refused to conduct Wagner, as commanded by Prague's Nazi occupiers, during the entire period of the war. He finally fled the Czech capital after famously refusing to bark the required *Heil Hitler* at a Philharmonic concert attended by high Nazi officials.

Much more personally, the Czech Philharmonic was a great orchestra from my dear mother-in-law's, Margit Raab Kalina's, home country. She was my inspiration for this event. It would only be appropriate if her countrymen were to have the honor of performing on this historic occasion.

When I approached the management of the orchestra with this momentous invitation, they reacted positively, sending me a telegram to that effect. They did add that the orchestra's acceptance of this invitation would have to be approved by their new Chief Conductor, a German named Gerd Albrecht. It was in Herr Albrecht's contract, I was told, that such permission had to be given. The orchestra assured me, however, that they believed this would be only a formality. They were certain that anyone could see what a great opportunity this would be for any orchestra, even one as universally esteemed as the Czech Philharmonic.

Nothing is ever simple in the politics of the arts. No sooner was Herr Albrecht apprised of this Papal invitation than he declared that the orchestra was not free to go. They had rehearsals scheduled for an upcoming tour and would be unable to accept. Period.

I was very disappointed, as I knew many others involved would be as well. However, I was willing to move on to any one of the great orchestras I felt would jump at this chance to make musical history. But it wasn't that simple.

Many members of the Czech Philharmonic and high officials of the government of the Czech Republic did not want to let this opportunity pass them by. Players in the orchestra and government representatives pleaded with Albrecht to relent. They believed it was such a unique invitation that they in turn even raised their concerns with the President of the Czech Republic, none other than the great playwright and human rights activist Vaclav Havel. President Havel reacted with civil outrage. After initial personal entreaties to Herr Albrecht had failed, Havel went on national television to accuse the conductor of "besmirching the reputation of the Czech nation" by refusing this extraordinary Papal invitation. A German-Czech feud broke out that dug up negative feelings between the two countries, long buried in the years since World War II. The German press by and large supported Albrecht. The Czechs, by contrast, largely took President Havel's side. Herr Albrecht grew more and more incensed. He even accused the Czech secret police of bugging his phone, which was a bit out of date in 1993, three years after the "Velvet Revolution" that had rid the Czech Republic of its Communist-era secret police.

The orchestra itself was divided, some siding with Herr Albrecht, some not, and the controversy grew and grew. In the end, sadly, the Czech Philharmonic did not join us in Rome. Gerd Albrecht had won the fight. But he had lost the war. He never recovered his standing in the Czech community at large, and he resigned his post with the orchestra not long thereafter.

Upon hearing the Czech Philharmonic's final decision, I immediately approached my next choice, the Royal Philharmonic Orchestra
of London. I called their experienced Chairman Alan Hammond, and
he and his orchestra quickly accepted. In the great tradition of the
London orchestras, the RPO is player-run and self-governing. The
musicians themselves, through their player-run board, have a significant role in decisions about which major engagements to accept and
which to decline. I couldn't have been more pleased.

The program for the concert was the next item on my artistic
agenda. I have never been as daunted by the choice of musical repertoire in my entire life. How do you represent the Holocaust in music?
For that is precisely what the Pope believed music could do: reach out
wordlessly to bridge this age-old religious and historical divide. How
do you honor the martyrdom of millions of Jewish victims and yet
instill hope in the children and the children's children of those who
miraculously made it through? These were questions to which I needed
to find just the right answers. The wrong music, evoking horrible
memories of unseen horrors, would have drastic consequences in the
charged atmosphere then prevailing between Catholics and Jews.

My first thought was to perform the Adagio from the Tenth
Symphony of Gustav Mahler, a single monumental movement of a
planned gargantuan four-movement magnum opus. It is like the trunk
of a primordial tree, whose remaining musical branches and beautifully colored, carefully detailed leaves, were never to see the light of
day. This opening expanse from his Tenth was Mahler's attempt to
depict in music the human encounter with our tortured existence here
in this world, and his vision of a place of peace that might just possibly
exist beyond. It is at once apocalyptic and resigned. I was sure this was
the right work to represent the unanswerable questions that will be
posed by the Holocaust to everyone forever: How could this happen?
How could one group treat another as though they were not human?
From what place in the mortal condition does such a horror spring?

As with every aspect of this concert, I brought my ideas
back upstairs to the Apostolic Palace at the Vatican. I shared my
Mahler Tenth idea with Monsignor Dziwisz. He asked me to tell him

something of this work, which he said he did not know, so that he could better present the idea to the Pope. I told him my understanding of Mahler's vision and a bit about the biography of the composer as well; in short, everything I could think of that would help him evaluate this choice. Monsignor Dziwisz asked me to come see him again after he had had a chance to speak with His Holiness.

When I next saw him, not long thereafter, Monsignor Dziwisz asked me a simple question: "Hadn't Mahler converted to Catholicism in order to become the Director of the Vienna State Opera? Maestro, far be it for us to advise you on strictly artistic matters. I am sure this is a most appropriate work for this important concert. But those days are behind us. Such religious tests are no longer part of our lives in this era. Do you think, Maestro, that this will send the right message to the Jews who might attend, especially the survivors who will be present that evening: that they be forced to convert in order to be accepted to any position in society? Again, please understand, I do not wish to interfere, but might you not be able to suggest some other work which did not come with such a history? Just for this occasion. Maestro, your repertoire is large, I know. Might you not find a less difficult choice?"

I was stunned. As wise as I knew Monsignor Dziwisz to be, this thoughtful response must clearly have come from the Pope. His Holiness' empathy for the feelings of the survivors of the Shoah was powerful. My lack of forethought about just this essential ingredient of the musical offering for that sacred evening was personally disappointing.

And he was, of course, correct. Mahler, who had been born Jewish, and had written music intensely influenced by his Jewish upbringing, had grown more and more interested in other spiritual traditions, especially Christianity. He may well have converted to Catholicism on his own at some point in his life. But the sudden decision to do so in 1897, just to meet the qualification to ascend to the most esteemed conducting position in the musical world at the time, most likely did not represent the sincere coming to Christ that the Pope would surely have warmly welcomed. And he was so right: the survivors who would gather in the Vatican's hallowed halls that coming

April would assuredly not have seen our choice of Mahler's Tenth as the welcome for them as Jews that the Pontiff so sincerely intended.

So, Mahler was out, for that Papal Concert, at least. It would wait for its appropriate place, on another day.

A better choice immediately came to mind, and I should have thought of it immediately. Beethoven's Ninth is *the* universal statement of the brotherhood of all mankind and has been accepted as such almost from the time it was written in 1824. Its deeply moving third movement, the monumental, stirring Adagio slow movement, perfectly balances grandness and universality with an intimate human dimension—a musical combination so deeply needed to soothe the souls of all who would be present on that special night in Rome. Beethoven was the answer, of course. But why hadn't I thought of that earlier? It took a nonmusician, the Roman Catholic Pope, to teach that sensitive lesson to his Jewish Maestro.

The rest of the program came much more easily. I knew that I would want the Bruch: Kol Nidre, a wordless setting by a Catholic composer of the most important Jewish prayer from our Day of Atonement—Yom Kippur. The inclusion of this work had a special significance above and beyond the Hebraic origins of its well-known melody. Owing to its composition, Bruch's music was banned by the Nazis. He was presumed to either have been Jewish or to have harbored Jewish sympathies, both of which made him anathema to the National Socialist regime. It was therefore most important that this work be on our program. It was also of special significance that this work had formed a part of our Templ Synagogue concert in 1990, one in which the Pope had played such a vital role.

When the wonderful American cellist Lynn Harrell, whose playing I had admired for so many years, agreed to participate, I was thrilled. Not only is Lynn an extraordinary artist of impeccable musical credentials, but he is also the former student of a Holocaust survivor, Lev Aronson, with whom he had studied in Dallas. Under the guidance of Aronson, Lynn's artistic awakening had been accompanied by a powerful understanding of the connection of musical expression to this greatest of twentieth-century tragedies.

I was thrilled as well when Richard Dreyfuss agreed to recite the Kaddish as part of a performance of a portion of Leonard Bernstein's Symphony No. Three, also subtitled "Kaddish." As Dreyfuss said, he received a thick fax filled with words like Pope, Holocaust, and Kaddish. He read these words, and it dawned on him just what he was being asked to do. He said yes. He knew he could be in no other place that night but with us, and with the watching world, in Rome.

Dreyfuss was considered by some Jewish friends and acquaintances to be a bit of a strange choice. Although born Jewish in Brooklyn, Richard was totally nonobservant. He told me that he had never in fact said Kaddish in a synagogue in his life.

But Richard Dreyfuss, the world-famous, Oscar-winning actor of *Jaws* and *Close Encounters* fame, is also a strong social advocate, a great believer in the power of peace and justice to overcome the might of the sword. Richard may have been unaccustomed to the ritual of reciting this sacred prayer, written as it was in Aramaic, the spoken language of Jesus, but to me he was the perfect person to bring the voice of the "everyman," believer and nonbeliever alike, to the remembrance of the millions of victims of racial hatred. Jews of all religious practice and many of no religious practice at all were murdered by the Nazis, who did not differentiate believer from nonbeliever in their savage rampage. Richard Dreyfuss would represent all Jews, religiously observant or not.

Next, we would perform a last bit of homage to the journey the Pope had led me on, the same setting of Psalm Ninety-two by Franz Schubert that we had performed in Notre Dame Cathedral before Cardinal Lustiger. The Pope's befriending of his Jewish Maestro was in my thoughts in choosing this work for our Shoah concert as well.

I was so pleased to be able to honor Leonard Bernstein. I never forgot his unknowing contribution to the very fact that I became a musician. Without his pitch-perfect advice to my mother, through his private secretary, those many years ago, this concert, and my existence as an artist, would have been utterly different.

Not only would we perform the excerpt from his Kaddish Symphony, then, but also Bernstein's beautiful, lyrical, quintessentially

American "Chichester Psalms." These settings of the ancient Davidian texts were in fact written to be performed at the Three Choirs Festival in Chichester Cathedral in England. Bernstein set the Psalms in their original Hebrew, mixing lines of a number of different Psalm texts and in the process creating just the right amalgam of joyful, celebratory prayer and soulful pleading for universal peace. He ends his work with a setting of one of the most important supplications in all the Psalmic canon: "Behold, how good and how pleasant it is for brothers to dwell together in unity." (Psalm 133). It would be a perfect ending to our Shoah concert, expressing a sentiment that, if fulfilled, would truly answer the fervent plea of "never again."

When it came time for the official Vatican announcement of the concert to go out, I was deeply honored when Cardinal Cassidy asked me to pen the words describing our event. The trust that this implied was a deep sign of how far His Eminence and I had come from our first awkward meeting two years before in his offices on the Via del Erbe.

I chose the words with great trepidation, attempting to encompass the immense tragedy that is the Shoah, and the hope that our common endeavor might just bring to our two forever-entwined, brotherly and sisterly faith communities. The official statement of the Vatican's Commission for the Religious Relations with the Jews of February 15, 1994, read, in part:

> The Shoah is a terrible abyss which has thrown a black light on the terrifying depth of human evil. Music, of all the arts, has the capacity to enter directly into the soul, to clarify the inner reaches of the spirit. It is hoped that the music chosen for this Papal concert will bring all who hear it together in remembrance of those horrendous events which must never be forgotten so that they may never be repeated.

April 7, 1994, dawned bright and full of hope.

CHAPTER

NINETEEN

I knew from my experiences at the Vatican that a concert in the presence of the Pope is astonishingly rare. There are precious few such events in a year, and those who take part in them, whether as participants or as members of the invited audience, consider themselves extraordinarily privileged. The Vatican is not a concert hall, I was often told. So such concerts were very special indeed, none more so than the Papal Concert to Commemorate the Shoah.

We had worked on this event for nearly three years and many of the details had been set, but I felt that there was one more important element missing from our plans.

Some months before our April 7 date, I asked Cardinal Cassidy whether it might be possible for the survivors themselves to be able to greet the Pontiff on the day of the concert. I thought, if there was a chance for these special people, who had suffered so much during the war, to come into personal contact with Pope John Paul II, then the message of our music that evening would be that much more powerful for them. His Holiness' compassion, his empathy, which I knew they would feel as I had, would greatly foster the historic outreach to the Jewish people that the Vatican intended this event to represent. The Papal audience would surely open their hearts to receive the hand of reconciliation that I knew John Paul so fervently wished to proffer.

Much to my astonishment, the answer came back in the affirmative. The Pope would receive the entire survivor delegation of more than 150 in an audience in the Apostolic Palace on the morning of the

Shoah concert. For the Pope to offer his precious time to this group, both at the concert and in a private audience, was extremely rare. It showed just how committed His Holiness was to making this historic day a thoroughgoing success.

At 11:00 A.M. sharp on April 7, we all filed into the Sala Clementina, the largest of the rooms set aside in the Apostolic Palace for receiving guests (and one I had entered for the very first time some six years before). All the survivors and their children and grandchildren entered a meeting they could not have imagined in their wildest dreams when they were surviving one single day at a time at Auschwitz, Treblinka, Sobibor, or Dachau. They drank in the richness of the frescoes and the grandeur of the forty-foot-high ceiling, but they watched even more intently as the Pontiff entered and sat down in his throne before them.

Two of us were chosen to address His Holiness: Rabbi Rudin and myself. Rabbi Rudin spoke of the history of Catholic-Jewish relations under Pope John Paul that had brought us to this great occasion. Speaking in Polish, I thanked the Pope for the trust and faith he had in me to have supported this great initiative through the many obstacles that had stood in its path.

Then Pope John Paul II rose and spoke in English, the second language of so many of the survivors and their relatives present that day. This was the moment everyone had been waiting for. The Pope spoke eloquently about the need to keep the memory of the Shoah alive, not just for its own sake but to ward off the newly nascent manifestations of anti-Semitism, which he said were still alive in the world. He spoke of the "common patrimony," the unbreakable bond, between Christians and Jews. And he quoted the last verse of the very Psalm (133) we would perform in Bernstein's setting that evening: "How good and how pleasant it is when brothers live together in unity." There was silence when he finished. Everyone stood there, drinking in the Pope's perfectly chosen words, which had so clearly come from his heart. Then the applause began. Whether this was proper by protocol, no one knew or truly cared. To a person, we wanted to show our deep appreciation for this man and for all he was doing to make things better between our two peoples. After some time the applause died down, and we all thought the audience had come to an end.

But then the Pope undertook something that none of us present would ever forget. Cardinal Cassidy gestured for those in attendance to line up, one by one, or by family group, and come forward toward the Pope. His Holiness wished for every single member of that audience, every survivor along with their spouses, their children, and grandchildren, to come to him. To be greeted by him. To be comforted in some degree by his presence.

And so we did, all 150 of us, each waiting our turn to greet the Pontiff. As we did so, in whatever language we wished, His Holiness listened intently and spoke to each of us in our own native language, whether German or Polish, Italian or French. But all the time, in whatever tongue, the Pontiff spoke the language of memory and of compassion. The look on all their faces was one of disbelief that they were being accorded this opportunity and profound gratefulness for the Pope's clearly demonstrated empathy. Some were too timid and merely accepted the Papal blessing. But many told His Holiness where they were from, what camps they had been in, how many of their relatives had died. Pope John Paul stood there and greeted survivor after survivor, sometimes looking them in the eye, sometimes looking down in profound sadness, often seeming to be close to tears. They approached, said their peace in brief, and left with the feeling that the Pope had personally heard their voice, that they mattered, and that he had embraced their ancient pain but also their hope for a better future for all mankind.

At one point, the Prefect of the Pontifical Household, whose job it is to keep the Pontiff on schedule, tried to urge the Pope to move things along. These exchanges had gone on for more than half an hour. But His Holiness insisted on hearing from each survivor who wished to be heard. Last of all, the Family Levine.

When my mother-in-law, Margit, approached the Pope, he reached out to her and greeted her as if their last conversation had been a few days ago, and not almost six years before. He spoke to her softly, with special attention, as she thanked him from the bottom of her heart for having made this day possible. The Pope pointed to me and said, "Your son-in-law has made great contributions to this day. He has done so much. You should be very proud of him." Then he turned to my wife, Vera, thanked her for coming, and especially for bringing her mother and our children. He kissed first two-year-old Gabriel, dressed in a blue sweater knit for him by his Grandmother Margit especially for this occasion. Then he greeted our elder son David, who was almost too shy in the Pope's presence but who knew at the age of nine how important this day was for his family and for the memory of the murdered relatives whom he had heard about from his grandmother but whose descendants he would never know.

Finally, His Holiness warmly shook my hand, thanked me for bringing him the idea of the Shoah concert, and for helping to make this day a reality—a day His Holiness said he hoped would bring some measure of peace to those he had just met. He wished me luck for the very special performance he would attend that night. And then he was gone.

I believe that audience was as important for the Pope as it was for the survivors themselves. He had seemed eager to express his compassion and his sorrow for all that these men and women had suffered. He had seen what had happened to their fellow Jews in the terrible years of the war whose horrors he had also personally witnessed. He had lost close friends, both Polish and Jewish. He had seen unspeakable acts inflicted by man upon his fellow man, separated from this horror only by the fence of a quarry where he labored in his Nazi-occupied homeland. He seemed to carry with him always that terrible pain.

After the Pope was finally whisked away, we all walked out of the Sala Clementina with a powerful memory of a lifetime and the beginning of a newfound peace. And still, we were only halfway through this unforgettable, historic day.

Our dress rehearsal that morning went off without a hitch. The playing of the Royal Philharmonic Orchestra was everything I could have hoped for. We worked intensively, carefully, making our music come alive with well-honed professional care.

When I finally walked onto the stage at the Sala Nervi that evening, the feeling was very different from that of the Papal Concert in 1988. The atmosphere in the Aula was solemn, and not at all celebratory, as it had been the time before. In front of the concert platform was a six-candle menorah: one for each of the six million Jews murdered in the Shoah. Instead of a single Papal throne, as in 1988, this time, in the middle of the hall, there was a Persian carpet, on which there were three equal thrones: the one on the left, I was told, was for President Oscar Luigi Scalforo of Italy, the one on the right, for Rav Toaff, and the one in the middle, no higher than the other two, for His Holiness.

In rows in front, and to the Pope's left, sat the survivors from the Roman Jewish community. They had chosen to wear identifying blue-and-purple-striped bandanas around their necks, with a gold seal across the back. Just in front of them sat the international survivors delegation, with Margit sitting in the first row looking around, seemingly in awe of the whole scene arrayed before her.

A red carpet ran from the Pope's throne to the front of the stage. We had been told that after the performance His Holiness might wish to come forward to greet all of us artists, to thank us for giving our talents for this sacred occasion. And if he did, he would come towards us on this carpet.

A sense of great anticipation ran through the crowd, and through the orchestra and the chorus as well. This would be no ordinary professional engagement. Something extraordinary, something historic was about to occur, and we were going to play our artistic part.

From the back of the hall we could hear the applause start and then grow louder and louder. The hour had arrived. It was 6 P.M. and the Pope, followed by the Chief Rabbi and the President of Italy, were making their way down the aisle to their seats in the center of the Auditorio. Instead of the warm smile that I had seen so often, His Holiness looked extremely serious, as if the weight of this Shoah commemoration were already on his mind, before we had even begun.

I looked just behind the Pope for the familiar face of Monsignor Dziwisz, but he was nowhere to be seen. I had been calling "upstairs" frequently since my arrival in Rome to begin our rehearsals, only to be told, in Vaticanese, that "he did not respond." I was so disappointed that it appeared he would not be present for this event to which he had given so much.

After His Holiness and his esteemed guests had taken their places and before a note was played, a group of six survivors came forward, one by one, either alone or with a member of their family, to light one of the candles on the menorah in remembrance of their martyred relatives, and all the six million. One of these was Margit. She walked forward, her hands shaking as she brought her candle up to the level of the giant candelabra. I cannot imagine what she was thinking, but the intensity of her expression told me all I needed to know. She had lost more than forty members of her family in the Shoah. Her parents, her brother, all her aunts and uncles, and all their children, save one uncle, had been murdered by the Nazis. And now, here she was in the Vatican, saying a silent prayer in their memory. I watched and wondered where I would find the emotional strength to conduct the concert, so drained was I from the emotions of that moment and the unfolding scene.

When all six candles had been lit, I turned and looked at the Pope. I caught his eye for an instant. He looked back with a sad but grateful look rather than his usual smile of encouragement. But I felt his warmth and support nonetheless. It occurred to me that he too was experiencing the emotion of this moment in a very personal way, and feeling it very deeply. Memories of his Jewish friends lost in the war seemed to be deeply etched in his face as he waited for our musical rite of memory to begin.

I bowed to His Holiness and turned to face the Royal Philharmonic Orchestra. There, in this group of musicians, many of whom had traveled professionally around the globe, were faces with lips pursed, heads down, in silent contemplation of what they were about to do. I looked first to Hugh Bean, one of the legendary concertmasters of the British orchestral scene, who had had a long and distinguished career with another of London's great ensembles, the Philharmonia Orchestra. Hugh's musicianship, like that of the rest of this ensemble, was superb. He had been the concertmaster for the legendary German-Jewish conductor Otto Klemperer, who was himself a Holocaust survivor. Whether that was on his mind or not, his expression the entire evening was one of intense concentration. This evening's music-making would be so much richer for his invaluable artistic contribution. Now it was time to begin our part, to make the music that would be the language of historic remembrance and sacred reconciliation.

We started our concert with Bruch's Kol Nidre. Lynn Harrell, who I know had performed the piece many times before, played fervently, imbuing this special work with all the inner understanding that his teacher, Lev Aronson, had taught him about the pain of his horrific wartime experience.

The greatness of the Royal Philharmonic really showed in the performance of the Adagio from Beethoven's Ninth Symphony. This last symphonic opus of Beethoven had always held a special place in my artist's soul. I had conducted this great symphony many times. But here in these hallowed halls, with this audience of survivors and the Pope, it moved me like never before. The RPO seemed inspired as well. This had to be the Beethoven's Ninth of our lifetime. The first violins sang their main theme and its quickened variations in one rich, seamless line; the woodwinds and violas played their hearts out in the song-filled contrasting middle section; and the brass and timpani made their shattering climax as telling as I have ever heard it performed. I like to imagine Beethoven, who was always a son of the Church, smiling down on us, proud of the distinguished part his music had played in our common spiritual journey that night.

We followed our Beethoven Nine with a performance of the Schubert 92nd Psalm, which had been such a vital part of the concert in Notre Dame in 1989. Its Hebrew text seemed a seamless piece of our evening of prayer in the Vatican.

Richard Dreyfuss recited the Kaddish, as part of the Bernstein Symphony No. Three, in a more dramatic way than is typical of synagogue practice, evincing sympathy from this particular Vatican audience, which included many Jews for whom this prayer was as familiar as their own names.

When it came time for the Bernstein Chichester Psalms, we had our first surprise. Live performance is always fallible.

We are only human after all.

At the beginning of the Second Movement of the Psalms, twelve-year-old Gregory Daniel Rodriguez, the boy soprano, was supposed to begin singing (in Hebrew) the famous words of the Twenty-third Psalm, "The Lord is my shepherd, I shall not want." His voice should have been heard right after the strumming of a single chord on the harp and the lightest hint of triangle and suspended cymbals. In rehearsal, things had gone exactly the way Bernstein would have wished. We had no reason to expect anything else. Gregory was a solo singer from the Metropolitan Opera, one of the most storied opera houses in the world. He had sung many times at the Met both in live performance and in their famous Saturday afternoon international broadcasts. He was as experienced a young pro as we could find, with a bell-like voice to match.

The rehearsal, however, had been in an empty Sala Nervi. There were no distractions from the musical task at hand. The evening of the concert was a wholly different thing. Instead of the empty chair that had been set out in the middle of the Aula during the rehearsal, His Holiness Pope John Paul II, Christ's Vicar on earth, now sat, not fifty feet away on his throne. Gregory was a devout Catholic, raised in a traditional home and educated in Catholic schools by nuns and priests all his life. To him, all through his school years, the Pontiff had been a beatific picture on the wall of every classroom in his parish schools. Revered, to be sure, but distant. And now he was there, in the flesh, sitting right in front of him.

Gregory opened his mouth at the appointed moment in Bernstein's ancient-sounding music, and not a note came out. Nothing, not a syllable. He stood, staring slack-jawed at the Pope seated on his throne, unable to take his eyes off the Papal presence. A musical bar went by, then two, an eternity of time on the concert platform. There was not even an orchestral underpinning to distract from the ongoing minidrama, just that lone harp and faint percussion, sounding in imitation of their biblical ancestors. Gregory's silence was going out to millions upon millions of faithful listeners around the world.

I looked into his face, trying to draw his eyes away from the Pope to meet mine. I smiled my best, most comforting smile, and finally, his concentration returned. His beautiful voice came pouring forth and filled the huge Sala Nervi as we knew it would. Gregory still looked dazed, but he finished his performance with aplomb. He had been, in that instant, the innocent shepherd boy of the Psalmist, and not the seasoned professional he had tried so hard to be for us and for the world that night. Luckily, we had recorded the dress rehearsal and were thus able to save the recording for the subsequent delayed U.S. broadcast. His musical reputation was none the worse for wear.

The evening's music-making ended with the hushed a capella setting of the same 133rd Psalm quoted by the Pope that morning in the audience: "*Hine ma tov u manayim, shevet achim gam yachad*" — How good and how pleasant it is when brothers live together in unity. The Royal Philharmonic's muted solo trumpet finished magnificently what was a solemn night of Jewish prayer in the Vatican. A night when musical incantations captured the pain and the hope of humankind, in memory and in quiet confidence, that for this moment, at least, would give reality to the phrase "Never again."

As the applause for our performance faded away, His Holiness rose, solemn-faced but determined to give expression to our common thought. He began to speak in Italian:

"We are gathered tonight to commemorate the Holocaust of millions of Jews. The candles which were lit before us are there to symbolically demonstrate that this hall has no limits. It contains all the victims themselves: Mothers, Fathers, Sisters, Brothers, and Friends. In our memory, they are all here with you. They are all here with us."

After he finished, after all the tears were wiped away, the Pope came forward to greet us all. He received Richard Dreyfuss, Lynn Harrell, Gregory Rodriguez, Don Pablo Collino (the conductor of the Choir of Saint Peter's Basilica), and myself. He gave a special greeting to Gregory Daniel Rodriguez, patting his young cheek, showing his artist's sympathy as a former performer himself.

Then he came with me on stage, and greeted all the front desk players of the Royal Philharmonic. Some seemed to avert their eyes, as if the meaning of the occasion was still on their minds, and the moment called for humility, above all else.

The Pope put his arm around me and whispered in my ear, in Polish, "*Dziekuje. Dziekuje bardzo*"—Thank you. Thank you very much. The word *bardzo* the Pope enunciated with strong emphasis, looking me in the eyes in a way by now familiar to me, but no less affecting after six years of feeling its underlying powerful emotion. His words were simple yet entirely sufficient. It was all that needed to be said. He walked down the stairs and out of the Aula, having touched us all, and we him, I do so profoundly believe.

Backstage, in my dressing room, I was able to welcome some of the most important figures who had made this event a reality, and who had been with me on the long journey to help it come to pass.

Cardinal Lustiger came and put both his arms on my shoulders, holding me at a slight distance. Tears were in his eyes. I cannot imagine what this day had meant for him. Here was his Church commemorating the martyrdom of his many relatives, most of all his mother, who had been taken from him so early by the horrible whirlwind. "Thank you, Gilbert," he said. "Thank you for this evening. Gilbert, you know, when you first came to me with this idea, I thought you were crazy. Yes, crazy. I really never thought this day would come. But now it has, and it has brought my family together, here with me in the Vatican. My Jewish cousin, Arno, has come here to Rome from Frankfurt. He came to the Vatican on this night to remember with me all the family we have lost. And now, Gilbert, we must go forward. This work is not yet done. Let this be the start and not the finish of bringing us all together. Shalom, Gilbert. Shalom."

Then Cardinal Cassidy came forward and bent down towards me as I sat down, recovering my strength. "Maestro," he said, "thank you. Without you, we would never have even begun this. We would never have started down this path." What a generous statement, I thought, from someone whose responsibilities to keep Catholics and Jews on the road to reconciliation had made this Shoah concert a journey that was so personally difficult for him.

Finally, after everyone else had left my dressing room, I walked over to Margit, who was sitting quietly by the side, lost in thought. I bent down to her, gave her a big hug, and said simply, "I did this for you." She looked at me with a combination of thanks and deep sadness. She was near tears. She had been waiting so long for such a day, for the Vatican to take note of what she and her relatives had been through. This would not bring them back, but it might bring her some peace. That at least was my most fervent hope. It is what had inspired me and, I believe, the Pope to bring this concert into being.

The next day, I finally reached Monsignor Dziwisz by telephone. He congratulated me for a wonderful concert, apologized for not being present, and said that he had watched it on television from the Papal Apartments. It turns out that Monsignor Dziwisz and the Pope had been doing a bit of spring skiing in the Italian Alps the week before the Shoah concert. Monsignor Dziwisz had somehow managed to wrap himself around a tree. His face was black and blue, and his shoulder bumped pretty badly, but otherwise, he said, thank God, he was intact. The accident had prevented him from attending the concert in which he had played such a vital role.

In fact, Monsignor Dziwisz told me, the Pope wished to thank me in person. He informed me that I would be received in private audience by the Holy Father, the very next day. I had hoped that I would have such an opportunity. Not so much to receive His Holiness' appreciation but to offer instead my profound thanks for his having made this occasion historic by his presence, and for his having trusted me in a way that I am not sure I would have trusted myself, to bring this concert to fruition.

In anticipation—or in hope—of a post-event audience, I had gone the week before to an antiquarian bookshop in Rome's Jewish Ghetto, near the Via del Portico d'Ottavia, just behind the Great Synagogue. It was there that I thought I might find just the right gift of thanks for His Holiness. And sure enough, I did: a very rare facsimile of the ancient Sarajevo Haggadah. The Haggadah is the prayer book which we use on the occasion of our Passover Seder. Every Jewish household has many copies of the Haggadah, one for each participant in this special meal. Some Haggadahs are kept in families and used at Seders for years and years. At the second-night Seder we attend every year at the home of the Schiffmans, our close friends in Boston, the Haggadahs are inscribed with our Levine family names, signed year by year, going back to our very first Seder with them in 1984.

There are a myriad of modern editions of the Haggadah prayer book, from Maurice Sendak's beautifully illustrated volume to one with Elie Wiesel's wonderfully annotated, deeply poignant Holocaust commentary accompanying the text. Each Haggadah tells the story of our exodus from Egypt, led by God, and declaims the ancestral tale for each new generation of Jews. For Christians this book is equally important, because the Seder was also the Last Supper that Jesus shared with his disciples before his Crucifixion.

The Sarajevo Haggadah is perhaps the most famous example of this book. It is not just that it is the most wondrously illuminated manuscript in the Jewish liturgical canon, it is also a book with a rich and courageous history all its own. It is thought to have been produced in Barcelona in 1350, in the time of Moorish Spain, a period known for interreligious tolerance among Muslims, Christians, and Jews. After the Christian Conquest, in 1492, this special Haggadah is believed to have been smuggled out of Spain by Jews fleeing the Inquisition. It made its way over the centuries to Sarajevo, then under Ottoman rule and later becoming part of Yugoslavia. In 1941 it was hidden by the Muslim director of the museum in Sarajevo from the Nazi commandant of the conquered city. Finally, in 1992, it was left miraculously undisturbed as unrecognized debris on the floor of the same Sarajevo museum during the ransacking by marauding Serbian armies, who were laying siege to the city during the terrible Balkan civil wars. The Sarajevo Haggadah is thus the very symbol of the survival of the Jews and the Jewish faith, under one despotic ruler after another. And it has been protected along the way, often at great peril, by the kindness and concern of guardians of the other Abrahamic faiths, Christian and Muslim alike.

Pope John Paul had been deeply moved by the plight of Sarajevo during the civil war. He had attempted to fly into Sarajevo to celebrate Mass and show his support for the besieged population of this multi-religious city, only to be threatened with the killing, not of himself, but of those who would come to worship with him. His compassion for all the suffering citizens of that ancient "Jerusalem of Europe" was clear for all to see. This was a gift that, I felt, would mean the most to His Holiness after our Concert to Commemorate the Shoah. "Never again," for Pope John Paul II, included the citizens of all faiths inhabiting and trying their best to survive in Sarajevo in 1994.

When I met the Pope in the Apostolic Palace, I gave him the Sarajevo Haggadah, now bound in the finest brown leather binding any Roman craftsman could create especially for His Holiness. John Paul held this ancient manuscript and asked me exactly what it was. He looked at me with gracious thanks for having thought to share this with him. In putting it in his hands, I said, "Your Holiness, this is the Sarajevo Haggadah. An ancient version of the book we use every year when we celebrate our Seder." With that brief explanation, a look of recognition came over His Holiness' face. Seder, Haggadah—these were words the Pope already knew.

"You have given me the greatest honor I could ever have as an artist and as a Jew," I said, pausing for a moment as I thought about what I had just said. The Pope looked at me with empathy. I went on.

"Your Holiness' presence made our concert a part of history. It will never be forgotten. No one can ever say that the Shoah never happened. No one can ever say again that the Church does not have the deepest, most profound compassion for the memory of the six million Jews who were murdered. This was your gift to the Jewish people and to the world. I thank you so much for giving me the honor of helping you to bring this to life."

His Holiness was silent. He looked me in the eyes and smiled warmly. Finally, he said, "Maestro, thank you again for all you have done. That was indeed a most important event. Without you, I don't know how we could have accomplished it."

Then the Pope started looking through the pages of the Sarajevo Haggadah, stopping at this page and then that, drawn as so many others have been before him to the glowing, painted illustrations richly arrayed throughout the manuscript. Leafing through the book, he also asked about the text, and the way he did so told me that this was perhaps not the first Haggadah he had ever seen. The story of the exodus from Egypt is after all a part of Christianity's Bible as well. It's Old Testament. It is the story Jesus shared with his disciples at his Last Supper before his Crucifixion. This was His Holiness' sacred book as much as it was my own.

And in the homes of the Pope's Jewish friends, when he was growing up in Wadowice, there were surely many Haggadahs. Those friends and their families had all celebrated the Seder by taking turns, as all Jews do, reading and singing from their own Seder prayer books. These were friends whose tragic loss he must have experienced with great pain as they were swept up, one by one, in the insanity of the Shoah.

Even as he enjoyed these friendships with his Jewish neighbors, he was pursuing his Catholic education and then his calling to the priesthood. To the young Karol Wojtyla there would have been no contradiction in this. He could have warm friendships with Jews and become ever more devout in his Catholic faith. One thing did not preclude the other. It is said that his relations with his Jewish friends were as natural as those with his fellow Catholics. In any case, that is how I had felt he treated me since the day we had met in his Papal library in 1988. He saw me as a fellow human being to be judged by the content of my character, not by the religion I professed. He even seemed pleased that my Jewish faith burned in me ever more brightly.

Now holding the Haggadah, Pope John Paul thanked me once again. He was clearly moved by this gift, and for that I was grateful. But I suspect he was also reminded of the people of Sarajevo, for whom he had consistently shown such great concern in recent months.

There could not have been a more satisfying conclusion to this Papal Concert. This warm and personal audience, and His Holiness' generous thanks, were all that I could have wished for. The travails of the last three years had been, in the end, worthwhile. I was as content as I thought I could ever be. But then who could have expected a surprise like the one that was about to come my way.

CHAPTER

TWENTY

On the day after the event, the Shoah concert was reported by major newspapers and television and radio stations throughout Europe and North America. Dozens of countries had broadcast the concert live, and many more did so over the weeks and months that followed. Time Warner produced a documentary in which my mother-in-law was featured, telling with poignant, unadorned directness a brief part of her terrible ordeal at Birkenau. Also on this documentary, Meyer Gottlieb, a top film executive in Hollywood, told his own powerful story. He said that during the Holocaust, he had been a freezing, starving Jewish child, living in constant fear, feeding only on the faint remnants of hope. He had prayed then just to be able to live one more day. And now here he was, a grown man, meeting the Pope in the Vatican, having lived long enough to experience an almost unimaginable Papal Concert to Commemorate the Shoah.

PBS aired the concert in their own version especially produced by John Walker of "Great Performances," and a CD was released with special spoken commentary by Richard Dreyfuss, Lynn Harrell, and myself. Clearly, it had been a major media event, but its lasting influence went far beyond its widespread fame.

As I toured the United States and Europe, Jews would come backstage after concerts to say "Thank you for the Vatican Shoah concert!" Then they would invariably add, "Pope John Paul. What an amazing friend he is of the Jewish people!" Through this one noble gesture, the

Pope had begun to change the Jewish perception of the Roman Catholic Church. The atmosphere of distrust that had hung in the air between our two ancient faiths was beginning to clear. Now we could agree to disagree but always in the context of brotherly respect. Catholics, too, would come up to me and say how proud they were of their Church and tell me how important the concert had been to them as well.

Even some of the Jewish organizations that had refused to support the Papal Concert were now voicing their approval, after the fact. I received letters from some of the most prominent Jewish leaders in America and abroad, saying what a blessing the concert had been to Catholic-Jewish relations and, more importantly, how meaningful it had been to so many of the survivors whom they knew. This near-universal praise made all the difficulties we had encountered along the way to the Shoah concert quickly fade away.

During the summer of 1994, I visited Castel Gandolfo for a more relaxed celebratory conversation with Monsignor Dziwisz. Such visits were easier now. We didn't need a problem to arise for us to enjoy each other's company.

Monsignor Dziwisz and I sat in one of the castle's small, elegant reception rooms, beaming back and forth at each other, so pleased with what we had accomplished together. I told Monsignor Dziwisz all about the positive comments I had heard, both from Jews and Catholics, in the months since our concert.

Monsignor Dziwisz answered me in a way that moved me almost to tears. "His Holiness was deeply moved by your concert. We all were. You were right, Maestro, music was just the right language to express these profound sentiments. His Holiness is so grateful for all you have done."

With these words, spoken by Monsignor Dziwisz, but bearing the sentiments of His Holiness, I knew that my journey from America to Kraków to Rome had all been part of a plan, which before that time I could not have fully comprehended. It had helped to lead, under the inspiration of this great pope, to an evolving rapprochement between Christians and Jews, which had been achingly unattainable for such a very long time.

My friendship with Monsignor Dziwisz had deepened also, in large part because Pope John Paul had been the force behind it all. Without him, of course, there would have been no Papal Concert. But Monsignor Dziwisz and I had walked through the fire together to realize this vision and had come out stronger and more united on the other side. How impossible it had all seemed. Now it was so easy to share a laugh.

At the end of our conversation, Monsignor Dziwisz walked me to the small elevator that would take me down to the entrance to Castel Gandolfo. As I was about to board, he stopped me, smiled a secret smile, and said, "Oh, Maestro, something quite special will be happening soon. It may take a bit of time, but I think you will be very pleased." Before I could say, "What are you talking about?!" he had allowed the door of the elevator to close behind me, leaving me dumbfounded and intensely eager to find out just what he meant by "something quite special." I saw his gentle grin and slowly waving hand fade through the passing glass as the elevator began its descent to the ground floor and the castle's main entrance.

I walked back out past the Swiss Guards and into the tiny square of the town of Castel Gandolfo, high above the beautiful blue of Lake Albano. I'm sure the view was as marvelous as always. But I didn't notice a thing. I drove south along ever-crowded streets back into Rome, and flew home to New York, in bated anticipation the whole long way.

One morning, some six weeks later, in mid-September, Vera picked up the phone in our Upper East Side apartment. "Hallo, Madame," a deep voice said. "May I please speak with Gilbert? It is Cardinal Lustiger, calling from Paris."

"Yes, yes, of course," Vera said, calling me quickly to the phone. "Hurry. It's Cardinal Lustiger." Vera stage-whispered, "He hardly said hello to me. He must have something important on his mind."

"Good morning, Eminence," I said, "or it should be 'good afternoon,' isn't it for you?"

"Gilbert," Cardinal Lustiger said, pronouncing my name with a soft G à la française. "I am calling with congratulations. I have wonderful news. His Holiness has wished to invest you as a Knight-Commander of the Pontifical Equestrian Order of Saint Gregory the Great. The official Vatican documents to this effect will be sent to you shortly, but I wanted to call you myself to share this special news. And I am so pleased, because the Holy Father has chosen me to present you with this honor at a ceremony in Paris. We will talk about all the details later. Again, congratulations! *Auf Wiedersehen*, Gilbert." And he rang off.

I held the phone to my ear long after the dial tone had begun to sound, as if to hear some further explanation for what I had just been told.

"Vera," I said. "You won't believe this. Do we have champagne? No, of course not, it's much too early. Vera, I am to be knighted by the Pope!"

"You're kidding!" my wife said. And I think she meant it. To Vera, being European, this was incomprehensible. She would believe it only when it actually came to pass.

Sure enough, as if written in a fairy tale, ten days later, as I was about to leave our apartment building, the doorman said to me, "Mr. Levine, there is an oversized white envelope that came for you this morning. It wouldn't fit in your mailbox. Would you like it now, or should we keep it until you return?"

"Now, please, yes, now!" I said.

The envelope was indeed very large, and crafted of very fine heavyweight paper. It was from Nonciature Apostolique en France, the Embassy of the Holy See in the French Capital. It was addressed to His Eminence Cardinal Jean-Marie Lustiger and then forwarded on to me. I didn't want to open it; the envelope was so beautiful. I just wanted to stare at it for a little while longer.

But then, right there, in the lobby of my building, I sat down on the leather couch and carefully opened it up. Inside, beneath a fine protective liner, was a Latin-lettered parchment, emblazoned with the Papal Seal. The calligraphed words read in part:

"*Ioannes Pavlvs II Pont. Max—Gilbertum Levine e Foederatis Civitatibus Americae Septentrionalis-Eqvitem Commendatorem Ordinis*

Sancti Gregorii Magnum"—In the name of John Paul II, Roman Pontiff, Gilbert Levine of the United States of America is made a Knight-Commander of the Equestrian Order of Saint Gregory the Great.

The envelope also contained a book with a history of the Knighthood and a description in words, as well as a drawing, of the knightly uniform that I was presumably meant to wear. It was all surreal. I turned right around, went back upstairs, and showed this to Vera.

"Now do you believe me?!" I said to Vera. "To tell you the truth, I didn't believe it until today myself. But now it must be true. I am holding it in my hand."

Then I sat down with my sons, David and Gabriel. I told them that their dad was going to be knighted by the Pope.

David said, "Like those figures we saw in the big market in Kraków, with their suits of armor?"

"No, David," I said, "not quite like that. I don't think Pontifical Knights dress like that nowadays, but I'll have to check it out. But listen to me, it's very important. Don't go telling anyone in school about this. They won't believe you, and they'll make fun of you for making things up. OK? For now, let's make it our family secret."

David nodded, and Gabriel, who was then in preschool, said he would also not say a thing.

"But Daddy, you'll be a knight?" Gabriel added, just to make sure.

"Yes, Gabe, it's unbelievable, but it's true," I said, and watched the amazed and oh-so-proud looks spread across both their beautiful faces.

The next day, I phoned Paris to express my profound gratitude for such a great honor.

Cardinal Lustiger said, "Don't thank me, Gilbert. You should thank the Holy Father. Such honors are only in the gift of His Holiness. He loves you, you know that. And it is he who has asked me to confer on you this Knighthood. We have tentatively set the date of December twenty-second for your Investiture. Is it convenient for you to come to Paris on that date?"

"Convenient?" I shouted. "Of course. Yes, I'll be there. But, Your Eminence, I do understand it is the Pope who has done this, but I would very much like to repay you also, for your friendship, for your encouragement, for helping me all these years in Kraków, in Paris, and the Vatican. Tell me, is there something I can do to show you but a small part of the respect and friendship you have shown to me?"

"You know, Gilbert, there is something," the Cardinal said, a bit hesitantly. "For us here in Paris, Midnight Mass at Christmas in the Cathedral of Notre Dame is very important. I have always thought it would be wonderful to have an orchestra and choir perform one of the great masses, perhaps of Mozart or of Haydn, as part of our celebration of the Mass. Would you consent to do this? If we were able to have one of the admirable orchestras of Paris come and perform with you, would you conduct the Midnight Mass? It would mean so very much to everyone in Notre Dame that night."

"Yes, of course, Your Eminence," I said immediately. "This would be my greatest pleasure. I am a musician. It will give me great joy to make music for you as the tiniest repayment for the honor you will bestow."

"Good, then it is settled. We will work on the details. My secretary will be in touch."

When I got off the phone with Cardinal Lustiger, I realized just what I had agreed to do. I would be conducting a Catholic Mass, not in a concert form without any recitation, as I had done before at the Vatican for His Holiness' tenth anniversary, but in Notre Dame Cathedral as part of a service, the celebration of the Holy Mass. I had never before done such a thing in my entire artistic life. As I imagined all the things that could go wrong, I began to get very nervous about it, fully three months before the fact.

CHAPTER

TWENTY-ONE

When my family and I arrived in Paris in December 1994, it was freezing. I had never known that Paris could be so bone-chillingly cold. But the frigid arctic air was warmed considerably by the lights of Paris at Noël. Bright white lights were everywhere, on the trees lining the Champs-Élysées, which were festooned with glowing bulbs strung from limb to limb. They lit the windows of all the fashionable stores and illuminated the facade of Notre Dame and every other major church in the city. Paris in the snow and ice was bathed in Christmas lights, which made it, oh, so warm and inviting.

The ceremony of the Investiture of a Pontifical Knight usually takes place in a cathedral as part of the Catholic Mass. In my case, because of Cardinal Lustiger's gentle sensitivity, my ceremony would take place in the largest, most formal gilt-edged room of his residence, right next to the room where we had had our first real encounter, some five years before.

Friends had flown in from across Europe, Israel, and the United States. This was an important part of my story, and they all wanted to be part of it. Daniel Berger flew in from Philadelphia. Dan, a lawyer by profession, was a friend of twenty years or more, who had been with me for every Vatican concert, and most of the major concerts I had conducted in Poland and around the world, since 1988. Nahum and Sheila Gelber flew in from their home in Jerusalem. The Gelbers had been part of a group of Jews who had "found" me in Kraków when they randomly walked into a Kraków Philharmonic concert and couldn't believe their eyes and ears: an American Jew conducting his Polish orchestra. They adopted me and I them. I even shared the bottle of the Lubavitcher Rebbe's blessed vodka with them and a group of American and Israeli Jews who had gathered in my hotel suite just for this communal purpose. To Nahum, the fact that I had the *heckscher*, the blessing of the Rebbe, was as important as that I was the chosen conductor of the Pope. And Sam and Judy Pisar came over from their elegant townhouse in the Sixteenth Arrondissement of Paris. Sam is an internationally known lawyer and a prominent Holocaust survivor, and Judy, his wife, is a music lover par excellence, who was an acolyte of my musical inspiration, Leonard Bernstein. Also present were members of the press, including Jim Bitterman of ABC and John Tagliabue of the *New York Times* and his wife, Paula Butturini. The room was filled with all these friends and many more, including of course the man who would officiate at that evening's ceremony.

After we had all assembled, Cardinal Lustiger raised his hands and brought the room to silence. He asked whether there was anyone who would wish to present me for investiture as a Pontifical Knight-Commander of the Equestrian Order of Saint Gregory the Great.

Jacques Barrot, one of my closest friends in France, who had been with me at World Youth Day in Denver, then formally presented me to the Cardinal for Knighthood. Jacques was at this time a Catholic layman of great importance and a man who wore an incredible number of important political hats in his country. In December 1994, Jacques was, simultaneously, the head of the French Christian Democratic Party; a member of the Assemblée Nationale; the Mayor of Yssingeaux; and the Governor of the French Department, or province, of Haute-Loire. It would be as if he were the head of the Republican Party, a congressman, a mayor of a small city within that congressional district, and the governor of the state in which that city was located. Jacques then was by any standard a very prominent member of the French political and lay-religious establishment. He was especially chosen by Cardinal Lustiger for this night's task because of his close relationship both to me and to His Eminence.

Jacques' brief statement, official yet heartfelt, spoke of what I had accomplished for French culture through my concerts at Notre Dame and my other concert appearances, both in Paris and throughout France. Especially memorable, he said, were those at the Festival de La Chaise-Dieu, an annual musical event staged in a magnificent medieval cloister in the Auvergne, close to his hometown in central France. Jacques noted the tremendous importance for France of the Catholic-Jewish dialogue, in which, he said, I had played such an important and constructive part.

Jacques' speech was followed by a statement from Rabbi James Rudin of the American Jewish Committee, read to the assembled audience by Judith Pisar. I would venture to say that mine was the first ever Pontifical Knight's Investiture where a rabbi's statement was part of the official program. Rabbi Rudin's letter was an appreciation for what my work in Poland and at the Vatican had meant to the Jewish community. He congratulated me on the courage it took to go to Kraków in the first place, in the midst of the Cold War. He remarked on how the idea of the Shoah concert had grown out of my friendship with Pope John Paul II. "Blessed with the divine gift of music," Rabbi Rudin wrote, "Maestro Levine recognized that perhaps only through that gift could the Shoah be commemorated. And his relationship with the Pope was more than mere friendship. Together, they made their shared dream into a wondrous reality."

I couldn't help but think how different that sentiment might have been if our concert had not been such a success. I had not forgotten just how skeptical most Jewish organizations had been before the fact. But it had turned out well, as was clear from another letter sent to me on this occasion from the same Miles Lerman, the Chairman of the United States Holocaust Memorial Council, who had written his note of grave caution before the fact. Now Miles wrote, quite candidly, "With your sensitivity, tactfulness and patience, you have succeeded (in spite of all the politics) in a Holocaust memorial concert in the Vatican, which by all standards should be considered a major breakthrough."

After the letter of Rabbi Rudin, Cardinal Lustiger proceeded to my actual investiture as a Pontifical Knight-Commander of the Equestrian Order of Saint Gregory the Great. Without the panoply of the church service it was much less directly religious than would ordinarily have been the case. His Eminence read the Papal decree aloud in Latin and then translated it into French. Then the Cardinal placed the medallion of the order, hung from a red and gold ribbon, around my neck. The medallion bears a representation of St. Gregory on one side, and on the reverse the motto "*Pro Deo et Principe*"—For God and Prince. He also presented me with a sword, whose handle is made of mother-of-pearl adorned with a medallion of the order. Finally, Cardinal Lustiger gave me an elongated black beaver-felt hat, which one normally would associate with Admiral Lord Nelson. This, as suggested to me by Jacques's wife, I placed on the head of my ten-year-old son David. Three-year-old Gabriel got to hold the ceremonial sword, still sheathed in its leather scabbard, keeping it safely away from his nose with both his little outstretched hands.

After this small bit of levity, Cardinal Lustiger's speech was, in contrast, as moving a moment as I could remember in all the six years of my improbable relationship with the Roman Catholic Church. His Eminence spoke to the assembled group about how he had met me here, in this house where the ceremony was now taking place. He talked of how my going to Kraków had reminded him so poignantly of his own family's reverse journey out of Poland so many decades before. He had watched my relationship with His Holiness grow before his eyes. He said he was "stupefied" to learn that I, a Jewish conductor, had become, in his words, one of the "*interlocuteurs du choix du Saint Pere*" (that is, one of this Pope's most select advisors). He said he had never seen anything like this in all his years. Then he embraced me, putting his arms around me, and whispered in my ear, "Brother. You are always welcome in this house."

I was struck at that moment that Cardinal Lustiger had used the familiar German *du* instead of the more formal *Sie* when he addressed me. By longstanding European custom, now that my "superior" had addressed me in the familiar, we were bound together in a bond that takes years, if ever, for Central Europeans to form. In Germany, or in France, in fact, when a friendship moves from formal to familiar, a toast is often made. Here, in this golden hall, Cardinal Lustiger had cemented our familial relationship on the very day the Pope had made me a lay member of the Church's nobility. It was a fairy-tale knighthood capped by the priceless gift of His Eminence's deepening friendship.

After the Cardinal's presentation, James Hogan, the Cultural Attaché at the United States Embassy to France, read a letter sent on the occasion of my Knighthood from President William Jefferson Clinton. Pontifical Knighthoods are fairly rare; in fact, they had been conferred on Jews on only three previous occasions in the entire history of the Church. Mine, it turned out, was the very first one ever accorded an American Jew. So this had evidently even come to the attention of the American President.

President Clinton wrote:

I am delighted to congratulate you as you are invested as a Pontifical Knight-Commander of the Equestrian Order of Saint Gregory the Great. As the first Jewish American to receive a papal knighthood, you continue to serve as a bridge between people of different beliefs and backgrounds—a symbol of our common humanity. Hillary joins me in extending warm wishes for continued success.

Cardinal Lustiger had prepared me earlier in the day for just how rare this bestowal of a Papal honor on an artist truly was. It seems His Eminence had been doing a bit of research of his own into musicians knighted by the popes over the centuries. Not only was my Knighthood unprecedented in American Jewish history, but Cardinal Lustiger had found out that mine was the first Pontifical Knighthood to be accorded a non-ecclesiastical musician since Mozart. And Mozart's Knighthood, the Cardinal had told me with a bit of a smile, had been bestowed not by the Church itself, let alone by order of the Holy Father, but by a member of the Black Nobility. These were lay Catholic figures of noble rank, principally in Rome, who in Mozart's time, around 1770, had been empowered by the Vatican to grant such pontifical honors without prior papal approval. But then Mozart was a genius, perhaps the greatest composer of all time, and he was only thirteen at the time of his Investiture. His ambitious father was sufficiently impressed with this papal honor, however, that he commissioned a portrait from an artist in Bologna with the young genius decked out in the uniform of his new pontifical noble rank. How he had gotten his uniform made in such a short time, we will never know.

After President Clinton's letter was read, a bound sheaf of congratulatory letters from American Senators, celebrities, and musical colleagues was then presented to me. Sir Georg Solti, my mentor, sent his congratulations, as did Senator Carl Levin. Carl and I had met when he and his wife, Barbara, came to Kraków as part of a congressional delegation. Senator Levin is a classical music fan, and he and Barbara had attended a Kraków Philharmonic concert—Brahms First Symphony, if I remember correctly. The next day I had shown the Levins around my new hometown, and we had since become fast friends. Carl wrote:

"The honor for Maestro Levine is first and foremost recognition of a fine conductor and musician, but its symbolic significance surely is there as well."

Barbara Walters had written a warm and charming note. Governor Mario Cuomo of New York and the Ambassadors, both American and Israeli, to the Holy See, as well as professors from Harvard, Princeton, and Yale, among many others, had also added their warm praise. Finally, Richard Dreyfuss summed things up in a statement that was as personal as it was affecting:

"Gilbert Levine allowed me to be part of one of the most remarkable events of my life. It was through his efforts and vision that two ancient communities were brought together in an historic and inevitable evening. For that, we all owe him. And for that, this great honor is so richly deserved."

Finally, Cardinal Lustiger asked if I had anything I might wish to say. I did.

"Words cannot express the profound gratitude that is in my heart at this moment. Gratitude towards His Holiness Pope John Paul II, towards His Eminence Jean-Marie Lustiger, and towards all those, particularly my wife, Vera, who have brought me to this honor. Words cannot express this for me, because ever since I can remember, it has not been words but music that has had the mystical power to encompass depths of feeling and, yes, even thought. From my earliest years, music and spirit have been enveloped one in the other. Music has been my path to 'at-one-ment.' It is, I believe, a language of God. It is whole and mysterious, sweet and awesome, unimaginably peaceful and singularly terrifying. All without words.

"Saint Gregory the Great, for whom this order is named, is said to have received his inspiration for the Gregorian Chant which bears his name from a white dove perched on his shoulder that sang into his ear. From God, to nature, to one man, to all men. I cannot help but feel a close bond with him in this. I feel my whole life has led me here, where spirit and music come together in the service of something higher.

"For me, this Knighthood is much more than an honor. It is an obligation. I take this obligation on with great joy. I will try to fulfill the trust this honor implies. A trust to make my music serve that which is good. That which is larger than all of us."

A round of toasts was offered, with wine selected from among the Cardinal's favorite vintages. His Eminence and I bid our brief farewells, and I was off into the Parisian cold to drink champagne with friends, and to seek out the courage to face my next challenge: conducting a Christmas Mass in Notre Dame.

The Cardinal had arranged for me to conduct the Orchestre de la Bastille, the extraordinary orchestra of the Opéra National de Paris. This ensemble plays almost every evening in the pit of one of the great opera houses of the world, and on select occasions they appear with important conductors in concert and on recordings. But even for them, performing for Midnight Mass in Notre Dame was a first. Our rehearsals were anything but routine. Notre Dame has an acoustic meant for reverent prayer, not for a symphony orchestra, as I had learned when I conducted the Kraków Philharmonic there in 1989. The musical sounds we made resonated from stone to stone, on and on, in that immense Gothic cathedral. The gentle joke was that if you liked the music you heard, you only had to wait six seconds to hear it all again. Still, we were not there for the acoustics but for the incredible atmosphere of the Cathédrale Notre Dame de Paris, one of the most famous cathedrals and one of the most famous edifices of any kind in all the world. And even more, it was Christmastime.

We were helped in our accommodation to the acoustics of the cathedral by the Maîtrise de Notre Dame, the wonderful choir which sings at every major service. They knew the cathedral's "voice" as well as anyone. They were in their own spiritual home.

I chose for this most special occasion the "Coronation Mass" of Mozart, one of the great examples of liturgical music in the entire classical canon. It was music literally fit for a king or, in fact, for an emperor, having been performed for the coronations of both Emperor Leopold II of Austria and his son Emperor Francis II. When I told His Eminence of my choice, he was pleased, but then he asked what to me was a very strange question: "Gilbert, please tell me, how long is the Sanctus?"

I should have known that this event was going to be something entirely different. Normally, the timing of a particular movement of a classical piece is never a decisive factor. There are many performances of the Mozart Coronation Mass in concert halls all over the world. I had in fact conducted it quite often with the Kraków Philharmonic and other orchestras, once even on Korean television. And I had never, ever been asked just how long this portion or that might be. But then this was no concert performance, ordinary or otherwise. And Cardinal Lustiger's question was meant to elicit very practical information related to his celebration of the Mass. It also let me know just how different this particular performance was going to be.

"Levine Soars in Twin Cities Debut ..." My international career in Kraków and my spiritual journey to the Vatican and His Holiness began with a single series of concerts in America: conducting Shostakovich's Fifth Symphony with the Minnesota Orchestra, April 1984.

First American conductor in the East Bloc. My debut concert as Music Director of the Kraków Philharmonic, conducting Mahler's Third Symphony in Philharmonic Hall, December 1987.

Pope John Paul II, my wife, Vera, and I following my first tête-à-tête in His Holiness'
Private Library in the Apostolic Palace at the Vatican, February 1988.

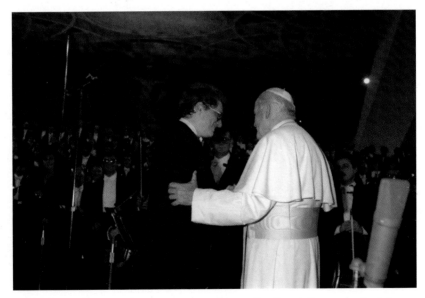

Pope John Paul congratulates me on stage after my first Papal Concert in the Sala
Nervi at the Vatican, December 3, 1988. Brahms' Ave Maria and Dvořák's Mass in
D were among His Holiness' favorites.

PREFETTURA DELLA
CASA PONTIFICIA

PROGRAMMA

LA RAI - RADIOTELEVISIONE
ITALIANA SABATO 3 DICEMBRE 1988,
ALLE ORE 18, NELL'AULA PAOLO VI
IN VATICANO, OFFRIRÀ UN
CONCERTO SINFONICO IN ONORE
DI SUA SANTITÀ

GIOVANNI PAOLO II

KRZYSZTOF PENDERECKI
STABAT MATER
PER TRE CORI MISTI A CAPPELLA

JOHANNES BRAHMS
AVE MARIA
PER CORO FEMMINILE
E ORCHESTRA

ANTONIN DVORAK
MESSA IN RE MAGGIORE
PER SOLI CORO E ORCHESTRA

DIRETTORE
GILBERT LEVINE

SOLISTI:

SOPRANO: ADELINA SCARABELLI
MEZZOSOPRANO: ANNE GJEVANG
TENORE: EZIO DE CESARE
BASSO: JAMES JOHNSON

ORCHESTRA SINFONICA E CORO DI ROMA
DELLA RAI - RADIOTELEVISIONE
ITALIANA

CORO DELLA FILARMONICA
DI CRACOVIA

MAESTRI DEI CORI:

FULVIO ANGIUS - HENRYK WOJNAROWSKI
STANISLAW KRAWCZYNSKI

VATICANO, 18 NOVEMBRE 1988

The trifold program, engraved on thick, cream-colored, deckle-edged stock, for the first Papal Concert at the Vatican, in honor of Pope John Paul II's tenth anniversary, December 3, 1988.

During the October 1990 Bishops Synod at the Vatican, His Holiness and I (speaking Polish) discuss my idea to offer a Concert of Remembrance and Reconciliation in the Templ Synagogue in Kraków. Cardinal Lustiger looks on intently.

The Kraków Philharmonic and I rehearse for our Concert of Remembrance and Reconciliation in the Templ Synagogue in Kraków, October 26, 1990.

Cardinal Lustiger and I celebrate after my concert at Yale University, November 2, 1992. His Eminence was honored as a Chubb Fellow.

He stole the show! Pope John Paul II interrupts "his Maestro" at World Youth Day in Denver, 1993.

My mother-in-law,
Margit Raab Kalina,
is received by His
Holiness at the first-ever
papal audience for
Holocaust survivors
and their families,
April 7, 1994.

Pope John Paul II; Rav Elio Toaff, the Chief Rabbi of Rome; and Oscar Luigi
Scalforo, the President of Italy sit on three equal ceremonial thrones as I conduct
Beethoven's Ninth Symphony with the Royal Philharmonic Orchestra at the Papal
Concert to Commemorate the Shoah, April 7, 1994.

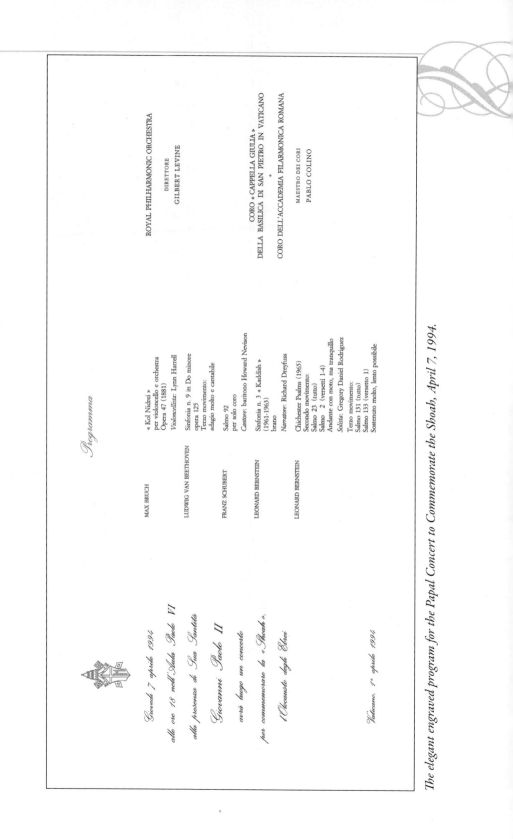

Programma

Giovedì 7 aprile 1994

alle ore 18 nell'Aula Paolo VI

alla presenza di Sua Santità

Giovanni Paolo II

avrà luogo un concerto

per commemorare la «Shoah»,

l'Olocausto degli Ebrei.

Vaticano, 1° aprile 1994

ROYAL PHILHARMONIC ORCHESTRA

DIRETTORE
GILBERT LEVINE

CORO «CAPPELLA GIULIA»
DELLA BASILICA DI SAN PIETRO IN VATICANO
*
CORO DELL'ACCADEMIA FILARMONICA ROMANA

MAESTRO DEI CORI
PABLO COLINO

MAX BRUCH
«Kol Nidrei»
per violoncello e orchestra
Opera 47 (1881)
Violoncellista: Lynn Harrell

LUDWIG VAN BEETHOVEN
Sinfonia n. 9 in Do minore
opera 125
Terzo movimento:
adagio molto e cantabile

FRANZ SCHUBERT
Salmo 92
per solo coro
Cantore: baritono Howard Nevison

LEONARD BERNSTEIN
Sinfonia n. 3 «Kaddish»
(1961-1963)
brano
Narratore: Richard Dreyfuss

LEONARD BERNSTEIN
Chichester Psalms (1965)
Secondo movimento:
Salmo 23 (tutto)
Salmo 2 (versetti 1-4)
Andante con moto, ma tranquillo
Solista: Gregory Daniel Rodriguez

Terzo movimento:
Salmo 131 (tutto)
Salmo 133 (versetto 1)
Sostenuto molto, lento lento possibile

The elegant engraved program for the Papal Concert to Commemorate the Shoah, April 7, 1994.

Kaddish echoes in the Vatican. Actor Richard Dreyfuss recites Kaddish to a portion of Leonard Bernstein's Third Symphony, at the Papal Concert to Commemorate the Shoah.

Pope John Paul II addresses Vatican officials, rabbis, Catholic and Jewish laity, and survivors of the Holocaust from around the world at the conclusion of the Papal Concert to Commemorate the Shoah. In the foreground is the Holocaust Menorah, with one candle lit for each million of the six million who were murdered.

Italian survivors of the Shoah, wearing their distinctive blue neck scarves, listen to Pope John Paul's speech at the Papal Concert to Commemorate the Shoah.

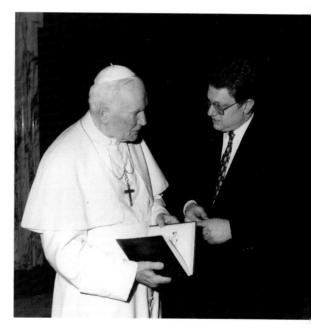

His Holiness and I discuss the facsimile of the Sarajevo Haggadah, a fourteenth-century illuminated manuscript of the Jewish Passover ritual, which I presented to the Pope in gratitude for his belief in and support for the Papal Concert to Commemorate the Shoah.

At his Archbishop's residence in Paris, Cardinal Lustiger presents me with the honorific sword at my Investiture as a Knight-Commander of the Pontifical Equestrian Order of Saint Gregory the Great, December 1994, the first such papal honor accorded a non-ecclesiastical musician in more than two hundred years.

Inside his private chapel in St. Peter's, Pope John Paul and I prayed silently and mourned the assassination of Prime Minister Rabin in 1995. Afterward His Holiness asked, "If he is gone, can there be peace?"

In June 1995, the Bavarian State Orchestra and I bow after performing Schubert's "Unfinished" Symphony at our concert "In Memory of the Victims of the Holocaust" in Munich. We are in the Ludwig-Maximillian University, the center for the "White Rose," the Nazi-era students' resistance movement.

Pope John Paul II listens as the Philharmonia Orchestra and Chorus and I perform Haydn's "Creation," in honor and celebration of His Holiness' eightieth birthday, May 18, 2000. As an encore, we sang "Sto Lat!" (Happy Birthday) in his native Polish.

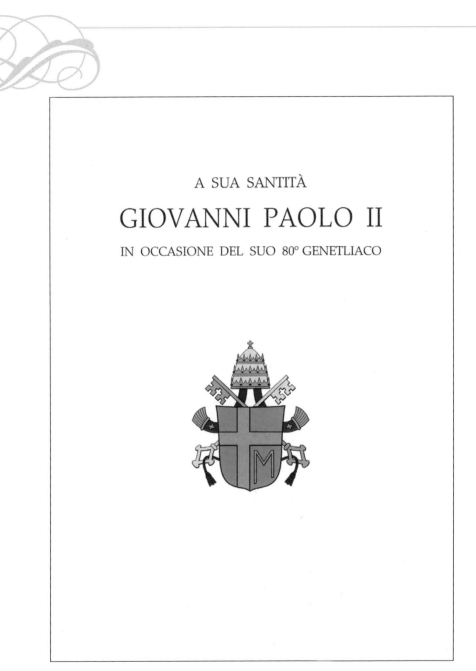

A SUA SANTITÀ

GIOVANNI PAOLO II

IN OCCASIONE DEL SUO 80° GENETLIACO

The front page of the forty-page, lavishly illustrated program booklet for the Papal Concert in honor of Pope John Paul's eightieth birthday, May 18, 2000.

The hierarchy of the Roman Curia—the Cardinals, Archbishops, and Bishops who govern the Holy See—were an all-important part of the 7,500-person audience attending the Sala Nervi concert in honor of Pope John Paul's eightieth birthday.

In the Papal Study at Castel Gandolfo, His Holiness and I discuss a concert I conducted at the Church of Saints Peter and Paul in Kraków. The Staatskapelle Dresden and the Munich Bach Choir joined me there to perform the Brahms Requiem to mark the first anniversary of 9/11.

"Reconciliation." Pope John Paul II, with Abdulawahab Hussein Gomaa, Imam of the Mosque of Rome, and Rav Elio Toaff, Chief Rabbi of Rome, preside at my performance of Mahler's Second Symphony ("Resurrection") with the Pittsburgh Symphony and choirs from Pittsburgh, London, Ankara, and Kraków at the Papal Concert of Reconciliation, January 17, 2004.

My wife, Vera, and I, with Archbishop Dziwisz in the background, at our last audience with Pope John Paul II, January 20, 2004.

PREFETTURA DELLA CASA PONTIFICIA

Concerto della Riconciliazione

Concert of Reconciliation

קונצרט הפיוס

حفل موسيقي من أجل المصالحة

alla presenza di Sua Santità

Giovanni Paolo II

Città del Vaticano - Aula Paolo VI
sabato 17 gennaio 2004 - ore 18,30

The front page of the forty-eight-page program booklet for the Papal Concert of Reconciliation, January 17, 2004, which contained beautiful four-color paintings by Brother Kenneth Chapman accompanied by selections from Pope John Paul's many writings on peace and reconciliation.

As part of our last audience with the Pope, our sons, David and Gabriel, converse with His Holiness. He always showed them affection, warmth, and great interest in their development.

His Holiness with Vera, Gabriel, David, and I on January 20, 2004. I am about to present Pope John Paul II with a specially bound conductor's score of John Harbison's "Abraham," which had had its premiere at the Papal Concert of Reconciliation three days before.

Our music-making was functioning that evening as the accompaniment to the most sacred rite in the Catholic liturgy, the celebration of the Eucharist. Mozart himself knew this very well when he composed this masterpiece. He would never have imagined it being performed outside a church service. This great orchestra and I would be lending our musical voices to the much more important proceeding that Cardinal Lustiger and his concelebrating priests would be undertaking that evening: welcoming the birth of Jesus in one of his most beautiful houses of worship in the world. Music, for this special occasion, would be the servant of the word. The precise length of the Sanctus, a part of the Mass that, as I had learned at World Youth Day in Denver, traces its origins to the Jewish liturgy of the Kadosh, was therefore essential information for His Eminence as he planned his liturgical service. He needed to know that our music would not interfere with the proper celebration of this Holy Rite. My answer, that the Sanctus of the Mozart Coronation Mass would last only a minute and a half, seemed to quiet whatever concerns he had about the appropriateness of the work I had chosen for this wonderful occasion.

Thus chastened, I paid close attention to everything His Eminence said in our one and only conversation about my duties in the cathedral that night. In this, too, I was thinking about Mozart, who by contrast had had a frosty relationship with the Archbishop whom he served, Hieronymus Colloredo in Salzburg. Count Colloredo would later, proverbially, kick perhaps the greatest musical genius who ever lived out of his house and thus out of his noble service, for the sin of undue pride. Mozart wanted to have his music heard by all the world. Prince-Archbishop Colloredo simply wanted his servants to know their place.

But I was in the hands of a true friend. Cardinal Lustiger asked me to watch him carefully. He in turn would keep his eye on me, so as not to let me go astray. His Eminence also asked how much music we had for the Communion Rite. I looked at him blankly. He smiled, and said not to worry. When he gave the signal, we should play through passages of quiet contemplation, and then, when we ran out of music for this place in the service, the organist of the cathedral would play on, improvising if need be, until every one of the five thousand or more in attendance had received Holy Communion. It was all so very new to me, even after my six years in the Catholic world. It would be as if I were conducting this work for the very first time. And in a sense I would be. Music in service to God was meant to be just that. I was in for an exciting, if nerve-wracking, new musical experience.

When I arrived on Christmas Eve, I saw the miracle of candle-light setting stone afire. The entire cathedral was set with votive candles, at every level, high into the vaulted ceiling. Notre Dame seemed to float on a bed of gentle flame. The church was filled to overflowing. Thousands of Parisians, French from outside the capital, and foreign tourists jammed in, until I thought the huge doors separating Notre Dame from the Grand Place outside would never close. That didn't stop people from crowding forward. And in those days before the JumboTron, the Place du Parvis Notre Dame was filled with tens of thousands who would listen to the service and our music on loud-speakers placed outside, in weather not fit for an Eskimo. *Cold* was a word that did not begin to encompass the freezing weather of that magical Christmas Eve.

I entered the church by the side entrance and looked for Cardinal Lustiger. I was told he was *"très occupé"*—very busy. Of course he was. This was Christmas Eve, and this was his realm. This was a night he would share with his flock, the entire Catholic population of the city of Paris and all France. There would be ten or more concelebrating priests, some from his Archdiocese and some even from foreign countries, whom His Eminence had invited especially for this occasion.

All this pomp and circumstance made me even more nervous. I needn't have worried. As it happened, we began our music-making with the levée, a concert meant to bring all those assembled up to the spiritual level of the Mass. We performed glorious music of Mendelssohn, Bach, and Berlioz, whose music had filled this and so many other great French cathedrals through the years. By the time the Mass began, we were well into our music-making, and it all went so much better than I could have imagined. In any case, my chest stopped pounding after the Kyrie, the opening movement of the Mozart Mass. We settled in to making music, so transcendent that even after repeated performances it still sends chills down my spine to think it was composed by a mortal like ourselves. I reveled, but I could not quite relax until the last Dona Nobis Pacem that ends Mozart's gorgeous Mass.

As Cardinal Lustiger recessed out of the cathedral, leading his train of priests and acolytes into their vestry, he gave me a knowing, brotherly smile. He thanked me with his eyes for the music we had provided and gave me a visual pat on the back for getting through his Catholic liturgical labyrinth. I had not come in with music in the wrong place. I had stopped and started where I was supposed to. And for all this, I said, *"Laus Deo"*—Thanks be to God. It had been quite a week. Again, my family and friends and I repaired to a great Parisian restaurant, this time Lucas Carton, and the champagne flowed into the early hours of Christmas Day. But as grateful as I was for the gift of the Papal Knighthood, and for the remarkable chance to please my Cardinal friend by bringing Mozart to his Mass at Notre Dame, my journey in service to His Holiness, and the true meaning of this high honor, would soon begin to unfold in even more surprising ways.

The Papal Concert to Commemorate the Shoah continued to reverberate in many ways long after the last notes faded away on April 7, 1994. In addition to the continuing admiration for this remarkable event that I heard from Jews, especially from survivors, it had been rebroadcast over and over on PBS through the auspices of WNET President Bill Baker and his fabulous team at Thirteen in New York. The impact of television in spreading the good word to millions across the United States and around the world had never been so clear.

After the Papal Shoah Concert my mother-in-law, Margit Kalina, seemed to be a changed person. She was calmer, outwardly at least, more at peace. On the wall of her small, otherwise blank-walled bedroom in her apartment in New York, next to the pictures of her mother and father, and her brother Poldi, all murdered by the Nazis, there now hung a picture of herself with Pope John Paul II. Her forty relatives could never be brought back, let alone the scores of their descendants who would never be born, but her experience with His Holiness had answered at least one of her prayers: her silent plea that someone hear the voices of her loved ones crying out and honor their memories, so that they might not have died in vain. I believe that, in a way, just as I had done the concert for her, so in part had Pope John Paul. And she knew and felt that powerfully also.

Elie Wiesel, who had regrettably not attended the concert in Rome, now warmly welcomed its success. In early July 1994, Vera and

I were invited to an elegant soiree at the country home of two of Elie's closest friends. After dinner, Elie quietly took me aside. He thanked me most sincerely for the concert. Then, in his friend's small den, we put a videotape into their machine and watched the Papal event. Elie told me how deeply moved he was by the way in which we had rightly honored the Shoah and the memory of the six million in the very heart of Christianity, in Rome.

The publicity surrounding my Papal Knighthood was also extensive. The *New York Times* published a story, as did many other mainstream newspapers around the country. But none of these caught my eye like the story that appeared in *America*, the national Catholic weekly published in the United States. There on the cover of this Jesuit magazine was a picture of me in my finest summer whites, with an article entitled "The Pope's Maestro." I don't know why I was so surprised, except perhaps that I hadn't thought the significance of my Papal honor would be understood so quickly and so well inside the Catholic Church. My relationship with His Holiness was evidently newsworthy in its own right, but it was also a lesson in brotherly respect and understanding that the broader Catholic world, outside the Vatican, seemed now to be welcoming most openly.

The Knighthood and the Shoah concert also generated several musical offspring. I was invited to conduct concerts to commemorate the Holocaust in cities across America and in Europe. Cardinal Keeler invited me to create a concert for him in the glorious Basilica of the Assumption in Baltimore, America's oldest Catholic cathedral. And, after the American Jewish Committee had awarded me their Interreligious Award for 1994, the AJC's Twin Cities Chapter asked me to conduct an event for them in Saint Paul, Minnesota. Both of these were considered to be of such significance that NPR elected to broadcast them nationally.

The Baltimore Symphony made a wonderful partner for the concert, which we called "A Symphony of Psalms: A Celebration of Our Common Heritage." We performed the exquisite "Symphony of Psalms" by Stravinsky, Brahms' psalm settings from his "German Requiem," and two pieces from the Papal Concert to Commemorate the Shoah, Schubert's Psalm 92 and Bernstein's Chichester Psalms. In an interesting innovation, Cardinal Keeler and Rabbi Alexander Schindler, the head of the Union of American Hebrew Congregations, recited the psalms in English before we performed each of their texts in the works' original language: Latin, German, and Hebrew.

In Minnesota we had the most welcome participation of the Saint Paul Chamber Orchestra, a great American ensemble. Through Bernard Gersten, the Executive Producer of Lincoln Center Theater, we were able to entice the distinguished American actor Sam Waterston to come to the Twin Cities to recite poems written by children who were murdered at Terezin during the Shoah. When interspersed with the incidental music from Beethoven's Egmont, a drama about true heroism in the face of terrible tyranny, these became a searing depiction of the extremes of the human spirit—the depth of human depravity and cruelty, and the courage and hope that can shine through even in the darkest of times.

But it was a concert in Munich, performed on June 20, 1995, that was the most difficult and the most important of the offspring of the Papal Concert to Commemorate the Shoah in Rome. It would be the first-ever concert to commemorate the Holocaust in the capital of Bavaria, where the Nazi movement had been born.

Not long after April 1994, Jack Eisner, who had organized the participation of survivors from around the world for our Papal Concert, invited me up to his fancy apartment on Fifth Avenue high above Central Park. Jack asked me to sit down. He told me he had an idea.

"Gilbert, you know, the fiftieth anniversary of the liberation of Flossenbürg is coming up next year. That's the last place I was held. I was liberated from there. It was a small camp, near Munich, but this anniversary means a lot to me. Would you consider doing a concert there to commemorate that liberation from Flossenbürg? Maybe we could do it even in Munich, which is a couple hours away. They have good orchestras there, in Munich, no?"

I was very uneasy. This seemed a step too far. Munich for me was two places. First of all, it was the most elegant city in Germany, with a grace and charm as a cultural center that no other city, not Berlin nor Hamburg, could match. It was home to a great opera house, the Bavarian State Opera, and—Jack was right—it boasted at least three important symphony orchestras and was visited by many major touring ensembles. In fact, just before the Papal Concert in December 1988, I had brought the Kraków Philharmonic to the new Philharmonie concert hall in Munich as the final event on our German tour. But still I was unsettled by Jack's heartfelt proposal.

Munich was also the birthplace of the Third Reich—the Beer Hall Putsch, the Brown Shirts of Hitler's first thuggish cadres, the very heart of evil. That was now sixty years ago, true, but still it somehow shook me to the core. I could go to Munich and happily participate in their newly resurrected preeminent place in European cultural life. But its history in World War II haunted me in a way I could not fully explain, and that feeling rose up in me in response to my friend Jack and his need to search for closure at Flossenbürg. A Holocaust concert in Munich. I wasn't so sure.

"Jack, I just don't know. Didn't we achieve all that we needed to at the Vatican? Isn't this really a step too far?" I asked.

"Gilbert, maybe so, but let's see. Come with me. Let's go together there to Munich. I have a contact. Someone high up on in the Ministry. Let's go talk to him. I think it could work. OK? Please!" Jack implored.

I couldn't say no, not to Jack after what he had contributed to the Papal Concert, and so off we flew to Germany.

We arrived at the Bavarian Ministry of Education, Public Worship, Science, and Art and were escorted in to meet a certain Herr Manfred Heger. He greeted us rather coolly, with proper respect, but nothing more. Jack and I were disappointed with this low-key reaction to Jack's impassioned plea for a Flossenbürg commemorative concert. More importantly, though, Herr Heger was not the person Jack had expected to meet, and this made him very unhappy.

"I was expecting to meet the Minister. In any case, someone very high up. I was promised that he would be here. I came all the way from New York with Maestro Levine here, and I want to see the person in charge." Jack's veins rose in his neck as he addressed Herr Heger.

It was clear to me that Herr Heger was a bureaucrat doing his job, nothing more, nothing less. He had been delegated to receive us, and he was doing his duty. As Jack remonstrated, Herr Heger sat calmly, seeming to let it all roll off his back. It was soon clear to me that this was going nowhere. After ten minutes of Jack demanding to see the Minister and Herr Heger saying that would not be possible just now, Jack got up and stormed out, dragging me along. Herr Heger stood up behind his desk as we exited his office, incongruously thanking us for our visit. He seemed genuinely surprised by this turn of events, but it was too late.

Out on the street, in front of the Ministry, Jack explained that he had written everything in a letter to the Minister and had received what he had believed was an encouraging reply from someone in the Minister's office. He thought that surely if he came all this way he would be meeting with someone important, someone who would understand what this was all about, someone who would help him realize his idea. Now, after his encounter with Herr Heger, this would be it for Jack. He was out, he was through. And before I knew it, as quickly as we had arrived in the city on the River Isar, we were back on a plane, winging our way to New York.

As I sat next to him on the plane, I had the feeling that something much deeper was going on inside Jack Eisner, something had caused him to come to Munich already at full boil. True, Herr Heger had not been so very sympathetic; yet he was, after all, doing his duty. But after what Jack had suffered during the war, after watching so many of his family and friends murdered before his eyes, to Jack Eisner that correctness was an insult in itself. It was unacceptable. Heger's reaction had ended the whole idea. Jack seemed completely crushed.

On our way in the taxi from Kennedy Airport, Jack exclaimed, "Gilbert, the Germans! I just couldn't take it. It was like I was back in the war. It was too much!" As I listened sympathetically, I thought about Jack as a survivor of the Holocaust. To me, that gave him very special rights, particularly the right to see the world in a way that those of us who have not come so close to the heart of darkness cannot ever hope to fully comprehend.

Jack begged my forgiveness for having gotten me involved and said we would find someplace else to do another concert together. "Gilbert, we will do it again. We'll just find a better place!"

I can't say that I was entirely disappointed with the way things had turned out with Jack in Munich. I had a lot on my plate just then, and I had my own Munich Holocaust demons to deal with as well.

Back in New York, I returned to my work and my life, trying to put our whirlwind trip to Germany out of my mind, when the telephone rang in my apartment. A woman with a German accent asked, "Gilbert Levine? Is this Maestro Levine?"

"Yes? May I ask who is calling?" I replied. I don't know why, but I felt my hackles rise.

"This is Ulrike Hessler, from the Bavarian State Opera. This is Maestro Levine? Yes? I understand you were in Munich recently, at the Ministry, to talk about doing a concert here. A Holocaust concert, yes? I am calling to say, I hope you will still reconsider doing this. It would mean a great deal to many people here if you did. Including, I must say, myself."

I was surprised. And I was still somewhat unsettled by my recent trip to Munich. "Frau Hessler," I said, "I guess you know I was in Munich with Jack Eisner, a Holocaust survivor, and yes, he and I met at the Ministry with someone who did not seem so very interested in such a concert. I have to tell you, Mr. Eisner was deeply offended."

"Well, that is why I am calling. Herr Heger thinks you may have misunderstood him. And I, as I said, am personally very interested in this idea. Can we at least talk about it?"

For some reason, I was both wary and a bit afraid of this woman. I didn't know her at all. But I also felt a grudging acknowledgment of the courage it had taken for her to call after what she must have heard from Herr Heger about his meeting with Jack and myself in Munich.

Frau Doctor Hessler went on, "You know, I think there may be something very important here. I am a member of the Munich chapter of the Overseas Board of Tel Aviv University. I have many friends in the Jewish community, both here in Germany and in Israel. I believe we can do something historic together. Please think this over once again."

Finally, I said, calming down just a bit, "Yes, I understand. Many thanks for your call. Really, I appreciate it. May I think about this, please? May I call you back? There are some people here that I need to speak with."

"Yes, yes, of course. Thank you for thinking about this. Let us speak again soon," she said, and rang off.

I got off the phone in a bit of a shock. Who was this woman? Her voice was so calm, and I sensed that she was sincerely interested in bringing something good out of this very bad situation. But the answer to her request would have to wait just a little while.

First I had to call Jack. We had not spoken since we returned from Germany. He was still very upset. I told him about the call I had received that day, and I was really surprised by his response.

"Gilbert, you know, I think you should go ahead and try. Maybe you can do it. Maybe this was just too much for me. Maybe I was foolish. Who knows? The memories for me are still too fresh. But if you think something good can come out, then go. Try to do it. Go see them. Listen, you did it in Rome. Nobody thought you could. But you did. Why not in Munich too? I know you'll make us proud. That you'll honor us there. Go and try." Then he said, in Yiddish, "Go in good health."

I heard resignation in Jack's voice, maybe even a bit of fatalism, that he could not go "there"; but maybe I, who was a generation removed from the pain he still suffered, maybe, just maybe I could. Perhaps Jack realized his limits and hoped for a better future brought forward by those with younger eyes than his own. Those who had not seen what he had.

With Jack's reaction in mind, on my next trip to Rome I raised the idea of a Holocaust concert in Munich with Monsignor Dziwisz. His answer was very quick, as if he were one step ahead of me.

"Yes, you know, Maestro, that is a wonderful idea. Maybe you can do in Munich something like you did here in Rome. It won't be easy, but then, we know that, no? And you will have the support of a very good man, Cardinal Wetter, the Archbishop in Munich. He will be very helpful, I am sure. Go, and you must let me know how this progresses."

So with these two vital blessings, I now went to Munich to personally encounter Frau Doctor Ulrike Hessler. When you meet Ulrike Hessler, you are first impressed by her elegant carriage. She is tall, thin, and oftentimes bespectacled. She shows intelligent sympathy and great authority at the same time, a very rare combination of attributes. In person, as opposed to on the telephone, she made me feel at ease. At our very first meeting I knew she was right. It would be possible to achieve something important, especially with her as my new German partner.

I told Ulrike that I had spoken with Jack Eisner and that he had agreed I should go and see where this idea might lead. And I related to her that after my talk in the Apostolic Palace we would have the support of the Catholic Church at the very highest levels. I said that I would like to "re-produce" the Papal Concert to Commemorate the Shoah of April 1994, but with a specifically German character and cast. It should be a program that represented the Holocaust from the German cultural perspective. I suggested that we perform Bruch's Kol Nidre and Bernstein's Kaddish Symphony excerpt, just as we had done at the Vatican. But I proposed that we also do Mahler's "Kindertotenlieder" (Songs on the Death of Children) and Schubert's "Unfinished" Symphony on this Munich concert.

Ulrike thought this program seemed most appropriate and told me what she had in mind from a performance point of view. The Bavarian Government, despite what Jack might have thought after the meeting with Herr Heger, was most eager to see this concert go forward successfully. The Ministry had even offered its own Bavarian State Orchestra, the orchestra of the Bavarian State Opera, where Ulrike was head of the Office of Communications, to perform at the event. The Bavarian State Opera would make available any soloists engaged by the Opera that we might need, and they would organize the concert in the hall of my choice.

I was astonished. All this was more than I could ever have expected. The Government of Bavaria, on its own initiative, was taking the concert very seriously.

I thanked Ulrike. It all sounded wonderful. I said, "I know your orchestra by reputation. They are excellent, and I am sure you will find wonderful soloists from among your ensemble as well. Regarding the hall," I said, "might I suggest the Philharmonie? I conducted the Kraków Philharmonic there on tour a few years back. I really loved the acoustics."

"Well, yes, perhaps. It is a very good hall, but it is maybe not the best place. It's so new, and not so very appropriate for this concert."

"OK, then what about the Herkulessaal?" I replied. "It's older and also a renowned concert hall here in Munich. A lot of musical history has taken place there."

Ulrike demurred once again. "Yes, the Herkulessaal is wonderful, just not quite right for this occasion either." I felt like I was back at the Vatican suggesting places for the Papal Shoah Concert.

I found myself repeating the same question I had asked in Rome. "Well, Frau Dr. Hessler, do you have an idea?" We had just about run out of halls in Munich, that I knew of.

"Yes," Ulrike said. "I do have an idea. I think this historic concert, the first-ever Holocaust memorial concert in Munich, should take place in a very special hall and one that is uniquely appropriate for such an event: the Great Hall, the Aula, in the Ludwig-Maximillian University. The hall most closely associated with the 'Weisse Rose,' the 'White Rose.'"

She needed to say no more. It all became so clear to me. Of course. The White Rose. That was the German student resistance movement that had flourished for a brief time from June 1942 to February 1943 at the famous Munich university where the *aula* Ulrike was now proposing was located. In that building, right outside the Great Hall, Hans and Sophie Scholl, brother and sister, and their stalwart comrades led by their professor (a musicologist!) named Kurt Huber, had bravely defied the Nazis. There they had distributed leaflets decrying the persecution of the Jews and the abrogation of civil rights so dear to their notion of Germany's best historic ideals. From that balcony, right next to the Aula, Nazi-resisting students had been thrown to their deaths by members of the Hitler Youth. There was indeed no better place for this concert, no place more meaningful for Germans to remember the very best of their forebears' resistance to such all-pervasive evil.

That spirit of resistance could be summed up in the leaflets that the White Rose had distributed, leaflets that led directly to the students' arrest and execution at the hands of the Gestapo. They were courageous and honest beyond all measure. Their leaflets read, in part:

> Isn't it true that every honest German is ashamed of his government these days? Who among us has any conception of the dimensions of shame that will befall us and our children when one day the veil has fallen from our eyes and the most horrible of crimes—crimes that infinitely outdistance every human measure—reach the light of day?—From the first leaflet of the White Rose

> Since the conquest of Poland three hundred thousand Jews have been murdered in this country in the most bestial way. . . . The German people slumber on in their dull, stupid sleep and encourage these fascist criminals. . . . Each man wants to be exonerated of a guilt of this kind, each one continues on his way with the most placid, the calmest conscience. But he cannot be exonerated; he is guilty, guilty, guilty!—From the second leaflet of the White Rose

It was this history of the White Rose and these extraordinary sentiments that made the Aula the perfect place for our Munich Holocaust concert.

"And in any case," Ulrike told me, "the University itself has offered the hall as part of its sponsorship of this event. They will join the Bavarian Ministry and the Bavarian State Opera as the entities organizing this historic concert. And the proceeds from ticket sales will go to the Fund for Anti-Semitism Research at Tel Aviv University."

Wow! I couldn't believe my ears. I only wished Jack Eisner had stayed the course and been at my side to hear this marvelous news.

Ulrike said that she thought that, as Monsignor Dziwisz had said, Cardinal Wetter would be as helpful as we needed him to be, but that the difficulty might come from the Jewish community. She just did not know how eager the Chief Rabbi would be to get involved.

"You will have to go to the Jewish Community Center and present yourself to Frau Charlotte Knobloch, the President of the Bavarian Jewish Community, to see what she could do to induce the Rabbi to agree to attend. But watch out for Frau Knobloch. She is a formidable woman. First, she will have to size you up for herself."

Thus forewarned, I went to the Jewish Community Center in Munich to have a kosher meal with Frau Knobloch. She is a Munich-born Jew who had endured the Holocaust and returned to help with the resuscitation of the Jewish presence in her home city and in the surrounding Bavarian province. This reflowering of Jewish culture had been no easy task, and her iron will had been a great asset in these postwar struggles. In 1995 she still carried those efforts on with great force of will, just as she does today.

As we ate, Frau Knobloch and I talked. She told me, "You know, I followed your event in Rome. That was something special. It had great meaning for us here in Germany, what this Pope has done. And so, I will do what I can to assist your event in Munich as well. In any case, you have a wonderful helper in Frau Doctor Hessler. She is such a friend of our community. But the Rabbi, he has his own opinions. He is a bit more conservative than I am. I will tell him that I met you, and I believe this concert will be a good thing. I will tell him that you are a man with a kind heart, and I will suggest to him that he should attend. But we will just have to see how he reacts. He will have to make up his own mind." Frau Knobloch was all that Ulrike had said she was and more. After meeting her, I knew that it was much better to have her as a friend than any other way.

My rehearsals with the Bavarian State Orchestra were a joy. I must say, from my side, I brought a lot of preconceived notions to this music-making. First, there was the memory of Richard Strauss, one of the twentieth century's most important composers. He had had a very close association with the Bavarian State Opera and its orchestra, and had served briefly and most unfortunately in the 1930s as the President of the Reich's Musikkammer, the body ceremonially overseeing the Nazi government's oppressive musical regime. Some still held it against him that he had remained in Nazi Germany throughout the war.

Then there was the extraordinary coincidence that this had also been the orchestra of my esteemed mentor, Sir Georg Solti, from 1946 to 1952. Maestro Solti (born Gyorgy Stern) had fled the Nazi invasion of his native Budapest, lived out the war years playing the piano in Switzerland, and then, as a total neophyte, was rewarded with the exalted Music Directorship of the Bavarian State Opera and its Bavarian State Orchestra by the American military authorities who then occupied Bavaria. By 1995 Maestro Solti had become, of course, one of the towering figures in the classical musical world. He had been the extraordinarily successful Music Director of the Chicago Symphony from 1969 until 1991, had graced the cover of *Time* magazine, and could choose to be a guest conductor of pretty much any orchestra in the world. I never had the chance to talk to the Maestro about this Munich Holocaust concert with his old orchestra: he died not long thereafter. But the irony and the appropriateness of their participation would, I believe, not have been at all lost on him.

I was delighted by the Bavarian State Orchestra's ease and familiarity with the works on our program. The Mahler particularly seemed familiar to them. In fact, Mahler had composed his "Kindertotenlieder" in a tiny mountain chalet in Maiernigg in the Austrian province of Carinthia, just a few hours' drive from where we were now rehearsing his songs in Munich.

During our rehearsals, we had had an interesting discussion with the member of the Bavarian Jewish community who, through Frau Knobloch, had volunteered to recite the Kaddish during the Bernstein, as Richard Dreyfuss had done at the Vatican. This man kept insisting that he should read the words in German. "Everyone there will understand them that way, no?" he had said.

I explained that the idea was to recite them in memory of the six million, in Aramaic, the language that all of the Holocaust's victims (whether they were from Germany, Austria, France, Poland, Hungary, Greece, Bulgaria, Holland, Belgium, or any of the other countries that had had their Jewish citizens murdered by the Nazis) would have understood. And besides, I reminded him, Aramaic was the daily language of Jesus. It was the linguistic tie that binds all Christians to Jews. He finally agreed, and recited the prayer in Aramaic as he did in synagogue multiple times every day of his Jewish adult religious life.

The atmosphere before the concert was full of anticipation. Dignitaries from the Bavarian Government were present. The Minister himself, Hans Zehetmair, the personage whom perhaps Jack Eisner had thought he would meet, was in the first row. Alongside him was Ulrike Hessler, and next to her was Peter Jonas CBE, her boss as the Intendant of the entire Bavarian State Opera. I knew Peter only slightly from his days as Administrative Assistant to Sir Georg Solti at the Chicago Symphony, during the time I first came to know the Maestro before beginning my work with him in Europe. Peter, looking very distinguished, a bit more gray-haired than I had remembered him, also looked slightly unsettled by what was about to occur. Perhaps he just didn't know what to expect, not having been intimately involved in the event's preparations.

His Eminence Friedrich Cardinal Wetter, true to what Monsignor Dziwisz had promised, came early and was seated in the center of the audience on the right side of the aisle. Frau Knobloch was there early as well. But the seat next to her was empty. We were all waiting for the Chief Rabbi to appear. Finally, almost at the last moment, he walked in quietly and took his seat just across the center aisle, opposite Cardinal Wetter. No one could remember ever having seen these two most important religious leaders of Bavaria at a public event together before. It was a historic occasion, if only just for that.

As at the Shoah concert in Rome, everyone sat in silence as six chosen survivors stepped forward and lit the six candles in the menorah.

The sight of those candles burning in this hall, in this building, beside that stairway leading to the balcony that had seen so much pain and suffering, was almost too much to bear. I hoped that the Scholls, their brave comrades, and their music professor mentor all were looking down at us with pride. What we were trying to do was at least partly in their honor.

The whole musical program proved to be exactly right. The cellist for Bruch's Kol Nidre, Franz Amann, a soloist from the orchestra, confided that he had never fully understood the meaning of this work until he had performed it as part of this "Concert in Memory of the Victims of the Holocaust," as it was called. And the mezzo-soprano, Daphne Evangelatos, told me that the shattering words of these songs which depict Mahler's intense pain on the inexplicable death of children had never affected her as much as they did on this occasion. She sang the last lines of "Kindertotenlieder," "No ills can now betide them, for God's own hand will guide them, they rest as on their mother's breast," so achingly that one would have thought she would break down. But it was the rest of us she left near tears.

The performance of the Schubert went as well as I could remember. There was something so appropriate about playing a symphony that ends softly but says much that is powerful along the way. Contrary to common thought, Schubert "chose" not to finish this work. He did not die or become incapacitated before he could do so. He wanted it to end without a clear and forceful resolution, but in quiet resolve and at peace, leaving the listener much to contemplate after the last orchestral chord fades away.

After the performance, Ulrike and her husband, Michael, came to greet me. He said he had never heard the piece conducted that way, that it sounded as if he were hearing it for the very first time. His and Ulrike's professional praise was music to my ears, coming from people so attuned to German art and music.

But the evening's most affecting moment happened, not in the Aula itself, but on the way to my car in the rain that night. Peter Jonas, the great Intendant of the Bavarian State Opera, shielding me from the downpour with his umbrella, walked with me side by side. As I was getting into the car, he leaned down from his great height, with tears seemingly glistening in his eyes, and said, "Thank you so very much for what you did here. Thank you for this evening of wonderful music-making. It meant more to me than you can ever know. You see, Gilbert, my father was Jewish. He was a German Jew from Hamburg. He survived the war, escaping with his life from the Nazis. I have told almost no one about this. I don't exactly know why. But that you could do this concert, here in this special hall, brings my father's memory back to me so vividly. I thank you from the bottom of my heart."

Peter and I had hardly exchanged a word in all the years that we knew each other. I had worked hard on this concert with his great institution, but mostly with his right-hand lady, Frau Doctor Hessler. I had had no inkling of what Peter's own attitude towards this event might have been. Now, after our brief postconcert talk, that at least was just a bit clearer to me. Maybe that is why he had seemed a bit unsettled as he waited for our music to begin.

But more than that, now I knew why I had gone through with this concert. In a sense, I had done it for Peter Jonas—for not ever letting memory die. And for Jack Eisner, and all the survivors, and for their loved ones, families, and friends. And finally, for a whole generation of Germans who were Jews. German Jews and their descendants who were not allowed to live to see this day.

Ulrike, Michael, and I shared a private late night supper at an Italian restaurant down the street from the Vier Jahreszeiten Hotel, the wonderful Munich hostelry where I had hung my hat during my stay. We toasted to our success, but I raised a glass more than once to our friendship. For that is what Ulrike and I had become. Friends.

The first chance I got, I went to Rome to report back to Monsignor Dziwisz. I started to tell him all about our evening. He laughed and stopped me short. "Maestro, I know. I have already heard. Bravo to you on your important success in Munich. Now then, Maestro, what's next?"

I looked at him and said, "Well, Monsignor, interesting you should ask. I may just have a few more ideas I'd like to share."

CHAPTER

TWENTY-THREE

S aturday evening, November 4, 1995, my wife and I were in our
kitchen preparing a dinner at our home for our new friend
Winnie de Montesquieu and his young son. They were visiting
New York, and we had promised to show them the same hospitality
in our home that Winnie had shown us when we had been welcomed
to his flat in Paris. We had met Winnie when I was conducting the
Messe de Minuit at Notre Dame. Winnie is the Baron de Montesquieu,
heir to an ancient aristocratic title, and as such was fascinated, he said,
to find out how it felt to be the actual person in a family who had
achieved a noble rank. I was sorry to disappoint Winnie by telling him
that since the nineteenth century Pontifical Knighthoods could not
be passed down from father to son. The Levine noble line would most
likely stop with me.

Not only were we preparing dinner for Winnie and his son,
but my bags were packed and ready in the next room, for I was on my
way to the Vatican the very next night. I had a very full schedule
planned out in Rome. A meeting with Monsignor Dziwisz, a coffee in
the private apartment of Cardinal Cassidy, a meeting with Dr. Solange
de Maillerdoz, the Head of International Relations for Vatican Radio,
and a luncheon appointment with two good friends at the Vatican, Dr.
Marjorie Weeke, the Head of Audio-Visual Services at the Pontifical
Commission for Social Communication, and her boss, Archbishop
John Foley, the President of that important Vatican office. By seeing

Drs. Weeke and de Maillerdoz, I was meeting with two of the most highly placed laywomen in the Vatican's rarified hierarchy.

At some point in our dinner preparations, Vera and I decided to find out what was on the news. What we saw when we tuned in stunned us. Prime Minister Itzhak Rabin of Israel, the 1994 Laureate of the Nobel Prize for Peace, had been assassinated at a peace rally that very evening in Tel Aviv. This was unimaginable. Why would anyone want to do such a thing?! Then we heard that the killer was a fellow Jew, a right-wing fanatic who could not abide Rabin's efforts to bring peace to the Holy Land. I was furious, in shock, and completely uncertain about what to do next.

All through our dinner we debated. Should I cancel my trip, or should I go? But then I was going to the Vatican, not to Israel, and the officials I was going to see were not in the Vatican's diplomatic service. My personal shock and grief would remain just that, personal, whether I was in Rome or New York. I wasn't such good company that evening, but I hoped that the Baron de Montesquieu understood.

The following night I boarded my nonstop flight to Fiumicino Airport, from where I set off straightaway to my home away from home, the ivy-walled Hotel Raphael, next to the Piazza Navona and a mere ten-minute walk from the Vatican. After a quick shower and change I made my way across the bridge over the Tiber and passed the Castel Sant'Angelo, turned left, and walked in the direction of Saint Peter's. Just before entering the Via della Conciliazione, I turned right to find the modern building that houses the Catholic Church's voice heard round the world: Radio Vaticana.

Dr. de Maillerdoz greeted me in her cramped office with a wonderful welcome and a broad smile. I was subdued. I couldn't hide from Solange, by now a good friend, that I was deeply troubled by what had taken place in Israel. Dr. de Maillerdoz is a refined noblewoman from an important old Swiss family, who had spent many years in Vatican service. Her extraordinary linguistic skills include French, German, Italian, English, and I was sure, some Latin as well. That polyglot nature and her empathetic personality made her perfectly suited to her job of bringing the Vatican's message to people around the world. She expressed her condolences, although I am American, not Israeli, and gently went on to our agenda for the day.

Vatican Radio was interested in knowing whether my Church-related concerts of the previous months in Baltimore and Saint Paul, which had already been broadcast in the United States, might be suitable for worldwide distribution via Vatican Radio. Solange wanted to know whether I was happy with the musical level of these performances. She wanted my approval before going ahead with the necessary contractual arrangements for broadcast.

My answer was that I couldn't have been more pleased with the Baltimore Symphony and the Saint Paul Chamber Orchestra. If everyone else was happy with the technical aspects, I told her, I was certainly happy to see them shared worldwide.

My next official meeting, a rather informal get-together with Cardinal Cassidy, took place in his large elegant apartment, just inside the Vatican, in the building which had once housed the Holy Office, the dreaded Inquisition that had terrorized church heretics and my Jewish forebears for hundreds of years. Putting that history firmly out of my mind, I rode the elevator up to His Eminence's apartment and was shown into his drawing room. His Eminence walked into the room, his arm outstretched.

"So wonderful you have come, Maestro. I am so pleased to be able to welcome you to my home," he said, smiling broadly and openly, as Australians seem to be so able to do.

We had not seen each other since the Shoah concert of 1994, and the Investiture of my Papal Knighthood. This private coffee was His Eminence's most personal way of saying "well done" once again.

We talked for three-quarters of an hour about the change in Catholic-Jewish relations since our event in April 1994. We reminisced about the event itself, and laughed now about the near misses—mistakes we had thank God avoided, which could have proved so detrimental to our cause. We even talked about music, a love His Eminence and I could share with ease. But most of all Cardinal Cassidy told me of the incredible beneficial effects our concert had had on his work with the Jewish community worldwide.

"The issues still remain difficult," he said in his easy, Aussie-inflected English, "that's for sure. They're not so easy to solve after hundreds of years. But it's like we are brothers and sisters now, engaged in a back-and-forth. It can get pretty heavy still, but it never gets angry, like it sometimes did before. It's what the Holy Father has always wanted, I believe. A dialogue where we could air our differences, and move towards some sort of reconciliation. The Shoah concert has been a great help in all this. And, as I said after the event, we would never have started with that concert if it hadn't been for you."

At the end, when I was about to leave, Cardinal Cassidy said, "Terrible about Prime Minister Rabin! I thought we were finally getting somewhere. Please do say hello to Monsignor Dziwisz for me." I looked at him, just a bit puzzled. How did he know where I was headed? I wondered, but then I knew. I didn't have to ask. This was the Vatican. It was like a small village, and everyone knew everything about everybody, or so it seemed.

I took the elevator down to the bottom floor, and fairly ran across the back of the Vatican, passed three sets of Swiss Guards and the Sediari to get to my five o'clock appointment with Monsignor Dziwisz in the Apostolic Palace. Out of breath, I arrived in his small office, by now so familiar, and waited for the clock to strike the hour.

When he walked through the door at the rear of the room, he too wore a broad grin. This was the first time we had actually seen each other since my knightly investiture. He congratulated me, staring at the rosette, the symbol of my noble rank, that glistened in my lapel. Then he too mentioned Prime Minister Rabin, as if feeling my anguish.

Diffidently, I asked, "You know, Monsignor, I am sure this is not possible, but it would mean so much to me to be able to thank His Holiness personally for the extraordinary honor of this Knighthood. It is not at all necessary. There is nothing in particular for me to discuss with His Holiness just now. But I feel I owe him so much."

Monsignor Dziwisz looked at me for what seemed like a very long time. I returned his gaze, thinking how serious he seemed, that something else entirely seemed to preoccupy him. I feared I had asked too much.

Finally, he said to me, "Maestro, can you come tomorrow to Saint Peter's? His Holiness will be there. Please come to the side entrance of the Basilica, the one on the south side. Someone will be waiting for you there at 12:30 P.M. I believe His Holiness will see you. Maestro, *a domani!*"

I was so pleased with the news that I might possibly be seeing the Pope that it took me a while to realize just what might be in store. For the first time in all my years of knowing him, if I met His Holiness the next day, I would not be seeing him in the Apostolic Palace, or in the Aula Paolo VI, but at Saint Peter's Basilica. Then I thought, what had Monsignor Dziwisz meant when he said, "I believe His Holiness will see you"? I was concerned about the serious look on his face. He clearly had something on his mind. He didn't need to share it with me, of course. Only the Pope would finally decide. But my nervousness grew with each passing hour. It would be difficult to sleep that night.

The next day, at the appointed hour, I presented myself at the South Portal of Saint Peter's. I was met there by an officer of the Swiss Guard, who walked me through a covered hallway away from the entrance, out underneath Bernini's magnificent Monument to Alexander VII, across a short open space to the large wooden organ works off the south side of the apse of the Basilica. I was now just a short distance from the Baldacchino, the stunning canopy above the Papal Altar that dominates the middle of the largest church in all Christendom. There I was left alone.

I could hear the singing and recitations, resounding off the Basilica's hard stone floor, of the Papal Mass being said at the funeral for a Cardinal who had died a few days before. If I craned my neck to my right, I could see His Holiness in white vestments and the many high-ranking Vatican Cardinals in their bright regalia celebrating the Mass along with him. In the front rows of the Basilica were many, many Bishops and Archbishops, some of whose faces I recognized but many, of course, I could not. This was a very High Mass indeed, an important Church occasion. Obviously. I just had no idea at all what I was doing there.

Up until that day, Saint Peter's to me was a beautiful architectural marvel filled with superb treasures: Michelangelo's Pieta, sculptures by Bernini, and so many others. I had visited it many times while I was in Rome but always as a tourist. But I had never attended a Catholic Mass here, let alone one celebrated by His Holiness, and I felt somehow that a mistake had been made. Perhaps I was in the wrong place after all, regardless of what Monsignor Dziwisz had asked me to do.

I waited some twenty minutes for the Mass to end, and the Papal party to recess. His Holiness walked by me with three priests in attendance, Monsignor Dziwisz among them. Neither the Pope nor Monsignor Dziwisz looked my way, nor would I have expected them to. Then the Pontiff and this very small retinue came to a point just ahead of me, turning right towards a marble wall opposite where I was standing. An unseen hand opened a door in that marble wall, a door that had not before been visible. The Pope walked through this door with his short priestly train in tow. No sooner had the marble door opened than it closed again, leaving no sign that there had ever been an opening in that stone wall at all.

Meanwhile, the Cardinals, followed by the Archbishops and Bishops, continued to recess. Among the Cardinals were several whom I knew, including Cardinal Cassidy. As His Eminence walked by me at a stately pace, he turned and caught sight of me, standing by the side of the organ. The smile that had greeted me the day before in his apartment was now all but gone. Instead, he looked at me as if to say, "What are you doing here? This is not your place." I looked back and opened my arms with hands held out as if to say, "Beats me! I have no idea!" He half smiled back, still clearly puzzled by my presence.

Finally, when everyone had left, when all the dignitaries had exited Saint Peter's, I turned to the officer of the Swiss Guard, who was still standing watch, although whom he was guarding was now not so very clear. He stood between me and the door in the wall that was no longer there, and said not a word.

I got his attention. "Perhaps I should go," I said. "His Holiness is clearly very busy now. I can come back another day. Whenever he wishes. Or not at all ..."

The Swiss Guard quietly said, "Please wait here. Maestro, it was requested that you remain right here."

Five minutes went by. Then ten. By now, the Basilica was completely silent. Every last person, whether priest or worshiper, had long since left. I grew smaller and smaller as I shrank with the embarrassment of being in the wrong place at the wrong time. But still I waited, feeling more and more curious.

At last, the invisible door in the marble wall opened once again. Monsignor Dziwisz peered out from behind the door and signaled me with his index finger to follow him back inside. I felt like looking around to see whether there was someone else behind me. This just didn't feel right. But I trusted Monsignor Dziwisz completely, so I followed him inside.

When I walked across the threshold, I found myself in a very small chapel filled with light, despite the curtains that covered all the windows. Three priests and His Holiness were gathered in a room not bigger than an intimate study. On the far wall of windows to my left stood two priests: Monsignor Piero Marini, the Pope's liturgist, and Archbishop Dino Monduzzi, the Prefect of the Pontifical Household, whom I had come to know during the preparations for my Papal Concerts. They both looked at me as if to say the very thing that was on my mind: "What on earth are you doing here?"

Monsignor Dziwisz, however, knew why I was there. He welcomed me warmly, and I could tell he wanted me to feel at ease here in this most private and sacred space. I suddenly felt as if I were in the Holy of Holies, that place in the Temple in Jerusalem where only the Chief Rabbi could enter, and only on Yom Kippur. True, I didn't see the golden cord that the Chief Rabbi let out behind him so that he could be rescued from his encounter with God. But the marble door that was not a door gave my imagination room enough to run.

In the middle of the chapel, his hands clasped in front of him, his eyes tightly closed, sat His Holiness, deep in prayer. He seemed oblivious to all that was going on around him. He certainly took no notice of me as I entered, as quietly as I could.

Monsignor Dziwisz gently guided me towards the praying Pontiff. He carefully positioned me so that I was looking directly into the face of the Pope, and not towards the figure of Jesus on the cross that hung on the wall of the chapel.

I stayed looking into the visage of the Pope as he prayed to his Christ for a very long time. The room was completely silent. No one moved. I could hear my own breath. The Pope prayed silently, not even moving his lips. I found myself drawn deeper and deeper into him, into his prayer. At the same time, in some mysterious way his prayer was becoming my own. I searched my litany of Jewish prayer, then silently said the Kaddish, that ancient prayer in Aramaic that His Holiness' Savior would have said over and over in his daily life as a pious Jew. But soon after that I ran out of worded prayers.

As I stood there, moment following moment, my prayer turned with seamless ease into pure music, the real and true language of my spirit. I imagined in my mind's ear the most beautiful music of God. And then I thought of a place in the Adagio of Bruckner's monumental Symphony No. Nine, the most spiritual work of that most spiritual of all composers, a work Bruckner himself had dedicated to "A Loving God." In this passage, about midway through, aching high strings descend against a rising bass, forming the sonic image of peace in sound. This music now sang in me so strongly that I thought that it must be filling that small sacred room to bursting, that everyone in that chapel could hear Bruckner's immense heart-filled voice. All must be hearing what I was hearing, its placid, soulful call to God. I was lost in this powerful reverie for what seemed like an eternity. The music soared, on and on.

Then, as the Pope was moved from his sitting position to one of kneeling at a prie dieu, Monsignor Dziwisz moved me sideways, inching me forward just enough so that I would remain in my position gazing at the Pontiff. By now the Bruckner Adagio's fluted voice had all but stopped, replaced by silent prayer and, then, by stillness itself. In this stillness, I imagined myself not as one man alone, but it was as if I had been accompanied here, in this Papal Chapel, by millions and millions of my fellow Jews. My mother-in-law, the six million murdered. And the millions of my forebears, who could not have imagined this moment when I, a Jew, would be praying silently with the Vicar of Christ on earth in his Holy of Holies, in Saint Peter's Basilica at the Vatican in Rome.

At last, as if breaking our silent trance, His Holiness was finally helped to his feet. He walked over to me and grasped my hands, looking deep into my eyes. He looked at me with such a penetrating gaze, in fact, that I had to look down, almost ashamed of how small I felt next to him in that room.

Finally, the Pope asked, "With him gone, can there be peace?" The question hung in the air, seemingly for an eternity. I sensed immediately that he was referring to Prime Minister Rabin, but he must have known I could not possibly have an answer. I don't really believe he was asking me. It was the question on his mind and in his prayers that day. But I was surely not the right one to ask. He continued to look at me until I finally raised my eyes to meet his.

And just at that moment, as quiet as it had been before, that small room suddenly became alive again. His Holiness looked at my rosette and proudly congratulated me on my Knighthood. I showed him a video of the Papal Concert to Commemorate the Shoah. I had had so little inkling of what was to happen that I had brought it with me to my Papal audience that day. The Pope seemed pleased and took the gift, quickly handing it to Monsignor Dziwisz. He thanked me again for the concert. I in turn thanked His Holiness from the bottom of my heart for the incredible honor of the Knighthood but even more for the privilege of having been entrusted with the Papal Concert to Commemorate the Shoah. His trust was more valuable than all the honors in the world.

Our friendly conversation went on for a bit. The Pope inquired, "Maestro, how are your sons doing?" Then, he asked me to remember him to my mother-in-law, Margit. "Please tell her that I pray for her." His Holiness smiled strongly, his smile reaching all the way inside me, as if he knew just how moved and how shaken I still was by what had just occurred. And as quickly as that, the Pope and his retinue were gone.

I found my way out of Saint Peter's and across the open space, passed the Vatican Gas Station to the Palazzo San Carlo, where Palestrina, the great Renaissance papal court composer, had once lived and where my friends Dr. Marjorie Weeke and Archbishop Foley now worked. I plopped myself down, exhausted, in a chair in Marjorie's office and said, "You won't believe where I have just been, and what I have just experienced." After knowing me and my relationship to the Pontiff, I am not sure anything would have surprised Marjorie. But this experience clearly did.

Over lunch at a favorite restaurant, I Quattro Mori, just outside the Vatican walls, I related my encounter with His Holiness that morning after Mass. Marjorie said she had had no idea such a chapel existed. His Excellency Archbishop Foley, who had been present at the Mass, said he knew that it existed but that he had never seen it himself. I was left with many, many more questions, but in the end they came down to just one.

Later that afternoon, still very much in a daze, I called Monsignor Dziwisz on the telephone. I asked simply, "What was that? What happened in the Pope's chapel this morning?"

"Maestro, don't you know? We both pray to the same God." I thought I could see him smile through the phone, a warm smile of compassion for my still bewildered state. Then he said a fond *Buona sera*, Maestro, *a la prossima*—until next time" and rang off.

The next day I was back on a plane to New York. I believe we did in fact touch down at Kennedy, but I was still up there in a daze for many months thereafter.

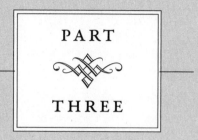

PART

THREE

Creation

CHAPTER

TWENTY-FOUR

For Pope John Paul II, the year of the Great Jubilee 2000 was of supreme importance. He had written about it and spoken about it almost from the time he was first elected to the See of Saint Peter in 1978. For His Holiness, part of the significance of this year came from the Bible (the Torah, in fact), when a Jubilee meant that slaves would be freed and the poor taken in. It was to be a year of celebration and a year of repentance. This Great Jubilee, the two thousandth year since the birth of Jesus, had so much more significance for him than any other such festival year. Pope John Paul II wished that the year of the Great Jubilee would be nothing less than a new beginning, a fresh start, for all humankind.

After he was diagnosed with Parkinson's disease in 1993, as his robust, athletic health began slowly but surely to fail, he spoke about his destiny being fulfilled if only he could lead his Church through the Millennium Year.

Everyone who cared for him or who had heard his voice knew what this Year 2000 meant to him. I counted myself as belonging to both these groups. So I took on the cause of the Jubilee Year as my own.

For months after I had prayed with His Holiness in his private chapel in Saint Peter's, I had thought about what it had really meant. I thought long and hard about Monsignor Dziwisz's statement, "Maestro, don't you know? We both pray to the same God." After the Papal Concert to Commemorate the Shoah, after all the Pontiff had done to bring our two peoples together, Dziwisz's simple, clear, perfectly chosen words now made profound sense.

I also recalled feelings of calm and completeness that had come over me many times as I stood in His Holiness' meditative presence. It was a feeling of peace that I had never known before—except, of course, in music, for as long as I could remember.

As I prayed with Pope John Paul in his private chapel, as I was drawn deeper and deeper into his silent devotion, I heard the sounds of the ethereal Bruckner Ninth coming from someplace deep inside, opening me up further and further to the world of the spirit. That meeting, that "at-one-ment" with His Holiness, had inspired me and challenged me in every aspect of my life in the months that followed, as it does to this day. What I hadn't understood right away was just how it would affect my essential core, my music-making. Over the course of the next years that too would become ever more clear.

Early in March 1996, I was scheduled to record the Tchaikovsky Third Symphony with the Royal Philharmonic, the same orchestra that had performed with me at the Papal Concert to Commemorate the Shoah. Our recording sessions were set to take place at Henry Wood Hall, a recording venue I knew well from my work as assistant to Klaus Tennstedt during his tenure as Music Director of the London Philharmonic Orchestra. From the outside, Henry Wood looks like the Trinity Church of the Anglican faith that it once was. But Trinity fell into terrible disrepair after a disastrous fire there in 1973, and when it was rebuilt, it had been reconfigured as a venue for rehearsals and recordings for London's top orchestras. I had been there many times in the years before I met Pope John Paul II, and had thought nothing of the building's original purpose. Now, for these Tchaikovsky recording sessions, when I approached Trinity Church Square, I saw a house of worship. The building hadn't changed; I had.

There is nothing liturgical about the Tchaikovsky Third. Nothing overtly spiritual either. It is a symphony based in part on both Russian and Polish folksongs, to which the great English conductor and impresario Sir Henry Wood (he for whom this orchestral venue was now named) had almost arbitrarily appended the title "Polish." The work is as far from being a mass or a cantata as anything can be. But like all music of enduring worth, it has the capacity to ennoble the human spirit. Well performed, it makes us larger. To plum its depths as performers, we have to be open to freely explore our own.

I had conducted this work many times and had been rather well received in doing so. I had even brought this "Polish" symphony with us as the major work of the Kraków Philharmonic's USA/Canada tour in 1993, when we visited many of the most important concert venues on the North American continent. At that time, two leading music critics of the venerable *New York Times*, John Rockwell, who reviewed our preconcert performance in Kraków, and Bernard Holland, who wrote about our New York performance at Avery Fisher Hall in Lincoln Center, had been most generous in their praise.

But now, with the world-renowned Royal Philharmonic Orchestra, these sessions were totally different. I felt an openness to the spirit of the work, a way of letting it breathe that suddenly seemed natural. And the RPO breathed the music right along with me. The third movement, the Andante elegiaco, sang as I had never been able to make it sing before. It revealed its soaring soul. And the grandeur of the first movement's Allegro had the feel of the profound Slavic spirit that I believe Tchaikovsky had had uppermost in his mind.

Our producer, the estimable Heinz Wildhagen, who had produced so many important recordings for Deutsche Grammophon, was smiling from ear to ear. After each take, he would call me on our private conductor-to-producer phone to offer his deep satisfaction. And when I went into the control room with members of the RPO to hear playbacks of our work during our breaks, we knew why Heinz had seemed so pleased. There was something truly very special going on in those sessions, something the musicians attributed to our collective professional skill but which I knew had been inspired by another source. In my mind, at least, I felt I had learned so much more about my art from that inspiring November day with His Holiness in Saint Peter's.

When the reviews came out, we were all thrilled. The *Times* of London gave us Three Stars, their highest rating. The *Philadelphia*

Inquirer wrote that there was "amplitude and warmth to the Royal Philharmonic's performance," and the *American Record Guide* opined, "There cannot be a more beautiful recording, both in sound and in sensitivity to the emotions." See, I said to myself, they heard it too. The Shoah concert, our other Papal events, the communion with His Holiness in his private chapel had all helped me hear this music in a way that was somehow much richer than I was able to before.

As I went about my professional engagements over that spring and summer, I kept thinking about the Pope and the coming Jubilee. I would travel back and forth to the Vatican to speak with Monsignor Dziwisz, hesitantly sharing ideas about what might come next. I wanted to build on what we had accomplished, but after the Papal Concert to Commemorate the Shoah, nothing I suggested seemed quite right. Finally, on one of my trips to Rome, I summoned my courage and asked, "Monsignor, I wonder whether you can tell me, will there be concerts in the Great Jubilee? Is this part of His Holiness' plan? Would there be a possibility that I could offer my gifts in service to His Holiness and his mission once again during this most important of celebratory years?"

"Well, Maestro, the Jubilee will be very different from the other occasions for which you have conducted," Monsignor Dziwisz said. "This will be an enormously important year for the whole Church and, we feel, even for the whole world. You should know, Maestro, that the Holy Father has appointed a committee of Church leaders, the Central Committee for the Great Jubilee, to plan all the activities for the year 2000. It is headed by Cardinal Etchegaray and includes Cardinal Cassidy, whom you know well, I believe. They will decide finally on what will take place, within the guidelines, of course, which have been established by the Holy Father. And as you may know, plans have been in the process of formulation since 1994, so they are well under way. But Maestro, please, you know the respect and affection in which you are held here. What did you have in mind?"

"I think I do know how important this Great Jubilee is to His Holiness," I answered. "For example, I know how deeply he believes in the importance of dialogue and common understanding among the peoples of all the monotheistic faiths. So, my idea is to perform 'Creation' by Joseph Haydn. It sets the first verses of the Book of Genesis, a text that tells a story that is holy to all three monotheistic faiths—Judaism, Christianity, and Islam. I believe it would be perfect for performance before the Pope in the Year of the Great Jubilee. And my vision, Your Excellency, is for a pilgrimage of 'Creation' performances in cathedrals on three continents: in Baltimore, in London, here at the Vatican, and even on to Jerusalem, Bethlehem, and Nazareth in the Holy Land."

"Interesting. Yes, this may well fit into the concepts the Holy Father has set forth. If you would, Maestro, let me see this in writing. Please send me this idea in the form of a letter. I will see whether we can go to the next step," Dziwisz said politely.

This was a first. I had never been asked to submit a proposal to the Pope in written form. Always before, even if I brought a document to one of my meetings with Monsignor Dziwisz, it was only to show it to him personally. I would slide the written material across his desk, and Dziwisz would read it most carefully, noting absolutely every nuance in the writing, in whatever language the letter or document was written. This in itself was an amazing feat. At that time, I didn't know how well the good Monsignor actually spoke English. I had heard him say only a very few words; our conversations had always been in Italian or in Polish. But his understanding of the written English word is astonishing. He will read a letter or a complex document and go to the crux of the matter it describes. Then he will ask the absolutely right questions that get at the heart of the issues at hand. His intelligence is keen, almost as keen as his understanding of the human character. These are just two of Stanislaw Dziwisz's many remarkable attributes that served John Paul so well for so many years.

I could only imagine two reasons for Monsignor Dziwisz's request. One was that now, in 1997, meetings with the Pope were becoming rarer. And not just for me. Monsignor Dziwisz was guarding John Paul's time and energy extraordinarily carefully. Second, as Monsignor Dziwisz had said, this was to be a Vatican process far more complex internally than even the Papal Concert to Commemorate the

Shoah had been. It was possible that for this reason Monsignor Dziwisz wanted a written record of just what I had in mind. The letter I wrote included the following paragraph:

> Such an event could bring together God-fearing people of all monotheistic faiths, grounded in the shared belief that this, the Bible's beginning story, is the first of God's gifts of life and soul to mankind. Past centuries have witnessed deep division and misunderstanding, and yes, even unspeakable cruelty. We forget this, as His Holiness has said, at our great peril. But the new Millennium should usher in a new era of greater under-standing, mutual respect, and love among all God's children. This "Creation" concert would embody this, His Holiness' fervent wish, for the year 2000 and beyond.

I sent this letter on July 3, 1997, together with a recording—not my own, alas, but the best one I knew of—with the Berlin Philharmonic under their great chief conductor, Herbert von Karajan.

Then I waited. Weeks went by. Then months. I heard nothing from Monsignor Dziwisz throughout the entire summer. In late September, just before heading to London to record Wagner with the London Philharmonic Orchestra, I made a quick sidetrip to Rome.

"Maestro," Monsignor Dziwisz said, "His Holiness appreciates your idea very much. I think the next step would be for you to kindly visit His Excellency Archbishop Crescenzio Sepe, the Secretary General of the Central Committee for the Great Jubilee Year. His is the appropriate office to continue your dialogue about your most interesting proposal."

When I had proposed the Shoah concert to His Holiness, the answer had come back immediately. Now, things would take time. Patience is an ancient Vatican art that I would now have to cultivate most reverently.

Then, in early January 1998, as I sat in my study in New York, looking forward to my next trip to the Vatican later that month, the telephone rang. A strong British-accented voice said, "Maestro, this is

David Whelton, Managing Director for the Philharmonia Orchestra. I have heard wonderful things about your recent sessions with the London Philharmonic. I wonder if on your next trip through the U.K. we might have a chance to meet. I'd like to tell you about the Philharmonia Orchestra. From what my colleagues have told me about you, I think you would like working with our orchestra very much indeed." In our recordings of excerpts from Wagner's *Tristan, Tannhäuser*, and particularly of his most spiritual music-drama, *Parsifal*, the musicians of the estimable London Philharmonic, had seemed transformed. After one particularly beautiful take, the Principal Cellist of the LPO, Bob Truman, had asked me, "How is it that the music seems to float? I have never felt it this way it before." Clearly, positive resonances of those London Philharmonic recording sessions had whetted David Whelton's appetite to begin our musical collaboration.

It happened that I was flying to Rome to finally meet with Archbishop Crescenzio Sepe, at the introduction of Monsignor Dziwisz, so David and I agreed to meet in London on my way over to Italy. The Philharmonia Orchestra was founded by the formidable record executive Walter Legge to make recordings for major record labels in the early 1950s. As utilitarian as that sounds, those recordings, with conductors as legendary as Toscanini, Furtwangler, Klemperer, and von Karajan, were among the most celebrated of that period. The Philharmonia had gone on to work with many of the great maestros of the second half of the twentieth century, so I was very pleased by David Whelton's call. He and I sat and talked about music for more than an hour, ensconced in the deep green leather of overstuffed high-backed chairs; we were in the ground-floor lounge of the Caledonian Club in Halkin Street. He told me about his orchestra's tradition in the German classics, about projects he saw me undertaking with them, performing Strauss and Mahler and Brahms. I told him that I had been an admirer of his orchestra from my youngest years, and that one of the three classical recordings in my home growing up had been the Brahms First Symphony with the New Philharmonia and Maestro Otto Klemperer. Both of us seemed to be speaking each other's language. I left for Rome with the feeling of having added another wonderful orchestral home.

At the meeting in the Vatican I would have my first chance to talk with Archbishop Sepe about "Creation." His Excellency is a dark-haired, round-faced southern Italian from Salerno, not too far from Naples. I had good friends, the Forenza family from Naples, whom I visited quite often on my trips to Italy, so our conversation started off with a discussion of the unique culture of that special city and its enticing cuisine, which we both much too greatly admired.

His Excellency began his explanation of the Grand Jubilee by stating that competition for the very few concerts which might find their way onto the official schedule in 2000 was intense. He named a number of my most illustrious colleagues, saying that they too wished to participate and that each idea had to be carefully weighed to decide which ones were most appropriate. He raised the name of the great Riccardo Muti, his fellow southern Italian, with particular pride. As a first step, Archbishop Sepe asked me to submit to him a formal proposal of the work I wished to perform for the Holy Father and the musical forces I would propose to bring for this most special occasion. This proposal would take its place among the official submissions he had received thus far.

Almost as soon as I was out the door of Archbishop Sepe's office, I telephoned David Whelton and related to him the substance of my Vatican meeting. He told me that he would have to consult with his council of management but that he thought the Philharmonia would be delighted to perform for the Pope should we be fortunate enough to be invited to do so. I had hardly unpacked my bags after my flight back to New York, when a letter arrived from David. It read in part:

"The Philharmonia is the proud bearer of the conducting tradition of von Karajan, Klemperer, Muti, and Von Dohnanyi, a tradition which fits your own. The opportunity to perform with you at the Vatican as part of the Millennium celebrations would undoubtedly be a highlight in the history of the Orchestra."

I was thrilled to have the Philharmonia as my musical partner, and so now we were set. I wrote to Monsignor Sepe, proposing the

"Creation," and the Philharmonia Orchestra, and then began to practice my art of patience anew.

The Ambassador of the United States to the Holy See, the elegant Louisianan Corrine C. "Lindy" Boggs, wrote a letter to Cardinal Etchegaray, the President of the Central Committee for the Grand Jubilee. No decision. The British Ambassador Mark Pellew, the Philharmonia's diplomatic Holy See representative, if you will, likewise wrote to the Vatican Secretary of State Cardinal Sodano. Still no definitive reply. I kept Cardinal Lustiger informed, as well as Cardinal Cassidy, who was a member of the Central Committee. And of course, I spoke frequently with Monsignor Dziwisz. Time and again I was told I would just have to wait. A decision would be made at the appropriate time in the appropriate manner by the appropriate authority. And then it would be transmitted "as is customary in such cases." I had faith that in the end it would come out alright, in large part because Monsignor Dziwisz had told me, "His Holiness appreciates your 'Creation' idea very much." But the wait was still very tough to take.

In the meantime, I had another quite intriguing project, which had come to me quite by accident. While on vacation in Southern California, I had driven down the coast from the posh enclave of Newport Beach through one high-toned enclave after another with my good friend John Miley. Our plan was to stop at the wonderful old Franciscan missions along the way. San Juan Capistrano, San Luis Rey di Francia, and San Diego de Alcala. I had had the vague idea of doing some concerts in a venue as peaceful as I could find, far from the hustle and bustle of our frenetic world.

We visited Mission San Juan Capistrano, which was pretty and interesting, but rather touristy. It still had a functioning parish church, but it was mostly a place of historical interest in a sea of antique dealers. Then we headed on down the coast, past San Clemente, where President Nixon had had his Western White House, through the vast expanse of Camp Pendleton, a major Marine base with, it was said, frequent live-fire artillery practice, and on to Oceanside, a Southern California city that the boom of the postwar years seemed to have forgotten. From Oceanside we turned inland just a few miles to Mission San Luis Rey.

Situated on a hill in the middle of nowhere, the alabaster-walled Mission Church, a National Historic Landmark, is the first thing one sees. Although architecturally beautiful, San Luis Rey seemed to be a place long forgotten. It had been founded almost two hundred years before by the Franciscans, as were all the missions, as the Spanish conquistadors made their way up the coast. The mission had ministered then to the poor and the dispossessed. But unlike San Juan Capistrano, this was no museum. San Luis Rey was still true to its founders' purpose. And to me that made it all the more captivating.

In the midst of the riches of the South Coast, San Luis Rey was a mission on a mission. Here was real Franciscan outreach to migrant workers, indigenous peoples, and the poor of Oceanside, a town as far from the glitz and glamour of Orange County as one could get. This was it. We would never travel on to San Diego de Alcala. I had found what I was looking for.

The leader of the Franciscan Friars Minor at San Luis Rey was Father Ben Innes. If one imagined a Franciscan monk, Friar Tuck from Robin Hood would come to mind. Stout and kindly, and truly pious. That is Father Ben. He is a cigar-smoking, brown-robe-wearing, Birkenstock-shod graduate of the University of Oregon, who found God, as he says, when he saw a halo around the moon. I don't know what Ben saw when he first saw me and, more importantly, when he first heard my story of my relationship with Pope John Paul, but it wasn't a halo, I would suppose. For one thing, I am not sure he believed me. My being Jewish probably didn't help.

What came out of me, however, was even more suspicious. I told Ben that I had fallen in love with his mission at first sight, and that I wanted to make music for him and his community. I went even further into the impossible. I told Ben that my plan was to bring the Capella Giulia Choir of Saint Peter's Basilica there to San Luis Rey.

It made no sense, of course. The mission was not a place for classical concerts; it was a place of simple prayer and outreach to the downtrodden. And the Capella Giulia had never been in the New World in all its five-hundred-year history. The choir had worked with me on the Papal Concerts I had conducted in Rome. I loved their life-affirming Choirmaster, Monsignor Dom Pablo Collino. But travel all the way to this remote Mission to perform classical music, including their specialty, the works of Palestrina? This was crazy. The only people who didn't believe that were me and, well, Father Ben. For some reason, he didn't shoo me out of his office. For some inexplicable reason, we were kindred souls from the first time we laid eyes on each other.

When I next traveled back to Rome, in March 1998, it was to witness the Episcopal Ordination of my friend of ten years, soon-to-be Bishop Stanislaw Dziwisz. The Pope had decided to elevate his three most trusted aides, Monsignor Dziwisz, his liturgist Monsignor Piero Marini (who had been with me in the private chapel in Saint Peter's three years before), and Monsignor James Harvey, an American from Milwaukee soon to be named Prefect of the Pontifical Household, to the rank of Bishop in the Roman Catholic Church. In the Church a man is initially ordained into the priesthood, where many gladly serve for a lifetime. A select few are ordained again when they attain episcopal rank. In a richly traditional ceremony, they become Bishops or Archbishops, and are thereafter considered members of the Roman Catholic hierarchy. In very rare cases the Roman Pontiff himself will choose to celebrate this Mass of Episcopal Ordination.

As I soon learned, from the time the Pope names a new Bishop until his Mass of Episcopal Ordination, the newly elevated priest is referred to as Bishop-Elect, a cumbersome title he thankfully has to carry for only a brief time.

Still, when I saw my friend Bishop-Elect Dziwisz in his Papal Palace office, two days before the ceremony, to congratulate him on his coming elevation, it was as if nothing had changed. He was modest about his new rank, almost diffident. He didn't want to hear my praise and congratulations. I don't think he had ever wished for the Pope to elevate him in this way. He would do whatever his Holy Father wished. If he could be of more use to His Holiness by becoming a Bishop, then that is what would be.

Before going "upstairs" to see Dziwisz, I had spoken with Monsignor Pablo Collino about bringing the Choir of Saint Peter's to

San Luis Rey. His answer, in his Spanish-inflected Italian, was, "Yes, Maestro, of course. For you, we would do it. But, you know, we need a permission. We can't just take off from our duties in the Basilica di San Pietro. We participate in the Mass there every Sunday. It is our duty."

"Pablo, I know. But let me speak with Bishop-Elect Dziwisz. I would be most interested to see what his reaction might be."

Now I told Dziwisz about Mission San Luis Rey, about Father Ben, and the wonderful work the Franciscans were doing there. I had found out, I said, that they were going to be celebrating the two-hundredth anniversary of their mission that coming June.

"Wouldn't it be wonderful if we could bring a musical part of the Vatican across the ocean to be shared with those Franciscans and their faithful? Wouldn't that be a great gift?"

"OK, Maestro, I see; it is a good idea. I will help you if I can. I am sure there might be a way that permission could be granted. I will contact the Cardinal Archpriest of Saint Peter's. Let us see what can be done."

Before I left his office that day, Bishop-Elect Dziwisz stopped me and said, "Maestro, some days ago someone presented a gift to the Holy Father. We would like you to have it. We thought it might find better use with you." He reached over to the small table to his right, the one with the old Baroque clock. From it he took an object which had not even caught my eye, so accustomed was I by now to sitting in that room in rapt conversation with my friend. But the object was one my mind could not grasp as belonging to that room, to this place, to the Vatican. What Dziwisz handed me took my breath away. It was a bronze menorah, the ritual candelabra that we Jews use at Chanukah, the festival of lights. This menorah was very heavy. It looked old. It was cast in the ancient design depicting two lions holding the *shammas*, or ritual lighter of the eight lamps that represent the eight days of our holiday. I looked at Dziwisz, and he looked at me. This was a truly remarkable gift. I had no idea who had given it to the Pope. I presumed it was a Jew. At first, I thought, I cannot possibly accept this. The person who gave this gift to the Pope was undoubtedly hoping that it would somehow find its way into a special room in the Papal Palace, that it would be kept by His Holiness as a kind of objet d'art. I knew, however, that to the Pope this was not some quaint religious relic but an integral part of a living faith. He knew what Judaism meant to me and my family. He knew that we would use this menorah as part of our celebration of a holiday that brings only joy and happiness, especially to our children. This menorah carried with it such symbolism. It betokened a level of respect for my Jewish faith on the part of His Holiness that was as clear as it was rare. I knew that I had to accept it in the spirit in which it had been given. I walked out of the Vatican that day with my extraordinary gift carefully wrapped, and safely stowed under my arm.

Two days later, on March 19, 1998, I had the privilege to witness the Papal Mass of Episcopal Ordination of Bishops Dziwisz, Marini, and Harvey in a magnificent ceremony in Saint Peter's Basilica. The beauty of the vestments, the uplifting music of the Sistine Chapel Choir, and the solemnity of the Mass itself were deeply moving. The Pope bestowed on each new Bishop his crosier, or pastoral staff, his distinctive bishop's hat, called a miter, and his episcopal ring. When it was Bishop Dziwisz's turn, he seemed to be in tears, so carried away, it seemed, by the emotions of the day. All three Bishops then lay prostrate before their Holy Father in a sign of their obedience to the supreme leader of their Church. Finally, the scores of their fellow Bishops in attendance, as well as a great many Archbishops and Cardinals, approached each new initiate, laying on hands as a show of their episcopal brotherhood. This ritual took many minutes, as each prelate seemed to wish to impart a special blessing to these three men, who had been their faithful friends in curial service to Pope John Paul for so very many years. This was the first time I had ever actually attended a full Papal Mass in Saint Peter's. I was there at now-Bishop Dziwisz's special invitation, so although I felt like an outsider, in religious faith, I felt the warm welcome of one who is most welcome at court. His Holiness Pope John Paul II's bestowal of this great honor on my very dear friend is a memory I will carry with me for the rest of my life.

Three months after that Papal ceremony in Saint Peter's, I was back in Southern California. Bishop Dziwisz had indeed worked his magic. The Capella Giulia of Saint Peter's Basilica received Vatican permission and flew to the New World to join members of the Los Angeles Philharmonic, a group of wonderful young international soloists selected by the great London agent Jenny Spencer, and me for three days of glorious concerts celebrating two hundred years of Mission San Luis Rey de Francia. We performed works of Palestrina, who had been the conductor of the Capella Giulia in 1551; of Mozart, including his Symphony in D (K. 81), which he had written in Rome at the time he received his Papal Knighthood in 1770; and of Haydn, who had written his Lord Nelson Mass in 1798, the same year of the founding of Mission San Luis Rey. As one last treat, the Principal Bassoon of the Los Angeles Philharmonic could not perform on these concerts, so my old teacher Stephan Maxym from Juilliard, who had retired as Principal Bassoon of the Metropolitan Opera and moved to Southern California to teach at USC, filled in for him. Looking across the orchestra at my first mentor, performing with the person who had saved me for a life in music, was an enormous thrill. These first performances of the Capella Giulia in the Americas were a perfect rarity. And so I was not surprised at all when the concerts were broadcast, first across America by NPR and then, under the auspices of Vatican Radio and Dr. Solange de Maillerdoz, throughout the world.

Finally, in December 1998, a year and a half after first having proposed it to Monsignor Dziwisz, I received the letter, Vatican Protocol No. 5651/98, signed by His Excellency Archbishop Crescenzio Sepe, officially inviting the Philharmonia Orchestra and myself to perform Haydn's magnificent oratorio "The Creation" at the Vatican on May 18, 2000, the eightieth birthday of His Holiness Pope John Paul II. A musical pilgrimage of a lifetime, to Baltimore, London, Rome, and beyond, was soon about to begin.

Almost immediately after I received the letter authorizing the Jubilee Papal Concert, we began holding meetings, first at the Vatican, with Bishop Dziwisz and with Archbishop Sepe, then in London with David Whelton and the Philharmonia Orchestra. A single concert for His Holiness in Rome televised worldwide was a major project, but planning a whole "pilgrimage" of concerts, in Baltimore, London, Rome, and, we fervently hoped, in the Holy Land, was an undertaking of a completely different order of magnitude. For one thing, except for London, no concert organization in any of these places could take on the day-to-day preparations that are essential to a successful musical event. For another, we had no money for any of this.

Despite (usually erroneous) assumptions many people make about the Church's excess wealth, as I knew well, we would have to find financial support for our pilgrimage of concerts from the good graces of those generous enough to donate to a project that expressed the Pope's vision of a world entering the new millennium with more love and less hate in its collective heart.

In each city on the planned pilgrimage, every aspect of these events would fall under the aegis of the highest local Catholic authority. In Baltimore that was William Cardinal Keeler. Cardinal Keeler and I were by now old friends. As then Archbishop Keeler, the President of the U.S. Conference of Catholic Bishops, he had been responsible for making arrangements for me to conduct for the Vigil at World Youth Day in Denver in 1993. He had also been of immense support to me during the arduous run-up to the Papal Concert to Commemorate the Shoah. And it was Cardinal Keeler who had welcomed a major televised interfaith concert by the Baltimore Symphony to his basilica in 1995.

Cardinal Keeler once again opened wide the doors of the Basilica of the Assumption in Baltimore for the inaugural event of our pilgrimage of concerts, scheduled for March 26, 2000. In preparation, he and I met many times at his residence on North Charles Street, just around the corner from the basilica itself. From the second floor of his house, His Eminence could walk through a door that connected directly into the rear of the sanctuary. Sometimes we would break bread in his dining room, and at other times partake of a quiet drink in his living room or a coffee in his homey kitchen on the mansion's ground floor. Our ability to share ideas, to be open with each other about the sensibilities of our respective religious communities, is something that would have been unthinkable to me even a few years ago, let alone before I had gone to Kraków. This was a real friendship, yet one where I never failed to call him Your Eminence and he always chose to call me Maestro.

The Basilica of the Assumption of the Blessed Virgin Mary was the first major metropolitan cathedral constructed in the United States after the adoption of the U.S. Constitution. Completed in 1821, it was the work of Benjamin Latrobe, the architect chosen by Thomas Jefferson to design the Capitol in Washington, D.C. To Cardinal Keeler, and to so many citizens of Baltimore, their basilica was the finest representation of religious liberty in America, standing as a magnificent demonstration of Maryland's historic role as the cradle of tolerance for people of all faiths in the predominantly Protestant society of the early years of the republic. We couldn't have chosen either a better place for the inaugural concert of the Jubilee Creation tour, or a better representative of the ideals for which it stood than His Eminence William Cardinal Keeler.

Cardinal Keeler worked tirelessly to help bring our concert to fruition and to have it be seen as an event to which the entire American public could lay claim. He raised funds from a broad range of individuals and corporate entities, both in Baltimore and elsewhere, and he sometimes brought me along to meet his generous donors if he thought that might be helpful. I remember well our visit with Michael Bloomberg, the future Mayor of New York City, at his Bloomberg LP corporate headquarters on Park Avenue in New York. His Eminence told me downstairs before our meeting that he thought Bloomberg would be open to helping out, but that given the fact that our events were to take place in Baltimore, London, Rome, and the Holy Land, his expectations were modest. At the meeting, we did our best to describe the vision of the concerts as a way to bring the members of all three Abrahamic faiths together, to show what unites them rather than what keeps them apart. Bloomberg listened carefully and quietly, both to His Eminence, who spoke of Pope John Paul's fervent wish that this venture succeed, and to me, when I described the artistic vision of "Creation" and the power of music to bind human souls together. As we spoke, Bloomberg showed little emotion. We couldn't tell how our request was being received, but when we finished, he sat down at a simple desk in a small private office and wrote out a check. He rose, thanked us for coming, and placed the folded check into the breast pocket of His Eminence's Roman-collared black suit, bidding us a most polite good-bye. When we got down to the lobby, Cardinal Keeler took the check from his pocket and gasped. He didn't show me the amount but told me that Michael Bloomberg had just given him a donation that was fully ten times the amount he had thought we could expect. I could tell Cardinal Keeler was dumbfounded, but then he said this was a sign that our great musical-spiritual enterprise would surely succeed. We both knew we still had a long way to go in order to bring the whole Philharmonia Orchestra and its choir from London to Baltimore, but we hoped that if we could raise such a donation from Michael Bloomberg, then our pilgrimage of tolerance and mutual respect between Jews, Muslims, and Christians would surely reach its goal.

Cardinal Keeler's help did not end with Mr. Bloomberg. His Eminence also arranged for Maryland Public Television to broadcast the concert for PBS. Our complete performance of Haydn's "Creation" would be seen all across America. Now all we had to do was to prepare a performance that would be worthy of an audience of millions.

"Creation" is a massive work of musical art, comprising three parts divided into thirty-four musical sections, for full orchestra, large chorus, and either three or five soloists, depending on how the parts of the biblical roles of Raphael, Uriel, Gabriel, Adam, and Eve are divided. (We chose the version for one soprano, one tenor, and one bass soloist, so as to ease the logistical burden on our enormously complex musical pilgrimage just a bit.) The whole of "Creation" lasts nearly two hours in the complete version we were preparing for our tour. The Philharmonia and I had our work cut out for us, but we were eager to dive into this beautiful, imposing music.

Our first rehearsals took place in London the week before the concert. We had two rehearsals with the choir alone, then three separate rehearsal sessions with the Philharmonia Orchestra. Our preparations were complicated by the presence of a camera crew from *60 Minutes*, America's most important and most popular television news program. During the previous summer of 1999, I had been contacted by their producer to see whether I would consent to a profile of me to be entitled "The Pope's Maestro," using our Creation Pilgrimage as their principal source of material. I was thrilled, of course. Their conductor profiles are very rare and have only included such colleagues as Daniel Barenboim, Valerie Gergiev, and Gustavo Dudamel, among very few others. After a wonderful dinner in London with their correspondent, the music-loving, war-zone-covering Bob Simon, and his indefatigable South African-born producer Michael Gavchon, I readily agreed. Michael, Bob, and their crew were to be with us every step of the way.

The *60 Minutes* program meant that I had to wear a contact microphone on my lapel to record every word I spoke both in rehearsal and in one-on-one conversations with members of the chorus or orchestra, or with their management. I soon forgot that I was wearing the mike. I've never heard a bit of what was recorded in this way, but

I can only imagine what they have on me in their files. Indiscretions of the microphone, indeed!

In any event, the rehearsals went wonderfully well. The Austro-Hungarian Haydn's music flowed easily from these accomplished English musicians and choristers. Late in his life, Haydn spent more than five years in almost constant residence in London, writing a series of the greatest of his 104 symphonies as well as other major works for the most famous British orchestra of its day. There, in the English capital, Haydn had become enamored of the very high professional level of the orchestra for which he wrote his "London symphonies."

Between the London rehearsals and the Baltimore concert, I stopped in New York to meet with the television director Alan Skog, who had come highly recommended by the folks at "Live from Lincoln Center," and Bill Baker, the president of WNET Thirteen, the PBS flagship station that would broadcast our concert in New York. Alan was the most meticulous director I had ever worked with. He came and sat with me in my study and asked me question after question about my conception of the Haydn "Creation," so that he could mirror my ideas in his televised version of our performance. I felt great confidence in him from the start.

Haydn's "Creation" begins with a representation of chaos that is justly famous, and was astonishing in its boldness to the audience in 1800. We musicians began our performance in the unlit basilica in a darkness so deep we had to use stand lights to see the music before us. At the words "Let there be light" from the first verses of the book of Genesis, Haydn lets loose with a huge burst of musical energy scored for full orchestra and chorus that is as illuminating as the primordial stew had been dark and opaque. In our concert, at the words "Let there be light," hundreds if not thousands of klieg lights, specially designed by Alan and his television team, began to illuminate the Baltimore Basilica, first with blue lights, then with brilliant whites and yellows, turning night into day, just as the Scripture says. In anyone else's hands this would have been garish overkill. In the hands of the expert

Maryland Public Television/PBS crew it created a stunning effect on the awestruck audience at each of the two Baltimore performances and, I have heard, on the millions who watched on television.

Before the concert, Cardinal Keeler invited me to a dinner he was hosting for the assembled religious leaders. There were Rabbis, Imams, Protestant clergy, and members of the Catholic hierarchy. Regrettably, I could not dine with them, but I was happy to welcome them to the first concert of our pilgrimage and to ask them to pray for its success in London, Rome, and the Holy Land. This was just the kind of interfaith gathering that His Holiness Pope John Paul would have wished to see.

The Philharmonia Orchestra's warmth of tone, lightness, and precision made them a great Haydn orchestra, but the revelation was the Philharmonia Chorus. They enunciated the words of the Book of Genesis with such clarity and with such love of the English language that even these standard, well-known texts sounded vibrant and new. The soloists for these performances, soprano Janice Chandler, tenor Richard Clement, and bass John Relyea, were all excellent. If there was a standout, it was the Canadian John Relyea. John, with whom I would have the pleasure to work a number of times in subsequent years, sang the parts of Raphael and Adam with a rare combination of archangelic authority and deep humanity. The last B-flat chord that ends "Creation" seemed to last a full ten seconds as it reached the heights of the cupola before finally dying away to tumultuous applause.

Cardinal Keeler waited until all the guests and well-wishers had gone before he invited Vera and me to come back to his home and have a celebratory drink with him. His Eminence seemed to be most pleased with the pilgrimage's inaugural concert. But both of us knew our work had only just begun.

After the second performance, I was surprised by a tap on the shoulder as I greeted well-wishers "backstage" in the vestry of the basilica. When I turned around, I was met by the warm *abbraccio* of Senator Carl Levin of Michigan, who had come up from Washington especially to attend our concert. I had not seen Carl since we shared a dinner in Greektown in Detroit after the Orchestra Hall stop on the

Kraków Philharmonic's 1993 North America tour. This night, in Baltimore, he reminded me of our first meeting in Kraków in 1988, when he and his wife, Barbara, had come to Poland on a congressional tour with other U.S. lawmakers and had come backstage to greet me after one of my Philharmonic performances. The next day we had toured Kraków together. I had especially wanted to show them Kazimierz, including the Templ Synagogue. In a sense, Carl and Barbara had been along on this whole Kraków journey with me.

The day after the second basilica performance, as I walked on the newly revived Baltimore waterfront, I met dozens of members of the Philharmonia, from both the orchestra and the choir, also out enjoying a late-morning stroll before their flight. Each of them thanked me. They had enjoyed the music-making and, they said, had appreciated the beauty and significance of the basilica as the setting for their artistic work. I wished each of them well on their transatlantic journey and said that I looked forward to seeing them all in London in under two weeks' time.

Our concert in Westminster Cathedral was to be an entirely different affair. For one thing, preparations for the event had first been undertaken with His Eminence Basil Cardinal Hume. I had met with Cardinal Hume on a number of occasions before the concert, and I had found him to be a warm, empathic priest, much in the Benedictine mold of the monk he had once been before his elevation to the Catholic hierarchy. I was also happy to be working on this event with the very Cardinal I had seen on television in 1978, when he had kneeled before his newly elected Pope. Sadly, in June 1999 Cardinal Hume died. His successor, Archbishop Cormac Murphy-O'Connor, was named just two months before our event was to take place. The staff of Westminster Cathedral soldiered on with the preparations for the concert, and the Archbishop did the best he could, but through no fault of his own some of the joy was taken out of the event in London because of the death of Cardinal Hume.

Westminster Cathedral is a church with a most interesting history. Owing to events that took place five centuries before in the reign of King Henry VIII, there had been no Catholic cathedral built in the United Kingdom until Westminster Cathedral was consecrated in 1910. No pope had visited a British cathedral until John Paul's visit to Westminster in 1985, and no British monarch had visited a Catholic church until Queen Elizabeth II accepted the invitation of Cardinal Hume to visit Westminster Cathedral, in 1995. Westminster was thus an important symbol of the newly emerging English Catholic Church. Our British stop on this Philharmonia Orchestra Jubilee Creation Pilgrimage was as much a sign of ecumenical progress, a musical sign of better Christian understanding, as it was of outreach to Judaism and Islam.

Haydn would have felt right at home in this setting. A devout Catholic, Haydn had spent half a decade writing music in a London atmosphere that, in the last decade of the eighteenth century, must have been much less welcoming for his fellow Catholics than it was in 2000. Haydn was so devout in fact that he told a friend that when he was encountering creative problems during the composition of "Creation" he would kneel down and say his rosary, which he said always solved his musical writer's block. Nevertheless, he composed his "Creation" following the Old Testament text of Genesis as re-created by Milton and Dryden, both loyal subjects of the Church of England, headed by their respective English monarchs. Haydn knew a great text when he saw one, and his heart knew no religious prejudice, as far as one can tell.

When I arrived in London, I was prepared for an atmosphere that was somewhat less amiable than the one in Baltimore but looking forward to presenting "Creation" with the excellent Philharmonia players once again. Little did I know just how much re-creation this would involve, however. I arrived at the first of my two rehearsals thinking I would just be touching up the performance we had prepared so well in our five rehearsals and two performances of the previous month. I knew the soloists would be different because their schedules did not permit the Baltimore concerts' soloists to perform in London and Rome, but I accepted that fact. I was particularly looking forward to working with the amazing British bass Sir John Tomlinson, whose work I had admired for many years.

During my stay in London, in the middle of our intense preparations for the Westminster concert, I got a call in my hotel from a new friend in New York, Jonathan O'Herron, a Managing Director at Lazard Frères, the worldwide investment banking firm. John and I had met at an interfaith dinner in New York some months before, and he, a devout Catholic, had offered to help Cardinal Keeler and me with the "practical" aspects of this Papal Pilgrimage in any way he could. One of John's clients was Fiat, in Turin, Italy. To make a circuitous story less winding, John had contacted Guido Vitale, his Lazard Frères partner in Milan, with whom he worked on the Fiat account. Guido had thought that another client of his, the international financial giant UniCredito Italiano, might well be interested in helping to sponsor our tour. If this support could be secured, John said, it would, along with what Michael Bloomberg had so generously given us, complete our support. John asked if I would be willing to fly to Milan to meet with Lucio Rondelli, the President of UniCredito Italiano. Signor Rondelli had wanted to meet the artistic creator of this series of events, to hear firsthand the creative vision behind them.

"John, I'm in the middle of this tour. I have the London concert coming up in a few days. Is this really important?"

"Yes," he said. "I believe it could really make the difference. Only you can describe the vision that you and the Pope have for this Jubilee Pilgrimage. He wants to meet only you. Please do go. I think it would be so worthwhile." I couldn't believe it, but I said yes. I knew from what John said that this could be very important.

When I went into the first London rehearsal, there was another and completely unexpected surprise. As I looked out over the Philharmonia Orchestra that gray April day, I saw only ten out of the seventy players I had worked with in Baltimore. Through a very strange booking arrangement, I would be rehearsing this "Creation" with an almost entirely new orchestra, with only two rehearsals, one of which was our "run-through" dress rehearsal in the cathedral itself. This particular version of the Philharmonia had not performed "Creation" in a number of years. And capable as they were, we fairly scrambled to get everything together for the performance. Everything turned out well. The chorus was the same as in Baltimore, and the soloists performed wonderfully, especially Sir John. Our reviews were very good. We had performed a veritable musical miracle, but I scratched my head as I left the church that night. I couldn't figure out why I had faced an almost completely different orchestra.

The next day, I called my friend Jenny Spencer, who in addition to being a well-known concert agent had also worked in the management of the London Philharmonic, which is where I had first made her acquaintance.

"Jenny," I said, "I don't understand. I work like crazy with one group of musicians who are the Philharmonia. We do two great concerts after five intensive rehearsals. Then I show up and find a totally different orchestra for our London concert. What was that about?"

"Gilbert," Jenny replied, "don't you remember? I told you months ago. Be careful. Make sure the Philharmonia Orchestra is tied for these concerts."

"'Tied,'" I said. "Now I understand. I was certainly tied. So was Haydn. Tied up. That was outrageous!"

"Yes," Jenny said. "Welcome to the London orchestral world. I'm sorry, but I'm sure the concert was great. Just look forward to the next one in Rome."

"Yes, of course I will. But who knows which Philharmonia will be showing up."

"I know, bit of a puzzle, that. But you'll see; it will all work out. The Vatican will be wonderful, I'm sure. And now you'll know better for the next time." Jenny rang off with a smile of encouragement that came right through the phone.

The atmosphere at my meeting with David Whelton the next day in the Festival Hall was understandably a bit tense. He assured me that the orchestra I would have in Rome, at the Vatican, would indeed be the same one I had had in Baltimore. I was relieved but still puzzled, yet with all I had on my plate I decided to let it go.

⁓

Two days after the Westminster concert, I was off for my quick trip to Milan. Guido Vitale, John O'Herron's Italian partner, met me at my hotel and thanked me for making the trip. "Thank *you*," I said. "If this is successful, you will make many people, including those close to the Holy Father, very happy indeed."

UniCredito's Lucio Rondelli couldn't have been more gracious. He apologized for bringing me all the way from London. But, he said, he needed to hear from me personally about this Papal Creation Pilgrimage.

I spoke as strongly as I could in favor of our work, about my relationship with His Holiness and the concerts I had already performed for him at the Vatican and elsewhere. Then I spoke to him about Haydn's "Creation," about the special work that it is, and what it meant to the Pope to see this vision of a world brought closer to peace, through music, realized. I told him just how much was riding on the success of our venture and on the outcome of our meeting in Milan that day.

Luckily, very luckily, Signor Rondelli was persuaded. His company, UniCredito Italiano, and its closely affiliated sister institutions, including Polish bank PeKaO, donated a magnificent sum that would enable us not only to perform for the Pope in Rome but to continue our journey onward.

The minute I left the offices of UniCredito, I went back to my hotel to telephone Bishop Dziwisz with the good news. If he had been nervous about our not having the funding for the concert, he did not betray it over the telephone. I was pleased, to be sure, but I think, from his serene tone of voice, that he had believed all along that the money would come to us. He didn't seem to doubt that such a remarkable project to advance a vital part of His Holiness' interfaith agenda would remain an orphan. Someone important would adopt it as his own.

CHAPTER

TWENTY-SIX

On the way from London to the Vatican for the Papal Concert, the *60 Minutes* staff convinced me to make a detour and travel via Kraków. I was frightened, and resisted the idea. I had not been back since my last concert with the Kraków Philharmonic in January 1993. Although I had been invited to conduct the orchestra numerous times, most notably to participate in their fiftieth anniversary celebrations in 1995, I had never accepted. My memories of the secret police and all that they had threatened in my life were simply too strong. "Rocks will fall on your head. You will not know from where they came." The voice of my mother-in-law, Margit Kalina, still rang in my head, even now, two years after she had passed away. To me Kraków meant glorious musical and cultural memories that faded into the darkness of Communist oppression.

But Michael Gavchon and Bob Simon promised me that the Kraków of 2000 was totally different. And anyway, they said, we would all be together. Who would dare harm me if I had CBS News in tow?

On May 14, 2000, I boarded a British Airways flight from Gatwick to Kraków and landed some two hours later at the newly named Pope John Paul II Airport. As I soon found out, not only the name had changed. There were no more guards with guns standing every fifty feet. In this era, before 9/11, the Kraków airport was as normal as any in Western Europe. The border guard behind the little booth who checked my passport was no longer the intimidating secret police-affiliated defender of the Communist state. This young man checked my passport, taking note, it seemed, of the numerous Polish visas still decorating its pages, stamped it, and waved me through.

In the minivan *60 Minutes* had hired for Bob, Michael, the crew, and myself, I sat as close to the CBS folks as I could. I still felt I needed protection. The Polish countryside on the way into Kraków looked the same as it had when I had left. Only when we got into town could I see the incredible difference between the Kraków of 1993 and that of 2000. There were more neon signs around the Rynek square at the center of town than I would have seen in Stuttgart. Even the Sukkienice, that medieval guildhall, was surrounded by a hundred outdoor tables, topped by parasols protecting their customers from the sun, which poked through the clouds on that fine Polish spring day. As the hours passed, and we began to visit some of the places that had made Kraków home for me, I could feel the tension dissipate. I wanted to accept Kraków for the modern central European city it was fast becoming, and I found that I could if I just let myself go.

The next day, after filming with *60 Minutes* on some of the ancient streets that lead away from the Rynek towards Wawel Castle, we made our way back towards the central square, just to shoot background footage of me walking through the center of the city. Bob Simon and his crew were walking behind me when I noticed a familiar figure walking towards us across the square. It was an older priest, dressed in simple black with Roman collar; he was trailed by a younger priest, whom I also vaguely recognized. Before I knew it, I was face to face with His Eminence Franciszek Cardinal Macharski. I don't know who recognized whom first. I was certainly more out of context for him, seven years after I had left his city, than he was to me. In an instant, however, we were locked in conversation, as if no time had passed at all.

"Welcome, welcome," His Eminence exclaimed in English. "How is it, Maestro, that you are back here with us in Kraków? To what do we owe this visit?" I pointed to the camera crew from *60 Minutes*, and being a public personage, he immediately understood.

"Your concert for the Holy Father is coming up, no? On His Holiness' birthday, May 18, isn't it? I will be there, of course. I know the Holy Father is looking forward very much to this occasion," Cardinal Macharski went on.

"Yes, Your Eminence," I replied, also in English. "I too am looking forward to that day. It will be great, I hope. And we have given concerts already in Baltimore and London. We are on a musical pilgrimage for the Year of the Great Jubilee. It would give me enormous pleasure to add such a concert in Kraków to our tour. Would you wish this, if it were possible?"

"Yes, Maestro, this could be interesting. But would you kindly write me a letter proposing this, and I will see what can be done." And with this, His Eminence continued on his way across the Rynek in the direction of the Kuria, the elegant Kraków building that housed both his residence and his offices and the place where I had met him almost thirteen years before.

The whole encounter was astonishing, especially the way we had started almost from where we had left off. It was as if our conversation had only been on hold for the seven years since I was last in his city. I was amazed at my own temerity to have raised the idea of a Kraków concert, a prospect that unfounded fear would have kept me from even contemplating only forty-eight hours earlier. I had anticipated my *60 Minutes*-inspired trip to Poland with dread. Now I was proposing that our pilgrimage might come full circle, ending where my story had begun.

I didn't know if it could really happen, but the thought was very exciting. As I contemplated a concert in Kraków, with a great international orchestra in one of the most magnificent churches of this glorious Polish jewel of a city, my artist's imagination began to go into overdrive. And I knew the Pope would love the idea as well.

That night in the hotel, I happened by the room that Bob, Michael, and their crew had turned into their mobile editing room. Through the door I could see them watching me on a small television monitor. Michael saw me approaching and made a gesture that indicated immediately that I was not welcome, so off I shuffled to my large but empty room. As I lay in bed waiting for sleep, I stewed. What were they really up to with this program about me? In the dark, my mind went back to *The Insider*, a movie I had recently seen about a whistle-blower in the tobacco industry who had been betrayed by *60 Minutes* and CBS. Was some version of that going to happen to me? What if they were really using me to get the great journalistic "get," an interview with the Pope? What if they harbored anti-Catholic sentiments that would come out in the end? I couldn't help but think of those hundreds of *60 Minutes* gotcha interviews with Mike Wallace shoving microphones in people's faces.

The next day, on our flight from Kraków to Rome, I stood up on the small Polish plane and confronted Michael Gavchon.

"Michael, what's your real agenda here? What do you and Bob really want out of this story? Come on, tell me," I demanded.

Michael Gavchon is a very experienced television journalist, who is calm under pressure. He has covered his fair share of wars and conflict zones. He was not about to be put off by a slightly paranoid conductor in the middle of filming a story he had been working on for months.

"What do you think we want?" he asked calmly. "Do you think we have come all this way, interviewed and filmed you in all these different cities, just to sandbag you? Maestro, is that what you really think?"

"No, I suppose not," I answered, only slightly mollified. "But you have to admit you guys do have a bit of a reputation for pretty tough journalism. Tough but fair, you would probably say. But I guess you're right. You've been absolutely up front with me so far. I am just a tad nervous is all."

"Maestro, you have a concert coming up, bigger than any of the others. The Pope is going to be there. Your orchestra, the choir, great soloists. You have lots to think about right now."

He was right, of course. I had a great, important concert—the Pope's Birthday concert—for worldwide broadcast. And I needed to be ready for that.

I went back to my seat, took out my conductor's score to "Creation," and heard the music fill my head where fear had almost taken over.

As our plane came down across the Alps and flew over the Lazio plain, as the incredible azure of the Mediterranean came into view, I knew I would soon be home. Not my home in New York, but a place in which I had come to feel comfortable, nonetheless. Soon I would be in my Room 405 at the Hotel Raphael, with its balcony overlooking the German Augustinian Church and the tiny street called Largo Febo, just off the Piazza Navona. I would arrive at the hotel, change my travel clothes for Roman casual, and go out for a stroll to the best gelato bar in all Rome, called by its quaint English name, Old Bridge. I would choose from the incredible aromas of chocolate, pear, *melone*, and *stracciatella* and slowly amble back to the Raphael following the Vatican's massive outer wall, then walking by St. Peter's Basilica off my right shoulder.

Crossing the bridge over the Tiber, I would walk down the Via dei Coronari, with its antique stores, one hard on the other, and settle back into my room to wait out the warm Roman night. No, Michael was right. Whatever *60 Minutes* had in mind I could handle. It was the rest of the goings-on at the Vatican that should be my preoccupation.

CHAPTER

TWENTY-SEVEN

I saw Bishop Dziwisz at 11:00 on the morning after my arrival from Kraków. We had seen each other many times that fall and spring. I had discussed with him even the smallest detail of every one of our Creation Pilgrimage concerts so that he could keep His Holiness apprised and offer his sage advice. On that day, May 16, I first had to tell him about my encounter with Cardinal Macharski. Bishop Dziwisz wondered at the coincidence of our meeting. He knew how rare my visits to Kraków were, and just how busy Cardinal Macharski is every day. Bishop Dziwisz thought that the Pope would love the idea of adding a concert in our "home" city to our Jubilee events schedule. His mind immediately began to go over the churches we might use. He named them out loud, one beautiful sanctuary after another. He let me know, of course, that the final decision would rest with Cardinal Macharski but that in his mind, the Basilica of Saint Mary, one of the Pope's favorite Kraków houses of worship and one of the most famous in all of Poland, would be a wonderful place for such an important occasion. But then we both remembered we had a very big concert coming up in just two days.

"Maestro, is there anything I should know? Anything that has not yet been taken care of for our event on Thursday?"

"No, Your Excellency, everything seems to be under control. The Philharmonia Orchestra and Chorus should be arriving later this after-noon, and we will be rehearsing tomorrow and Thursday morning in the Sala Nervi. Marjorie Weeke has, as always, been very helpful, as have so many others in the Vatican. I do hope His Holiness will be pleased."

"Well, Maestro, I have heard wonderful reports from Cardinal Keeler about your concert in the basilica in Baltimore. I remember His Holiness' visit there. Do you know that on the one single day of the Papal visit His Eminence and the Holy Father took their lunch in the homeless shelter in the basement of the basilica? I am so glad there was an event in that wonderful church. That must have been a very special occasion. And Archbishop Murphy-O'Connor was also most complimentary. Your London performance also went quite well, by his account."

"Yes, we were pleased with both concerts. The one in America was broadcast widely, and there were many interreligious personages present at the invitation of Cardinal Keeler. And in London ..."

"Yes, I read the review. Your performance was a great success, I think. So the newspaper said. Maestro, I am so looking forward to your concert here at the Vatican."

"One thing, Excellency, I should apprise you of. I have prepared a little surprise for His Holiness. After we finish Haydn's "Creation," and after His Holiness speaks, we have a small addition to the program. I hope you will not mind. In honor of his eightieth birthday, I have taught the Philharmonia Chorus to sing "Sto Lat." They will actually sing it in Polish. I have given the orchestra their music for this also. Please, may I ask you, if this meets with your approval, please don't tell His Holiness. We would wish to play and sing it for him as a surprise."

"What a wonderful idea, Maestro. No, I will not say a word. I think His Holiness will be very happy with this 'gift.' Is there anything else?"

"Yes, Excellency. One last thing. I must soon go to the Holy Land to see the Latin Patriarch, and also the Papal Nuncio, about our concerts in Bethlehem, Nazareth, and Jerusalem. Would you be so kind as to give them information that I will be coming? My schedule calls for me to travel there in June. I would be so grateful."

"With pleasure, Maestro. I think you will receive a warm welcome from Patriarch Sabah. He is a very good man. I know he will be in sympathy with our project. And the Nuncio, Archbishop Sambi, is an old friend. He is open-minded and a strong believer in the Holy Father's interfaith work. I think you will find both of these men to be excellent partners in this project ... So again, we will see each other in the Aula on Thursday. If there is anything else, you will call, yes? Thank you for all you have done to realize this Creation Pilgrimage. The Holy Father is so pleased. It is truly a great and important series of concerts."

I left the Apostolic Palace and walked straight across Saint Peter's Square to the office of Dame Marjorie Weeke. She was, as always, a potent force to be reckoned with in the Vatican. With just two days left, I would need her help should anything untoward suddenly surface in her area of expertise.

Marjorie's job was to keep the media in their proper place at the Vatican. She was very busy with our event. The RAI, Italian national television, would be televising our concert and offering it to broadcasters around the world via Eurovision. *60 Minutes* needed her assistance as well, however. As an American with long experience with all the U.S. networks, she knew their presence was something special. They had asked her for permission to put their own cameras in the Aula for our concert. She saw that *60 Minutes* got everything it needed to make its story on me reflect most respectfully on the Vatican as well, while keeping them out of the way of the RAI.

The afternoon of that first day in Rome was in fact my *60 Minutes* D-Day. The "big interview" with Bob Simon was scheduled to be shot in an elegantly frescoed foyer of the lower lobby of the Hotel Raphael. The lighting alone took hours to prepare. I was more nervous than I had ever been for just about anything in my life. When it came down to it, though, Bob Simon, who is as sharp a questioner as can be found on the air, was careful and straightforward in his in-depth probing. I felt he wanted to achieve for his viewers a level of insight into my relationship with the Pope that was open and honest, but not unfairly intrusive, as I had originally feared. I knew that he was Jewish and from the Bronx, and that in some ways, although he probably wouldn't want to admit it, he could identify with what this entire Vatican experience must have been like for me. This gave him, I felt, an interesting perspective from which to ask great questions. The interview lasted two hours, under hot lights, in a relatively small, close-up space. But I never felt like there were any gotcha moments. In the end, Bob was fair and I was left in one piece, just as Michael Gavchon had gently implied I would be on our flight to Rome two days before.

I walked out of the interview, went upstairs, changed into my rehearsal clothes, and went straight over to the Vatican to begin my work with the Philharmonia Orchestra and Chorus. To my relief, I recognized the members of the orchestra sitting on the concert platform in the Sala Nervi as the same ones who had performed with me in Baltimore. We nodded to one another in mutual respect. I could relax. This Papal performance would be well prepared.

The soloists for this Vatican concert were, once again, different from those in Baltimore or London. Here with us in Rome was Harolyn Blackwell, an American Catholic who had joined me seven years before to sing before John Paul at World Youth Day in Denver. We also had the remarkable elegant English tenor Philip Langridge, whose portrayal of the title character in Benjamin Britten's "Peter Grimes" is rivaled only by that of Britten's longtime companion, Peter Pears. And then there was Hakan Hagagard, the Swedish baritone, whom I and just about everyone else in the opera-loving world had come to know through his humor-filled Papageno in Ingmar Bergman's legendary cinematic adaptation of Mozart's "The Magic Flute." In the final analysis, I am always artistically seduced by beautifully enunciated, wonderfully sung British English. I couldn't stop smiling as I heard the words of this anglicized biblical text roll off Mr. Langridge's tongue. When he let loose his clarion voice, singing, "In splendor bright is rising now the sun and darts his rays," he made me, and even his British colleagues in the Philharmonia Chorus, break into broad smiles.

On the evening of the performance, His Holiness showed his eighty years only in that this time he did not, as he usually did, enter from the back of the Auditorio and make his way up the aisle shaking every hand as he passed by on his way to his normal seat in the center of the hall. This time, he walked out from offstage, coming from the same direction we artists had, to tumultuous applause, which filled the Aula and went on and on. I looked out over the enormous audience and saw many friends and acquaintances from far and wide who had flown in especially for the concert, including my good friends Joe and Claire Flom from New York.

Finally the Pope sat down in his large thronelike chair, surrounded by his closest aides and high Vatican officials, Bishop Dziwisz just behind him. The instant Bishop Dziwisz gave a nod, off we went, unfolding Haydn's magical representation of the creation of God's universe in strong, yet delicate musical language meant, as the composer wished, for everyone to understand.

The orchestra had grown even more accustomed to my tempos and gestures in this work, and the chorus sang with what seemed to me to be an extra measure of spiritual fervor. The only strange acoustical note was sounded by the harpsichord, which plays during the recitative portions of the work, a kind of musical declamation particular to the Classical period. This ancient-sounding, key-plucked eighteenth-century instrument seemed oddly out of place in a work performed in that immense modern hall before a crowd of 7,500. The quaint sound so well produced by the Philharmonia's harpsichordist was captured beautifully, however, for the worldwide television audience.

For this Papal event we performed only two of the three parts of Haydn's magnum opus. Papal Concerts, I had learned, should generally not exceed an hour and fifteen minutes. And this year, especially for a pope husbanding his energies for the great work he still had left to do, we were only too happy to make a small musical accommodation. Something tells me that the deeply Catholic Haydn would have been thrilled just to have this significant portion of his masterwork performed for the Pope in Rome, the entire Vatican hierarchy of his

Church, and millions upon millions of listeners and viewers of all faiths the world over.

At the end, the applause rang out long and loud. I knew we had done well, but the only review I was interested in was the one coming to me from the great personage on the throne to my left. During the entire performance, as I caught glimpses out of my eye, the Pope had seemed especially engaged. He enjoyed the music, following the text of Genesis in this exquisite musical setting with intense concentration. And his fond thumbs-up gesture towards me at work's end was all the approbation I needed.

In His Holiness' speech following the performance of the Haydn, he spoke eloquently about creation and the meaning of the Genesis text as so beautifully set by Papa Haydn. Then he thanked all of us for bringing him the wonderful birthday gift of this music. As he turned to take his seat, the Philharmonia Orchestra and Chorus and I began to perform the Polish birthday song "Sto lat." The text in English does not begin to capture with what gusto it is sung at every Polish special celebration:

> Good luck, good cheer, may you live a hundred years.
>
> Good luck, good cheer, may you live a hundred years.
>
> Good luck, good cheer, may you live a hundred years.
>
> One hundred years!

Bishop Dziwisz had kept his word: the Pope was not merely surprised, he was flabbergasted, and he broke out in a huge smile that stretched from ear to ear. Every Pole in the Aula had begun to sing along. I was singing too, almost losing my place as I stared at John Paul's beaming face. Applause rang out and wouldn't stop, even as he raised his hands begging for this show of affection to end. Finally Bishop Dziwisz called for the soloists, certain select members of the orchestra and chorus, and myself to approach His Holiness.

When I came to the Pope, he greeted me with a warmth that was as direct and sincere as it was deeply profound for me. Bishop Dziwisz then asked me, in a rare and great honor, to introduce the soloists and the other musicians to the Pope. This honor in fact continued backstage when I introduced His Holiness to the many people gathered there to express their personal birthday wishes, and to receive his Papal blessing. Among these lucky few were President Rondelli of UniCredito and his senior management team from Milan; Jonathan O'Herron and his wife, Shirley, as well as his Lazard Frères Italian partner, Guido Vitale; and my good friend Daniel Berger and his fiancée, Janet Stanwood, who true to form, had made their way to Europe once again to be present at one of my major concerts. Such loyalty and lasting camaraderie is irreplaceable on a journey as strange yet wonderful as the one which I was on.

The Pope was soon gone out the door and back to his Papal Apartments. Many of my friends and I went off to a reception at the Hotel Columbus, *due passi*, as they say, just a few steps down the Via della Conciliazione from where we had just performed. This reception was hosted by His Eminence Cardinal Keeler and was attended by many of the same members of the American Church hierarchy who had been so helpful, including the rector of the North American College, Monsignor Timothy Dolan, now Archbishop of New York.

Michael Gavchon had been so right. This Papal Concert was by far the most important one of our Jubilee Creation series.

As if the *60 Minutes* profile wasn't proof enough, the press interest surrounding the event was enormous. Newspapers throughout the world ran stories. The one that touched me most was in my very own hometown paper. On the day of the concert, the *New York Times* ran an interview by their Rome/Vatican correspondent, Alessandra Stanley. She quoted Cardinal Lustiger as saying the concert for the Pope's eightieth birthday was a "Cardinal's plot." True, many of the Pope's most trusted advisors were part of the planning of the event, but it was His Holiness himself who had wished to show the world his profound desire for peace and understanding among the adherents of all the world's great monotheistic religions by having Haydn's "Creation" performed. He could well have asked for a Te Deum, or a Mass, both of which—or many other Catholic works—would have been suitable. But His Holiness had wished for a work with a broader meaning, and I had been honored to fulfill his request. The importance of the concert itself was mirrored once again in the *Times* the very next day, when the front page of the May 19 edition showed a picture of me, conducting "Creation" for His Holiness, in full color, above the fold. Two major stories in two days in the *New York Times*. I was delighted and amazed.

On that day, May 19, my family and I were invited to a postconcert, celebratory private audience with His Holiness. This time, as we entered the Pope's library, he reached out to my sons—Gabriel, eight, and David, fifteen—greeting them first and remarking on how they had grown since he had last seen them, in 1994. He asked after David's violin-playing and Gabriel's chess prowess. I almost wished that we had brought along a violin on which David could play the Pope his Bach, or a chess set so that my young wizard Gabriel could test his patient skills against those of the Bishop of Rome. Of course, I would never have done so, but Pope John Paul had such a fondness for young people that I actually think he might have enjoyed it, if his time and energies did not have to be so carefully husbanded.

His Holiness was all smiles when he greeted Vera. For a woman with a Ph.D. in Slavic Languages and Literatures from Yale, this encounter could be almost taken in stride. It was not her first meeting with the Pope, after all. But for someone who as a little girl sat in the back of her native Bratislava's Catholic churches, peering in amazement over the back of the last row of pews at pristine, white-clad brides standing with their straight-necked grooms, the couple taking their everlasting marital vows before their local parish priest, this was still a remarkable occasion. As it was for me. For as many times as I had met His Holiness, I never lost the sense of wonder that I was in the Pope's presence. I never knew if each time could be my last time, and with that sense came a deep need to savor every single moment. To remember all I could. To build my memory of this unique relationship so that I could cherish it all the more when finally it was done.

When at last John Paul got around to greeting me, he did so with an outstretched hand, bearing a whole set of Papal medals, in gold and in silver, in thanks for the concert of the night before. These Pontifical Medallions of the year of the Great Jubilee were made even more valuable coming from the Pope's hand. But as grateful as I was for these tokens of the Pope's esteem, I felt that His Holiness' happiness and pride with what we had accomplished, trying to realize our common dream of peace through music, were reward enough to keep me going.

After giving me his gift, His Holiness asked me about our events in Baltimore and London. He told me he would be so very pleased if there might be a concert in his beloved Kraków, that he had already been informed that such an invitation might possibly be forthcoming. But most of all, the Pope gave me his blessing again for the success of the next part of my journey: the Jubilee Creation concerts that would follow in his own recent groundbreaking footsteps in the Holy Land.

When he had landed in Israel two months before, at the exact time as the Philharmonia and I had embarked on our own Jubilee Creation Pilgrimage to the New World, His Holiness had said to the assembled dignitaries:

> I pray that my visit will serve to encourage an increase of interreligious dialogue that will lead Jews, Christians and Muslims to seek in their respective beliefs, and in the universal brotherhood that unites all the members of the human family, the motivation and the perseverance to work for the peace and justice which the peoples of the Holy Land do not yet have, and for which they yearn so deeply. The Psalmist reminds us that peace is God's gift: "I will hear what the Lord God has to say, a voice that speaks of peace, peace for his people and his friends, and those who turn to him in their hearts." May peace be God's gift to the Land he chose as his own!

I could not have imagined then, standing beside the Pope, what violence and turmoil I would yet encounter in our quest to make the music of peace in Jerusalem the Golden.

CHAPTER

TWENTY-EIGHT

In June 2000, I landed at Ben Gurion Airport near Tel Aviv, in the heart of modern Israel, and from there began my literal ascent to Jerusalem, a city uniquely holy to all three great monotheistic faiths. It is an ancient place, battled over furiously for almost two millennia, a place to which pilgrims of all descriptions have journeyed since time immemorial.

To get to Jerusalem from the airport, my taxi took Israeli Route 1, which runs from the west near Tel Aviv almost all the way to the Jordan River to the east. The route snakes its way up from the populous areas near Israel's coast, through an area of relative wilderness, directly to the walls of the ancient city. Along the way there are numerous villages, like Abu Ghosh, for example, traditionally inhabited by Arab Christians. In those sleepy-looking towns, church steeples rather than minarets foreshadow the Christian holy sites that lie beyond the Jaffa Gate, Old Jerusalem's only portal leading back to the sea. I was disturbed to see, lining Route 1, what looked like the carcasses of Israeli tanks left over from the War of Independence in 1948. (I later found out they were the burned-out remains of supply trucks used in that war, which had been armored to protect them from snipers as they made their way to the Holy City.) Whether they are too heavy to remove or, better, one hopes, left as a reminder of the tragedy of war, I did not know. But they certainly made a strong impression on me as I began my mission of peace in the Holy Land on behalf of the Pope.

When I arrived at the King David Hotel and was shown to my room, I opened the shutters and looked out over the Old City panorama spread out far beneath me. The most dominant landmark, besides the city's walls themselves, is the golden Dome of the Rock, the mosque built atop the ruins of the Temple of Solomon that is an unmistakably strong, almost dominant Muslim architectural presence. But the mosque is almost matched by the presence of numerous bell towers of the many churches that rise above the walls of the Old City, magnificent buildings such as the Roman Catholic Dormition Abbey on Mount Zion, which is said to be the place where Mary fell asleep for the last time, just before she was taken into Heaven. Or the ornate tower of the Cathedral of Saint James, headquarters of the Armenian Patriarchate. Christians are important here, these towers seem to say. Hidden from view that day but very much on my mind was the Wailing Wall, the Western Wall of the Second Temple, the place where we Jews believe we are closest to God. Religious Jewish Jerusalem, the most ancient of all three faith presences, is by far the most understated, despite the ongoing conflict that might indicate otherwise.

The following morning I walked through the Jaffa Gate into the Old City proper, turned left, and made my way up a narrow street to the headquarters of the Latin Patriarch of Jerusalem. His Beatitude Michel Sabbah was the first Palestinian ever to hold that exalted title since it was established by the Crusaders in 1099. I was met at the entrance to the Latin Patriarchate by its Chancellor, Father Raed Awad Abu-Sahlyeh. Father Raed was young, in his midthirties, tousle-haired, fast-talking, and energetic. He welcomed me with open arms, literally embracing me as he said in heavily accented English, "Brother, welcome to our home."

I almost wanted to look around to see whether Father Raed had somehow mistaken me for someone else. But I guessed that Bishop Dziwisz had indeed prepared the way. I was clearly expected that morning.

Father Raed led me through the narrow hallway, past the entrance to their cathedral on the right, and ushered me into a small, simple, but functional meeting room—a far cry from the Vatican and its ornately decorated Papal Palace. I waited for some minutes while Father Raed went off to see about the Patriarch. I was expected, he said, and would be brought into His Beatitude's presence quite soon. "His Beatitude—quite a title," I thought, and one I knew was reserved for the leaders of only four specially designated historic dioceses of the Catholic Church. As I waited impatiently, I began to imagine my coming encounter.

His Beatitude was said to be as much a proud Palestinian patriot as a leader of the Roman Church. I am Jewish—my name would tell him that—but I was sure Bishop Dziwisz would have made that clear as well. Would politics be a part of our meeting? Would he embrace our vision of brotherhood, or would he be skeptical about the entire project?

Finally Father Raed came back and led me across the hallway. As we entered the large reception room of the Patriarch, I noted its spare, understated style, muted Persian carpets on the floor, and the chairs lining the walls, Arab style. One large chair sat in the middle along the far wall, in which, I presumed, His Beatitude would take his rightful place. He entered from the hallway down which I had come, with Father Raed trailing just behind. He was short and round-faced, with a tight smile and stern bespectacled eyes. His long black cassock was adorned with a large silver pectoral cross. A red bishop's skullcap rested on his balding head.

His Beatitude came towards me, opened his hands, and offered me a firm handshake. He offered no *abraccio*, but it was a warm welcome nonetheless. His Beatitude introduced me to His Excellency Kamal Hanna Bathish, the Vicar General of the Latin Patriarchate, the Patriarch's right-hand man, and invited me to sit in the chair alongside his. This was as high-level a reception as I could possibly have imagined.

Patriarch Sabbah began our discussion by saying he had heard about the concert for His Holiness' eightieth birthday. He told me that Bishop Dziwisz had indeed written to him about me after my last visit to the Apostolic Palace in May.

"Maestro," His Beatitude said, "we will do everything to help you. We all think such concerts could be a strong sign for peace. The Holy Father's visit here in March has shown us the way, yet again. What can I do to make your visit most effective?"

"Your Beatitude," I answered, "I would wish to perform concerts in all three great places of pilgrimage: Bethlehem, Nazareth, and here in Jerusalem. We need to find just the right church in each place. I had thought of the Church of the Nativity in Bethlehem, and the Basilica of the Annunciation in Nazareth, and I would be open to any suggestion you might have for the concert here in Jerusalem."

"Yes, Maestro, yes. I see. Let us take this one step at a time. There are many problems. We live in a sea of problems. Each of these places has its difficulties. I think, yes, we can overcome them. But the proper people must be approached in the proper manner. I am not the final authority here. There is the Palestinian Authority in Bethlehem. They must approve any concert in Bethlehem. Then there is the Bishop of Nazareth. He must agree to your giving a concert in his church. And of course, the Israeli Government. I suppose they would need to be involved. And most of all, there is the Custodia Terrae Sanctae, the Franciscan Custody of the Holy Places. Its head, the Custos, Father Giovanni Battistelli, must give his approval for any of the places you have mentioned. We are brothers in protecting and administering the ancient churches. I will help you to meet them, and I will support your project as strongly as I can, as I have said. I believe with all my heart in the way of peace. Father Raed will help you with everything. Maestro, I wish you Godspeed."

And with that, he left. Father Raed, true to His Beatitude's word, sat down to go over the details of my coming busy two days in the Holy Land.

"First, Maestro, you must go to Bethlehem to meet Christiane Dabdoud Nasser," Father Raed said. "She works for the Palestinian Authority as the head of their Bethlehem 2000 Project. Ms. Nasser can begin to work with you to plan the concert in Bethlehem. I will call her right now, and see whether she is free even today. We need to start right away."

He picked up the telephone that was on a small table in the Patriarch's reception room and called Christiane Nasser. He spoke a few words of Arabic into the phone, and got off in a hurry.

"She is excited. She too has heard about your project. She wants to see you right away. Can you go directly? She will wait for you at 11:30 A.M. in her office in Manger Square in Bethlehem."

"Yes, yes, of course. That is why I am here." I got to my feet, thinking it was now 10:30 A.M. Bethlehem is only a few kilometers from Jerusalem, but it was impossible to tell how the traffic would be, especially in and around Jerusalem. I rushed to the door and was about to leave when Father Raed stopped me.

"I almost forgot. There is someone else you must meet." I looked around to see that a youngish Arab man had entered the room. He was clearly a layman, as he wore no priestly garb. "This is Wadie Abunasser. He is Executive Director of the Committee for the Great Jubilee here in the Holy Land. Wadie, this is Maestro Gilbert Levine, the conductor who has performed so often for the Holy Father. He has been sent here from Rome to plan some wonderful concerts.

"Maestro, Wadie will pick you up tomorrow at your hotel and take you to Nazareth. You will meet with Bishop Marcuzzo there at 11:00 A.M. Now, do please go; there is no time to lose. Call me about anything you need. Anything. Please, I am here to help you."

"Yes, thank you so much. And please thank His Beatitude also."

I reached out to shake Mr. Abunasser's hand, and told him I would look forward to seeing him at the hotel the next day. As I was about to leave, I remembered and turned to face him. "What time?" I called out. "What time do we have to leave?"

"8 A.M. I will pick you up at 8," Wadie shouted out to the back of my head, as I rushed into the narrow street that led to the square just inside the Jaffa Gate. I quickly searched for a taxi with a white Palestinian license plate to take me to Bethlehem.

Once before, on my voyage of discovery with my friends Jacques Barrot, a major French political figure, and his wife, Florence, at Easter in 1990, I had had a chance to encounter Palestinians in a way few Israelis ever can. I was present at meetings in the French diplomatic mission to Jerusalem, where Palestinian officials and important members of Palestinian civil society had opened their hearts and voiced their concerns to Jacques, in his capacity as head of the French Christian Democratic Party. Back then, however, I was but a fly on the wall. My French was fine, so I understood everything that was said, but my role was simply to listen, to witness, and then perhaps to give Jacques my Jewish perspective on what had been discussed. Now, as I sped toward Bethlehem, I realized I would be at the center of an enterprise that would depend very much on Palestinian cooperation and initiative to succeed.

The Holy Land that I saw from the taxi on the way to the birthplace of Jesus was a land seemingly at peace. The Judean Hills stretched out beckoningly on my left, as the walls of Old Jerusalem faded in the rearview mirror. There had not been any fighting between Palestinians and Israelis in years. It seemed that everywhere I looked as we entered Bethlehem, there were construction cranes, which are the clear markers of major economic activity. Prosperity, it seemed, was finally beginning to touch the Palestinian street. My taxi driver, a thirtyish-looking man from Ramallah, told me that his dream was to save eighteen thousand dollars so that he could buy a condominium for his family in his hometown. He said he wished his kids could get an education so that they could have a better life than he had. These seemed like the dreams of taxi drivers everywhere, whether in New York, or Paris, or Tel Aviv.

I arrived at the offices of the Palestinian Authority in Bethlehem and was shown upstairs to meet Christiane Nasser, an elegantly dressed woman in her late thirties, I surmised, whose English was ever so slightly accented, but not by her native Arabic. To my ear, at least, I detected a clear French influence. Ms. Nasser was exceedingly well briefed. Even before I said anything, it was clear that she knew why I had come. As a Catholic with close associations to the Patriarchate she had heard all about the Papal Concert at the Vatican. As the head of the Church Relations Unit of the Bethlehem 2000 Project, she wanted, she said, to do anything she could to bring such an event to her native town.

She immediately introduced me to Dr. Nabeel Kassis, the Minister in the Palestinian Authority in charge of her department. Dr. Kassis also pledged to do all he could to bring our event to Bethlehem.

Christiane offered to give me a small tour of Bethlehem, and we walked out of her office, turned left into Manger Square, and came almost immediately to the Church of the Nativity, where I thought our concert should take place. We entered the church, which was smaller than I thought it would be. But I felt its beauty and its powerful tradition, nonetheless. Its double rows of columns were stained towards the top with centuries of dark discoloration. It did not appear that this ancient sanctuary would give us the space we needed for our "Creation" performance. It would have to be carefully assayed, of course, but since even now, at midday, the church was overcrowded with tourists, any such assessment would have to await a quieter visit.

From there Christiane led me to the Church of Saint Catherine, right next door, a lovely church whose modern Gothic revival architecture did not give it quite the same atmosphere as the Church of the Nativity we had just left. We looked around and did some quick calculations about the space that might be made for musicians and choristers around the altar in St. Catherine's, then made our way outside.

Once back in Manger Square, Ms. Nasser invited me for a coffee, and introduced me to the complexities of Christian Bethlehem. Christiane told me that the Church of the Nativity was controlled by the Orthodox Church. We would never be able to get permission for a concert there. But perhaps, if we were fortunate, St. Catherine's, a Roman Catholic church, would be a possibility. She asked whether I had met with the Custos. I told her that Patriarch Sabbah had mentioned Father Battistelli but that I had not yet had the pleasure.

"Well, you see, Maestro, it's like this. His Beatitude is the highest Church official in the Roman Catholic hierarchy here. He is the head of all the Catholics in the Holy Land. But the Custos, he is charged by the Holy Father with maintaining and protecting all the holy sites, including the Church of the Nativity and the Church of the Annunciation in Nazareth. Did the Patriarch explain that to you?"

"No," I said, "our conversation was not so detailed. He had indicated it would be important for me to meet him, but he did not say precisely why."

"You will find out soon enough. But please be assured that we, here at the Palestinian Authority, will do all we can to help you with your 'Creation' concert. It would be such an honor for us to be able to include this in our plans for the Great Jubilee."

I asked Christiane about modern-day Bethlehem, about all the construction cranes I had seen on my way into the city.

"We are in a very good period right now. We are building hotels, a new convention center. We look forward to even more tourists," she said, with a laugh. "We are very optimistic. Your concert, with an international orchestra and choir, here in our Manger Square, would fit in so wonderfully with the future we hope we are building."

"Well, I hope so, too. I have come this far to see that we succeed. Just a quick question: Do I hear a French inflection in your English?" I asked diffidently.

"Yes," she smiled. "I am really bilingual, I guess trilingual—if you think my English is OK—as is my whole family. But we are very fond of French culture. I really hope my children can study at the Sorbonne."

I thanked her for the coffee, and for the beginning of what I hoped would be a very fruitful friendship, then found a taxi so that I could return to Jerusalem.

When I returned to the King David Hotel, there was a message from Father Raed.

"Maestro, how did it go in Bethlehem with Ms. Nasser?" Father Raed asked when I called him back. "The Patriarch wants to know."

"Fine. I believe we have a good beginning. When do you think I can meet the Custos? His Beatitude had told me that would be important, and now Ms. Nasser told me the same."

"Well, Maestro, not this time, I'm afraid. The Custos, he is very busy just now. When will you come back? Soon, I hope. You will meet him then, I am sure. In any case, tomorrow you will go to Nazareth to meet Bishop Marcuzzo and to see the basilica. Wadie will pick you up at your hotel. Please call me before you leave for Rome tomorrow afternoon?"

"Yes, I will," I said, not remembering when I had told Father Raed about my travel plans. All I could think of was that the village that is the Vatican extends its borders all the way to the Holy Land.

Later that afternoon, I met with both the British and the American Consuls General in Jerusalem. I saw the American, Gerald Feierstein, who served as the American representative to the Palestinians, in his West Jerusalem office. Jerry confirmed my impression that peace and prosperity seemed to be breaking out all over. He said my concerts would come at just the right time. His British counterpart, Robin Kealy, agreed. He was especially interested in our plans because a major British orchestra was to perform these concerts with me.

The next day, as promised, Wadie Abunasser picked me up at 8:00 A.M. in the lobby of the King David. Wadie is an Israeli Arab, educated in Israeli universities and fluent in English and (I presumed) Hebrew as well as his native Arabic. As one of the principal coordinators for John Paul's visit to the Holy Land that March, he was as well positioned as could be to assist us in making our pilgrimage concerts a reality.

But Wadie is first and foremost a Palestinian. He wanted to introduce me to the West Bank, to see it through his eyes. So he chose a route from Jerusalem to Nazareth that went by way of Jericho, all the way to the east, and north along the Jordan River, instead of the route most Israelis would have taken, namely, doubling back into Israel and driving up the center of the country.

I was fascinated. Everything I saw was new: Arab villages. Some Israeli settlements. Again, the great Judean Hills. As we drove, Wadie poured out his heart.

"We Catholics believe in nonviolence. We are for peace. The Patriarch, he is talking all the time about Palestinian rights, yes, but only achieved through peace. The Christian presence in the Holy Land is so important for this. We want to see a peaceful solution to all the problems here. And we are under such pressure. Our villages are emptying out. Whole communities are emigrating. Even to America. You will find more Palestinian Catholics abroad now than here. This is terrible, not just for us. But for everybody. I hope the Pope's trip here last March will convince people to stay. I am so glad he has sent you to us. Maybe these concerts can show our people that the outside world cares about us more than for just a few days."

As we approached the city of Jericho, I saw nothing of the biblical wall, or of the Prophet Joshua himself, but I did see a new, fancy-looking casino. It was an Israeli casino, Wadie told me, which was generating business for Jericho and the whole of the West Bank. He was not a fan of gambling, he assured me. But the Oasis Casino, as it was called, approved by none other than Yasser Arafat himself, was a promising sign of Palestinian economic development. Wadie wished it were a shopping mall, but he hoped it promised prosperity nonetheless.

We turned back towards Israel, crossing the heartland of the West Bank, finally arriving at the residence of the Bishop of Nazareth, His Excellency Giacinto-Boulos Marcuzzo. Bishop Marcuzzo was born in Italy but had spent many years in service to the Latin Patriarchate. He showed me his basilica, which like the Church of the Nativity was his for religious worship, but which was overseen by the Franciscan Custodian of the Holy Places, Father Battistelli, whom I would not be able to meet on this trip.

Bishop Marcuzzo shared with me some of his many troubles in Nazareth—troubles with Catholic emigration, and with a growing Muslim presence in what had been a majority Christian city. There was now a movement to build a large mosque directly across from the basilica, one that would perhaps be even larger than the great church itself. Things were changing in Nazareth, His Excellency told me. And he was not sure the times ahead would be easy. We agreed to stay in touch, but I had the feeling I was leaving behind a man in the middle.

My whirlwind visit was now drawing to a close. I phoned Father Raed one last time before I boarded my flight to Rome.

"Everything went well," I said. "Everyone from the Patriarch, to Christiane Nasser, to Wadie and Bishop Marcuzzo, have been as helpful as they could be. I will report to Bishop Dziwisz that we are on our way."

The day after I arrived in Rome, I went to the Apostolic Palace to meet with Bishop Dziwisz and tell him all that had happened in the past week. He was amazed, both at the rapidity with which I had managed to see so many of the important personages in the Latin Patriarchate, and with the seeming progress I had made toward realizing our treasured Holy Land concerts. He counseled patience with the Custos.

"Yes, Maestro, Father Battistelli is very busy. But I am sure the next time you go he will find the time to see you. Do let me know when that might be. I will tell him again how very important these concerts could be in continuing the Holy Father's search for peace."

I flew back to New York feeling a sense of accomplishment almost too good to be true. The scene on the West Bank was so peaceful. The prosperity that was blossoming was all too promising. Everyone was talking of peace. Would it remain so? We would all have to wait and see. But outwardly, at least, there was not a cloud in the Middle Eastern sky in July 2000.

In the middle of August I received a letter from Christiane Nasser with an official invitation from the Palestinian Authority to perform the Haydn "Creation" as part of their Bethlehem 2000 series. She wrote that St. Catherine's would indeed be the most appropriate place for holding this concert, and that she "hoped that the Latin Patriarchate would help us in securing that venue." This last phrase struck me as strange. What resistance would the Latin Patriarch need to help us resolve? She was, she had told me, very close to Patriarch Sabbah. It was he who had sent me to her in the first place. To what could she be referring?

So I planned my return trip to Israel for September, eager to get to the root of whatever problem seemed to be brewing. Over the summer, the Camp David summit among the Palestinian President Yasser Arafat, Israeli Prime Minister Ehud Barak, and American President Bill Clinton broke up without any clear resolution. It was world news, of course, but I had no idea just how much of it would alter our own Holy Land plans.

On my way to Jerusalem, I stopped in Rome to meet once again with Bishop Dziwisz, then doubled back to London to confer with Serge Dorny, the Managing Director of the London Philharmonic Orchestra (LPO), which had become our official pilgrimage orchestra, replacing the Philharmonia, whose schedule that fall made it all but impossible for them to continue.

The LPO was an orchestra I had admired for many years. I had been assistant to Sir Georg Solti when he had recorded "La Bohème" with them during my student days. I had been a protégé of their Music Director Klaus Tennstedt, assisting him in the early 1980s on his legendary Mahler Symphony cycle. Then, in 1997, I had had the great pleasure of making music with the orchestra myself, recording excerpts from Wagner's "Tristan," "Tannhäuser," and Siegfried Idyll with the LPO in a series of sessions that have lived on in my memory as some of the most satisfying music-making of my life. I was very much looking forward to setting out with the London Philharmonic on the next leg of our pilgrimage journey.

I flew from London to Israel via Copenhagen, which was a roundabout route that must have made sense for some tight scheduling reason or other. The choice proved extremely interesting, however.

I am well known for keeping to myself on flights. I get lots of work done, studying scores in the silence at 35,000 feet. On that day I would have been just as happy reading Beethoven as talking to my seatmate, a well-dressed Arab gentleman in his forties, but I answered when he asked, in strongly accented but fluent English, "How are you? And what takes you to Lod airport today?"

"I am on my way to plan a series of concerts in Bethlehem, Nazareth, and Jerusalem," I said.

"Ah, what kind of concerts?" he asked inquisitively.

"Classical concerts, to celebrate the year of the Great Jubilee. I will be there representing Pope John Paul. The concerts are being planned with the Vatican."

The floret of my Pontifical Knighthood glistened in my lapel, and I noticed that my seatmate had stolen a look in that direction. I am not sure he knew exactly which rank or distinction it signified, but I believe he factored it into the next comment he made.

"I will tell you, sir. I have close connections with the Palestinian Authority."

"Oh, yes?" I said. "I am working with them in Bethlehem. Minister Kassis is to be our host there, I believe."

"Minister Kassis, yes, I know him quite well. A fine gentleman. When had you been planning to hold these concerts?"

"It has not been finally decided, but I suppose they will take place in October. That is the period we're aiming for."

"Listen, sir, I don't mean to interfere. I am sure these will be wonderful events, ones with deep meaning for everyone. But I don't think you will be able to do them in October."

"Why?" I asked, somewhat surprised.

"Just please remember what I say. You would be better off to avoid this next period." He gave me a knowing look, nodded his head, and then went back to his book.

We said no more during the flight but bid each other a polite good-bye as we exited the plane.

The next morning I began my very busy day with a meeting with His Beatitude. From there I would go on to meet with the Papal Nuncio, Archbishop Pietro Sambi, the Pope's ambassador to both Israel and the Palestinian Authority; my new friend Christiane Nasser; Consul Generals Feierstein and Kealy, as well as an official of the Israeli government.

The Patriarch was as friendly and solicitous as he had been that last June. But as we discussed places for the Jerusalem concert now, in September, nothing seemed to quite work out. This place was too cool in October, that place too small to fit the orchestra and the choir. Instead of leading me to the "perfect" location, as His Holiness had done in 1994 at the Vatican, or even as Ulrike Hessler had in Munich, His Beatitude offered no solutions. None. He asked that we stay in touch and keep on looking for just the right places. His words seemed to imply an indefinite delay. The strange words of my flight companion started to rattle around in my head. Maybe this was not going to be possible after all.

I met Archbishop Sambi at the Nunciatura, the Vatican's embassy on top of the Mount of Olives in Jerusalem. His Excellency was open and friendly, and he offered the full assistance of his office in "your wonderful project." I liked him immediately, as Bishop Dziwisz had told me I would. We promised to stay in touch as things progressed.

When I told Christiane Nasser what the Arab gentleman on my plane had said, she had no inkling of what it might mean. She was wanting to go ahead and figure out all the details of the Bethlehem event. The same was true for the British and American Consul Generals. As I've thought about it in hindsight, they either had no insight or more likely did not choose to share whatever they might have known as to why there might be any impediments to our plan for a series of October events.

The next day, however, at 10:30 A.M., I finally met with Father Battistelli. As we spoke in Italian, it seemed to free him up to be more candid in his assessment of our prospects.

"Maestro, I cannot say anything about Jerusalem. That is for His Beatitude to decide, if as I suspect, you are not requesting to perform in the Church of the Holy Sepulcher. No?"

"No, of course not," I replied. Not only was it much too small, but it is shared by six or sometimes more Christian denominations, all with a claim of their own small part on that labyrinthine church.

"No," I repeated emphatically, "that is not in our plans."

"Well, I can tell you, Maestro, there are difficulties in Bethlehem and in Nazareth, in both the Church of the Nativity and in St. Catherine's, and in the Basilica of the Annunciation in Nazareth. I don't see how those would be possible either."

"But Bishop Dziwisz had indicated to me that you might be able to render your assistance to this project ..."

"Yes, I know. But it is I who must manage the terrible difficulties we find ourselves in. I will explain to Monsignor Dziwisz when I see him next in Rome. I am sorry, Maestro, but this is just not the time." And with that, our conversation was over.

Father Battistelli's assistant showed me to the door, offering his apologies in beautiful, flowing Italian all the way out to the street. His words were calculated to soothe my painful disappointment.

"We know how much this means to the Holy Father. It is just not possible. Please, Maestro, do try to understand. Perhaps another time. *Chi lo sa*?—Who knows?"

After my meeting with the Custos, I went off to a prearranged lunch with my friend Nahum Gelber. He and his wife, Sheila, own a number of homes throughout the world, none more beautiful than their home in the storied Jerusalem artist neighborhood of Yemin Moshe. Nahum was bringing along Zusia Rodan, the manager of the Jerusalem Symphony, whom he said I just had to meet. After my disappointing conversation with the Custos, I was in no mood to make small talk. The Jerusalem Symphony, while quite a good orchestra, was not then on my radar screen. Nahum is a wonderful good friend and a great fan of the Jerusalem orchestra. I did not want to disappoint him, so I went.

Over lunch, Nahum and Zusia enthused about the orchestra and did their best to entice me to consider conducting them one day. But through it all, I just could not pay much attention. My mind was in the clouds of darkness that had hung over the meetings I had just had with His Beatitude and with the Custos. I could not help thinking about the admonition of my Palestinian travel companion. "Just remember what I say. You would be better to avoid the next period."

All this took place on September 27, 2000, the day I left the Holy Land for Kraków. On that very day also, as yet unknown to the world at large, a Palestinian security officer on a joint patrol with Israeli forces turned his firearm on his Israeli counterpart and murdered him. The very next day, Ariel Sharon, the leader of Israel's Likud Party, accompanied by more than a thousand security officers, paid a most unwelcome visit to the Temple Mount, the Haram al-Sharif, to assert the Jewish right to visit that hotly disputed holy ground.

The uprising known as the Second Intifada had just begun, and with it, ended our foreseeable plans for peace through music—*pax per musicam*—through our Jubilee Creation concert in the Holy Land.

Matters only went from bad to worse. On October 12, two Israeli reservists were lynched by a Palestinian mob in a Ramallah police station. The image of the blood-stained hands of the killers being proudly demonstrated to the crowd below, as the corpses of the two Israelis were dragged through the streets, was as depressing as it was barbaric. How fast the seeming idyll of my June visit had deteriorated into chaos. I thought of my Palestinian taxi driver, who then had dreamt of buying a condominium in that same city of Ramallah. Where would his oh-so-normal dreams be now? I thought of Wadie Abunasser and his fervent wish for change through peaceful means. Of the Patriarch for whom nonviolence was a profound truth. I wept for Christiane Dabdoub Nasser and her whole family. Where would they ride out the storm of violence that would surely engulf my city of David, her city of Jesus, the world's Bethlehem?

On my way back to the United States, I met in Kraków with Cardinal Macharski, who in the intervening months had kept on with his preparations for a grand concert in St. Mary's Basilica. In my conversation with the Cardinal, I dared not talk about the violence in the Middle East. I'm sure it would have brought him terrible sadness, as I knew it would His Holiness. I could only imagine how great was the Pope's heartache for the land he prized as the origin of hope for all humanity.

When I returned to New York, I was spent. All of our Holy Land dreams were dashed. All that time and effort for peace that I and so many others had invested had, at least for now, come to naught.

A few days later, I was in the music room of our apartment on the East Side of Manhattan, preparing for my next engagement, when the phone rang. It was Zusia Rodan, the manager of the Jerusalem Symphony, whom I had just met in Israel less than a month before.

"Maestro, I know you will think I am crazy, but I had to give this a try. Our new chief conductor has just cancelled the opening concerts of our season. He says he is too scared to risk coming to Israel in the middle of all this violence. I know you are very busy, that this is such short notice, but would you consider coming and conducting in his place? We would do whatever program you wish. It would mean so very much to us, and to everyone here in Israel. Will you please come?"

"Zusia, I am so busy just now. And I only just got back from your country. I have so much on my plate."

"Yes, I know. I am sure this would be very complicated for you. But it would mean so much for us if you would come. Join us. Please, at least think it over!" Zusia implored.

"OK, tell me again the dates of the concerts. I will call my wife. And tell me where I can reach you. I promise, I will call you back one way or another. Zusia, you *are* crazy, but I will think about it."

The truth is, I knew I would go the minute he asked. Somehow I believed that I had to be there, that it was my place, and that something good, very good, could come out of something that seemed on the face of it to be so terrible. I wasn't sure why, but I believed it was fated, beshaert, as we say. That I had met Zusia, and that he had called me now. All of it, beshaert.

I put down the phone and called Vera. Her reaction was swift and sure. "Are you out of your mind? Have you been watching the news? You know what's going on there. What can you do to help? Isn't there someone in Israel who can conduct these concerts? Call a colleague. Phone a friend. There must be someone in Jerusalem or Tel Aviv who can step in to help them out. Let's give them some money. Israeli orchestras are always in need of donations. There must be something else we can do. But please, this is nuts."

"No, Vera, I know this sounds crazy. But I am meant to do this. I have to go to prove that even in this terrible time something can be done for peace. And for me, music is what I can do. Please, I won't go if you tell me absolutely no, but I really think this is the right thing to do. Trust me. It will be OK. I can feel it."

At dinner that night we talked it through again. I even asked my sons, Gabriel and David. They were both very nervous, to be sure, but somehow they too knew I would go if I felt so strongly. Finally, Vera relented. I would be in Jerusalem, after all. Far, far from the West Bank. What could happen to me there?

"Go," she said, "if you must. Just come back in one piece!"

The next morning I called Zusia, who I think had fully expected me to turn him down. He was shocked. Shocked, but happy beyond belief.

"Maestro, Gilbert—may I call you Gilbert?—that's fantastic! Everyone will be so pleased. What program do you wish to conduct? We have a pianist, Daniel Gortler, engaged to play Mozart; I hope we can keep that on the program. He is very gifted. What else would you like to conduct?"

"Zusia, I have thought about it. I want to conduct Eroica, Beethoven's Third Symphony. To me, it is about the will of all human beings for freedom and peace. It is a universal statement. That is what I want to do."

"Done. We will do it. My staff will call about the arrangements. I look forward to seeing you in two weeks' time."

I hung up the phone, nervous and a bit scared, but also with a sense of great anticipation. I wanted to be there already, to stand up for peace in the middle of this war.

On October 20 I took the morning flight to London, over-nighted at the Ritz, and had a quick meeting with the London Philharmonic, hoping against hope that we could still agree to perform our Holy Land concerts later that month, which were still nominally on the books. I am not sure I was so very persuasive. In the end, the orchestra did indeed pull out. Serge Dorny's letter to my London assistant, the indefatigable Sue Banner, was sensible enough: "At the moment we are not sufficiently confident of the stability of the region. We would be thrilled to join Maestro Levine in Israel at a future date once the situation has stabilized."

I pushed on, again through Copenhagen, to Tel Aviv and then Jerusalem. At Ben Gurion Airport, it didn't feel to me as though the country was under siege. Life in Israel seemed normal; the cars jammed the highways; and people flooded the streets as they did on any ordinary day.

But Jerusalem was different. My rehearsal with the orchestra was taking place in a city very close to the "front lines" of the fighting. Zusia, members of the orchestra, and members of the orchestra's board of directors, including Haskel Beinish and his wife, Dorit, who was the Chief Justice of the Israeli Supreme Court, all came to me at the beginning of our rehearsals, at the intermission of our concerts, and afterwards at their homes as well, to welcome me and to thank me again and again for being so brave.

In turn, I told the orchestra members and everyone associated with them that I was proud to join them in this terrible time. And as I had told Vera, I said that I felt I was meant to be there with them. That it was beshaert. I also said that I wanted to dedicate our concerts that week to the search for peace. The violence had to end, and to me, peace and nonviolence were the only answer to solving the difficult problems in the long term.

Some of the orchestra members lived in towns that were now under threat. Their cars were stoned as they came out of the tunnel that led to their homes. Their families were under siege. I felt it was the least I could do to stand by them and help them through these trying days.

The night of the first rehearsal, Nahum Gelber and his wife, Sheila, invited me to accompany them to a charity dinner to benefit Shaarey Zedek Hospital, one of Israel's finest. It was to be held at the Israel Museum in the heart of West Jerusalem. Everybody who was anybody in Israel was there, including high-ranking members of the government. About midway through the proceedings we all heard an extremely loud noise, a rumbling overhead that shook the building. Some of us rushed outside to see what it was. We looked up in the sky towards the noise, only to see massive helicopter gunships heading east towards the fighting on the West Bank; they were flying just a few hundred feet above us. The sound of these massive flying battle-ships was deafening. Their rotors whooshed the air as if they would blow the cars in the museum's parking lots around like toys. I watched in fearful fascination. Nahum came outside to drag me back in. Now I knew why the orchestra was so pleased that I had come. Now I knew why I absolutely needed to be there with them.

The night of the concert, four days later, was even more eventful. As I arrived in the parking lot in the back of the Henry Crown Concert Hall, I heard loud but dull pops, bangs, and thuds repeating over and over at fitful intervals. I looked around to see where the sounds were coming from but couldn't see anything. Zusia rushed me inside. Once we got into the hall and I was safely ensconced in my backstage dressing room, I asked Zusia what I had heard out there.

"Oh, don't worry. That was just garbage men. You know, moving their garbage cans back and forth over the ground. They are working late tonight."

I am no expert in the sounds of sanitation, but that just didn't seem right to me. Finally, Ruti Malach, another member of the Jerusalem Symphony staff, came into my dressing room, closed the door, and said, "Gilbert, I heard what he said. Zusia was just trying to keep you calm. But I think you must know the truth. Here where we are, we are very close to Gilo in the southern part of Jerusalem. Right opposite Gilo is Beit Jala, on the West Bank. The Tanzim, Muslim fighters associated with Yasser Arafat's al-Aqsa Martyrs' brigades, have taken over houses in Beit Jala, a Christian town, and are trading fire with the Israel Defense Forces in Gilo. The battle is horrible. Families on both sides, Palestinians and Israelis, are in their basements. It is chaos there. That is what you are hearing. I'm sorry, we really didn't want to scare you. Actually, we thought you might just leave."

"No, I am here, and I will stay. If you are here, so am I," I replied, with a bravery I barely mustered.

Then I thought about the details of what she had just said. Beit Jala. That name rang a loud bell. It was the home of the only Roman Catholic seminary in Palestine. It was where His Beatitude the Patriarch Sabbah had studied for the priesthood. And Father Raed and Bishop Bathish as well. My God, I thought, that is a Catholic town, and those priests, and Christiane Nasser, must have relatives and friends there. This must be a nightmare for them. I can only imagine what they are going through right now.

The following day I tried to reach Christiane on her cell phone. It was switched off. How frustrating! My only hope was that that meant she was out of the country, in Paris, perhaps, with her children. Anywhere, I prayed, but here.

I finished my concerts with my respect for the musicians of the Jerusalem Symphony growing with every passing day. Our Eroica, which I had conducted so many times before, seemed this time to be imbued with an exceptionally heroic cast, which the full house at the Henry Crown Concert Hall seemed to share. The second movement, the Marche Funebre, encompassed a fullness of sound that was not merely musical but spiritual. It seemed to cry out for peace as much as it mourned the losses of war. I had chosen appropriately, and the musicians seemed to feel that strongly as well.

As I came to know, the Jerusalem Symphony is a wonderful orchestra, and these Israeli musicians played marvelously at those concerts. I was so proud I had come to Jerusalem to be with them at this terrible time.

When I returned to New York, I received a call from a producer at National Public Radio. He said he had heard about my concerts in Jerusalem from the Israel Broadcasting Authority. NPR now wished to include our Jerusalem Symphony season-opening concerts on their *Symphony Cast* series. I was thrilled. The message of our music-making during those awful days would be spread far and wide. I asked whether they would consider calling their broadcast a "Concert for Peace."

Yes, was NPR's instant reply. The orchestra gave its permission immediately for this broadcast, and so would I. I believed there was a profound message from that crisis-torn part of the world, which needed to be heard above the guns. And now NPR thought so too.

And so our normal subscription concert, opening the 2000–2001 season of the Jerusalem Symphony, was broadcast all across America in the second week of September 2001, days before the tragic events that were soon to unfold.

CHAPTER

THIRTY

In December I was off again for London and Kraków to prepare
for the last of our Jubilee concerts, in the Basilica of Saint Mary
on the Central Square, the Rynek, in Kraków.

My rehearsals in London with the world-class London Philharmonic were a joy. My friend Gillian Brierley, from Glyndebourne
Opera, came to one of our Beethoven Ninth rehearsals. As I caught
her eye, I smiled a quiet smile of deepest artistic satisfaction. And
Gillian told me later that she could sense the close rapport between
myself and the orchestra. Even more, she could hear the fruits of that
rapport in our compelling music-making together. The LPO is an
extraordinary ambassador of the great British orchestral tradition.

After just a few more sessions, our whole entourage—the orchestra, their glorious London Philharmonic Choir, a great group of international soloists, my family, and I—were winging our way eastward on
a charter flight to Kraków. St. Mary's Basilica in Kraków is the most
beautiful church in a city of magnificent houses of worship, both
Christian and Jewish. And Cardinal Macharski's invitation for us to
make music inside its walls was as rare as it was exciting just to think
about. Our concert was to serve a dual purpose. We were to help
the people of Poland commemorate the millennial anniversary of the
Roman Catholic Diocese of Kraków, and we were to participate in
the greatest concert series ever assembled in their country, put together
to celebrate Kraków's reign as the European Cultural Capital in the
year 2000.

The London Philharmonic and I would join some of the greatest orchestras and conductors in the world: the Berlin Philharmonic, conducted by Bernard Haitink; the New York Philharmonic, led by Kurt Masur; the Concentus Musicus Wien, then the world's premiere early-music ensemble directed by their founder, Nicholas Harnoncourt; among many others.

Our program, the last of the Kraków Year 2000 Millennium series, consisted of a performance of Bogurodzica, a Polish Marian Hymn thought to be at least a thousand years old; the second movement of Henryk Górecki's Third Symphony, the "Symphony of Sorrowful Songs," which is by far one of the most popular works of twentieth-century music; and Beethoven's Ninth Symphony, the "Ode to Joy."

The night of the performance, December 28, 2000, was frigid, and only slightly warmer inside the unheated basilica itself. The Rynek was filled to capacity with thousands upon thousands of people who could not make it inside the sanctuary, filled as it was to overflowing. Cardinal Macharski sat in the first row, bundled up in his winter coat. Everyone was shivering with cold until the first notes of the chorus rang out in the church. The London Philharmonic Choir had learned the words of Bogurodzica, the Polish hymn, reading it in transliterated form on the sheet music set in front of them. Not so the Polish audience in the basilica that night, which rose row after row, as if as one, singing the hymn more from the soul than by heart. It was an extraordinary, stirring start to our evening of historic and poignant music-making.

Sofia Kilanowicz, the wonderful Polish soprano, then sang the Górecki in a way that would break your heart. The words of the text are those of a Polish girl sentenced to death, awaiting her fate in a dark cell at Auschwitz. She begs her mother not to cry, that her soul is in the hands of the Virgin Mary. Górecki ends the movement with her singing the opening lines of the Ave Maria prayer in her native Polish. There was not a dry eye in the house.

Finally, we performed the Beethoven Ninth's hymn to the unity of all humankind. Its galvanic opening movement rang off the walls and high ceiling of that ancient church, as did the propulsive Scherzo with its driving, pounding beat. The great London Philharmonic Orchestra played the soulful Adagio so beautifully, as if they too understood how special our concert was that night. And then, the finale, the famous "Ode to Joy." It ends, "There above the stars our creator must dwell. In praise of joy, the very font of God." I think our Polish audience could have as easily sung along with the choir; Beethoven's last symphonic masterpiece is as well known and well loved in Poland as it is all over the world.

At the concert's end, the Mayor of Kraków made a speech for the assembled audience and for the worldwide television audience as well. I couldn't quite make out what he was saying. Twice I thought I heard my name. But I was "backstage," behind the scenes in the vestry of the church, and couldn't really hear. Finally, a member of the television crew came up to me, asking, "Maestro, why didn't you go out when your name was called?"

"I don't know. I didn't really hear. What was it about?"

"The Mayor has awarded you the Millennium Gold Medallion of the City of Kraków. It's quite an honor, bestowed on a very few."

"Wow, I had no idea. It must have been strange when I didn't appear. No one told me."

"No, Maestro, it was supposed to be a surprise."

Later at a reception across the Rynek from the church, the Mayor honored me with his city's highest millennium honor, and I, who had lived and worked and been so afraid for so long in that city, held back tears as he placed the Gold Medallion in my hands and led the applause of all who were there assembled.

After Vera and my sons and I enjoyed a few days in Paris over New Year's, we travelled back to New York. I unpacked my bags and began to decompress. What an incredible year 2000 had been. It was the year of the Great Jubilee to be sure. It had been filled with promises kept and with music, I hoped, well made. Although there had been tragedy mixed in, we saw at least the faintest glimmer of peace, nurtured by our music.

As an epilogue to this millennium year, my family sat in our den on January 6, 2001, and watched along with twenty-plus million Americans as the CBS *60 Minutes* profile of "The Pope's Maestro" flickered across our television set. True to their word, Bob Simon and Michael Gavchon had honored my story in a beautiful segment, as filled with music and spirit as I could ever have imagined.

And I have never, in all my years appearing as a conductor or as an interview subject, felt the power of television as I did after that *60 Minutes* story aired.

The next day, our butcher, who before this had hardly known my name, asked me, "So, Maestro, what's the Pope really like? That must be an incredible experience to know him as you do."

"Well, he's the most wonderful human being you'd ever want to meet. And me, I'm the luckiest guy in the world."

PART

FOUR

Resurrection

CHAPTER

THIRTY-ONE

In 2001 my son David was a junior at the nonsectarian Saint Ann's School "for talented children," as they described themselves, in Brooklyn Heights. Usually, he would take the subway to school, about an hour door-to-door, as he never ceased to complain, from our home on Manhattan's Upper East Side. That Tuesday, September 11, 2001, I felt sorry for him. He had slept in just a little, and begged me for a ride to school. So we set out onto FDR Drive, which runs down along the East River, crossed the Brooklyn Bridge, made the little jog left and then a right turn into Brooklyn Heights, reaching the Pierrepont Street main classroom building of St. Ann's at about 8:00 A.M.

I kissed my sixteen-year-old scholar a quick good-bye and drove north, bucking the morning rush hour traffic back across the bridge, reaching the Manhattan side again at about 8:25. I marveled at the dazzling clear-blue sky of that late summer morning, and the stark, thrusting skyline of the World Trade Center towers and their sister skyscrapers clustered in the financial district of lower Manhattan. I buzzed straight back up the FDR, arriving at my home at about 8:45 A.M.

No sooner had I made my second cup of coffee and begun a slightly delayed perusal of that day's *New York Times* than Vera called me from her midtown office in a panic.

"Gil, turn on the television now," she said. "A plane just flew into the Twin Towers. I can see the smoke from my office. It's awful!"

303

I turned on the "Today Show," which had remained on the air past its normal cut-off time, and saw their cohost Matt Lauer and his crew looking on in horror, the NBC cameras fixed on the inferno that had transformed the North Tower of the World Trade Center. Just after I tuned in, at 9:03 A.M., a shadow cut across the middle of the television screen, appearing from just behind the South Tower, and a huge fireball erupted, spreading plumes of white ash out from the point of impact in all directions. The South Tower began to smolder, and then burn, with terrible, thick black smoke billowing now from both towers. As the towers burned, black dots could be seen falling from the windows. Occasionally, a close microphone would pick up a loud thud as one of the dots hit the pavement below. The dots were people, who were choosing a quick death over the slower, unspeakable fate of burning alive. Within an hour and a half, both towers pancaked, folding in on themselves. Businesspeople and janitors, restaurant patrons having breakfast in Windows on the World, and incredibly brave firemen and policemen going the "wrong" way, into the towering inferno, would all perish in a few short moments.

Everyone who saw it, I believe, will never forget it. They will remember exactly where they were, whether they were watching from halfway around the globe in Hong Kong or London, from San Francisco, or from the Vatican. September 11, 2001, felt like November 22, 1963, when John F. Kennedy was assassinated, a moment frozen in time and a day that would have grave consequences far beyond what was clear at the instant it happened.

But from where I sat, from where Vera and every other New Yorker was sitting that day, this wasn't Dallas in November 1963. This wasn't an assassination of a President; it was an attack on all of us. It was about our families. Our loved ones. Friends and colleagues in the towers, in the financial district, around the whole southern end of Manhattan; and to us, in our family, it was about our children, one just across the East River in Brooklyn Heights, and one uptown in Manhattan.

Vera and I were panic-stricken. First, what about our David? St. Ann's is so close! Is he safe? How would he ever get home? We called him on his cell phone but couldn't get through because at the instant of the second crash, cell phones stopped working.

Vera called the landline at the school again and again, and of course the line was busy. Then we called our younger son Gabriel's school, Hunter College Elementary at Park Avenue and Ninety-fourth Street. He was far from lower Manhattan, but we had to make sure he was OK. No answer there, either. Everyone, it seemed, was, like us, in panic mode. It would be hours before we could get in touch with either of our children. Those hours for us, as for so many millions of New Yorkers, were terrifying.

In the end, the Levines were all safe, thank God. But the atmosphere in both schools had been one of confusion and fright. What about the parents of the kids in both schools who worked in the World Trade Center itself? What must these children have been thinking? What panicked screams must have echoed all across those school corridors and cafeterias, where the kids were gathered as they were told the news and terror struck their hearts as they wondered whether their dearest loved ones had lived or died. Were they late to work that day, and now safe, or were they early birds, eager to get to work, and therefore condemned?

Although the bridges and the subways were closed between Brooklyn and Manhattan, at least for the first few hours, David had been allowed to leave St. Ann's and go to a friend's house in Brooklyn Heights, where he was able to call both of us on a landline. Eventually, in the very late afternoon, he made his way home, flecked in ash from the burning towers, which was blown south across New York Harbor, towards the Promenade in Brooklyn Heights. He and his friends, and just about everyone else in the neighborhood, had gathered along the river to watch the ongoing tragedy unfold not a mile from where they stood.

For days thereafter, even all the way uptown where we live, a slightly sweet odor permeated the air. I immediately thought that it might be smoldering flesh, charring in the incessant fires that burned day and night beneath the wreckage of the towers. The deeply penetrating smell lasted for almost three weeks after the attacks. Even with the windows closed, I could not keep the smell outside.

My visits to Auschwitz came to mind. That seeming smell of flesh on fire was like nothing I had ever sensed before. But my imagination ran to what it must have been like fifty-five years ago, when the Birkenau ovens were going full blast, twenty-four hours a day, for months and months at a time.

American flags were hung from every building in Manhattan and all across New York. The sight of our proudly waving flags and the smell of what I took to be burning flesh made for terrible, complex sensory overload. In the first days after the attacks, everyone seemed to be out in the streets, searching for open markets, open restaurants. Or just wandering the streets trying to find cleaner air to breathe. As I walked in my neighborhood, I constantly drew in that smell of death. There was no getting away from it; it was suffocating. But Manhattan was sealed off. We were trapped, at least for the first few days.

Most important, though, we were all safe. We could stroke our sons' hair and thank God we were all together. Then it began to sink in. They had killed in the name of God. Our same God. The God of Abraham. They had chanted *Allahu Akbar*—God is Great—as they blew themselves and three thousand of their fellow human beings to smithereens. How could they have done that? What God would demand such an act?

"Maestro, don't you know, we pray to the same God," Bishop Dziwisz had said to me that November day six years before when I had prayed with His Holiness in his private chapel in St. Peter's. Was this that same God? It must be. But what kind of god could hear such a supplication as a way to find redemption through the death and destruction of the attackers' fellow human beings? That His adherents would invoke His name in the moment of committing such heinous crimes was incomprehensible. How could one kill in the name of God? What could the Pope be thinking now?

Almost immediately, I began to think about what the answer to those acts of unthinkable inhumanity might be. Not an answer for everyone, but for me. I am a musician—first, second, and third. As my teacher Nadia Boulanger used to ask, "What would you say you are if you are awakened in the middle of the night? What would be your first thought?" A musician, I am sure, would be my answer. So for me, the opposite of all that madness, all the hatred, was music. The sound of terror, of metal on metal, and the horrendous noise of the buildings' collapse and the thud of flesh on concrete, could only be replaced by the musical sounds of peace. I had to find the right musical spirit to fill this terrifying terrorist void.

I called the Vatican and told Bishop Dziwisz I would come as soon as I could. That wouldn't be so easy. Travel was restricted for some time, but within a month of the attack I was in Rome, asking how I could help in whatever His Holiness' answer to this barbarity might be.

The Pope had spoken about little else. At his Wednesday audience on September 12 he spoke out against intolerance, and for peace. Peace was the only answer. He did so again and again, on every occasion he could find thereafter.

A month later, on October 11, 2001, he told the Synod of Bishops gathered in the Sala Nervi, the Auditorio Paulo VI, where I conducted my concerts at the Vatican: "It is now one month since the inhumane terrorist attacks which occurred in different parts of the United States of America. We implore tenacity and perseverance by all men of goodwill continuing on the paths of justice and peace."

He would not stop passionately promoting the cause of peace; if there was even one person within the sound of his voice, the Pope wanted to be heard. And of course, there was not just one; there were millions. But he believed the message needed to be repeated over and over again until every person on earth had heard his plea.

As I spoke with Bishop Dziwisz again and again, we discussed the possibilities for a musical event. Finally, after more than six months of back-and-forth, I came up with a plan that I thought His Holiness might feel was appropriate.

"Excellency," I said to Bishop Dziwisz, "I want to conduct a concert in Kraków, a city the whole world knows is so close to the Pope's heart, on the occasion of the first anniversary of 9/11. It should be held in one of the magnificent churches there, and broadcast from there, throughout the world. His Holiness would, I imagine, offer a message on that important day, and his words could be sent out just prior to our musical offering for peace. Words of peace, followed by music of peace. Music for tolerance and mutual respect for all God's children. I remember your words so well, Excellency. 'We pray to the same God.' That would be our theme. What do you think? Might this be the way to add a musical dimension to His Holiness' constant plea for peace? I want to add my voice to his as best I can."

Bishop Dziwisz didn't hesitate. "Yes, yes, I think this might be very good. Kraków. Yes, I think His Holiness might well like this idea."

"Then, please, Excellency, ask His Holiness whether we should go ahead with this. I am ready to do all I can to realize this project."

It was now nearly midwinter in 2002. By this time, my private meetings with the Pope were becoming less and less frequent. "He cares for you greatly, Maestro," Bishop Dziwisz would say. "Do understand, but His Holiness' energy must be guarded so very carefully." I was not blind; I saw what the world was seeing. The Pope's health was not what it had once been. And in any case, my relationship with the Pope had become such that we could easily and transparently communicate through the good offices of Bishop Dziwisz. By now, after thirteen extraordinary years working together, Bishop Dziwisz and I had become close friends. My trust in him and his clear and direct relation of the Pope's sincerest wish was, by now, complete.

A week later, not being able to wait even one day longer, I was on the phone to Rome.

Bishop Dziwisz told me, "Yes, Maestro, the Holy Father wishes me to tell you that this idea of yours, a concert in Kraków to remember the victims of September 11, would be welcomed most warmly. It is up to His Eminence Cardinal Macharski, of course, to make all the necessary decisions, but what would you think of the Church of Saints Peter and Paul? His Holiness has a deep connection to this church. He celebrated Mass there many times during the period when he was a priest in Kraków. You know this church, I think. You have conducted there before, no? The acoustics are OK, are they not? And although the church is undergoing renovations, I believe they are almost complete. In any case, I have already spoken with Cardinal Macharski. He is awaiting your visit to Kraków to speak about all the details. Call me at any time to keep me informed."

Two weeks after that, I was on my way to Kraków to see how our idea might proceed.

When I met him in his office on the second floor of the Curia Metropolitana down the street from the Philharmonic Hall, Cardinal Macharski told me straight away that he welcomed the initiative, coming as it did with such a strong Papal blessing. And, His Eminence thought, the Church of Saints Peter and Paul, while not nearly so magnificent as Saint Mary's Basilica, nor as historic as Wawel Cathedral, would, as Bishop Dziwisz had said, make a wonderful location for our concert.

From the Cardinal's office, I went to the Consulate General of the United States. Within minutes of raising the Pope's idea with Consul General Siria Lopez and her staff, I had the support of the United States. Siria thought this would be great for Polish-American relations and that her colleagues at the U.S. Department of State would help in any way they could. She would even approach the Polish authorities to gain their approval as well. This was all music to my ears.

Everything now seemed to be settled. The date, of course; the place. The support of the Pope, the approval of the Cardinal, the warm welcome of the U.S. government, and the promise of Polish government involvement. It seemed that everything was all set to go. The only problem was that I had no orchestra and no choir, no television, and most of all, no money to pay for any of it. With mere months to go until 9/11/02, just about everything was in fact still very much up in the air.

On my way back from Kraków I stopped in Munich to see a wonderful new friend, Helmut Pauli, who had been introduced to me by Frau Dr. Ulrike Hessler, with whom I had worked on the Concert for the Victims of the Holocaust in Munich in 1995. Helmut was a highly successful concert impresario in Germany; his tousled hair above a round and friendly face made him look younger than his middle-aged years. Beyond his music business he was a man fully dedicated to the concept of a United Europe, the European Union.

The moment I told him about the idea of a European concert to commemorate the terrorist attacks of 9/11, of the blessing of the Pope, the offer of the church in Kraków, and the U.S. and Polish interest, he was off and running with many ideas of his own.

"Maestro, what if we were to make this an event of the European Union, offered in solidarity with America?" Helmut said in his mellifluous German. "What if we were to find a European orchestra and a European choir? Perhaps they could actually donate their services to this cause? I don't know if you are aware, but I am the head of something called Europamusicale. It is the musical arm of the European Union. I like your idea; I want to help. I believe I can do this." In Helmut's enthusiasm I met my own. I was ready to believe anything he said.

It was now July. We had not more than two months to go before 9/11/02, and both of us had busy schedules of "regular" concerts ahead. Helmut organized an extensive series of concert offerings in various cities in Germany for the coming 2002–2003 season, and I had a whole host of concerts in my normal concert calendar as well. I was especially looking forward to a season-opening gala concert with the Montreal Symphony later in September. Helmut and I were both a little crazy for running with this ball.

Over the course of the next two weeks, Helmut contacted various orchestras with which he had close relationships. An astonishing number of very reputable European ensembles were ready to join us and, as Helmut had promised, wanted no fee at all. To me, though, none of the orchestras he named seemed to be right for such an important concert. This event was to be broadcast worldwide. The musical forces had to be world-class. Many times, as we spoke on the telephone between Munich and New York, I could hear Helmut's exasperation with me grow and grow.

"Maestro, what do you expect?" he said more than once. "That an orchestra of world stature will suddenly just happen to be free on precisely the date we need them?" And each time he suggested yet another orchestra, one he had most carefully chosen, I would most politely demur.

"OK, Maestro, let me just say this. The Vienna Philharmonic. Great orchestra. One of the best in the world. It is not available. Not a chance. They are booked up two, maybe three years in advance. The Berlin Philharmonic. Extraordinary orchestra, absolutely no doubt. Again, we have no chance. Not at this late date. They are booked God knows how far ahead. So what do you expect? The Staatskapelle Dresden will suddenly become free?" Helmut said facetiously.

And it struck both of us at the same time. Yes, indeed, the famed Staatskapelle Dresden, the oldest and many would say one of the very best orchestras in the world, might very well be available.

It was now mid-August, and a terrible, one-hundred-year flood had devastated cities up and down the Danube and the Elbe. Dresden was among the cities most severely hit by this terrible calamity. The scenes of destruction had been all over the news. The signposts of the city barely poked their heads above the deluge. Old Dresden, so painstakingly rebuilt after the fire-bombing of 1945, was seemingly swept away. The Zwinger Palace, the most famous edifice in the city and home to the priceless "Gallery of the Old Masters," filled with Rembrandts, Reubens, Vermeers, Titians, and Raphaels, was under ten feet of water. So too was the Semperoper, the professional home of the Sächsische Staatskapelle Dresden. The raging Elbe had taken its terrible toll.

For a month now, the famous opera house, where so many of the greatest works of the lyric genre had been premiered, including "Der Rosenkavalier" and "Tannhäuser," had been closed. No one knew when it might reopen. The Semperoper and all its musical activity was at a standstill. In this special circumstance, maybe, just maybe, the self-governing musicians of the opera's home orchestra, the Staatskapelle Dresden, would agree to perform with us in Kraków on such short notice. We decided, why not? Helmut said he would give it a try.

To his astonishment, no less my own, with not three weeks left until the 9/11/02 concert date, the Staatskapelle said yes. And in an amazing gesture of brotherly love (there is no other way to put it!), they would donate their services. The German state of Saxony, which financially supports the orchestra, would do everything in its power to help them make their way to Poland. I couldn't believe my ears. I think Helmut Pauli was even more astonished than I.

The next day, Helmut went from strength to strength. He called a meeting of the managing council of the Munich Bach Choir, with which he had had a long and fruitful managerial relationship. The famous Munich choral ensemble, which had made so many successful recordings over the years, likewise agreed to come to Kraków. And Helmut convinced the Bavarian government to join their Saxon colleagues in helping to make it all happen. We were almost there. Then, my London assistant, Sue Banner, went to work trying to find great soloists who just happened to be free in three weeks' time. Incredibly, Christiane Oelze, a great German soprano, and Wolfgang Holzmair, a distinguished Austrian baritone, agreed to come aboard. I could hardly believe our good musical fortune. A great orchestra, a wonderful choir, and two top-notch soloists. We would have a true musical feast to offer the world on this important and most solemn occasion.

The main work we would perform was Brahms' universally beloved "German Requiem." Although it bears the title of the Latin rite for the dead, Brahms chose texts from both the Old and the New Testaments. It is so profoundly rooted in the common Judeo-Christian tradition that Brahms himself once suggested to his publisher that it be called "A Human Requiem." The title "A German Requiem," which he finally settled on, comes from his setting these biblical texts in their German translation, for Brahms a vernacular language of direct communication with his broadly based German-speaking public. This work would be home territory for the two great musical ensembles, and for the two remarkable soloists who would come together in Kraków. They all agreed instantly with my choice.

But our program also needed to honor both Poland and America: the homeland of His Holiness Pope John Paul, the inspiration for our concert, and the home of the victims of the terrorist attacks in New York, Washington, and western Pennsylvania.

We chose Henryk Górecki's Totus Tuus, a hymn to the Virgin Mary setting a text that was the very motto of the Pontificate of John Paul, "All for You, Mother of God"; and Samuel Barber's Agnus Dei, a choral setting of perhaps the most famous piece of twentieth-century American music, Barber's Adagio for Strings.

As the day of the concert drew near, we received an immense outpouring of support from all over the world. Our endeavor had captured the imagination of leaders both in Europe and the United States in a way we could hardly have imagined. The Secretary General of the United Nations, Kofi Annan, sent his heartfelt wishes for the success of our important event, as did Mayor Michael Bloomberg, who had helped so generously with our Papal Concert in 2000. The State Ministers of Saxony and Bavaria, the U.S. Ambassador to Poland, Christopher Hill, and the Polish President, Aleksander Kwasniewski, all attended or sent their representatives and, in many cases, their practical support as well. The American Consulate General devoted innumerable hours to our effort.

The concert would be broadcast by Polish Television, with links to all of Europe via Eurovision, and His Holiness' message on the anniversary of the attacks would be aired, via direct link from the Vatican, just prior to the concert broadcast itself. Everything was in place, just waiting for the music to begin. It was a minor miracle we had come this far.

We would have to rehearse quickly in the two days we had to prepare. And all the rehearsals would have to take place in Sts. Peter and Paul in Kraków, as a devastated Dresden still offered no place for its extraordinary orchestra to make its music.

CHAPTER

THIRTY-TWO

The Church of Saints Peter and Paul, in Kraków, a Baroque church dating back to the seventeenth century, was lovingly lit like an architectural jewel by Polish television. Special lights highlighted statues of saints and frescos. Even the organ works in the back of the church were lit to wonderful effect. A single chandelier hung in the middle of the Baroque-era sanctuary, a lone survivor, perhaps, of the Communist era. It looked almost out of place. The plain gray stone walls of the church itself were left unadorned, with just a few icons and paintings dotting the walls. Its very simplicity was perhaps the reason John Paul had wanted that particular church.

As our rehearsal began, I could hear the very special sound of the Staatskapelle come alive before my ears. The sound was ancient, unique, and infinitely refined. It was as if these living Staatskapelle musicians were adding their own artistry to the long line of musicians who had gone before them. There was an incredibly rich warm glow to the strings. The Staatskapelle woodwinds seemed to be made from dark, aged limbs, and the brass sounded burnished, polished into a deep, ancient gold. They all played as if they were performing chamber music, ears perked up, listening to every nuance of the music they were making.

At first I just listened also, wanting to hear the complex combination of the hundreds of performances of the Brahms Requiem that this orchestra had presented—not these particular players, but all the Staatskapelle musicians who had passed down their insights and traditions from teacher to student in an unbroken line for more than four hundred years. They had a history that predated Brahms by hundreds of years. Their Music Directors included none other than Weber and Wagner. Bach had sought, without success, to be made their musical leader. He had written his greatest work, the B Minor Mass, as his unsuccessful audition piece! I listened, and I began to see where my ideas about a piece I had conducted many times could meld with theirs.

At the intermission of the first rehearsal, Ulrike Hessler, who had flown to Kraków especially to be with us, asked me when I would begin rehearsing. "There is so little time, Gilbert. You have so few rehearsals. Shouldn't you be stopping to rehearse with them?" she asked, with evident concern. I nodded, knowing that she was right, of course; there was work to be done, but only now that I had heard what these remarkable musicians had to offer could my ideas be put into play to create a performance that was greater than the sum of its parts.

And so we began our work together. I would gesture wordlessly. They would respond, reflect my musical wish, and add something extra of their own. A word was exchanged here and there. But only very rarely. Few words were needed. Brahms' musical lines shaped by the Staatskapelle's ancient sounds were liberated and clarified and created anew. Accents were honed and the broad-boned lines of Brahms' exquisite phrases were drawn out like lines of taffy, taut but never broken, from the beginning of a movement to its end. And that tension of the musical line, the *Spannung*, as they call it in German, was never broken, from the first repeated quarter notes in the cello and bass to the final radiant chord, more than an hour and ten minutes later, at the work's serene conclusion. All of this was in seamless ensemble with the beautifully prepared Munich Bach Choir and our two esteemed international soloists.

After the first rehearsal, a member of the orchestra came up to greet me. "Thank you, Maestro," he said. "Thank you for not conducting us."

I looked at him quizzically, as he went on. "No, Maestro, it is a compliment. So many of your colleagues don't understand. The key to working with the Staatskapelle is that we don't need conductors. We don't need time-beaters. We need musicians who will make music together with us. Inspire us. Phrase the music with us. Together we will make wonderful music, you will see. I think you will be very pleased with the way the evening will go."

The German word he used was *Zusammenmusizieren*. It is a long word for a precious concept: making music together. His words encapsulated perfectly what it was that I was feeling too. The glow that I had heard coming from all of these fine musicians now coursed through me, and it continued to inspire me as I went off to dine, and then rest, in a city where I had made so much music.

On the afternoon of the performance, just after my normal nap, there was a knock on my hotel room door. Our soprano, Christiane Oelze, stood there and almost hesitantly asked to come in. "Just for a moment, please, Maestro," she said in her accented but excellent English. "I don't want to disturb you."

"Yes, yes, of course. By all means. Is there a place in the score of the Brahms that we can go over together? I really adored what you did in the rehearsal this morning. Is my tempo in your movement too slow? Should we perhaps move it along a bit?"

"No, no, it is nothing like that. I really am enjoying the music-making. I just wanted to say that I read about your mother-in-law, that she had survived Auschwitz. I know we are doing this concert for the victims of 9/11, but in my mind, also, I will be singing for your mother-in-law, for the victims and the survivors of the Holocaust as well. In my family, we had members of the German Army during the Second World War.

"I feel somehow that this Brahms Requiem—you and I making music together here in Kraków, so close to the camps—that there is a deeper meaning to this. I just wanted to tell you how much this means to me to be here with you making this music together."

Her eyes were glistening. If our conversation had gone on any longer, I think she would have begun to cry.

"Fräulein Oelze," I said, "—Christiane, if I may—I am pleased and really honored that you chose to do this concert. I know how busy you are. And I have to tell you, I feel the weight of what you just told me in the incredible emotion you bring to the music. Your Brahms will tell this story to the world, without any words at all. I am looking forward so much to our music-making this evening."

I wanted to give her a hug. I wanted to reach out and comfort her, as the words of her movement in the Brahms Requiem said I should. But I was also so respectful of just how deep were her emotions at this moment. I looked her in the eyes, thanked her from the bottom of my heart for having come to Poland to be here with us, and wished her "*Toi, Toi, Toi*"—the German version of "break a leg."

The evening of the performance came, and I walked the few steps from the aptly named Hotel Copernicus (the great scientist had been a graduate of Kraków's famed Jagiellonian University) out into a small square where a large-screen projector had been set up so that the over-flow crowd could watch the concert outdoors on that cool Polish night. I crossed the Ulica Grodzka, passing between the line of beauti-ful statues of the Twelve Apostles that guard the entry to the Church of Saints Peter and Paul on either side, and walked into the sanctuary itself.

I arrived early, as is my custom, and went into the vestry, where I hoped to find a sliver of space to use as my private "dressing room." Some members of the orchestra had arrived early also. They were donning their formal concert clothes amidst their instrument cases, laid out here and there and blocking every conceivable straight line to the altar, where our concert would take place. Musicians in various states of undress, oblivious to the preconcert chaos, chatted amongst one another. As constantly touring international orchestral superstars, they had seen every manner of backstage accoutrement. There was nothing here to faze them. The music was what they had come for, not the backstage amenities.

The Munich Bach Choir, which would begin the program with our performances of the Barber Agnus Dei and Górecki Totus Tuus, were already in the process of dressing in another building alongside the church. Fräulein Oelze and Herr Holzmair would find yet another corner somewhere, if they could, when they arrived a bit later, having sensibly warmed up their voices in the quiet of their respective hotel rooms.

The television people were swarming all over. Their production trucks parked outside were buzzing with noisy activity. This was not a recording studio after all, but there were cables and microphones, cameras and lighting fixtures lying, blocking, and flying all around.

Barbara Pietkewicz, the Executive Producer of the broadcast for Polish Television, came up to me, thanked me for the idea of this concert, and assured me that everything was "under control." Dr. Lothar Mattner from WDR, West German Television, who was in charge of the international broadcast via Eurovision to the rest of the world, smiled at me in a way that I should have known was much too broad.

"Gilbert," Lothar declared, "it will be a wonderful performance. Everyone says so. I think so too. So, *Toi, Toi, Toi.*" Although he said nothing more, I had the feeling that he was clearly worried about something as he turned and left by the side door of the church, moving towards the production truck almost at a gallop. I was determined not to take his apparent nervousness to heart.

After the live broadcast announcements, which I did not hear, a production assistant wearing earphones nudged me out in the direction of the podium. This concert was live, and my normal few moments of quiet contemplation before I start a concert would have to be curtailed.

As I walked out, I saw the Staatskapelle arrayed before me to my left. They would be quietly sitting through the a cappella performances of the Barber and the Górecki. Behind them was the Munich Bach Choir, standing tall on their choral risers so that their perfectly pitched vocal tones would project out over the orchestra.

As I looked to my right, I saw a sanctuary filled to capacity. Diplomats and dignitaries sat up front, with as many citizens of Kraków as could find a place in this free-of-charge event sitting in the rows behind them. Among the crowd, I noticed several familiar faces. In the third row stage right, sat Henryk Górecki, the composer himself.

It is, for me, a rare privilege to have the creator of a work sitting in the audience. It makes for very special communication, as if there is a line between him and me that will be maintained throughout the performance of his work. For that reason alone, this was going to be a very special evening.

Just as I was about to turn towards the orchestra, I saw the tall, thin figure of Cardinal Macharski, dressed in simple black priestly attire, sitting near the front. His Eminence gestured to me, with a slight lifting of his hand and nod of his head. Welcome to Kraków, he seemed to be saying, just as he had some fourteen years before when we had first met in his office. I felt the warmth of his greeting, returned it with a small faint smile of my own, and turned to begin our musical tribute to the victims of man's inhumanity to man.

Barber's Adagio for Strings, the original form of our opening work, his choral setting of the Agnus Dei, is performed almost too often. In the days and months following 9/11, it was played countless times at many memorial ceremonies. But when the words of the Latin sacred text of the Agnus Dei ("Lamb of God") are sung to its plaintive, stirring strains, it comes alive anew. The music is literally transformed into prayer, and in this sacred setting, its shattering climax, followed by the most peaceful of all musical resolutions, was heartbreaking. The work ends with a setting of the words *Dona nobis pacem*—Grant us peace. It could not have been a more appropriate opening prayer to our evening of remembrance.

When we came to the Górecki Totus Tuus, I could feel the work's creator supporting me in every phrase. His setting of this Marian text is incantational. At the end, it repeats and repeats the name of Mary, over and over and over. The power of the faith behind the setting of this name is almost overwhelming. I felt John Paul, whose Marian devotion was itself the stuff of spiritual legend, also carrying me along through each line. Standing here in this church chosen by the Pope, conducting a work dedicated to His Holiness, celebrating Mary, the patron saint of the Polish Church, with the composer "by my side" was almost more than I could bear. The work carried me along almost as much as I conducted it.

With the opening of the Brahms, the Staatskapelle, which had now sat silently listening to their colleagues in the choir make their music for almost twenty minutes, could begin to spin their own musical tale. With their storied history they were near sovereign in their realm. And on this occasion, for this concert, they gave their collective all. They played their hearts out—and their souls, too. I have rarely been as invigorated by the sheer joy of music-making as I was that night.

We began the opening movement, with its slowly rising ebb and flow, setting the text of the New Testament Gospel of Saint Mathew, "Blessed are those that suffer, for they shall be comforted," leading seamlessly into the words of the Psalmist, "They that sow with tears, shall harvest in Joy." With those first phrases, the rich sounds of the Staatskapelle melded with the pure voiced tones of the Munich Bach Choir, I knew we had selected well. This would indeed be a most appropriate musical commemoration of 9/11.

When we came to the third movement, the great voice of Wolfgang Holzmair commanded that sacred space, filling the church to the rafters. "Lord teach me, that I may know that my life has an end."

The fourth movement, "How lovely is thy dwelling place," perhaps the most famous portion of the Brahms Requiem, had a lilt and a flow, a sweetness both in the orchestra and the choir, that I had never been able to achieve before.

Then Christiane Oelze, having waited patiently for four whole movements, stood and cast her spell on the entire audience, opening her voice and her soul both to the sanctuary and to the watching world: "You have only sadness, but I will see you again, and your heart will fill with joy." Now I knew exactly what she had been trying to say in words to me that afternoon. She brought such plaintive, gentle joy to these words that I thought I would burst as I accompanied her. The limpid, lush strings and soft winds, the hushed responsorials of the male choir, all came together in an unforgettable musical moment.

Once before I had experienced this work in this way, then not as a conductor but as a listener. I had sat in Carnegie Hall and heard the Berlin Philharmonic and Herbert von Karajan accompany the incomparable, fiercely compelling Leontyne Price. I had thought nothing would ever come close to that command of musical space, but now Christiane Oelze was doing it for all the world to hear.

We ended the performances with more strong contributions from Herr Holzmair, and a peroration in the last choral movement that left the church in hushed attentiveness, and left me fully at peace, as Brahms had so rightfully intended. For his is a requiem for us all, the living and the dead, sharing in our common, all too fragile, and fleeting humanity.

The silence that pervaded the church after the last chord died away was long and profound and so completely appropriate. It took a full fifteen seconds for the first tremulous applause to begin. We were all contemplating what it was we were commemorating that night. Barber, Górecki, and now Brahms, had all cast their spiritual spell. The applause that roared was as welcome for the release of tension as it was for the appreciation we as performers so willingly soaked up after our labor of love.

After the concert, as I was dressing amongst the orchestra, Eberhard Steindorf, the artistic head of the Staatskapelle, came to me and said how honored they were to have been asked to perform such a meaningful concert.

"No, it is I who am honored, Herr Steindorf," I said. "Honored that you and your colleagues would join me and us here tonight. You have given so much of yourselves artistically, at great sacrifice, and at a time of such travail for all of you back home. We are so deeply grateful to you. Please tell all your members just how touched I am by their performance."

Conductors don't often get a chance to express themselves in words. That's mostly for the good. We are about the music-making, after all. Our art should speak for us. But these words of gratitude, which I had wished could be spoken to the whole orchestra, I trusted would be taken back to the Staatskapelle Dresden, with all the sincerity and humility with which they were meant.

Finally, after almost everyone had left the church, I encountered my new friend, Lothar Mattner, of German Television.

"Lothar, what was that about before the concert? Something was going on, no?"

"Gilbert, now I can tell you. Something was wrong with the technical relay of our signal through Warsaw to Germany and out to all of Europe. I thought we wouldn't get it right in time. I smiled at you beforehand because I didn't want you to worry. We had some terrible moments, but somehow we managed. It worked. That is the most important thing."

The next morning, at precisely 10:00, I called the Vatican to report to Bishop Dziwisz on our great event in Kraków. I was patched through by the friendly sisterly voice of a Vatican operator to Castel Gandolfo, where Bishop Dziwisz and the Pope had retreated for a well-earned rest and respite from the infamous summer heat of Rome.

"Maestro, we have already heard about your event. Cardinal Macharski telephoned this morning. He was very pleased. I am told the message of your music was heard in many different countries. We are wondering, would you have the time to come to Castel Gandolfo, perhaps even tomorrow? I will look forward to your visit. And please, I am sorry to say, the Holy Father was not able to watch your concert. Would it be possible for you to bring us a video? I would be most appreciative. Please call me when you arrive in Italy, and we will set up a time for us to get together."

"Yes, Excellency, yes, of course. I will come, and I would be honored to bring a tape of the concert. *A domani.*"

I packed, and rushed off to the airport. If I hurried, I could still catch the Munich Bach Choir's charter flight back home to Munich, and from there catch a flight that evening to Rome. The Staatskapelle had returned to Dresden early that morning, so this would be my best way to travel south.

I greeted the members of the Bach Choir in the departure lounge and sat myself down next to Helmut Pauli for the hour-and-a-half flight to the Bavarian capital. Helmut took the opportunity to regale me in his melodious German about the sheer scope of the success we had achieved the evening before.

"Maestro," he intoned in his deep voice, "we reached far and wide with this concert. Just in Germany, the concert was broadcast on ARD, our most important national network, as well as on 3SAT and on Dr. Mattner's WDR in Köln. It was also seen on France 2, and TVE in Spain. Really, all over Europe. Even in Muslim areas such as Bosnia-Herzegovina and Turkey. The coverage in the press was also unbeliev-able. We had the cooperation of all the major newspapers in Europe: the *Times* in London, *Le Figaro* in Paris, *De Morgan* in Brussels, and of course the *Frankfurter Allgemeine* in Germany and *Gazeta Wyborcza* in Warsaw. There was even an announcement in the *Nepszabadszag* in Budapest. So you see, our event was covered by everyone."

I couldn't believe my ears. Helmut had accomplished so much in such a short period of time. And now he was telling this to me with such evident pride. We beamed at each other in shared satisfaction.

"And, Maestro, you should see the website we created for this concert. It has everything. A webcast of the concert, of course, will be online shortly. Interviews with you and the other artists, letters from the many statesmen who wrote in solidarity to our cause, and very importantly, the statement from His Holiness on the anniversary of 9/11. Everyone will know about the need for tolerance and mutual respect that this concert represented. That is the most important thing. People all over the world who didn't happen to see it on televi-sion, can now log on, hear the concert in its entirety, and hear from those involved about this dream for peace."

It took almost the whole flight for Helmut to tell me everything that had been done. He is more than an impresario. He is a European Musical Ambassador par excellence. And I was so proud to have worked on this project with him. We would have toasted with a glass of *sekt*, but it was much too early in the day.

That evening in Rome, I shared a meal with Dame Marjorie Weeke. Marjorie was one of most hardworking officials I had ever met in the Vatican. By now, in 2002, she had helped me with every one of my Vatican concerts, and with many other events around the world. She was a unique font of knowledge who could always be counted on to discreetly warn me off any flighty thought I had before it became an unfortunate, unrealistic plan. I told Marjorie all about the concert in Kraków.

"Oh, Gilbert, we know about that already. The Vatican is a very small village, you know. They say it went very well! You should be very pleased."

"But Marjorie, it was only last night."

"Yes, yes, but news travels fast here. Gilbert, you know that by now."

"Did I tell you I have been invited out to Castel Gandolfo tomorrow? Bishop Dziwisz wants me to bring him a tape of the performance for His Holiness."

"Now, Gilbert. Think about it. Do you really think Bishop Dziwisz would have had you fly all the way down from Kraków to deliver a tape? No, trust me, the Pope wants to see you. I know it's very rare these days, with his health situation and all, but that's what I would bet will happen. So dress accordingly. If I'm wrong, you tell me, but give me a call after and let me know."

The next morning, I called Bishop Dziwisz and made arrangements to get myself out to Castel Gandolfo for what I still thought would be a brief meeting with His Excellency, Marjorie's admonition notwithstanding.

I rode out to Castel Gandolfo by taxi, winding my way south the twenty-three or so kilometers to the area of Lake Albano. As I sat in the back of the cab, I dared to imagine a meeting with His Holiness. If I were to have an audience with the Pope, what would it be like? What changes might there have been in the two years since I had last seen him alone? Then, during the long way up the hill above the lake to the Papal Castle in the square, I put that out of my mind. I would be seeing my friend Bishop Dziwisz. That in itself would be a great pleasure. I could tell him all about our concert, give him the tape for His Holiness, and be on my way, back to New York.

When I approached the castle, I was immediately checked and rechecked by the Swiss Guards. After the formalities were dispensed with, I was greeted with a warm-hearted "Maestro, *Benvenuto*," and was ushered into the small elevator that would lead me to Bishop Dziwisz's sitting room on the floor above, the same one in fact where I had met him twelve years before.

His Excellency, waiting right outside the elevator door, greeted me with a broad smile and an outstretched hand, with which he led me into a small sitting room. But before I could hand him the videotape and begin to tell him about the concert in Kraków, he said, "Maestro, the Holy Father wishes to see you. He would like you to tell him personally all about the event in Saints Peter and Paul two nights ago. Would you kindly follow me?"

Marjorie's words flashed through my mind as I followed Bishop Dziwisz down the hallway towards the Pope's private study. Luckily, I had taken her advice and dressed in my most elegant suit and tie. It was hard for me to imagine what was about to occur.

The study was dark, even though it was five in the afternoon on this late summer's day. Lace curtains covered the windows, blocking out the bright light and the view of the lake far below. His Holiness rose from his seat behind his desk. His back was bent, his head tilting forward so that he saw me, and met my eyes, as he looked up from his clearly pain-filled posture. His handshake was less firm but no less warm-hearted than it had always been. But this was definitely not the athletic man I had met in 1988. The years had finally taken their toll. My father had had scoliosis, a disease that manifests itself with a pronounced curvature of the spine. I am no physician, but at first glance, up close, this was how the Pope looked to me on this day.

Bishop Dziwisz accompanied me into the study and looked on proudly as I presented His Holiness with the videotape of our concert. The Pope was still standing. Politeness, hospitality, and infinite graciousness had always been his hallmark. Finally, His Holiness sat down heavily in his chair, and indicated to me to sit beside him, next to his narrow desk. He got right to the point.

"Maestro," His Holiness said, addressing me as usual in his elegant native Polish. "I have heard such wonderful reports of your concert in Kraków. I am told it was broadcast widely. I have heard there were many important dignitaries there with you in Kraków. It seems it was a very significant occasion. I am only sorry that I could not view it on television myself. Thank you for this video. I will watch it with great interest. Tell me about the event and who was there."

"Your Holiness, first may I say, the choice of Kraków and of the Church of Saints Peter and Paul was perfect. Kraków embodies your spirit; your will for peace is so strongly felt there. You are a constant presence, as if you had never left for Rome. I believe and I hope that our music captured your spirit well. The Brahms Requiem, of course, was most effective, played by the great Staatskapelle Dresden and sung by a wonderful choir from Munich. But also the Totus Tuus of Maestro Górecki. I know how meaningful that prayer is to you. His work sets it so very beautifully. He is so devoted to Your Holiness. And we also performed a work by Barber, an American composer whose work I performed for Your Holiness in Denver."

"It sounds very fine. All of it. And yes, Professor Górecki. His music is very beautiful. Please go on."

"Your Holiness, I was told yesterday on the way here that our concert was seen in countries all across Europe. It will be seen also in the United States. It will even be on the Internet. The message of peace has been broadcast throughout the world once again. Yes, I think, Your Holiness, your message has been heard. And to answer your question, there were dignitaries from many different countries. From America, Germany, and of course from Poland. His Eminence Cardinal Macharski was a most important presence at the event. In all, many, many important personages were in attendance to hear this message of peace along with thousands both inside and outside the Church, and many millions, we hope, who saw it on TV."

My Polish must have been OK, because the Pope seemed to understand my words, although I am sure my awful grammar and my difficulty with Polish declensions were at their usual none-too-stellar level. In this too, though, His Holiness showed infinite patience and never let on if my linguistic foibles offended his ear.

"Maestro, this means so much to me," His Holiness replied, gesturing towards me with his right arm outstretched. "I believe that peace is the only answer. We must never stop trying to reach this goal. I pray for this every day. You know well that I believe that music can play a strong role in building bridges between peoples. We have shown this at your concerts here. I thank you so very much for all the work you do. What is next on your busy agenda?"

"Your Holiness, I am just recuperating from this concert in Kraków. I hope with all my heart it has had some good effect. With your permission, I will come to you soon with some ideas of what might come next. I hope they will meet with Your Holiness' approval."

And with that, His Holiness began his good-bye. He thanked me again for coming. He asked about my family, which he had never once failed to do. He expressed his sorrow at the passing of my mother-in-law, Margit, now almost four years ago. But he ended on a more uplifting note, inquiring smilingly after Vera and, of course, wanting to know about David and Gabriel.

"They are wonderful, Your Holiness," I replied. I was touched, as always, with his generous thoughtfulness. "We are happy and, thank God, all in good health."

He smiled and rose, helped to his feet by an aide, whose assistance the Pope seemed to wish to elude. He wanted to rise himself. He had been so physically strong and was still so strong of mind. He seemed to want me, his visitor, to see him the way he clearly still saw himself—vibrant and filled with a powerful, life-affirming force. It was also clear that he saw the future more clearly through his eighty-two-year-old eyes than did we who were so much younger.

I loved him powerfully for this. For not allowing his evident physical infirmities to hinder his life any more than was absolutely necessary. If anyone struggling with serious illness could see him in those years, they would have gained immense strength for their own lives, from His Holiness' remarkable example. "Be not afraid," he always said. He was showing us all how to age and how to deal with infirmity. How to celebrate the human spirit every day that we are blessed with the gift of life, even in the face of such challenging adversity as he was clearly facing now.

I was proud he had wanted me to see him. Proud I could share the success of our concert personally with him. Proud that he felt close enough to me to have received me at all. I would have flown all the way from anywhere just to have spent these precious minutes in his presence.

Bishop Dziwisz walked me back out to the elevator. He patted me on the back as I was about to leave. I turned to him and said, "Thank you for this, Excellency. You have no idea what this has meant to me."

Bishop Dziwisz smiled and said, "No, thank *you*, Maestro, for all you do. You must know how much joy you bring to the Holy Father."

I gave him an *abbracio* and bid him a very fond good-bye. This was yet another amazing day in a series I hoped would never end. But of course, I knew they would.

And I hoped and prayed this would not be the last time I would see the Pope.

CHAPTER

THIRTY-THREE

I was in and out of Rome between engagements all that fall of 2002. I met with Bishop Dziwisz in December. He kept saying over and over, "We hope and pray that it does not come to war. His Holiness prays for this above all else." As early as January 2002 at the World Prayer for Peace, when he had convened the heads of many of the world's religions at Assisi, Pope John Paul had said:

> Humanity is always in need of peace, but now more than ever, after the tragic events which have undermined its confidence and in the face of persistent flashpoints of cruel conflict which create anxiety throughout the world. In my Message for 1 January, I stressed the two "pillars" upon which peace rests: commitment to justice and readiness to forgive.

But war came nonetheless. By February of 2003 Secretary of State Colin Powell was making the case for war before the United Nations. On March 1, the Pope's personal emissary, Cardinal Pio Laghi, brought His Holiness' final plea for peace to Washington, but to no avail. On March 20, the "shock and awe" in Baghdad began. But the Pope's vision of brotherhood among Muslims, Christians, and Jews would not be denied.

On my next trip to the Eternal City, I made it a point to meet the U.S. Ambassador to the Holy See, R. James Nicholson. I had an idea waiting to burst out. And Jim was the first stop on the road to bringing it to fruition.

I made my way to the United States Vatican Embassy, just above the ancient Roman Forum. Past the high wall, and the marine guards, I went up the stairs of what could pass for a beautiful modern residence in this posh residential enclave, and to the rear office of the U.S. Ambassador. Jim Nicholson had come to this diplomatic post from his career as a longtime Republican Party official, most recently as chair of the Republican National Committee. Jim is a devout Catholic. His two allegiances, to the United States and to his Church, would be sorely tested in the months to come. I wanted to try, as an American patriot, to bridge this gap through music.

I proposed to Jim that I organize a Papal Concert to demonstrate the common origins of the three great monotheistic religions: Christianity, Judaism, and Islam. I believed that it was high time for me to bring an American orchestra to the Vatican for one of my Papal Concerts, and that by doing so, I would demonstrate the multireligious nature of America—that whatever one's political views, the United States stands for religious liberty, tolerance, and mutual respect.

Jim Nicholson was enthusiastic from the very beginning. He told me he would help in any way he could. "Do you have the agreement of the Holy Father? Have you spoken with the Vatican authorities about this?" he asked me.

"No, I haven't. But I believe with all my heart that the Pope will be interested. As you know, Jim, His Holiness has spoken about little else for many months now. He wants anything that will bring us closer to peace. I will be seeing Bishop Dziwisz this afternoon. I'll raise this idea with him, and give you a call as soon as I have a reaction from 'upstairs.'"

That afternoon at 5:00 I found myself once again in Bishop Dziwisz's office in the Apostolic Palace.

"So, Maestro, what have you brought us today? You said on the phone that you might have an idea for another concert. One that you intimated might be of interest, especially just now."

"Yes, Excellency, I do. What if we were to go one step further than we have before? With the Papal Concert to Commemorate the Shoah, His Holiness reached out, in a spirit of remembrance, to survivors of the Holocaust, and through them, to the whole Jewish world. In the Papal Concert for His Holiness' birthday in 2000, he stretched out his hand in peace to all three faiths in the year of the Great Jubilee. In 2002, in Kraków, at our Concert of Tolerance and Mutual Respect, we embodied His Holiness' message of forgiveness and unity in the face of the tragedy of the terror attacks of 9/11. What if we went one step further and, now, in the midst of war, demonstrated the common origins of Judaism, Christianity, and Islam, in a Papal Concert of Reconciliation, celebrating what unites our three monotheistic faiths?"

"Interesting. Very interesting. But too general. What specifically are you thinking of? What elements of the three faiths would show this, and how could this work in a concert? You know, Maestro, there is so much mistrust just now. The Pope is even called the leader of the Crusade in some circles in the Middle East. We would wish to do nothing to make these matters worse than they already are."

"No, of course not. That is the last thing I intend. Let me explain. The two concepts that I believe we share unequivocally, as adherents of all three faiths, are our common heritage in the Patriarch Abraham, about which His Holiness has spoken so often, and our common belief in resurrection."

"Resurrection?" Bishop Dziwisz asked, quite surprised. "How does that relate to Judaism and Islam?"

"Well, Excellency, we Jews pray for resurrection every day. Many times a day, in fact, in our prayers in the synagogue. Not through Jesus, of course, but for our souls' resurrection at the end of days, nonetheless. And, I have learned through speaking with an Imam, who is a friend of His Eminence Cardinal Keeler, that Muslims believe in resurrection, in their own way, as one of the five pillars of their faith."

"Very interesting. Very impressive, Maestro, if I may say so. I would like to bring this to the attention of the Holy Father. I believe he might be in favor of this idea. Would you be so kind as to write down what you have told me? Just a few pages that I may give to His

Holiness, so that he can give your idea some thought. Then we will see whether we can proceed."

"Great. It will be my great honor. I will have it for you very soon."

"Very well. *Do zobaczenjia*—until very soon—Maestro."

And with that, I was out the door, down the long flights of broad stone steps, and off, I hoped, on my next musical journey.

The very next evening I was invited to dine with Jim and Suzanne Nicholson at Villa Richardson, the home of American Ambassadors to the Holy See. It is a magnificent house that backs onto a sumptuous Roman garden filled with pines, citrus trees, and flowering plants of great beauty and seemingly infinite variety.

Over wine and cheese on their back veranda, I told Jim and Suzanne about my meeting with Bishop Dziwisz the day before. "I think this will work, Jim. I really do. I have to prepare this briefing paper for His Holiness. I believe, after all these years, that Bishop Dziwisz would not have asked for this if he didn't believe the Pope would indeed be interested."

"Well, let's get to the practical side. I understand from your previous Papal Concerts that this could take years! When do you think this might take place?" Jim asked.

"Well, I think His Holiness will want to have this soon. I really do. Maybe even early next year. Yes, it often does take time. The Shoah concert took three whole years. But this concert encompasses something that is on his mind and on his lips all the time. He speaks every chance he gets about the brotherhood of all the descendants of Abraham. He wants peace so badly. I think this will strike a chord. I think we'll be looking for an American orchestra very soon indeed."

"An American orchestra it must be. Yes. Which one did you have in mind?"

I told Jim I would have to think about this. We had to take this one step at a time.

On June 3, I returned to the Apostolic Palace with my missive for His Holiness in hand. I passed it across the table to Bishop Dziwisz and waited as he perused it, his comprehension of written English being as perfect as my spoken Polish still was not. Within the six pages, I had explained the Jewish and Muslim beliefs regarding resurrection as I had come to understand them after further consultation with the Cantor of the Fifth Avenue Synagogue, my friend Joseph Malovany, and W. Dean Mohammed and Mohammed Siddeeq, two leading Imams in the American Muslim community. I had also given some serious thought to the music that might be the medium for the Pope's message. The most appropriate choice, the immediately evident work, was the Second Symphony of Gustav Mahler, a work he had subtitled "Resurrection." For the Papal Concert, we would do the first, fourth, and fifth movements.

At the time Mahler completed the symphony, in 1884, he had not yet converted to Christianity. So I was curious to see whether there was a specific Christian message in this work. If this was the case, the work would not be appropriate, for obvious reasons, for this particular concert. I was amazed to find out that the inspiration for this imposing opus was in fact a poem entitled "Dziady" (Forefathers' Eve) by Adam Mickiewicz, a Polish poet of the first half of the nineteenth century, who just happened to be Pope John Paul's favorite author in his native language. Mahler had read this work in German translation, and had become fascinated with it. He used it as the inspiration for the gigantic first movement of his new symphony, a purely musical expression of the spirit of the poem. The fourth movement uses the words of a German folk song from *The Youth's Magic Horn* (a collection of German folk poems edited by Achim von Arnim and Clemens Brentano), and the fifth and last movement uses a poem by Friedrich Gottlieb Klopstock, "The Resurrection," as well as poetry written by Mahler himself. In this symphony, resurrection is seen as a universal concept, the ascent of the soul into the presence of God.

Beyond all this, the Mahler Resurrection Symphony is simply one of the most thrilling pieces in the entire classical music repertoire. It lasts more than seventy minutes, uses an immense orchestra of nearly one hundred, a chorus of as many as can be fit on the concert stage, and two great vocal soloists whose voices will soar above this entire musical ensemble. It would be an enormous honor and an exquisite pleasure to conduct this work at the Vatican for the Pope. If only he liked the idea!

When I passed my papers across the small table to Bishop Dziwisz, I could see his eyes move quickly down the first page to the religious explanations. Then, as he turned to the second page, I saw his eyes light up. He had found the reference to the poet Mickiewicz. He smiled from ear to ear.

"Yes, Maestro, I believe the Holy Father will find this extremely interesting. Give me a day or so, and I believe I will have an answer for you."

I waited in Rome, seeing friends at the Vatican and letting Ambassador Nicholson know that I thought things might go well.

Finally, three days later, I went upstairs once again to see Bishop Dziwisz. "Yes, Maestro, yes, the Holy Father welcomes your idea of the Concert of Reconciliation. He likes it very much. And the Mahler symphony, His Holiness does not know it. But the text seems excellent and most appropriate. The music, it is beautiful, no? You must think so, or you would not have suggested it. And, after so many years, we trust you with these decisions. As His Holiness has said many times, "You are our artist." So, we trust you. Maestro, the Holy Father has asked whether it might be possible to commission a new work for this concert, to be performed with the Mahler Resurrection Symphony? Think on this, won't you? Let me know if there is a composer whom you trust, whose work you know well, who might compose something quite special for this occasion. First, though, when do you think this might take place? We would wish it as soon as is practicable, given all the preparations that will need to take place."

"Early in the New Year, I would suppose," I answered. "That might be possible. Let me see what can be done, and you will tell me the precise date that is most favorable for His Holiness. His is, of course, the most important calendar. The only one, in fact."

"Yes, I will look at the diary of His Holiness and let you know. And which orchestra would you bring to us? It has been such an extraordinary pleasure to have the Royal Philharmonic and the Philharmonia Orchestra for your last two Papal Concerts."

"Excellency, this time I would like to bring an American orchestra. We are a country with a fundamental commitment to religious liberty. Where Muslims, Jews, and Christians of all denominations can live side by side, worshipping as they wish in complete freedom and without fear. This concert would be a wonderful opportunity to show the world the American commitment to religious liberty."

"Wonderful. I think that would be most appropriate. Maestro, I leave the choice, of course, to you. You will inform us of your decision at the appropriate time. But for now, you must go and get the approval of the two Vatican dicastries who are responsible for our relations with these two faiths, and which will organize this concert internally in the Vatican for us. They are Cardinal Kasper, the President of the Pontifical Council for Christian Unity, with whom I know you are well acquainted, and Archbishop Michael Fitzgerald, the President of the Pontifical Council for Interreligious Dialogue. You will get on well with Archbishop Fitzgerald. He is English and was a White Father doing missionary work in Africa. He has vast experience in the Muslim world. Go and see them, Maestro. I will tell both of them to expect you. They will help you with this important event, I am sure."

This was now 2003, not 1993. Rightly or wrongly, I no longer feared that my approach to these two very high-ranking Vatican officials would be nearly as awkward as my first encounter with Cardinal Cassidy before the Papal Concert to Commemorate the Shoah. I would go to them.

They would know who I was from my previous concerts for Pope John Paul, I hoped, and, in any case, Bishop Dziwisz would have told them why I was coming to see them. There would be no need for any 9 P.M. phone calls to Monsignor Dziwisz to reveal that I had avoided the ever-present pitfalls of the Vatican bureaucracy. I was now fifteen years into my journey into the world of the Vatican. I felt almost at home in Rome.

And true to my anticipation, my encounters with Cardinal Kasper, a genial German with a powerful intellect; Bishop Brian Farrell, the wise and welcoming Irish prelate who was the Secretary of the Pontifical Council for Christian Unity; and Archbishop Michael

Fitzgerald were indeed all easy, open, and extremely beneficial. Bishop Dziwisz had been right. I liked Archbishop Fitzgerald right from the start. I was at ease here with all three of these highly placed Vatican officials in a way I could never have imagined before.

These three high priests were as schooled in the complexities of the relationships among the three Abrahamic faiths as I was not. They asked question after question about the document I had prepared for His Holiness. Fortunately, they came to the same conclusion as I had. The two fundamental ideas underpinning the concert—resurrection and Abraham—were indeed common, in their own ways, to Muslims, Christians, and Jews, and could form the solid basis for an event that would welcome leaders of all three faiths to the Vatican sometime in the coming months. They pledged to do all they could to guide our initiative through the Vatican bureaucracy.

With the process of obtaining Papal and Vatican support now well under way, I began the musical and logistical preparations in earnest. As usual, I had no orchestra, no choirs, no soloists, and no money. This last could be quite a problem, especially if, as I had just promised Bishop Dziwisz, we thought to have an American orchestra flown to Rome especially for this occasion. What had I proposed? How could I possibly do this?

My next stop was Ambassador Nicholson. I already knew Jim would be pleased that the Vatican wished to have an American orchestra. And I had a great idea for just the one to invite. I had read in the *New York Times* an article about the terrible financial struggles of the Pittsburgh Symphony at that time. The PSO is one of America's finest ensembles. What a boost this would be if somehow we could find a way to bring them to Rome.

Jim Nicholson is a one-man dynamo. Strongly built, of military bearing, he sported a trim black mustache and a reserved mien. He is also a devout Catholic and a decorated veteran, who had served his country with distinction in battle in Vietnam. But above all, he is a doer. He knows everyone, and has a knack for connecting his "friends" in ways that can serve a higher good. Jim was on the case in a flash.

"Pittsburgh Symphony? You say it's a good orchestra?" he asked me.

"No, not good. Great. A great orchestra. And their artistic staff knows my work, and I certainly know theirs. It would be fantastic to have them with us. I just hope they'll be available." I paused and looked at him. "By the way, we have a date now. We've checked back and forth with Bishop Dziwisz, and the best date for His Holiness is January 17, 2004. We'll be threading a needle to have the Pittsburgh Symphony available on that specific date, with all the rehearsals we'll need for such an ambitious program."

Jim replied, "I know some people there in Pittsburgh. People who might be of some real help with this. Dick Simmons, the Chair of the orchestra's board, is someone I've had contact with over the years, but the people I know better are Senator Rick Santorum and the wonderful Bishop in Pittsburgh, Donald Wuerl. I'll call both of them, then I'll try Dick. We'll see real quick if this can work."

I started to leave Jim's office, thinking our meeting was finished.

"No, Gil, stay right where you are. I'll call right now."

And with that, Jim gave his secretary a number to dial and waited for the call to come through.

Within a few moments, Senator Santorum was on the line. "Rick, I am sitting here with Maestro Gilbert Levine. The Pope's Maestro, they call him here at the Vatican. Gil and I have been talking about bringing a great American orchestra to the Vatican for an important Papal Concert in January. And Maestro Levine thinks the Pittsburgh Symphony would be perfect. Rick, do you think you could help us out? I can call Dick Simmons, but my hunch is you may know him a little better than I do. Would you give Dick a call to see if his orchestra might be interested? The date is January 17. Coming right up. We know it's a long shot, but could you give it a try?"

I didn't hear what Senator Santorum said, but within days he had talked to Dick Simmons, who had in turn talked with Bishop Wuerl. Jim had followed up with a call to both, and it was all settled. It happened just that fast.

Of course, there were a thousand details to consider before anything could really move forward. Michael Bielski, who is the Managing Director of the Pittsburgh Symphony, has told me that he was on vacation at his house on a lake in the Berkshires in western Massachusetts when he got a call from Dick Simmons to ask him if the orchestra could possibly be free to go to an undisclosed place overseas for an undisclosed but very important event during the week of January 12, 2004. He was not to tell anybody about this, and he needed to give his answer within two days.

Dick Simmons is a powerful, self-made entrepreneur and a man of few words. As Michael tells it, when he asks you something, which is rare, he expects you to say, "Yes, sir! How fast do you want the answer?"

Within those two days, Michael came back to Dick Simmons with a tentative affirmative answer. If everything could be moved around, concerts in their already planned season cancelled, and personnel freed up, and if the money could be raised to cover all the costs of this overseas event, and if all the union rules governing such travel by a major American orchestra could be met, then, yes, this concert could be added to their already completely full 2003–4 concert schedule.

To Dick Simmons that was a yes. Now all we needed was the money. The Pittsburgh Symphony was deep in debt. The money would have to come from somewhere else.

In this regard, I had added an infinitely more ambitious artistic scheme that would raise the cost but was, I thought, essential to the worldwide scope of our endeavor. I wanted a truly international chorus: the Pittsburgh Mendelssohn Choir, as many as could come with us; the London Philharmonic Choir (which had been so terrific in the Beethoven Ninth concert from St. Mary's in Kraków); in addition to my old colleagues from the Kraków Philharmonic Choir. And if at all possible, I wanted a choir from the Muslim world; I thought perhaps from the Opera in Cairo.

"Gil, don't you think that's just a little ambitious? Couldn't we keep this simple?" Jim Nicholson asked, quite sensibly.

"Jim, I just saw Bishop Dziwisz this morning. The idea is to have all three religious traditions represented at this concert. The choir from Pittsburgh is a natural. They perform with their orchestra all the time. The London Philharmonic Choir is from an Anglican country but has people of all faiths represented, and the Kraków Choir is all Catholic, from the Pope's home city. That would be so special for His Holiness. And I think the conductor will be Jewish," I said with a grin.

"Yes, you are just a little bit crazy! I can see why the Pope thinks so highly of you. You think big. You know, I have a friend who is the Turkish Ambassador to the Holy See. Are there any fine choirs in Turkey?"

"Well, there are two that I know of. One in Istanbul, and one in Ankara. Perhaps your friend could try to interest one of those in joining us for this concert. It would be a first. Turkish artists performing at the Vatican. It's a great idea, and one I'm sure the Pope would love as well. Voices of all three faiths raised in the Vatican on behalf of reconciliation. Really great!"

"Fine, I'll try. I'll call my Turkish counterpart on Monday. But first there is someone I think you should meet. Are you free tomorrow early to meet Carl Anderson? He's the Supreme Knight of the Knights of Columbus. He's here in Rome just now, and I've already talked to him. If he likes you and likes the project, his organization could fund the whole thing."

"Yes, I think I can make the time," I said ironically.

"Fine. He's staying at the Hilton on the hill overlooking the Vatican. He's expecting you up there at 9:30 A.M. Let me know how it goes," Jim said in his flat, Midwest Iowa accent.

The following day, I made my way up to the Cavalieri Hilton. I had never stayed there, but it is a beautiful hotel, perched above all the hustle and bustle of Rome, with the dome of Saint Peter's as its background view.

Dr. Carl Anderson and his wife, Dorian, greeted me in the large lobby and invited me for a coffee. They are quiet, dignified people of great faith. The Knights of Columbus, a Catholic lay organization, is among the most generous donors to the Church. They had financed the renovation of the facade of Saint Peter's. They helped the poor worldwide. The Knights were the perfect sponsor for this world event, if only they would find it worthy.

Carl asked me about my relationship with His Holiness. He had heard some stories but wanted to hear directly from me. As I spoke about going to Kraków, my encounter with communism, and my providential first meeting with the Pope, I could see Dorian's eyes fill with tears. She was moved, and Carl, in his calm and dignified way, seemed to follow every word extremely carefully. I spoke for many minutes uninterrupted about the Papal Concerts I had conducted, about the vision of bringing people of the great faiths together in the Vatican, and about the Pope's commitment to tolerance and mutual respect among all the peoples of the world.

Finally, Carl said, "I think this concert can be very special. The time is right. If it is the wish of the Holy Father, I am quite sure the Knights would want to be a part of it. Let me confer with my colleagues back in New Haven, and I will let you know. But, Maestro, I very much want us to be a part of this. You can go forward with your plans in the knowledge that we will be with you. We will make it happen."

I reported back to Jim Nicholson about my meeting with Dorian and Carl. He acted as though he expected the news would be good. He told me he knew all along that it would go well. When I told Bishop Dziwisz, he was very pleased. The Knights, he told me, were the perfect sponsors for this Papal Concert. We were now truly on our way. Though there were still a thousand things to be done, I felt sure we would arrive at January 17 with an important Papal message of peace for a none-too-peaceful world.

One morning in the late spring of 2003, I was sitting in my study in my New York apartment when the phone rang. At the other end was Dennis O'Brien, a Senior Producer in charge of special events at ABC's *Good Morning America*, then hosted by Charlie Gibson and Diane Sawyer.

"Maestro, I saw your profile on *60 Minutes*," he greeted me. "I've seen your shows on PBS. And, I've heard all about you from our long-time Vatican correspondent Bill Blakemore, whom I think you know. Your relationship with Pope John Paul is amazing. I think our *GMA* viewers would be really interested in knowing more about it. It just so happens that we are planning a full two-hour broadcast from the Vatican this coming October to celebrate the Pope's twenty-fifth anniversary. Would you have time to sit down and talk with me about what we might do together to celebrate this important occasion?"

Of course I assented, and later that same week, over lunch at the now sadly defunct Café des Artistes, not far from the ABC studios opposite Lincoln Center, Dennis gave me his pitch.

"Maestro, my colleagues and I would like to have you be a part of our live show from the Vatican. Of course, we'd like to interview you about your relationship with the Pope, but we had another idea as well. It may be a bit impractical. We certainly have never done anything like it on *GMA*. In fact, I don't think anyone has done it on network television in a very long time. What would you think if we were to have you actually conduct an orchestra from the Vatican as part of our broadcast? Wouldn't that be perfect? *60 Minutes* called you the Pope's maestro, so here you'd be, doing what you do on *GMA*. What do you think?"

I loved its possibilities, but then there were the logistics. "Dennis, what a great idea! I only have about ten questions to ask you. First, where in the Vatican do you have in mind? And what orchestra would you have me conduct? An orchestra from Rome? An American orchestra? And what kind of music? Serious classical music? The kind I conduct for the Pope? On *Good Morning America*? Is that what you're thinking of doing? That would be a first, no?"

To me, this proposition didn't make much sense. *Good Morning America* is an extremely popular program, but it had not, so far as I knew, done much in the way of arts coverage, let alone classical music performance. PBS, yes; by 2003, I had conducted five concerts on that network. But classical music was not the normal fare of *GMA*. Dennis appeared to be proposing that *Good Morning America* was going to reach out in a way it had never done before. If this was for real, I was thrilled at the prospect of classical music finding a new, much larger audience in America. But I seriously doubted whether it was really possible.

Dennis O'Brien is a very persuasive man. "It's true, we have never done this before," he told me, "but I think it could work. You will have to be our guide, of course. You know the Vatican, so we would follow your suggestions, but we do have some ideas about three locales. You joked before, but we really would like to try for the Sistine Chapel and then, if that doesn't work, maybe the Apostolic Palace; and if not there, then Saint Peter's Basilica."

I looked at him in amazement. "Oh, is that all?! You've just named the three places I could never imagine getting permission for. I've never heard of an orchestra playing in the Sistine Chapel, or in the Apostolic Palace. And the only time I have ever heard of an orchestra playing in St. Peter's was the Berlin Philharmonic and Herbert von Karajan performing for a Pontifical Mass in 1986, celebrated by His Holiness himself. Dennis, forget it. I can't imagine any of these three places being remotely within the realm of possibility!"

He persisted, "But you know His Holiness, yes?"

"It's not so simple. There are rules and customs, and lines of authority within the Vatican. OK, let's say we even find a way to perform somewhere in the Vatican—the Sala Nervi, for example, where I have performed before. That might well be possible. But what orchestra would I be conducting?" My mind was racing, thinking of all the steps we had to go through every time we did a Papal Concert. "Really. It's not so simple. And I would have to have a world-class orchestra to merit a performance before the millions of viewers who watch your show every day. Do you know what that involves? Where would we get an ensemble of that quality on such short notice?"

"Well, we would be willing to fly one into Rome especially for this occasion. We have to be careful about our budget, of course, but we think this would be a very important part of a very special once-in-a-lifetime broadcast, and if you steer us in the right direction, we'll take it from there. We've been working on this Vatican show for a long time now. This would be the icing on the cake if we could pull it off. Suggest an orchestra. Let me see what I can do."

I still had my doubts, but my mind started to work on the problem. "OK, let's see. We have only a few months until October. Because it's such short notice, you might try one of the London orchestras. There are four great ones; perhaps one of them will happen to be available on the very date we need them. What about the repertoire though, the pieces I would conduct? Do you really want serious classical music on *Good Morning America*?"

"Yes, we want you, and we want the kind of music you would perform for the Pope on his anniversary. Music truly appropriate to that historic occasion. The world loves the Pope, and this is our way of saying to him and to our audience that we acknowledge the special place he has in the hearts of so many of our viewers, Catholics and non-Catholics alike. We want to do it right. So which orchestra would you want to have?"

"Well, let me think about this. You could start with either the London Philharmonic or the Royal Philharmonic. I loved working with the LPO on our Beethoven Ninth from Kraków. They would be perfect, if they are free. If not, then the RPO. They are really great as well."

"Yes, you know, I saw that Kraków broadcast on PBS. It was titled "A Thousand Years of Music and Spirit," yes? Beautiful church. Very beautiful show! You see, I did do my homework!" Dennis said with a smile. "And that orchestra was great. So, yes, the London Philharmonic would be perfect. I'll let you know as soon as we contact them. And, you, Maestro, think seriously about what you might want to conduct on national television for six or seven million people, all across America. This may be the first time many of them will be hearing classical music live."

I went back to my apartment crosstown in a daze. Serious music on network television! This hadn't happened since Bernstein on CBS. I started remembering those old *Omnibus* broadcasts, and the New York Philharmonic Young People's Concerts, which had inspired me to be a conductor way back when. What an incredible opportunity!

I called Bill Blakemore, who knew the Vatican as well as any American television correspondent; and of course he knew ABC, where he had worked for many, many years.

"Bill, do you really think they are serious? A top symphony orchestra on the ABC morning show appearing at the Vatican?"

"Yes, Gilbert, I have to say I do. They came to me first and asked me whether I thought you would agree. I told them, you'll never know until you try. So they called you, and here we are. Let me ask you, Gilbert. Do you think this can work with the Vatican? Do you think they will actually agree?"

"Well, believe me, as I was talking to Dennis, or rather listening to him talk to me of the dream he has for his broadcast, I was thinking we were way ahead of ourselves. First, before this goes any further, I will have to speak with Archbishop Dziwisz to see whether any of this is at all possible. Nothing will happen unless he says yes. He may think this is crazy! But I have to ask. If he agrees, I even have an idea about where we might do it. A kind of take-off on one of the ideas that Dennis had mentioned. As it happens, I'm traveling to Rome next week. I'll ask Archbishop Dziwisz, and see what he says. I'll let you know."

The next week I flew back to Rome, and the following day walked past the Sediari into the office of my friend.

"Maestro, so what brings you to us today?" Archbishop Dziwisz asked with some curiosity, speaking in Polish as was our custom. "Unfortunately, there is no news as yet concerning the Papal Concert of Reconciliation. It will take time. It always does, but you know that very well by now."

"Yes, yes, of course I do, Your Excellency. No, I am here about another completely different idea. I hope you won't think I'm being too audacious. An American television network, ABC, wants to celebrate the twenty-fifth anniversary of His Holiness' Pontificate with a whole program originating from the Holy See. But I'm not actually here about all of that, because I'm sure ABC will speak with the appropriate Vatican authorities about their general plans and will get all the permissions they would require. No, they have asked me if I would wish to conduct an orchestra, somewhere here in the Vatican, as part of that broadcast. They are willing to bring a great orchestra—we don't exactly know which one as yet—and the question is, would you think this is permissible at all, and if so, where might we possibly perform?"

"Well, Maestro," Archbishop Dziwisz leaned back and smiled at me. "I see you are indeed very busy! This won't interfere with your preparations for the Papal Concert?"

"No, I would not let that happen. I absolutely believe I can do this ABC concert and, of course, complete all the preparations for our Papal Concert as well."

"Well, then, I think some music in celebration of the Holy Father's anniversary is a wonderful idea. But you are not thinking His Holiness will actually attend, are you? I am quite sure that will not be possible. The Vatican's plans for the coming months have been fixed for quite some time, as you certainly understand. And so, where precisely do you think to have this performance? The Sala Nervi?"

"No, first, of course we do not expect His Holiness himself to be present. It would be a concert in his honor, to be broadcast to many millions throughout America, but with no expectation at all that he would be a part of it. The people of the United States, like so many millions around the world, love the Pope. ABC will be inviting viewers of this program to join in wishing him well and congratulating him for all that he gives to all of us. We would just hope and pray that he would be present in spirit.

"And, as to where we would perform, I hesitate to say. It's just an idea, but would it be at all possible to perform in the Cappella del Coro in Saint Peter's Basilica? I have walked by it many times, looking in through the Bernini gates. Sometimes I have even heard the sounds of music in my mind's ear. That beautiful chapel, I think, would be perfect for this anniversary celebration."

Archbishop Dziwisz surprised me with his ready response. "Yes, for my part, why not? It could be very beautiful, no? I trust you, and any musicians you would bring with you, would treat that sacred place with the utmost respect. But Maestro, it is not my decision. Not at all. You must contact Archbishop Marchisano. He is the Archpriest of St. Peter's. Only he can give you this permission. Write to him. Ask and see what he says. You will keep me informed, yes?"

I left the Apostolic Palace a little disheartened. I knew the Vatican is a place of careful prerogatives. Archbishop Dziwisz was making it clear that he could not make this decision and that he would not step into the sphere of the Archpriest. Still, to my ears, with fifteen years of Vatican experience, the conversation left me feeling that this potentially very interesting project was in a bit of Holy See limbo. To figure out what to do next, I went to see my old friend Marjorie Weeke.

"Of course, that is what he would say," Marjorie admonished me. "He likes your idea. Otherwise, he wouldn't have suggested how to proceed; but it isn't up to him. And the Cappella del Coro would be great. You are right. But Archbishop Marchisano isn't going to make this easy. He is incredibly zealous in guarding the sanctity of St. Peter's, and rightly so. But let me help you with this. I know him somewhat. I'll try to find the right occasion to ask his permission. Please leave it up to me. Let's see what happens. You never know until you ask." I took her word for it, and left it at that.

Just two weeks later Marjorie called to say we had permission to perform in the Cappella del Coro. I was about to ask her how she was able to do this. Did she speak with Archbishop Marchisano? Then I stopped myself. With Marjorie you didn't need to ask. She just knew the Vatican better than anyone else who was not a priest or a nun. And now she had found a way, once again.

I called Archbishop Dziwisz to tell him the good news. He seemed pleased. "Very fine, Maestro. So we will hear your music once again in the Vatican. This time in St. Peter's! I know the Holy Father will be pleased to hear this."

"Many thanks, Excellency. Your assistance has been invaluable."

"No, Maestro, as I told you, I had nothing to do with this. It was Archbishop Marchisano. I am pleased he has given you his permission. We'll look forward to seeing you soon."

I didn't quite believe him, but I was pleased that he and, evidently, His Holiness were pleased, and I left it right there.

Now the question was which orchestra. I called Dennis O'Brien at ABC once again. His voice warmed with pleasure as he told me, "Maestro, someone must be looking out for us. The London Philharmonic is free on the date we want, and very interested in joining us in Rome. We have a couple of details to work out, not least of which is your repertoire. The orchestra needs to know right away what you want to perform before we can finalize their participation. Have you given it any thought?"

Of course I had. "Yes. I can think of two pieces that I think would be perfect. Both are by great composers who write in an accessible style that your viewers will really appreciate. Mozart and Verdi. Here's the story. Like me, Mozart was also knighted by the pope. You probably remember that from the *60 Minutes* story. On the occasion of his visit to Rome when he received his papal honor, Mozart wrote a symphony in G. He was all of thirteen years old at the time, and it is still an amazing piece! We could perform that symphony in the Cappella del Coro with a modest size orchestra. I think it would be great. And as to the second piece, I myself have orchestrated one of the 'Four Sacred Pieces' of Verdi, the 'Ave Maria.' It was originally written for a cappella choir, as in Cappella del Coro, but my version is for strings. It is contemplative, really beautiful, and is based on a Marian prayer of the same name. As you may know, the Pope reveres the Virgin Mary, and she is the Patron Saint of Poland. The combination of the Mozart symphony, written by the master in gratitude for his Pontifical Knighthood, and the Verdi 'Ave Maria' in praise of the Virgin, would make a wonderful program to honor this Pope."

"Maestro, that sounds fine. But no one here at ABC will know either of these pieces. Would you please give us a recording so we can listen to them? Many of us will want to know what this will really sound like, most of all our director, Roger Goodman. He's the head of all the directors here at the network. He does our big special events. He will be directing this show for *GMA*. He is a pro, and an artist like yourself. You two will hit it off."

"Dennis, I look forward to meeting him," I answered. "And about the recordings, that's easy; I performed both the Verdi and the Mozart with members of the Los Angeles Philharmonic at Mission San Luis Rey in California a few years back. Terrific orchestra. And it just so happens that those performances were broadcast nationally on NPR. I have the tapes. I'll get them right over to you."

Within days I was in a conference room at ABC meeting with the staff of *GMA*, including Dennis, Bill Blakemore, Roger Goodman, and several others. Roger turned out to be a no-nonsense professional.

When we met, he immediately asked, "Maestro, what kind of space is this Cappella del Coro? It is stunning visually—I've seen the pictures—but how is it from your point of view? For you and your orchestra? What will it be like acoustically?"

"Well, I don't know," I had to admit. "No one knows, because there has never been an orchestra in the Cappella del Coro. Ever. In fact, the name comes from the celebration of certain specific prayers in that chapel, chanted as a 'choir' by the resident priests of the basilica. There is an organ there, but it is not a place intended for performance.

I think it will be very resonant, with a lot of echo. You'll need to close-mike us. But in the end, it should produce a wonderful sound."

To myself I thought, *Great question! This Roger Goodman is going to be good to work with. He really knows his stuff.*

While at ABC headquarters, I also got to meet, briefly, with the program's anchors, Diane Sawyer and Charlie Gibson. Dennis walked me around, and we literally poked our heads into their offices so that they would recognize me when we next saw each other in Rome. Charlie was going to interview me in Saint Peter's Square, and Diane was going to be the one to introduce the London Philharmonic and myself "on camera" from the Cappella del Coro.

Charlie Gibson is a fellow Princetonian from a class some years before mine. He is courtly and intelligent, smiling and friendly, and analytically cool. Diane Sawyer, on the other hand, is simply one of the most beautiful women I have ever seen in my life. Almost dazzlingly so. You might miss her wit and deeply thoughtful insights because you're so taken by her beauty. I didn't know if either of them would remember me when we next met, after just a minute or two of small talk in the offices of ABC, but I would certainly not forget them.

I flew to Rome in time to prepare for the rehearsal on October 12, 2003, which was also the day of the performance. We were set up in a large hall in the Governatorato, the building housing the governing body of the Holy See, situated up the hill from St. Peter's, deep inside Vatican territory. Although we had been lucky enough to get permission to perform in St. Peter's, we would not be able to rehearse in that sanctuary, busy as it was with Masses and other Offices of the Church being celebrated throughout the day. And thousands of tourists swarmed through that monumental church from the time it opened in the morning until it closed at 5:00 every evening. We would be let in afterwards to perform, but our rehearsal had to take place in the Governatorato.

During our rehearsal, we were under the protection of Cardinal Edmund Szoka, an American prelate who was close to His Holiness.

A seventy-five-year-old, plain-speaking, and somewhat stern Polish-American with the strong upper Midwestern accent of his native Michigan, Cardinal Szoka ran the Vatican city-state for the Pope.

To the members of the London Philharmonic and myself, he was a most charming host. He welcomed all of us to his palatial offices and said we should ask if there was anything we might need. In return, we made our rehearsal open to him and to any other priests, nuns, and any Vatican employees who wished to listen. And many did. Sitting in the few chairs that were set out around the orchestra were not only Cardinals, Archbishops, Bishops, and priests, all in the plain Roman collar of the Vatican's priestly workforce, but also several nuns, perched forward in their seats, eagerly listening as we went through the repertoire for our evening's music-making in St. Peter's.

ABC had decided to tape our performance before the live telecast because it was logistically easier, and it would afford the chance for us to record some additional music besides the Mozart and the Verdi.

Our rehearsal went wonderfully well. The music flowed easily. The London Philharmonic musicians played with warmth, care, and dedication, as I knew they would. After two and a half intense hours of rehearsal, we parted ways for two hours, to meet again at 7 P.M., when we would begin our taping in the basilica.

I am not used to such a short time between a full-fledged rehearsal and a performance, particularly one on television. On tour, my orchestra and I might get together on stage in a new hall for what is called a "sound check" to give us a chance to get used to the acoustics of the venue where we would be performing. But nothing is really rehearsed. We just play a few passages and listen to the echo in the hall. We might touch up a small passage to improve on how we had played it the night before, but nothing really serious.

However, the rehearsal that afternoon at the Governatorato had been no sound check. It had been a real, strenuous, full-out rehearsal of all the material we might eventually have time to record. And now I needed to rest.

The Vatican had provided me with a room at the Domus Santa Marta, just down the hill from the Governatorato. It's not really a hotel but in fact was built in the late twentieth century to house the entire College of Cardinals during the conclave that elects a new pope. In the old days, the Cardinals had slept on cots in the Sistine Chapel, right where they were voting. They waited there, behind thick, securely locked doors, for the Holy Spirit to inspire them to select the next Vicar of Christ on earth.

Since 1998, however, they would stay at the Domus Santa Marta during their sacred deliberations, and I was going to experience, if only for a couple of hours, what life was like for the Cardinals when they were engaged in their holy duties.

The rooms at the Santa Marta are spare. A small bed, a chair for sitting, and in my room at least, an antechamber with a desk and two chairs on either side. As I made my way to my room, I noticed that the hallways were all quite dark. It was hard to even see the entrance to my room off the dimly lit corridor. I couldn't help but imagine the kinds of holy intrigues that might have taken place in these sacred shadows.

I rested on my narrow bed as best I could, sleeping a scant half hour, then dressed in white tie and tails. Then I made my way across a plaza to a side door of St. Peter's. It was not the one I had entered in 1995 when I had had my extraordinary meditation with His Holiness in his private chapel. No, this door was also on the west side of the basilica but farther down towards Saint Peter's Square.

As I made my way towards that entrance, I saw a huge ABC television production truck. Dennis O'Brien and Roger Goodman were standing outside near a small stairway leading back up inside the truck. Pros that they were, they were chatting casually, as if they had all the time in the world. Everything appeared (at least to the uniniti- ated) to be under control. They kindly invited me into the truck to meet their colleagues. One of them was David Westin, the President of ABC News, who happened to be in Italy on vacation and had wanted to come by on this evening to listen to our music. Also in the truck were producers, technicians, and video and sound people from

GMA. It was clearly very busy, and this was Roger Goodman's directorial realm, so I did not stay long.

When I entered the basilica, the first thing I noticed was that we were almost totally alone. The London Philharmonic would not arrive for half an hour. The vast church was empty except for a few ABC camera and sound men, and the occasional Vatican security guard. The silence was nearly complete. The few people who were already there conversed in whispers, in deference to the holiness of this place. For the first time in my life, I almost didn't want to disturb the prayerful hush of the church with our music.

I took the opportunity to walk around the giant, empty sacred space. I strolled slowly, taking in its wonders, feeling almost alone, unencumbered by the thousands who would normally block my view.

I walked by the *baldacchino*, the immense stone canopy fashioned by the great Renaissance sculptor Bernini that covers the basilica's main altar. Its spiral golden columns support a stone awning that seems to float above the floor of the sanctuary, beckoning the prayers of an immense flock to join those of the now unseen celebrant in his daily sacred celebrations. The *baldacchino* is imposing, but it is dwarfed by the immensity of the basilica itself, whose exquisitely painted ceilings soar high above the altar, forming almost a sky inside the church.

While I still had this rare opportunity to wander the basilica alone, I walked the length of the nave to Michelangelo's Pietà, near the main entrance that leads to Saint Peter's Square. The pain in the downcast eyes of Mary, with the slain figure of Jesus lying across her lap, fills even a non-Christian like me with sorrow and deep empathy for the pain of humanity that is mirrored on the face of the Virgin. I stared at her for the longest time, her stone visage almost seeming to come alive, until I remembered that it was time to get to work.

When I walked back through Bernini's iron, bronze, and glass gates to the Cappella del Coro, the orchestra had just arrived and were setting up beneath the gold-encrusted organ works on the Cappella's far wall. The London Philharmonic seemed both oddly out of place and entirely appropriate for this five-hundred-year-old chapel. One could easily imagine just a small choir of men and boys raising their voices in prayer amidst the fifteenth-century Renaissance decor. In my mind's eye, the rich dark-brown wooden bodies of the LPO's stringed instruments blended in beautifully with the deep mahogany of the choir stalls of the chapel itself. Seated on the few chairs laid out by ABC for honored guests of this private "concert" were David Westin, whom I had just met outside, and Supreme Knight of Columbus Carl Anderson and his wife Dorian. Carl and Dorian are very much at home at the Vatican, so I should not have been surprised to see them. I welcomed them to our performance in the Cappella del Coro. We greeted each other with a knowing look, not letting on about the "Papal Concert of Reconciliation," which was still a secret.

Also just arriving was Diane Sawyer. She was even more beautiful in her elegant "on air" clothes than she had been in her daily attire at ABC back in New York. "Boy, do you clean up nice!" Diane said with a wide Southern grin. I couldn't say a word. I wheeled, and turned to face my orchestra, hoping that the blush on my face would fade very quickly.

We had just a few moments of sound check in the Cappella del Coro before Roger and his crew in the truck would begin to record. We went through the Mozart and the Verdi, just once, without stopping. Our rehearsal earlier that afternoon had been enough. The sound of the London Philharmonic echoed and echoed and echoed in the empty basilica. I was right: this would be a challenge for Roger and his ABC audio team. But I knew they would somehow rise to it.

It was only when we finally began our work in earnest that I noticed the incredibly strong, intense television lights that ABC had brought in to illuminate every detail of the sumptuously decorated Cappella and the huge expanse of the Basilica di San Pietro beyond, and of course, the London Philharmonic and myself.

I was sweating already, and the shirt beneath my tails was wet with perspiration even before I had conducted a note. I wiped the moisture from my forehead once, and then again. I remember thinking that this was unusual; I had conducted many concerts under hot television lights. But I assumed it would pass. There was music to be made, and in these wonderful surroundings who could think about anything but Verdi and Mozart and Pope John Paul, in whose honor we were performing that evening.

We performed the Mozart and the Verdi, and were told that the crew had gotten good recordings of those two works for their *Good Morning America* broadcast. Then we took a very brief break, during which the omnipresent Marjorie Weeke came up to me and asked, "Gilbert, are you feeling well? You look really pale."

I thanked her for her concern. "Yes, yes, of course. I'm fine. These lights are a little bright, but I'll be OK. I've done this many times before."

We went on with our music-making, performing Bach, more Mozart, and even some orchestrated Palestrina. About midway through one of our longer selections, I staggered backwards, almost falling off the podium. There was a gasp from the members of the LPO. I walked unsteadily out through the Bernini gates of the Cappella del Coro and flopped down in a seat on one of the hard benches that line the nave of the basilica.

Then everything went black. The next thing I knew, I was vaguely aware that I was in a small medical examination room just off the main sanctuary of St. Peter's. I was stretched out on an examining table; a doctor and a nurse were taking my vital signs and ministering to me as best they could.

Through a heavy haze, slipping in and out of consciousness, I heard the doctor say that they just didn't have the right equipment to treat me, and that they were transferring me as quickly as they could to a hospital nearby. I protested. I wasn't going anywhere! But luckily no one listened to me.

Instead, they immediately put me on a gurney and wheeled me out under the soaring ceiling of St. Peter's right down the center of the nave of the church, then out the door to a waiting Vatican ambulance, as the members of the London Philharmonic, the ABC crew, Carl and Dorian Anderson, David Westin, and anyone else who had been listening to our concert, watched with shock and concern.

The next thing I remember was the bone-rattling ride in the tiny ambulance over the ancient cobblestone streets that surround the

Vatican. The piercing, oscillating siren of that European ambulance seemed to cause an aural pain almost equal to whatever was ailing me internally.

I was in and out of consciousness for the short ride to the Hospital Santo Spirito, just a few blocks from St. Peter's. Although I don't remember, I must have been wheeled into the emergency room and assessed as being in need of immediate care, because the next thing I knew, I was in a cardiac intensive care unit with a kindly looking middle-aged doctor standing over me. I was gasping for air, sweating profusely, and my heart felt like it was racing out of control. After half an hour of fluids and whatever else was being administered to me intravenously, I still felt very weak, but I was awake enough to ask, in Italian, "Where am I, exactly? Who are you, and what's happening to me?" I was groggy, but I needed to get my bearings.

"I am Dr. Gianni Mayouf, a cardiologist here in the intensive care unit of Santo Spirito Hospital," the doctor answered, also in Italian. "I am told you were conducting an orchestra in St. Peter's and that you blacked out. You are getting fluids intravenously. They will help stabilize you. But for now, please just rest. I will come back in a few minutes to check on you. Do not worry. You are in good hands."

His voice was calm. Either I was out of danger, or he wanted me to think I was. So I settled in as best I could and tried to follow his advice. I was still feeling very weak and woozy.

When he came back fifteen minutes later, I was coming back as well. Back to life. Back to something approaching full consciousness. And Dr. Mayouf was giving me more details, this time in English. I was not sure I wanted to hear it all.

"Maestro, they tell me you were conducting in the basilica under very, very hot lights. And you were exercising very hard. You became extremely dehydrated. Well, that combination almost killed you. When you came here you were, I am sorry to say, a category 'Red.' Our most urgent level. You had a very, very high heart rate and a very, very low blood pressure. A potentially lethal combination," he continued, in a lilting accent that was both familiar but not Italian. "Now, at least, you have some color in your face. When you came here you were absolutely white. Again, I say, Maestro, just rest a little. I will be back again soon, and we will see what we will do. For now, just rest."

I finally looked around the cardiac unit and noticed there were others there. Of course, I was not alone. Most of the other patients were much older than I, and some seemed to be much worse off than I. I watched Dr. Mayouf as he worked. He showed each patient the same care and attention he had shown me. He was careful, calm, his manner in itself a comfort. He was in control and knew his business. We were all, thank God, in good hands.

When he came back for the third time (although I couldn't be sure of the count, because I had been unconscious on and off), I had more presence of mind to ask him some questions.

"Please forgive me, Doctor, but I sense an accent in your English that is not Italian. Where, may I ask, do you come from?"

"Well, Maestro, I am from Nazareth. I was born and grew up in Israel. I am an Arab Christian, a Catholic educated in Nazareth in the Franciscan school there. I went to university there, in that holy city, and then to medical school here in Italy. I am often on call at the Vatican. I know who you are also, of course. I know you are Jewish, and that you conduct often for the Holy Father. You know, I believe it is by his blessing that you were brought to me this evening. By the blessing of the Lord that you have come through this so quickly. Nothing is by chance. I am sure you were protected tonight. My colleagues and I have never seen someone who came in like you did, here to Santo Spirito, so sick, almost near death, I am sorry to say, who has recovered so quickly. Normally, we would have you stay overnight for observation. But you are now well. In a few minutes, in fact, you may leave. But please take it easy for a few days. I hope you can do at least that. This was a terrible scare, I am sure. But Maestro, here is my card. I have written on it all my contacts. Call me if you need me in the next few days, and then, when you are in Rome again, please call me. Anytime. I do not think it was chance that brought us together."

I looked at him for the first time able to see his face clearly. Clean shaven and of olive complexion, he seemed deeply moved. And I was also. I vowed to keep in touch with him. And I thanked him from the bottom of my heart for saving my life.

Astonishing. He was from Nazareth, from Israel. I thought of our dream of a concert in 2000 that had not been. I thought of the intifada that I had witnessed and that had scared me half to death. I thought of the Catholic priests and of the families under siege in the basements of Beit Jala, three years before. And now here I was, being saved by Dr. Mayouf of Nazareth. Dr. Hanna Mayouf, as he was called in Arabic. I knew now, as if I really needed any more proof, that there is indeed a God, and that he had shown his face to me that night, perhaps as never before.

When I walked into the waiting room, there was Marjorie Weeke, who had been there all along. We left Santo Spirito in a taxi. I was happy just to be alive. "Shouldn't you call Archbishop Dziwisz?" Marjorie asked. "Wouldn't he want to know what happened?"

I thought a minute, then said, "No, I don't want to bother him. He's got enough to worry about."

All the while, though, as we made our way back to the Hotel Raphael, I could not get Dr. Mayouf out of my mind. My heart rate had slowed down to normal, and now all I wanted was to rest.

None of the millions who watched my performances with the London Philharmonic on *Good Morning America* would have any idea how close I had come to meeting my maker. But then, it had all been for a higher cause, whether we had known it that night or not.

On the Monday after the incident in St. Peter's, a familiar baritone voice was on the phone in my hotel. It was Archbishop Dziwisz. Maybe Marjorie had been right. Maybe I should have called him after all.

"What happened, Maestro? I have heard you became quite ill in St. Peter's. How frightening! Are you all right now? We were very worried, you know."

"Yes, but I am fine now. I feel much better. But thank you so much for asking. And, Excellency, you won't believe it. It was an Arab Catholic, from Nazareth, who saved me. A wonderful doctor working in Santo Spirito. They said I was Code Red. I thank God for saving me. That's what the doctor thought. And I agree."

"Yes, thank God. It is wonderful you are all right now. We heard the story. And we are so grateful to this Nazareth doctor. I am very pleased he was able to help you. And His Holiness will be glad that you are well again. We were all very worried when we heard. And, Maestro, you have the Holy Father's blessing. Always. You know this. So, travel safely. We will see you soon. You have a very big concert coming up. His Holiness wishes me to tell you that he is looking forward very much to that special occasion! My regards to your family. Good-bye, Maestro, good-bye."

I was deeply moved by the concern of His Holiness and the Archbishop. But how did Archbishop Dziwisz know about the doctor? I would have known the answer if I only had thought it through. Hadn't Dr. Mayouf told me he was often called to work at the Vatican? And the Vatican is like a small village. So the answer was clear. Archbishop Dziwisz knew because there were those in the Vatican who cared, and because His Holiness cared about me also. And for that I was very grateful.

The next day, Tuesday, was the actual live-in-Rome *Good Morning America* broadcast, during which our performances would be aired. I arrived at St. Peter's, the scene of the drama from Saturday night, to find everyone very tense, not surprising given the logistics of a broadcast taking place in Rome and being beamed by satellite across the Atlantic to America, more than three thousand miles away.

Roger Goodman and Dennis O'Brien greeted me as if I had come back from the dead. They told me they were pleased that I looked so well, after having looked so ghastly when they had last seen me.

My live interview with Charlie Gibson was scheduled for the last half hour of the two-hour broadcast during the concert segment. So I had a bit of time before I had to head over to the front of St. Peter's to meet with Charlie. Roger and Dennis invited me into the ABC truck with smiles of deep satisfaction on both their faces. I couldn't figure out just why.

As we were still an hour or so before air time, he queued up my performances on a television monitor right there in the truck for me to see.

I couldn't believe my eyes and ears. Not only had we managed to perform both works superbly, despite my impending collapse, but Roger had captured those performances masterfully. He had melded the beauty of the music with the incomparable surroundings of St. Peter's. It was a perfect, magical blend of music and spirit, light and shadow, the glorious sounds of Mozart and Verdi in that ancient, majestic setting. Roger Goodman is a directorial genius. I was not surprised when Dennis told me they had gotten a slew of positive viewer comments about the two musical performances from the Cappella del Coro.

My interview with Charlie Gibson centered mostly on my "kinship" with Mozart through our shared Pontifical Knighthoods. That's about all Mozart and I shared, of course. But for that one day, I had done for him what no one in history had ever done for him before. I had performed the symphony which he had written on the occasion of his Papal Knighthood with the London Philharmonic in the Cappella del Coro of Saint Peter's Basilica. I think even Wolfgang Amadeus was smiling down in pleasure and gratitude on that wonderful October day.

CHAPTER

THIRTY-FIVE

On my flight from Rome back to New York after the *Good Morning America* concert, I was overwhelmed by deep feelings of sadness. For the longest time, I could not figure out why. The music-making in St. Peter's had been wonderful, and I had survived my brief brush with Code Red. Then I realized that it was my delayed response to Archbishop Dziwisz's telephone call: "His Holiness will be so glad that you are well again. We were all very worried when we heard. And Maestro, you have the Holy Father's blessing. Always. You know this."

Since 1998, the world had watched as Pope John Paul's illness became harder and harder to hide. He was stooped. He walked with ever greater effort, leaning on his cane. His words were more and more difficult to understand. The Pope's physical frailty, his mortality even, was now becoming clear. I was deeply touched that he had been worried about me, and I felt such sadness. How much longer could he go on? And then I grew calm as I realized the answer. As long as his spirit remained strong, everything would be all right. And his spirit seemed as strong as ever.

During the run-up to the televised concert in St. Peter's, a letter had arrived from the Vatican bearing the signatures of both Cardinal Kasper and Archbishop Fitzgerald, officially approving the Papal Concert of Reconciliation to take place on January 17, 2004. That was a good thing, because we had proceeded with the preparations at breakneck speed for months. The Knights of Columbus had agreed to sponsor the concert. The Pittsburgh Symphony had agreed to perform, as had the London Philharmonic Choir, the Kraków Philharmonic Choir, members of the Pittsburgh Mendelssohn Choir, and true to Ambassador Jim Nicholson's word, the Ankara Polyphonic Choir as well. John Harbison, one of America's foremost composers, had even composed a new work in an extraordinarily short amount of time. Everything was all lined up and ready to go, and now we had our official Vatican invitation in hand.

On November 7, 2003, only hours after we received notice of the *bolletino*, the eagerly awaited Vatican public announcement of the concert, we were permitted to hold a press conference in the ornate marble lobby of Heinz Hall, the storied home of the Pittsburgh Symphony. On hand to announce what had until then been a completely secret event were Richard Simmons, the PSO board chair; Carl Anderson, our Knights of Columbus knight in shining armor; and myself. Ambassador Jim Nicholson participated by telephone from Rome, and Bishop Donald Wuerl of Pittsburgh, who had to be elsewhere on official church business, sent his warm greetings and best wishes via video. Both the national and local press were on hand to tell the story to the world—and tell it they did.

The next day, and for the two months until our Vatican appearance, there was nothing as important in the Pittsburgh press as the Papal Concert of Reconciliation. It was front-page news. The television and radio stations, the mainstream press, and all the religious papers were filled with stories about how the concert had come to be. There were daily accounts of all our preparations, including the orchestra's journey to Rome. The whole city, including its enormous Catholic community, was behind the Pittsburgh Symphony in a way no one could ever remember.

Our concert in Pittsburgh on January 14 was a sold-out send-off. In Heinz Hall we performed the entire Mahler Symphony No. Two, "Resurrection," all eighty minutes of music, all five movements (only three of which, as determined by customary Papal Concert length, would be performed for the Pope in the Vatican). That complete performance was a special treat for our Mahler-loving Pittsburgh public.

However, we were not permitted to perform John Harbison's sacred motet, "Abraham." That was a Papal commission, which would have its world premiere at the Vatican in the presence of the Pope.

The Mahler Second with such a great Mahler orchestra as the Pittsburgh Symphony was deeply satisfying. And each member of that orchestra played in the tradition of all the musicians who had sat in their seats before them. They had passed their Mahler tradition down from generation to generation, mixing their experiences with those of their forebears.

Nothing pleased me so much as having a veteran member of the PSO bass section tell me that my Mahler reminded him of the music-making of William Steinberg, the orchestra's famed Cologne-born music director, who had last led them in concert more than a quarter century before. To me, that was one of the highest compliments I could ever receive.

A Mahler sound is like no other. It takes virtuosity, yes, but coupled with a sense of the style and ethos of the time in which it was written: Central Europe just before the turn of the twentieth century. My time in Kraków was essential to me now. I could bring that south- ern Polish, Galician, Austro-Hungarian musical sensibility to bear on all the long-line melodic story that Mahler tells so wonderfully.

The Pittsburgh entourage that flew to Rome in January was huge. It seemed like half the city had decided to accompany its orchestra on its historic date at the Holy See. The press contingent alone was enor- mous but so was the cadre of ordinary citizens, board members, and others who clamored for their coveted special seats in the Sala Nervi that January evening.

Michael Bielski later told me that the entire three days of the Pittsburgh Symphony's stay in Rome passed as if "time had stood still." They had clearly left their economic troubles behind, and welcomed the musical and spiritual experience that was to come, with open arms and hearts.

On the evening of the concert, as I waited with great anticipation with the assembled musicians on platform in the Sala Nervi, I won- dered about His Holiness. How would he look? Would he walk in?

Would he be supported by his cane? I had now not seen him in person in two years. What would time and travail have wrought on my beloved Pope John Paul?

The orchestra and the members of the immense choir, assembled from North America, Europe, and Asia especially for this command performance, seemed to grow tense in anticipation of His Holiness' arrival. As I looked around one last time, I felt the audience too beginning to grow quiet in anticipation.

The Sala Nervi seemed like a sea of covered heads, each person according to his or her faith tradition. To my left I saw the face of a beautiful Muslim woman, her head covered in an elegant orange silk scarf. To her right sat a row of rabbis, wearing yarmulkes of various colors, but mostly black, and one with a rounded top hat, signaling his strict orthodox Ashkenazi beliefs.

In another section was what seemed to be a sea of Bishops, Archbishops, and Cardinals marked by their purple and orange skull-caps, next to a small section of black head-coverings, some trimmed in white, of the members of the non-Catholic Christian denominations represented at the concert. Behind them sat row upon row of nuns, in all manner of habit, some in black, some in white, some in the blue and white habits of Mother Teresa's Sisters of Charity of Calcutta. The Aula was a sea of color waiting for the holy man in white to arrive.

In the midst of the seated clergy, I spied Bishop Donald Wuerl of Pittsburgh. He, more than most, seemed to be awaiting the coming concert with keen anticipation. It was his orchestra, after all, his beloved city that would be the center of artistic attention for all those in the Aula, and for everyone around the world who would be watching. His quiet pride shone on his smiling, modest, priestly face.

As I turned for the last time, I thought of all the wonderful conductors who had conducted for this Pope, legendary names like Carlo Maria Giulini and Riccardo Muti. Had they felt the same awe as I was feeling now? Had their orchestras, famed ensembles such as the Vienna Philharmonic and the Orchestra of La Scala, also sat on the edge of their chairs, like the Pittsburgh Symphony was right now? And my mentor, Sir Georg Solti, had he felt the exquisite specialness

I now was feeling when he led his renowned Chicago Symphony in their home city for the visiting Pope John Paul in 1979? Although this was my fourth Papal performance in this hall, I had lost none of the wonder of that first occasion in December 1988.

Finally, out of the corner of my eye, I caught the first glimpse of the Pope as he came through the same door through which the orchestra, chorus, and I had entered the Aula. He was flanked on his left by the Chief Rabbi of Rome, Rav Elio Toaff, dressed in an elegant black suit with a rich, silk charcoal-gray tie. Rav Toaff's presence was oddly familiar, since he had been an honored guest at the Papal Concert to Commemorate the Shoah back in 1994. On the Pope's right, however, was Imam Abdulawahab Hussein Gomaa, the Imam of the Mosque of Rome. As I looked at the Imam, dressed in a black caftan, with a black ecclesiastical collar, his head topped with a low white fez, I wondered what was going through his mind as he looked out over this multicolored, interfaith scene.

His Holiness was in the middle, not walking now, but wheeled forward in what looked like a rolling gold-upholstered throne. He was dressed in his usual white cassock, with a golden pectoral cross around his neck and a white sash emblazoned with his Papal Seal. He wore a white zucchetto, or skullcap, on his head. That head covering always reminded me of the *kippah* we Jews all wear in synagogue on Yom Kippur.

Although clearly not able to sit up entirely straight, the Pope looked out at the applauding audience with a warm, deep smile, lifting his right arm in greeting, his open hand reaching out as if he wanted to shake every outstretched hand in the vast audience arrayed before him.

The applause went on, and on, and on. It was directed at all three holy men, to be sure, but it was most especially meant, I felt, for His Holiness Pope John Paul II.

At last, the uproarious welcome died down, and Archbishop Dziwisz, sitting just behind the Pope, signaled me to begin the evening's music-making.

I bowed once more in the direction of the Pontiff, and he in turn gestured directly towards me. He was waving his hand, looking me upward in the eye, his face tilted downward by the curvature in his spine. To me, it looked as though he were reaching out towards me across the broad expanse between us. I felt as close to him in that moment as I ever had.

The Pittsburgh Symphony and all the choirs and soloists who had spontaneously stood at their first sight of His Holiness continued to stare in his direction, taking in the scene and the presence of His Holiness as if to store it in some precious place inside themselves, to be retrieved and savored again and again, after this experience was over. They seemed not to want to begin our evening's work. Finally, with a gentle gesture from me, they all took their seats.

At long last, I raised my arms in preparation for the opening of John Harbison's sacred motet, "Abraham."

It is a rare privilege to conduct the premiere of any work, especially one by such an important figure as John Harbison. But to bring to life the never-before-heard sounds that John had only imagined in his mind's ear, here in the Vatican, for this beloved Pope, was literally historic. The humbling dedication that Harbison wrote in his manuscript made the prospect all the more daunting:

> To His Holiness Pope John Paul II for his pontificate-long dedication to fostering reconciliation among the peoples of Abraham: Jews, Christians and Muslims, and with deep gratitude to Maestro Sir Gilbert Levine, for his 15-year-long creative collaboration with His Holiness, which led to the great honor of this commission.

I looked to see that everyone was ready, the Pittsburgh Symphony brass and the assembled choirs, and brought my arms down. Harbison's opening staccato chords crackled his music to life. The double chorus and two brass choirs antiphonally declaimed their loud, unanimous, affirmative intent: "And! When!" Chorus One asserts. "And! When!" Chorus Two answers purposefully, in stepwise descent. Harbison unfolded the text and the music as if they were always meant to be one:

And when Abraham was ninety years old and nine, the LORD appeared to Abraham, and said unto him, I am the Almighty God; walk before me, and be thou perfect. And thou shalt be the Father of many nations.

This text from Genesis is so simple yet so profound, binding together Muslim, Christian, and Jew, all the progeny of the one Patriarch, in an unbreakable historic union of brothers and sisters. And John Harbison's music perfectly captured that familial unity in our rich religious diversity.

The performance of a new work always raises the question of whether the audience will respond favorably. John Harbison, sitting there in the Aula that evening, must have been wondering the same thing. As his work ended with quiet resolution, intoning over and over the name of the Patriarch Abraham, I heard the vast audience begin to applaud. Their reaction was warm and sustained, which was of course satisfying. But there really was only one reaction that I cared about.

I looked over at the face of His Holiness, who was applauding our performance, and caught his eye; it was as if he wanted to give me his review, right there on the spot. His smile told me all I needed to know. He had approved the text beforehand, and now his smile showed me he approved the music as well.

The other reaction came from the Pittsburgh Symphony itself. Harbison's work is scored for double brass choir, thirteen players in all. So the eighty players who were sitting on the Vatican's stage waiting their turn to play in the Mahler were also hearing the world premiere performance of this work, along with the 7,500 people in attendance and the millions watching on television throughout the world. The orchestra's applause, demonstrated in the string players shaking their bows up and down in the air, and the woodwinds shuffling their feet, was a sign of approbation almost as important as that of the Pope.

After the birth of that new and wonderful work came the Mahler Symphony No. Two. We had performed it in Pittsburgh just three days before, but much had changed. For one thing, the choir was almost completely different. Only a handful of members of the marvelous Pittsburgh Mendelssohn Choir who had sung with us in Heinz Hall earlier in the week could accompany us to Rome, but the choirs of London, Kraków, and Ankara had all joined us just for the Papal Concert. In two marathon rehearsals, the three choirmasters and I had combined these three terrific, but very different, choirs, with their quite distinct choral traditions and Polish, English, and Turkish languages, into one cohesive, unified vocal ensemble, two hundred strong. If there were miracles in evidence that evening in this holy space, this was surely one of them.

The second challenge for the Pittsburgh orchestra and myself was the change of venue. Heinz Hall is an acoustical marvel, seating an ample 2,676 concertgoers. The Sala Nervi seats 7,500 and is anything but acoustically friendly to any musical event, let alone a complex classical undertaking like Mahler's Second Symphony. In addition, the Mahler score calls for an off-stage orchestra, which must be coordinated precisely with the huge orchestra on stage. In the Sala Nervi, that second orchestra was almost 150 feet away, and connected to me only by a closed-circuit television camera. What was a musical coordination feat in Heinz Hall became an extreme logistical challenge in the Aula Paolo VI.

More important than these logistics (which we thankfully could solve) was the question of whether the Pope would truly appreciate Mahler's work in all its full-throated intensity. He had approved the work based on his familiarity with the original Mickewicz poem "Dziady" and, frankly, based on his belief in me and our sixteen years of doing concerts together; but nothing like this had ever been performed for any pope in the history of the Vatican.

As we got under way, with the thunderous violin and viola tremolo and the pounding upward scales of the cellos and basses, I could only hope we would bring His Holiness with us on the extraordinary spiritual journey that is Mahler's Second Symphony. At the second theme of the first movement, when the violins begin their aching ascent to our first musical glimpse of heaven, I looked out over the strings towards the Pope sitting on his throne. His eyes were alternately open and closed, but just when I thought he might be off somewhere else, he began to move his head from side to side, almost in rhythm with the inner pulse of the music itself. He seemed enthralled. He seemed to be entering deep into the spirit of the music, into the meaning hidden within the notes. I had never seen him so absorbed in any musical work in all the years that I had made music for him as he was in Mahler's Second Symphony.

In the televised concert for PBS that was produced after the Vatican event, paintings especially commissioned by the Vatican for this occasion (and that were reproduced in the program for this Papal event) were shown. At the crucial section of the last movement, where the Last Judgment seems to be sounded and the call comes forth for all the souls of the faithful to meet their maker, the American television audience would see these paintings, one by one, in slow dissolve. The voice of the choir is intentionally almost inaudible. Coming from an immense chorus of more than two hundred, the effect of so little volume of sound produced by so many voices is unearthly. The paintings made a perfect complement to these heavenly choral tones.

In our live performance in the Vatican there were no such visual prompts. It is pure musical speech, entering the soul through the mind of the ear. And in this too His Holiness seemed to be right there with us, with Mahler, on the spiritual journey of the soul's ascent into heaven. Whether his eyes were open or closed didn't matter. I almost couldn't keep my eyes off him, so distracting was the intensity of his involvement.

As we neared the end, there came the final crashing chords and full choral and orchestral peroration: "Arise, arise my soul. What you have wrought will carry you to God." And it was over. The Pope joined the audience in standing up from his wheeled throne to applaud our performance, in what I hope and believe was his appreciation for the musical journey that we had just concluded with him.

When the applause finally died down, he sat and spoke words of peace that were at the very center of why we had initiated this concert in the first place:

I have taken part with deep emotion in this evening's concert dedicated to the theme of reconciliation among Jews, Christians, and Muslims. I listened to the splendid musical performance that gave us all an opportunity for reflection and prayer. I extend my greetings to the distinguished conductor Maestro Gilbert Levine, to the members of the Pittsburgh Symphony Orchestra and to the choirs of Ankara, Kraków, London, and Pittsburgh.

The history of relations among Jews, Christians, and Muslims is marked by both light and shadow, and it has unfortunately known some painful moments. This evening, we gathered here to give concrete expression to reconciliation, entrusting ourselves to the universal message of music.

The unanimous hope we express is that all peoples may be purified from the hatred and evil that threaten peace continuously, and so, be able to extend to one another hands that have never been stained by violence but are ready to offer help and comfort to those in need.

Yes, we must find within us the courage of Peace! We must implore on High the gift of Peace! And this peace will spread like a soothing balm if only we travel unceasingly on the road of reconciliation. Then the wilderness will become a garden in which justice will flourish and the effect of this justice will be peace. *Omnia Vincit Amor*!

The Pope's delivery was halting. He struggled mightily to find his breath. But there was no doubting the immense power of his words, or the powerful personal conviction with which they were delivered.

As His Holiness finished, Archbishop Dziwisz discreetly pointed in my direction for the chosen musical participants to approach His Holiness and receive his personal thanks. When the group, which consisted of Mark Huggins, the Pittsburgh Symphony co-concertmaster; our two wonderful German soloists, soprano Ruth

Ziesak and mezzo-soprano Birgit Remmert; and myself, finally made our way across the stage to where the Pontiff was sitting, Archbishop Dziwisz indicated that I (rather than, as was usual, a member of the Church hierarchy) was to introduce my colleagues to the Pope. This was a public gesture of trust before all those present and all the millions who were watching. I was deeply honored.

After introducing my three wonderful colleagues, I looked for the first time closely into His Holiness' eyes. It seemed to me that he had indeed been deeply moved. The music I had selected for him had made its intended impression. And the event that he had so courageously championed for many months had been well worth his intensive efforts.

He thanked me for all I had done, for the wonderful music we had made. And then he startled me with a remarkable request. "Maestro," the Pope said, "would you please give us an encore? Would that be possible? I would be so grateful if you could do that this time. Your concert pleased me so very much."

I was so stunned, I didn't move. I held his hand, which had been in mine the whole time, and almost didn't let go.

Finally, after what must have been far fewer seconds than it felt like, I answered, "Yes, Your Holiness, of course. We would be most pleased."

I walked back to the podium thinking rapidly about what we could possibly perform as an encore after the conclusion of a huge-canvassed work like the Mahler Second. Just as I climbed up to take my place, it hit me. We would reprise the last few minutes of the symphony itself, reliving for ourselves and for all assembled the final moments of the musical journey we had just concluded.

I quickly flipped through the final movement of the score, and spoke in a stage whisper to the immense orchestra and choirs, who were waiting with quizzical looks on their faces. They had observed the conversation between the Pope and me, but they could not have had any idea whatsoever of his request.

"Number 48. Can we please start again at rehearsal number 48?" I fairly yelled across the wide and deep expanse of the Sala Nervi stage.

Every single one of the musicians looked stunned. But soon they understood. The strings, who were arrayed right in front of me, heard me loud and clear. They noted the place in the score, and in turn passed the spot where we would start back over their shoulders to their colleagues in the woodwinds and the brass, who in turn passed it back to the three choirs who were sitting in long rows behind them. How it got to all two-hundred-plus choristers I will never know. Maybe it was the second miracle of the night, after the choir's unified performance after so few rehearsals.

In any case, we all found our place, plus or minus a few singers and instrumentalists who entered one by one, and by the time we reached the loud climax of that last movement of apotheosis once again, we had found one another, and Mahler. We had created an incredible musical end to a night of wonderful "at-one-ment" in the halls of the Vatican. The Pope's encore had its intended effect.

After we finally left the stage (after the Pope and his entourage had made their own ceremonious exit), I bid members of the Pittsburgh Symphony good-bye as some came, one by one, into my backstage dressing room to thank me for bringing them to Rome. I told them it was I who was grateful to them (and to their choral colleagues and the soloists) for their remarkable music-making. The choirs left quickly, out of the Sala Nervi by the door on the opposite side of the hall, to board the waiting buses and begin their journeys home: to Kraków, London, Ankara, and Pittsburgh. I hoped I would see them all again, orchestra and choirs, but at that very moment I had no idea where or when.

John Harbison came backstage with his wife, Rose, and his publisher, Susan Feder. They wanted to know what the Pope had said about his work. It was clear to me, as I told them: "Couldn't you tell, John? It seemed to me that he loved it." John nodded in deep appreciation.

The new President of the Pittsburgh Symphony Orchestra, Larry Tamburri, was in Rome as well, but he had only taken up his post at the new year. He came backstage briefly before heading off into the night to a party hosted by the orchestra to celebrate its triumph. What an initiation to his new job that Papal Concert in the Vatican must have been for Larry. After that, concerts in Heinz Hall would be a piece of cake.

The last to peek in my door was Michael Bielski, the orchestra's manager, who had worked so diligently with me over many months. I thanked him profusely, yet again, for his devoted service to this concert. Through our many trials and tribulations we had become fast friends, and we remain so to this day.

The Pittsburgh Symphony flew back to the United States the next day, but throughout the following week I would meet members of the orchestra's staff and their board all over Rome. Near the Pantheon, on the Via Veneto, in Saint Peter's Square, even in the Villa Borghese up above the Spanish Steps. They were everywhere. They seemed reluctant to let their Papal experience go. Michael Bielski had been right: for the people of Pittsburgh who had come to Rome, "time had stood still." They walked up to me on our family walks or while my family and I were dining in our favorite restaurants, curious and asking about how I had felt that night, and wanting, I suspect, to relive yet again the uplifting and magical feelings of that evening in the Aula.

For me, though, there was just one day off. The Monday after our Saturday concert I went right back to work. In my guise as on-air host of the upcoming PBS broadcast that would be created from this concert, I was to be filmed walking and talking in three of the most privileged places of religious importance in the whole of the Eternal City: The Sala Clementina in the Papal Apartments, the Great Synagogue of Rome, and the Great Mosque of Rome. All of this had been arranged, with the assent of His Holiness, through the good offices of Archbishop Dziwisz himself. The Pope knew the power of television to carry the message of our concert to millions across America, and he was seeing to it as best he could that all three faiths were equally represented in our presentation.

The Sala Clementina and the Great Synagogue were places I had known well, for more than fifteen years. The Great Mosque of Rome was something else again. Permission for a non-Muslim to enter this mosque is rare enough, but to be allowed to film there took the explicit permission of the same Islamic personage who had sat on the left side of His Holiness at the Concert of Reconciliation, the mosque's Imam, Abdulawahab Hussein Gomaa. His commitment to interfaith dialogue would now become even more self-evident.

When I arrived with my film crew in tow, the guardians of the mosque could not quite believe we had permission to enter the sanctuary. They called whomever they called, the Imam or his representative, I would suppose. The guards remonstrated on the telephone, in Arabic, with their consternation and meaning crystal clear. In the end, though, we were able to enter, just as the Imam had arranged.

I had never been inside a functioning mosque. But now I walked into a place of active worship where thousands upon thousands gathered each and every Friday for the Muslim day of prayer. The vast sanctuary was totally empty and elegantly bare. Only beautifully filigreed ceilings and lighted wall sconces suggested the path of a devout worshipper's prayers to Allah.

In this holy space, I spoke, on air, of the two themes of the concert: our common ancestry in the Patriarch Abraham, and our shared belief in the resurrection of the soul, through different means, of course, but towards the same end, a reunion with our creator above.

I left the mosque with a renewed respect for the prayer life of my Muslim brothers and sisters. Allah is indeed great. All three of our faiths can at least agree on that.

The next day, Tuesday, January 20, 2004, my family and I had an audience with the Pope. Archbishop Dziwisz had said that His Holiness wished to see us before we left for New York. "Maestro, please do bring your family," Archbishop Dziwisz said on the telephone. "They are with you, I know. I saw them at the concert. Your boys, David and Gabriel, have grown so much since they were last here with us. The Holy Father will very much wish to visit with them, and with your wife, Vera, of course, as well."

"Yes, we will all be there," I answered, happy as always to bring my family to see the Pope.

"So, Tuesday, at 11 o'clock, Maestro. In the usual place. We will see you then."

There was nothing unusual in his voice or what he had said, but still I began to get an odd feeling. Something about this meeting felt final. Some inner voice told me perhaps this would be the last time. But I told myself that couldn't be the case. People had been saying that the Pope had been dying for eight years or more. No, I told myself, he has more of a will to live than anyone I have ever seen. Besides, Archbishop Dziwisz had already asked me about my future concert ideas.

The taxi ride from our rented apartment in the center of Rome was longer than from the Hotel Raphael, where I usually stay, but I was very glad for the extra time, just to collect my thoughts. My mind went back almost exactly sixteen years to my first audience with a young, athletic Pope, just ten years into his Pontificate, who had looked at me in astonishment as I had told him what I thought God had in store for him: that God had made him Pope to bring our two peoples together after two millennia of mistrust. I could never have thought that that extraordinary meeting in February 1988 would have led me on the journey of a lifetime. I thought that I must cherish this meeting even more than I usually did. It could be my last. My whole story had been so improbable. I had no right to think that story would go on even one day more. I treasured these moments, and I would count the steps out of the Apostolic Palace once again, as always, trying to remember for the rest of my life every precious memory I had of this great man whom I had been so privileged to serve.

As we walked into Saint Peter's Square, Vera reminded me fondly of her first audience with the Pope, how we had found the gentle nun, and how she had been so trusting, leaving our little son, David, in the nun's sisterly hands while we went "upstairs."

"Where was that kindly sister now?" Vera asked me rhetorically. "Did she remember us? Had she followed your improbable journey? Could she have believed that now, sixteen years later, you had just conducted for her Holy Father in the Vatican, yet again, for peace?"

And then she spoke about her mother, Margit, how important the Pope had been for her, and how clearly dear she had been to His Holiness as well. Margit was gone now, but she never left our thoughts for long.

My boys were by this time twelve and nineteen. They had been so small, tiny children, when they first met the Pontiff that he could have bounced them on his knee. In fact, the Pope had held Gabriel in his arms at the audience for the survivors before the Papal Concert in Commemoration of the Shoah in 1994. He had kissed him so affectionately, like the grandfather on my side of the family whom my children had never known—my father—who had died before they were born.

Finally, lost in all these thoughts, we found ourselves deep in the palace walking toward the great wooden door that leads into the Papal Apartments. The Sediari led us in through the Sala Clementina, where I had been just the day before. But now I didn't even notice its awesome beauty.

We went through the beautiful Papal Palace and entered the Pope's private library, where Archbishop Dziwisz himself welcomed us. The room had changed little since the last time I had been there, except perhaps for the elegant Persian carpets, which covered the checkered marble floor. It was possible, I thought, that these carpets made it easier on the Pope as he perambulated around this space, meeting his special guests throughout the day.

As at my first audience in 1988, His Holiness was seated. But now, in 2004, he did not rise to greet us. The Pope was positioned in a large chair that was similar to the wheeled throne on which he had sat at the concert on Saturday night. Archbishop Dziwisz graciously announced us, and moved off to the side. As I drew near, I could see that the Pope's face was puffy and redder than I had remembered. His smile, though, was as warm and welcoming as ever. As he had done after the concert, Archbishop Dziwisz asked me to introduce my family to the Pontiff.

I spoke in English, in deference to my family. I realized it was the first time I had spoken with him in my native tongue since 1989, when he heard that I had learned Polish. "*Teraz tylko po polsku*"—Now, only in Polish—His Holiness had said, and from then on, that was how we had spoken.

My wife approached His Holiness with a broad smile. She was truly filled with joy at this meeting and showed it openly.

"I am sorry about your mother. She was a wonderful, brave woman," the Pope said, expressing his condolences. "I remember well her visits here to us. Especially at the Concert for the Shoah. Very moving and important." He told her how much Margit had meant to him.

As he spoke, the Pontiff labored over his words, but his shortness of breath did not prevent us from understanding fully what he had to say. Perhaps it was the intimacy of our surroundings here in the Papal library, but his speech seemed to come easier for him than it did after the concert. His head was bent downward, also painful to observe, but his affect was clear and present, and his mood upbeat.

He fairly beamed as he greeted each of my sons, as I updated him on their progress. "David is at Princeton now, Your Holiness. He is studying history and music. He thinks he might become a journalist."

"Yes," the Pope said with a smile, his voice again halting, his speech slurred a bit, but still completely understandable. "I remember you told me he played the violin. Does he play still? Has he played in your orchestra yet, Maestro?"

His Holiness pronounced *orchestra*, in English, as if the *ch* were the *ch* in *chest*. He had been doing the same thing for sixteen years now. In this, His Holiness would never be corrected!

"No, Your Holiness, not quite yet. But we will see," I answered, with a smile. "He is very serious about his studies."

"Yes, I am sure. Welcome," His Holiness said to David, who stood before the Pope dressed in his sharply tailored dark blue suit and orange and black Princeton University tie. "David, the King. A great name. I thank you, David, very much for this visit. Your father is so proud of you. He talks about you all the time."

Next, I said, "Holiness, this is Gabriel."

"Yes, of course. A chess player, no? Can he beat his father?" the Pope needled a little, a smile covering his wide open face.

"Yes, for some years now. He is just too good. And very good in school as well. He gets all A's."

"Ah. This is good," the Pope declared. "And Gabriel, this is also a special name. The archangel. He is holy to all three religions."

For his part, Gabriel just smiled his beautiful childlike smile, which I knew hid so well that he was taking in everything going on around him, with intense concentration and interest.

All this time, at Archbishop Dziwisz's urging, I was sitting in a chair to the Pope's right as we exchanged this familial chatter. It was a joy to be so near him and to witness his pleasure in seeing my family once again.

Finally, the Pope turned to me and said, "Maestro, I was pleased with this concert on Saturday. I pray that it opened the hearts of all those who were there. There is so much terrible hatred. Perhaps we have made a small step forward with this concert."

"Your Holiness, I hope and pray you are right. The atmosphere was remarkable. I felt, Your Holiness, that our music touched a chord. And everyone seemed moved by your speech at the end of the concert. You cannot imagine what gratitude I feel for the privilege you have given me. To make music for you, in the Vatican, to join you on your quest for peace is the greatest honor I could ever have."

I was speaking about the Papal Concert of Reconciliation, but I felt as though I was carried deeper and deeper into my memories of all we had accomplished together in the past sixteen years. I tried to hold these thoughts in check and strove to keep myself in the present, focusing on this lovely time in the Pope's library, conversing with him about what we had just done together three days before.

"Maestro, I know how difficult these are. These concerts," His Holiness told me. "I know how hard you work. But they are filled with such meaning. Your music is an important language. A way for peace. I thank you for this very much."

"No, Your Holiness, it is nothing. I would do it all again. Again and again. It is a privilege. The greatest I will ever know. Now, Your Holiness, if I may, I have for you a special gift."

With that, I offered the Pope an autographed copy of the score of John Harbison's "Abraham," beautifully bound in the finest brown leather I could find in Rome.

"Mr. Harbison has dedicated this to you, Your Holiness. And to us, to the work we do together. It is a symbol of all you have done to bring the peoples of all three great monotheistic faiths together over so many, many years. It is the musical representation of that vital work. I wanted you to have it, to remember our great evening. I have written some words inside, words that are for you alone, that try to express what is in my heart."

"Maestro, I thank you. I thank you very much for this, and for everything. It will be very dear to me."

And with that, Archbishop Dziwisz suggested we pose for a family portrait. Vera and I sat on either side of His Holiness, with our boys standing just a step back on either side. I wish I could say we all smiled broadly, the way one does at such important moments. But we didn't. We tried, but what seemed to come out of our faint smiles was sadness, in our faces and in our eyes. Afterwards, as I viewed the photographs sent by the Vatican's official photographer, I saw that sadness and perhaps concern on the Pope's face as well. Did he think this would be our last time together? Was this our real farewell? I kept refusing to imagine that would be so. We posed for several shots, all looking very much the same despite our strong collective efforts, and then, much too soon, our audience was over.

As I was preparing to leave, as the Pope leaned towards me to say his good-bye, I did something as necessary as anything I have ever done in my life. I bent down and kissed His Holiness on his hand for the first time. He patted my head with his other hand, bringing me to him, for one brief instant. We were bonded like that for a millisecond, and it was over. In that moment, I think we both knew what neither of us could say.

His cheek had felt soft, and warm, and oh so human. I will remember that human warmth as long as I live.

Finally, I said, *"Do zobaczenja"*—I'll see you soon—"Your Holiness."

He said, *"Do widzenia*, Maestro." Good-bye. Until we see each other again. He knew more than I did. That would never change.

I left his library with a heavy heart. We walked out slowly through all those regal rooms. None of us said a word.

CHAPTER

THIRTY-SIX

few days after my meeting with Pope John Paul, I paid what
I thought might be my last visit to Archbishop Dziwisz. After
we greeted each other warmly in his by-now familiar Apostolic
Palace office, I started to thank him for all we had done together, when
he interrupted me with a smile.

"Maestro," His Excellency began, "the Holy Father has asked me
once again to thank you for your wonderful concert, and also for the
visit of yourself and your family with him on Tuesday. He has asked
me to inquire whether there might be something else, another concert?
What might you now have in mind? And, Maestro, we have an idea
for you to consider as well."

I was dumbfounded. The holy man we had seen on Tuesday
seemed so frail, his physical strength greatly lessened from what it had
been when I met him sixteen years earlier. But clearly his spirit, his will
to forge ahead with his vision of music in the service of peace, despite
all his infirmities, was undiminished.

For a full thirty seconds, I was at a complete loss for words.
Finally, I asked, "What is it that His Holiness would wish me to
pursue?"

"Well, Maestro, you know that the twentieth World Youth Day
is coming up in Cologne in July of next year. Might this not be an
occasion—and the magnificent Cologne Cathedral a place—for a
wonderful concert to celebrate His Holiness' important meeting
with the youth of the world? We remember so well your music-making

379

for the Vigil at World Youth Day in Denver. Do you think this might be a possibility? If you agree, I would like you please to go to Cologne. Meet there with His Eminence Cardinal Meissner. He will help with this, I believe. Please do see what can be done."

"Yes, Excellency. Yes, of course. I will do this. Cologne Cathedral is a magnificent spiritual space, and it would be perfect for a grand concert. And I know, everyone knows, of His Holiness' love for the youth of the world. Let me go to Cologne, meet with His Eminence, and see what might be done. As to what I myself have in mind, no, Excellency, I have not had the chance to think about that. I will be in touch soon, and will share with you my ideas for what might be most interesting and appropriate. We can then see whether it meets with your approval."

"Well, good, Maestro. I will inform Cardinal Meissner that he may be hearing from you. Thank you for this visit. I hope to see you soon back in Rome to discuss these future concerts."

I left the palace still in a daze. When I had walked out of what I was still convinced would be my last audience with His Holiness, I could never have imagined that Archbishop Dziwisz would suggest more concerts. But clearly the Pope wished our common mission to go on—and on. A smile returned to my face for the first time since I had left His Holiness earlier that week.

When my family and I arrived in New York the following day, I had another surprise waiting for me, this time in my mailbox. Larry Tamburri, the new President of the Pittsburgh Symphony, who had seemed somewhat distant during our time in Rome, had sent me a note. It read, in part:

> Wow! Last week will certainly be among the most memorable of my life. I was deeply impressed by your passion, skill, and professionalism. What you accomplished in Pittsburgh and at the Vatican was historic. It was an honor for me to be a small part of this immense undertaking.

Once again I was shocked. I simply had had no idea that the Pittsburgh and Rome concerts would make such an impression on such a consummate professional orchestra manager. I had certainly felt that the Pittsburgh community had been touched deeply. I knew that from the day the announcement of the Papal Concert had been made back in November. But that the orchestra's top manager would be so appreciative was a major surprise.

To my amazement, by the following Friday, January 30, not quite two weeks after our event in Rome, I was back in Pittsburgh to discuss my future involvement with the PSO. I had lunch with a member of the symphony staff, then gave an interview for WQED, the local PBS affiliate, and had a private dinner with Bishop Wuerl. All three were interested in the same thing, albeit from very different points of view: How could we build on the incredible enthusiasm of the whole city and the orchestra that had been generated by the Papal Concert? How could we bottle the spirit of the concert in Rome? As I sat through the meals and meetings, I could feel the Pope's smile all the way across the Atlantic and right down to where the Three Rivers meet. His inspiration had spread. The work would go on, both in Rome and now, I saw, in America too.

Within weeks of the Papal Concert of Reconciliation, I was invited back to Pittsburgh to conduct the Verdi Requiem in Heinz Hall at the end of that very 2003–4 season—a special event that was not on their schedule and that was greeted skeptically, mainly because downtown Pittsburgh on a Saturday night in July is deserted. But as had happened so many times before, it all seemed to come together miraculously. We got our four top soloists on short notice and launched a serious concert in the sultry heat of a west Pennsylvania summer night. Such a feat had never been done before in Pittsburgh. But for Larry Tamburri, Michael Bielski, Dick Simmons, Bishop Wuerl, and myself it just had to be. Pittsburgh was on fire with the spirit of our Roman concert and demanded that we feed its appetite for spiritual music. We took a huge chance, especially in the normally risk-averse world of classical music.

On, July 10, 2004, Larry Tamburri had to come on stage to announce that the start of the concert would have to be pushed back by half an hour. The line at the box office, he told those already in the

hall, stretched around the block. A rumble of laughter and self-satis-
faction spread throughout the patrons already seated in their velvet-
covered seats at Heinz Hall. We were, astonishingly, sold out.

The members of the orchestra, who would normally be quite
upset with such a delay, were delighted. If this many ticket-buyers—
many of them, it turned out, new to the Pittsburgh Symphony—were
this interested in hearing them perform, then they would gladly wait
an extra half hour. The buzz of anticipation surrounding our performance built up to a fever pitch as we all waited to go on stage.

What was so different about what we were doing that night?
What was it in our outreach to this community that had inspired such
an outpouring of support? We should not have been surprised.

Pittsburgh is a city of deep faiths, with a huge Catholic population, and strong Protestant, Jewish, and Muslim communities as well.
Most had not attended the Symphony because the Symphony hadn't
seemed all that interested in them. There was, rightly or wrongly, an
aura of elitism that surrounded Heinz Hall. With their participation
in the Papal Concert, the Pittsburgh Symphony had showed that it
understood the link between music and spirit, a connection that was
compelling to the broader Pittsburgh community that had never set
foot in Heinz Hall. It had shown that the most important word in its
name was "Pittsburgh." And the Pittsburgh community had responded
to its orchestra's overture by mobbing their musical home.

I tried to speak directly to these newborn classical music fans in
the notes I wrote for that evening's concert program:

> Your Pittsburgh Symphony has been a great orchestra for a
> very long time. Sometimes though, it takes an extraordinary
> event to rekindle an appreciation for a gem in one's own midst.
> The Spirit of Rome has brought that renewed cherishing, but it
> has done more. It has reconnected the orchestra to its roots,
> for music and spirit have always been one.
>
> May your ear and your soul be refreshed and enlivened. May
> you hear the Spirit of Rome and the Spirit of Pittsburgh come
> together in the Verdi tonight. And may the union of

Pittsburgh with its great symphony continue to grow together and prosper for many years to come.

The performance was electric, from the hushed beginning in the cellos to the equally hushed full-orchestra conclusion eighty-five minutes later. The crowd seemed on the edge of their seats. The orchestra, which had not performed this masterwork in more than seven years, was in top form. The chorus, prepared expertly by their choirmaster, Robert Page, was amazing, as were our four internationally renowned soloists: Metropolitan Opera stars Sondra Radvanovsky, Jerry Hadley, and John Relyea, and Marianne Cornetti (a local favorite making her long-awaited Pittsburgh Symphony debut).

The next day the press was over the top. "Who would have thought that anything but a rock concert in July would have fans mobbing the box office like they were giving away caviar? That was the scene Saturday night when Maestro Gilbert Levine made his first appearance here since conducting the PSO's historic concert in the Vatican. A bone-shaking Requiem with the full power of Judgment Day, it spoke directly to the heart," thundered the *Pittsburgh Tribune-Review.*

Just a few months later, in early fall, I was back in the Vatican to follow up on my discussions with Archbishop Dziwisz about what might come next—and, of course, to inquire after the health of His Holiness. All that summer and fall the reports had been more and more unsettling.

"Maestro, the Holy Father is very strong," Archbishop Dziwisz told me. "Strong of spirit. He believes all is in God's hands. He works as hard as he can every day. He will do so until he cannot do so any more. I will tell him you asked after him. It will mean a great deal. And, now, how are our plans coming? The Holy Father will ask me about those as well."

"Well, Excellency, I believe it might be possible to have the concert His Holiness has suggested in Cologne. I have been there. The cathedral is magnificent, and I have met with both Cardinal Meissner and the Domprobst Norbert Feldhoff, the head of the Cathedral

Chapter. As Your Excellency knows, Domprobst Feldhoff is very important in this as well. Without his permission, no event can take place in his cathedral. But I think he is with us. So, I believe something very good can be done there. I have even spoken with the Knights of Columbus. They are prepared to sponsor the concert, and my German television producer, Dr. Lothar Mattner, says there would be great interest in broadcasting this concert throughout Europe, and perhaps in America. So, it seems, Excellency, that we are well on our way."

"Good, Maestro. Yes, very good. I knew His Eminence would welcome you and your music to his city. And I am happy to hear about the Domprobst. So Cologne is well under way. Now, have you had a chance to think about something else? Something that would continue what we set out to do in our Papal Concert of Reconciliation?"

"Yes, Excellency, I have. The fortieth anniversary of Nostra Aetate is coming up in November of next year. I know how important this Second Vatican Council document has been to His Holiness in laying the groundwork for all he and I have been doing in trying to bring peoples of different faiths together in mutual respect and love.

"So, I want to organize a concert to celebrate this important milestone, and I would like to do this in America. If His Holiness agrees, I would like to see whether we might do this in the Basilica of the National Shrine of the Immaculate Conception in Washington, D.C. I know His Holiness knows this place. He visited there during his very first Papal Pilgrimage to America in 1979. I believe the Knights of Columbus would again wish to sponsor this concert."

Archbishop Dziwisz promised to let me know if Pope John Paul approved of my suggestion.

On my next trip to Europe, in early January 2005, I stopped in Rome once again. Neither Archbishop Dziwisz nor I knew that this would be the last time I would see him in his office at the palace. The press had been reporting constantly on the Pope's health. Still, the world had lived with accounts of the Pontiff's physical decline for years. The real specifics of his condition were, of course, a tightly held Vatican secret.

"So, Maestro, since your last visit here I have had the chance to discuss your idea of a concert to celebrate the fortieth anniversary of Nostra Aetate with the Holy Father. He likes it very much, and he believes that the basilica in Washington would indeed be a most appropriate venue for this to take place. Since the anniversary itself is in November, would your concert take place then?"

"Yes, that's wonderful. I have spoken with His Eminence Cardinal McCarrick. I know he will be pleased with His Holiness' assent. And now we will look for a specific date in November of 2005. And, of course, we will keep you apprised."

"And what will be your musical program? Have you given this some thought?"

"Well, Excellency, I would think, to perform Beethoven's Ninth Symphony, the same work we performed in Kraków in December of 2000. It's a work that reaches out to people of all faiths with a great openness of spirit. And I have found some words written by our first President George Washington to the congregation of the Touro Synagogue in Newport, Rhode Island. The synagogue, it happens, is where my wife and I were married in 1976. Washington's letter offers words of comfort and support to the Jewish community of the United States. I think this would be a most appropriate message, in line with Nostra Aetate and with the deep wishes of His Holiness for better understanding among peoples of all faiths. We are hoping to find an American composer to set these words to music and have its premiere performance at this special event as well."

"Yes, Maestro. This sounds very good. Beethoven is of course perfect for such a concert. And, as to the words of your first President, I trust that they are indeed most appropriate. This sounds like it will be an important occasion."

Archbishop Dziwisz went on: "I have heard also from Cardinal Meissner that your plans for the concert in the Cologne Cathedral are proceeding quite well. He has told us that it will take place before the arrival of the Pope, and that you have decided on Beethoven's Missa Solemnis, a great and beautiful work. This will give a wonderful musical welcome, a foretaste of the openness to all and a sentiment that His Holiness wishes to usher in World Youth Day. I wish you very good luck with all your preparations.

"And, Maestro, I am most pleased to share with you that the Holy Father has it in mind that you should be awarded a further Pontifical honor. It may take some time. It will break a precedent yet again," he said with a wry smile. "You will understand better when it comes to pass."

And with that, we gave each other a warm hug of friendship and parted. I left the palace more confused than ever before. We were planning events, but His Holiness was so very ill. There was even talk of a further honor. So there was now a future where I had dreaded there would only be a past.

On February 1, 2005, John Paul was admitted to the hospital. Over the next two months, as he went back and forth from the Gemelli Hospital, there would be daily reports on his declining condition. They varied from guarded to grave. On March 13 he spoke from his window in the palace to the crowds in Saint Peter's below.

On Palm Sunday, March 20, he again appeared on the balcony. But this time, when he tried to speak, he could not muster his voice. Visibly shaken and distraught, he left the window that day, only to appear very briefly again on March 27, Easter Sunday. That was the last time he would be seen alive by the public.

All during this time from February through March, I was in New York, in a state of terrible sadness at the inevitability of the Pope's coming death. CNN and all the world's news channels were giving constant updates, but no one had truly authoritative news from inside the Papal Apartments. I couldn't get through either. My calls to Archbishop Dziwisz had gone unanswered for weeks. I dreaded the worst.

Early on the morning of April 2 in Rome, the bells started to toll in the Vatican, their solemn peals spreading outward to churches throughout the Catholic world. Pope John Paul II had passed away.

When I heard the news, I remember being numb, unable to speak for the longest time to Vera, to my sons, to my friends who called. I answered no one. It didn't matter that I had expected this news for many months, for more than a year since my last audience in January 2004: the Pope's death still came as a shock. We had said our good-byes without saying good-bye. My strong presentiment at the time had been right.

Now I realized that my meetings with Archbishop Dziwisz had gone on because His Holiness could not let go of life. Its force, the force of God, was within him and remained strong, no doubt, until the end. But now his life was over. He was gone.

The next day, still in a daze, I started to receive calls from the press. Would I speak about my friend, the Pope? they all asked. I would never presume to call him that, please understand, I would say, but if you wish, I will give my witness as best I can.

The two I remember best are my interviews on *Larry King Live* and on *Nightline* with Ted Koppel.

Waiting in the CNN greenroom, high atop Columbus Circle, Larry King walked in and treated me as if we had been friends for life. "Gilbert Levine. The Pope's Maestro! Pretty incredible story. But tell me, I'm from Bensonhurst; what part of Brooklyn are you from?" Larry asked in an accent redolent of our shared Brooklyn Jewish background.

"Well, I was born in Flatbush. To give you an idea, from the roof of my building on Sullivan Place, they tell me you could see the Dodgers play, for free. But we moved from there to the Five Towns on the Queens-Nassau border when I was very young."

"Still, once from Brooklyn, always from Brooklyn," Larry asserted. And instantly it seemed as though we were like two brothers separated by a lifetime's experience.

The interview itself went well. The conversation on air was little different in tone from the one we had had in the greenroom, but very much more to the point. Larry was interested in down-to-earth things. He posed questions like: The Pope's tailor made your jacket? Were you nervous when you conducted for him? How much of music did he understand? These were questions that everyone in his audience would have asked if they had had the chance. At the end, Larry King said, "I would like to do a whole show with you. What a great story this is. Thank you so much."

Nightline was a totally different story. Ted Koppel is one of the sharpest interviewers and perhaps even feared journalists in all of television. And for very good reason. He cuts through all the outer layers and goes right to the heart of the matter.

The preinterview was held in the *Nightline* studio, Ted Koppel peppering me with questions even as the lighting was being adjusted and the mike put into my lapel. There was no small talk. I didn't have any idea where he came from (London, I believe), and he seemed to have little interest in me as a person, let alone which Brooklyn neighborhood I came from.

I would be sharing the program, although not appearing on air, with Archbishop Desmond Tutu, who would be interviewed via satellite from his home in South Africa.

Koppel's questions went directly to the heart of John Paul's quest to bring the three great monotheistic religions together. This being 2005, post–9/11, Koppel was particularly interested in the Pope's outreach to Islam. I told him I thought it had been "unfinished business" for His Holiness, and that I thought it was the same for the world also. (Sadly, I feel it still remains so to this day.)

Koppel bored in. I stood up to his queries as best I could. He was after his story. I could only tell him what I knew. He wanted to give his viewers as complete an understanding of Pope John Paul and his view of other faiths as he could through my experiences. Of course, the Anglican Archbishop Tutu was infinitely better qualified than I was to speak from a position of religious authority. He spoke about the desirability of the next pope coming from Africa. In the end, I think I survived.

In any case, Ted Koppel and I became, if not friends, at least quite friendly. Our relationship, built in the crucible of that trying interview, was to bear fruit of an artistic sort later in 2005, when he would narrate the words of George Washington at the Nostra Aetate concert in Washington, D.C.

When I finally arrived in Rome on the morning of April 7 for the Pope's funeral the next day, I immediately called Archbishop Dziwisz. There was no reply. I next called Archbishop Harvey, the Prefect of the Pontifical Household.

"Maestro, I am so pleased you have called. It has been so busy here. You can imagine. We have instructions to find you a place of honor at the funeral tomorrow. Right up by the basilica, very near to where the Mass will be celebrated. If you wish, I can arrange for you to sit with the Jewish leaders who have been invited to attend."

"Excellency, yes, that is most appropriate. Somehow, I feel that is where His Holiness would have wished me to be."

"Very well, and since it is such short notice, if you would please, would you come to my office. You know the way. Your ticket will be waiting for you here. And, Maestro, you have our most sincere condolences. We know what a loss this must be for you."

"No, Excellency. It is a loss for the whole world. For you as well, I know. I will only be one of many millions who will miss him terribly."

That evening, I made a reservation to dine at my favorite Roman restaurant, Fortunato al Pantheon. As I arrived, Signor Fortunato himself greeted me with a strange request. "Please, Maestro, will you accompany me into our back room? There are some people here who would like to see you."

When I walked into the room, a large table of fancily dressed Italians stood and applauded me. They were the President of the Italian Chamber of Deputies and the President of the Senate of the Italian Republic and their distinguished guests.

"Bravo, Maestro. We all saw you on Larry King," the President of the Senate announced. "We are so pleased to see you, albeit on this very sad occasion. Please sit down with us to have a drink." I did so, thinking how very strange this all was. And when I got back to New York, I made sure to call Larry King's producer immediately. Larry's reach is truly international!

Early the next morning, I found my way to the Great Synagogue, where Jewish leaders from across the globe were assembling. I felt a little out of place as the only Jewish layman without official portfolio. But this was where and with whom I had to be on this most solemn day.

Accompanied by an elaborate security detail, we sped off through the snarled traffic, passing all the lights, sirens wailing, in our small minibus, which was flanked on each side, and front and back, by police cars armed to the teeth for this special task. Every precaution was being taken so that we would arrive at Saint Peter's on time and in one piece.

The mood among us was somber, yet grateful. John Paul was beloved by Jews worldwide as perhaps no pope before had ever been. I had experienced this growing sense of trust in him firsthand, over my seventeen years of work on his behalf. He would be sorely missed by my people, as he would be by the rest of the world.

The Rome we passed through was filled with millions upon millions of mourners. There were more people wishing to be near the Pope for his last rites than there were citizens of the Eternal City. The lines to view his body inside St. Peter's had stretched for nearly a mile in the short time he had lain in state. And now, on the morning of the funeral, his burgeoning flock of admirers filled every avenue and every small street leading to the Vatican from all the seven hills of Rome.

For the funeral, Pope John Paul's bier was brought outside, just in front of the main entrance to the basilica. The placement of the delegations of non-Christian faiths was said to have been planned by His Holiness himself. Whether it was he, or those acting on his behalf, we could not have been treated more respectfully. Our position was as close to his bier as any outside the highest of dignitaries. Lining the rows of seats just to the left of the casket were the heads of state from many countries. Opposite them were the members of the College of Cardinals. Close behind the heads of state were national delegations from countries like Poland and Italy that had close ties to His Holiness. And just to the left of those sat the Jewish, Muslim, and other interfaith delegations.

As I made my way to my seat, a nun in an ornate habit walked up to me, and reached for my hand. She introduced herself as Mother Tekla Familglietti, the Abbess General of the Holy Order of

St. Bridget. I knew her name. Everyone close to the Pope did. But we had never met. Mother Tekla was perhaps the closest female Vatican official to His Holiness throughout his Pontificate, and she had been with His Holiness, by his bedside, during his final hours. She wore the black headdress of her order, with its white cross amid a white circle, atop her head. As I looked towards her, her face seemed filled with deep compassion.

Mother Tekla said, "Maestro, you don't know me, but we all know you. I have been to all your concerts. I just wanted to tell you how very much you meant to him."

She didn't use the Pope's name, or refer to him by his title, but there was no need. She looked deeply in my eyes, which welled up with tears I could not hold back. She held my hand even more firmly, to comfort me, to calm me down, just as His Holiness himself had done at our very first audience. Mother Tekla seemed not to want to let me go. And I also did not want her to.

Finally, I said, "You cannot know how much what you have just told me means to me. Especially just now. I feel such an emptiness knowing he is gone. When this is over, I hope we will meet again. I know of you also. People say he loved you very much. I would love to sit down and talk."

She told me yes, that would be wonderful. But that we never did see each other again is not a surprise. The world after John Paul would be different for each of us. I knew life would never be the same again.

Across a narrow aisle, next to me on my right, sat the Polish delegation. Among them I recognized the former Polish President Lech Walesa, a close friend of His Holiness, and now a Polish hero and Nobel Prize winner. Sitting there also was former Prime Minister Tadeusz Mazowiecki, who had been one of the great leaders of Solidarity, and whose rise to power I had followed from my perch inside the Polish transformation from tyranny to freedom. Mazowiecki also had been a close friend of the Pope. I felt a kinship with those Poles, with their struggle, and with their nation in which I had lived so fruitfully and which had nurtured me so well.

As the funeral began, I saw the heads of state, kings and queens, presidents and dictators, Catholics, Protestants, Orthodox Christians, Muslims, Jews, Buddhists, and Hindus, who had all come to pay their last respects to a universally beloved religious leader. I recognized so many. Prince Charles, of course, and President George W. Bush. President Moshe Katsav of Israel was there as well, sitting right next to his arch enemy, Mohammad Khatami of Iran. Pope John Paul wouldn't have had it any other way. A striver for peace, even in death. It was said to be the largest-ever gathering of state leaders in world history.

Amidst all this ceremonial mourning, I saw, as everyone did, the open, terrible grief etched on the face of my friend Archbishop Dziwisz. He sat at the end of the front row of mourners, not far from His Eminence Cardinal Joseph Ratzinger, who celebrated the funeral Mass and gave the eulogy. Archbishop Dziwisz's eyes were constantly cast down. He looked shrunken in his grief. I don't know how he got through that long morning. I wish I could have somehow reached out to comfort him. Although he was only twenty-five feet away, we seemed separated by the ocean of our shared sorrow.

During the funeral Mass, I sang along with the chanting of the Litany of the Saints, which I had learned for my conducting of the Pope's Vigil Service at World Youth Day in Denver.

And then it was over.

The Pope's simple wooden casket, similar to those in which Orthodox Jews are buried, was carried by the Sediari back into St. Peter's for burial in the Papal Crypt. As Archbishop Dziwisz walked heavily behind the Pope's coffin, his purple skullcap was almost blown off by the wind, I could see. He grabbed at it, clasping it firmly to his head, as if losing that last covering would have revealed his deeply pained emotions to the vast crowd. In that instant, he looked like nothing so much as the humble priest I think he always thought himself to be. A simple servant of this great man who now belonged to the ages.

As I saw the Papal bier disappear inside the basilica, I wondered when, if ever, I would see my friend Archbishop Dziwisz again. He would be in mourning for a very, very long time, as would I.

After the door to St. Peter's was finally closed behind the cortege, I looked out to my left over the sea of people who had gathered from the four corners of the globe. There were countless colorful banners, some waving by themselves in the wind. But by far the most numerous were the red and white flags of John Paul's proud native Poland. As far as the eye could see, all the way down the Via della Conciliazione, past Castel Sant'Angelo to the Ponte Sant'Angelo, there were Polish flags. And sprinkled liberally among the crowd were almost as many banners, many hand-painted, held high by people from around the world. These read simply "Santo Subito"—Sainthood Now.

On December 6, 2006, nearly two years after our last meeting in the Apostolic Palace, I had finally found my way back to Kraków to visit my friend Stanislaw Dziwisz. In the interim, he had been appointed to lead the Catholic Archdiocese in the Polish royal capital by His Holiness Pope Benedict XVI. That spring, in the same Saint Peter's Square where the Papal funeral rites had been held, I had witnessed with enormous pride the grand ceremony, called a consistory, by which the Adjunct Prefect of the Pontifical Household had been created a Prince of the Church. From the youthful Father Dziwisz, whom I had first encountered in Rome in 1988, to the now augustly titled His Eminence Stanislaw Cardinal Dziwisz, Archbishop of Kraków, his had been a long and remarkable priestly road.

As I walked into the same rooms at the Curia Metropolitana Kraków that I had when I first met Cardinal Macharski at the very beginning of this magical musical and spiritual journey, I noticed that the Archbishop's study had been changed. It seemed simpler, more elegant, yet more humble, than I had remembered. To me, it seemed that Cardinal Dziwisz wished to live in a way that reminded him of his daily life with Pope John Paul. Or perhaps it was I who had changed, finding comfort and ease in these high church environs where my old friend now made his new home. When I first went to Kraków in 1987, I had never met a Catholic priest. Now, after seventeen years of Papal service, I was back where it had all begun.

Cardinal Dziwisz greeted me with sad but welcoming eyes. He looked much older. Grief had taken its toll. We spoke quietly, his first words seeming strange.

"Maestro, in which language shall we speak now? Would you prefer Italian or Polish?"

It is true that my Polish had deteriorated since the passing of the Pope, but I don't think that was why His Eminence asked me that odd question. It seemed to me that in the midst of the Italian-speaking Curia at the Vatican we had found our familiar connection through a shared Kraków experience by using His Holiness', and Cardinal Dziwisz's, native language. And now that he was back home, living in Poland again for the first time in more than two and a half decades, it was as if he needed to find the right language to continue our close but unique relationship as we followed our separate ways after John Paul.

In truth, we ended up speaking (and still do) a mixture of the two languages, sometimes mixing them in the same conversation, as if the two experiences of Poland and the Holy See are inextricably bound together in our minds and in our hearts. In any case, our relationship goes on. Our love of the Pope, shared by millions, is matched by our shared desire to see his powerful legacy flourish. Cardinal Dziwisz has published a book on Catholic-Jewish topics coauthored with an important rabbi. He has convened a meeting of the heads of many faiths in memory of a similar convocation called by His Holiness at Assisi in 1986. I have found as many ways as I could to make music that honors the profound influence that John Paul has had on my life and on my artistic vision. And together, His Eminence and I have gone on imagining events of music and spirit out into the future.

During the course of this first, quiet conversation in Kraków, I thanked His Eminence, and through him His Holiness, for the incredible honor that had been bestowed upon me the year before. In November 2005, His Holiness Pope Benedict XVI awarded me the Silver Star of Saint Gregory, the highest order of Pontifical Knighthood that had ever been accorded a Jew in the history of the Holy See. The ceremony had taken place after the concert to celebrate the fortieth anniversary of Nostra Aetate, one of the last to be planned with His Holiness' active involvement.

"Maestro," His Eminence said, "I know the Holy Father would have been so pleased with your Washington concert. Peace among all religions was so very close to his heart. And the Star of Saint Gregory, it was the gift of His Holiness, and you deserve this high honor for all you have accomplished. I am deeply gratified that Pope Benedict saw fit to honor our Holy Father's wish in this regard."

"If I could only thank His Holiness in person ..." I answered, stopping short as I saw the deep emotion coming over the face of my friend.

I waited. Then went on.

"And it was also so extraordinary to be able to perform the Beethoven "Missa Solemnis" in Cologne, as His Holiness and I had planned. We had the Royal Philharmonic, you remember, the orchestra that performed at the Papal Concert to Commemorate the Shoah. And the London Philharmonic Choir from our Reconciliation Concert. It was also a great honor that Pope Benedict XVI offered his deep insights on Beethoven's great work via video from Val d'Aosta. We all felt His Holiness' spirit with us in that magnificent, immense cathedral.

"Eminence," I said, "I have brought you a recording so you can experience our concert for yourself." As I offered him the DVD, I flashed back to 2002 when I had given a similar recording of our Kraków 9/11 concert to His Holiness at Castel Gandolfo. In that instant, I felt that Cardinal Dziwisz may have remembered that heartwarming moment as well.

He thanked me, and we fell silent. It was many moments before we looked each other in the eye again.

Then we rose and gave each other a warm hug, and I turned to leave. As I was about to leave his study, Cardinal Dziwisz stopped me and brought me back to his desk. He went through an open door into a neighboring room, looked for a small book on a crowded desk, and quickly scribbled something on a piece of paper.

"Maestro, here, these are my cell phone numbers, both the one for Poland and the one I use when I am abroad. Please call me, Maestro. We must stay in touch." And with that, he graciously saw me out of his study to the outer door that leads to the stairs that would start me on my journey back to New York.

Now, when I phone him, in whatever language I choose, he does not even need me to speak my name. "Eminence," I need only say, and his reply comes back immediately, "Maestro, welcome, from the heart! Thank you for calling. Are you here in Kraków? When shall we see each other next?" I always hear in his, the voice of John Paul. If not the Pope's actual voice, then surely one that embodies His Holiness' spirit. Cardinal Dziwisz has made it clear that my powerful Polish connection will go on.

So, I was especially moved when, in December 2009, Polish television (TVN) produced a documentary on my life and work with the Pope. It too was called "Papieski Maestro"—The Pope's Maestro. This was the first such program ever created about my life in John Paul's native land. The young Polish director, Aleksandra Bajka, was as sensitive and insightful as any journalist I have ever encountered. Her film told my whole story, from my earliest days, taking bassoon lessons in the pit of the Metropolitan Opera in New York, to my going to Kraków as Music Director of the Kraków Philharmonic. She told of my meeting Cardinal Macharski, my friendship with Monsignor Dziwisz, and finally, of course, my growing relationship with His Holiness. She even filmed me on Ellis Island in New York harbor, where my grandmother Ida Levine had landed as an impoverished immigrant, having left Warsaw for America in search of a better life for her and her family in 1907.

Two tableaux in Aleksandra's film stand out:

In one, I am standing at the crossroads of Krochmalna Street, where my grandmother had once lived as a Yiddish-speaking Jew in an almost completely self-enclosed Jewish city-within-a-city, in Polish Warsaw. During World War II, Krochmalna Street had been cut in two, with one end leading to a bridge into the Jewish Ghetto set up by the Nazis as a holding-pen to keep my people before they were shipped off to their annihilation at Treblinka and other death camps scattered around the Polish countryside. At the other end, Krochmalna had been utterly destroyed as the Poles, the Soviets, and the Nazis fought bitterly over Warsaw's liberation in the winter of 1945. In place of the rubble, a new Warsaw had been built up after the war, and the few blocks of the original Krochmalna Street that had still remained intact now intersected with a wide and spacious thoroughfare newly named John Paul II Boulevard. As I looked up at the street sign that marks this oddest of intersections, it seemed as though my family's entire history, from our simplest origins to my privileged Papal service, was mirrored in this most prosaic of municipal signposts.

The other, more surprising, tableau in the documentary was even more revealing. During her rare on-air interview with Cardinal Dziwisz, Aleksandra had asked His Eminence to describe my relationship with Pope John Paul. He had never spoken about this before in all the twenty-one years we had known each other. But now, on Polish television, Cardinal Dziwisz said, in the quiet reverential tone he always uses when speaking of Pope John Paul, "On the occasion of his first concert, he visited with His Holiness, and there began a deep spiritual friendship between Maestro and the Holy Father."

When I watched this film in the winter of 2010, I could not believe my eyes and ears. I had not heard words anything like that since the moment after my first Papal Audience in February 1988 when then-Monsignor Dziwisz had told me, "Maestro, the Holy Father has asked me to tell you that he thinks you have a great soul." I had kept those humbling words in my innermost heart all this time, never allowing myself to speak them out loud. And now Cardinal Dziwisz, the only person in the world who could bear such witness, was announcing to Poland and to the whole world what I had never dared say openly.

"A deep spiritual friendship," His Eminence had said.

My extraordinary journey of music and spirit into the hallowed world of Pope John Paul II transforms my life and my art to this day.

My seventeen years with John Paul taught me many things. The power of music and spirit to foster hope, transformation, healing, and love. The mysteries of faith, not one faith but three—Judaism, Christianity, and Islam. The potential for reconciliation and redemption, even in the face of the sadness and violence of both the past and the present.

My music-making now is different than it was. I am more patient. I listen for the stillness as well as the roar. I look for the longer story in the musical tales that are there to be told. I have learned to hear the meaning that lies cached beneath the surface of the notes. I know now that music is spirit made sound. That it has the power to make us whole. And yes, to bring us peace.

ABOUT THE DVD

A Thousand Years of Music and Spirit" was a historic concert performed in the Millennium Year 2000 in one of the most beautiful churches in the world, Saint Mary's Basilica, in Kraków, the Polish home city of His Holiness Pope John Paul II.

In that Jubilee year, Kraków reigned as European Cultural Capital, and as such was visited by many of the world's great orchestras, including the Berlin Philharmonic under Bernard Haitink, the New York Philharmonic under Kurt Masur, Concentus Musicus Wien led by Nicholas Harnoncourt, and the London Philharmonic Orchestra and Choir under the direction of Sir Gilbert Levine. It is this last performance, conceived under the guidance of His Holiness Pope John Paul II, which became "A Thousand Years of Music and Spirit."

This concert traces the last thousand years of Poland's history, both Christian and Jewish, from the chanting of "Bogurodzica," an ancient Polish Marian hymn of national unity, written almost a thousand years ago, to a performance of the second movement of Henryk Górecki's Symphony No. Three, "The Symphony of Sorrowful Songs," which gives plaintive voice to the lament of a young girl, awaiting her execution in a dank and dark prison cell at Auschwitz during World War II. The performance ends with the greatest hymn to humankind's hope in God's creation, Beethoven's Symphony No. Nine, "Ode to Joy." It is the most popular and uplifting work in all the classical canon.

The London Philharmonic Orchestra, the London Philharmonic Choir, and five wonderful international soloists joined Maestro Levine on this glorious occasion, which filled Saint Mary's with "A Thousand Years of Music and Spirit," in tribute to the universality of the spiritual message of His Holiness Pope John Paul II.

ACKNOWLEDGMENTS

The Pope's Maestro would not have been possible without His Eminence Stanislaw Cardinal Dziwisz. Neither the journey into the world of Pope John Paul, which is its subject, nor the book itself would exist without him. At every turn His Eminence has been my guide to the elaborately intricate world of the Vatican and of the Roman Catholic Church, worldwide. Cardinal Dziwisz's sagacity, his understanding of people, are humbling. It is no wonder he was His Holiness' most trusted aide for more than three decades. Stanislaw Dziwisz has been my window on what it meant to be a servant priest in the Catholic Church, and I believe I am for him the Jewish friend he did not have the chance to have, growing up as he did in post-Holocaust Poland. It was he who told me, "Maestro, yes, you must write this book. You have such a wonderful story to tell." I hope I have done the trust he has shown me over the twenty-two years we have known each other the justice it so richly deserves.

My loving thanks to my wife, Vera Kalina-Levine, who has been with me every step of the way as the story this book tells has unfolded. She allowed me to return to a Communist world she had been only too happy to leave behind. And she traveled the globe with me as I entered ever deeper into the world of Pope John Paul. It is she, too, who always reminded me to take good notes, and she who has read every word as it was written, offering her perceptive comments for every chapter as I finished it. Vera and my two enormously talented sons, David and Gabriel, have been the rock upon which my life has been built. Without them, and their constant encouragement, there would be no "Pope's Maestro."

My deepest gratitude to His Eminence Walter Cardinal Kasper, President of the Pontifical Council for the Promotion of Christian Unity; His Eminence William Cardinal Keeler, Archbishop Emeritus of Baltimore; His Excellency Donald W. Wuerl, Archbishop of Washington; His Excellency Dennis M. Schnurr, Archbishop of Cincinnati; His Excellency Bishop Brian Farrell L.C., the Pontifical Council's Secretary; His Excellency Bishop Denis Madden, Auxiliary Bishop of Baltimore and former Associate Secretary General of the Catholic Near East Welfare Association; and Father Ben Innes O.F.M., as well as Dame Dr. Marjorie Weeke and Dr. Eugene Fisher, who were invaluable in refreshing my memories of the Vatican and other church-related events with which they were so immensely helpful.

My reverent thanks as well to Rabbi Michael Schudrich, Chief Rabbi of Poland; Rabbi Mordecai Waxman of Temple Israel of Great Neck ז״צ״ל; Rabbi Chaskel Besser of the Ronald S. Lauder Foundation ז״צ״ל; Professor Alvin Rosenfeld of Indiana University; Cantor Joseph Malovany of Fifth Avenue Synagogue; and Eytan Halaban of Davenport College, Yale, who made sure my Jewish, Holocaust, and Holy Land facts were even-keeled.

I am honored and grateful that John Tagliabue consented to write the Foreword to *The Pope's Maestro*. John and his wife, Paula Butturini, were the first nonofficial Western contacts I encountered upon my arrival in Poland. For many years thereafter, John remained the ever-inquiring journalist, always analyzing my story to its core. But he and Paula also offered their friendship, welcoming me to their homes in Warsaw, in Rome, and in Paris. Through their wise and knowledgeable eyes, they helped me to understand the new worlds I was trying my best to come to grips with, day by day by day. That we are still (and even better) friends is one of the great rewards of my journey to Poland, the Vatican, and beyond.

My warmest appreciation goes to my editor, Sheryl Fullerton, who believed from the beginning that I could write this book—that my voice was the one that was needed to make my story sing. Her

Monday 2:00 P.M. phone calls, to wherever I was in the world, were just what I needed to enable me to write what I felt and believed, no matter how difficult that might be. Passers-by at a sidewalk café in Salzburg, just across the street from the Festspielhaus, have no idea who it was I was speaking with so animatedly, but showing a smile all the while. It has been a privilege to work with her and to become her friend.

Sheryl Fullerton was the best editor I could imagine for this book, and I am deeply in the debt of my indefatigable agent, Gail Hochman, for finding her. Gail's patient search for just the right publisher yielded such a fabulous result. I thank her partners at Brandt and Hochman as well, particularly her foreign rights specialist, Marianne Merola, who has believed in this book in many languages.

I extend my gratitude to Martin Gottlieb of the *New York Times*, who read early chapters and strongly encouraged me to persevere in writing this book myself. Dr. Patricia McFate, Ann Levine, Paul Rosenblum, Susan Feder, Frau Dr. Ulrike Hessler, and Professor Stephen Schiffman read larger and smaller portions of the manuscript (and in a few cases the entire work) in a timely fashion, always offering invaluable feedback.

Special thanks also to the Salzburg Global Seminar and its Senior Vice President and Chief Program Officer Edward Mortimer and his wife, Elizabeth, for offering me enormously helpful advice with the manuscript—and a wonderful room with a view at Schloss Leopoldskron, in which a goodly portion of the manuscript found form.

Many others gave advice on many subjects and checked the clarity of so many of my memories: Bill Blakemore of ABC News knows more about John Paul than any American journalist I know and was generous with both his time and his knowledge. Irena Grudzinska-Gross of Warsaw, now at Princeton, whom I have known since our days together at Yale; Leszek Wojcik of Lodz and Carnegie Hall Recording Studios; and Czeslaw Pilawski, former personnel manager of the Kraków Philharmonic helped refresh my memory of all things Polish. Salvatore Forenza and Aurelio Pappalardo were a phone call away to help with all things Italian. Helmut Pauli assisted with details of the 9/11 Concert with the Staatskapelle Dresden, and Richard Simmons, Michael Bielski, and Jody Doherty were most helpful with their memories of the Pittsburgh Symphony's Papal Concert of Reconciliation and their own Concerts of Music for the Spirit. And finally, Michael and Caroline Hornblow were a constant source of reference about my time in Poland and at the Vatican, both of which they know from the inside out, as well as from the outside in.

To all of the above I am also grateful for their friendship, which has in itself sustained me wonderfully over these many years since December 1987, when I first went to Poland.

THE AUTHOR

S ir Gilbert Levine is a distinguished American conductor who
has led major orchestras in the United States and abroad, including the Philadelphia Orchestra, Staatskapelle Dresden, San
Francisco Symphony, London Philharmonic, Pittsburgh Symphony,
Royal Philharmonic, Montreal Symphony, Philharmonia Orchestra,
Kraków Philharmonic, and L'Orchestre de la Bastille (Paris). Educated at Juilliard, Princeton, and Yale, Maestro Levine has conducted
numerous televised concerts on PBS and the European Broadcasting Union, and performed for His Holiness Pope John Paul II on
many occasions. He has been honored with the highest Pontifical
Knighthood accorded a non-ecclesiastical musician since Mozart.